DOCUMEN

The..., Concepts, and Skills
for the AP® Course

CORRELATIONS TO THE AP® US HISTORY COURSE

Key Concepts Alignment		
1.1–1.2	Ch.1	
2.1–2.2	Chs. 2–3	
3.1–3.3	Chs. 4–6	This textbook includes references to the Fall 2015 AP® U.S. History Curriculum Framework. Visit our website at **highschool.bfwpub.com /stacydocumenting1e** for the complete correlation.
4.1–4.3	Chs. 7–9	
5.1–5.3	Chs. 10–12	
6.1–6.3	Chs. 13–15	
7.1–7.3	Chs. 16–18	
8.1–8.3	Chs. 19–21	
9.1–9.3	Ch. 22	

Thematic Alignment	
NAT	Chs. 1, 2, 3, 4, 5, 6, 7, 8, 10, 11, 12, 13, 15, 16, 17, 18, 19, 20, 21, 22
MIG	Chs. 1, 2, 3, 6, 8, 10, 11, 13, 14, 17, 21, 22
WXT	Chs. 1, 2, 3, 4, 5, 6, 8, 10, 13, 16, 17, 21, 22
POL	Chs. 1, 2, 3, 4, 5, 6, 7, 9, 10, 11, 12, 13, 14, 15, 16, 17, 18, 19, 20, 21, 22
WOR	Chs. 1, 2, 3, 4, 5, 6, 7, 9, 10, 13, 17, 18, 19, 22
GEO	Chs. 1, 2, 3, 4, 6, 9, 10, 12, 13, 14, 16, 18, 19, 21, 22
CUL	Chs. 1, 2, 3, 4, 5, 6, 7, 8, 11, 12, 13, 15, 16, 17, 19, 21, 22

Building AP® Writing Skills	
Organizing and outlining evidence	Chs. 1–6
Combining evidence for effective support	Chs. 7–12
Conceptualizing historical thinking and writing	Chs. 13–19
The relationship between analysis and argument	Chs. 20–22

Documenting
United States History

Themes, Concepts, and Skills
for the AP® Course

Documenting
United States History

Themes, Concepts, and Skills
for the AP® Course

Jason Stacy
Southern Illinois University Edwardsville

Stephen Heller
Adlai E. Stevenson High School

AP® is a trademark registered by the College Board®, which was not involved in the production of, and does not endorse, this product.

Bedford/St. Martin's
BEDFORD Boston • New York

For Bedford/St. Martin's

Vice President, Editorial, Macmillan Higher Education Humanities: Edwin Hill
Publisher for High School: Ann Heath
Sponsoring Editor for Social Studies: Janie Pierce-Bratcher
Editorial Assistant: Rachel Chlebowski
Senior Production Editor: Peter Jacoby
Production Supervisor: Lisa McDowell
Marketing Manager: Julie Comforti
Marketing Assistant: Nont Pansringarm
Copy Editor: Rosemary Winfield
Indexer: Leoni McVey
Cartography: Mapping Specialists, Ltd.
Director of Rights and Permissions: Hilary Newman
Senior Art Director: Anna Palchik
Text Design: Lisa Buckley
Cover Design: John Callahan
Cover Art/Cover Photo: larry1235/Shutterstock
Composition: Cenveo Publisher Services
Printing and Binding: LSC Communications

6   24   23   22   21   20

For information, write: Bedford/St. Martin's, 75 Arlington Street, Boston, MA 02116   (617-399-4000)

ISBN 978-1-4576-2012-6

ABOUT THE AUTHORS

JASON STACY is associate professor of US History and Social Science Pedagogy at Southern Illinois University Edwardsville. Before joining the history department at SIUE, Stacy taught AP® US History for eight years at Adlai E. Stevenson High School in Lincolnshire, Illinois. Stacy has served as an AP® US History reader, table leader, exam leader, consultant, senior auditor, and question author for the redesigned AP® US History exam.

Stacy is the author of *Walt Whitman's Multitudes: Labor Reform and Persona in Whitman's Journalism and the First* Leaves of Grass, *1840–1855* (2008), editor of *Leaves of Grass, 1860: The 150th Anniversary Facsimile Edition* (2009), and coeditor of *Walt Whitman's Selected Journalism* (2015). His research has appeared in *Studies in American Culture, Social Education,* the *Walt Whitman Quarterly Review,* and *American Educational History,* and his reviews have appeared in *American Literature,* the *Journal of American History,* and the *Walt Whitman Quarterly Review.* Stacy is also a contributing editor for the Walt Whitman Archive.

Since 2009, Stacy has served as editor in chief of *The Councilor: A Journal of the Social Studies.* He is a former president of the Illinois Council for the Social Studies (2014).

STEPHEN HELLER has taught for twenty-eight years in the Chicago area, the last sixteen of which have been at Adlai E. Stevenson High School in Lincolnshire, Illinois, where he teaches AP® English Language and Composition. Heller has served as an AP® English Language and Composition reader, table leader, question leader, and consultant, and he recently completed a six-year term on the AP® English Language and Composition test development committee, where he also served as the College Board adviser.

Heller's publications include coauthorship of two textbooks for pre-AP® and AP® English—*AP® English Bound* (2009) and *Entering the Conversation* (2010). Heller also was the editor in chief for the College Board's 2007 workshop materials "Using Sources," and the College Board's 2013 workshop materials "Expanding Definitions of Argument," and he served as a contributing author to the College Board's AP® Vertical Teams for English workshop. Heller's additional publications have appeared in *English Journal*, *Social Education* (a piece coauthored with Jason Stacy), and the *Illinois Bulletin of English*.

Since 2007, Heller has teamed with Jason Stacy to teach American Themes in the AP® classroom, a course that examines the skills common to both AP® English Language and AP® US History, and for many years this course has been offered at Carleton College in Northfield, Minnesota.

PREFACE

Historical thinking is something we do naturally. We wonder about where we came from, why things are the way they are today, and what events in the past have affected the present and may affect the future. Historical thinking also expands our horizons, hones our reading and writing skills, makes us more logical thinkers, and helps us be better citizens in a republic where we all contribute to the nation's future.

There is nothing magical to thinking like a historian. With some practice, you will have the habits of mind that will allow you to understand and analyze voices from the past and to appreciate how your own voice fits into this grand and ever-growing documentary of American voices—both past and present.

This book will help you cultivate the historical skills that you will use to think critically and purposefully about the past and that you must master to pass the AP® US History exam. Cultivating these skills requires practice—practice in reading a wide range of texts and practice in employing historical thinking so that it becomes a habit of mind.

Overview of This Book

This reader complements your textbook and in-class work. The twenty-two chapters in this book follow nine time periods of United States history as defined by the AP® course:

Period One: 1491–1607

Period Two: 1607–1754

Period Three: 1754–1800

Period Four: 1800–1848

Period Five: 1844–1877

Period Six: 1865–1898

Period Seven: 1890–1945

Period Eight: 1945–1980

Period Nine: 1980 to the Present

Within each period are **key concepts** that form the outline of historical content for the AP® course. Here, key concepts are illustrated by documents, which are literally voices from the past. These documents may appear as written texts, drawings, photographs, old maps, or new charts or graphs. The purpose of the documents in each chapter is to help you develop your skills as a historical thinker.

How to Use This Book

1. Chapter Title and Introduction

Read the chapter title and introduction. Each chapter's title communicates the focus of the chapter, and each paragraph of the introduction connects to a **key concept** of the AP® framework. What is the difference between a concept and an event? A concept is larger, broader, and more thematic than an event. Many historical "facts" can prove a single concept. The more familiar you become with key concepts, the more versatile you become in thinking historically and developing original historical arguments.

2. Thematic Prereading Focus Questions

Each chapter features AP®-based **thematic questions** called "Seeking the Main Point" that help you connect the documents to the key concept of the chapter. These questions reflect the thematic learning objectives of key concepts in the AP® curriculum and will help you link the documents with the history that you have learned in class or in your textbook. Read these questions before you read the primary documents; they will help you draw deeper connections among the documents.

Here's an example of a prereading focus question:

> What were the gains and losses for Europeans, European colonists, and native peoples during this era of expansion?

A question like this at the beginning of the chapter will help you focus your reading as you begin to analyze the primary sources. This question tells you that you will have to be on the lookout for "gains" and "losses" for three groups—Europeans, Europeans in America, and native peoples. Keeping this question in mind helps you read the documents in the chapter *purposefully* because you will read with these concepts in mind.

3. Organization of Primary Documents

Each chapter has subgroups of documents. The documents within each subgroup are typically arranged chronologically so that you can monitor causal relationships and patterns of continuity (when things stay the same) and change over time. Many of the documents are textual; some are images (photographs, charts, and paintings).

Each document begins with a **headnote** that provides context for the documents by relating historical events and individuals that shaped the document. This information answers these fundamental questions:

- Who is the author or artist?
- What occasion influenced the creation of the text?
- What trends or phenomena preceded the creation of this text?

Each document is followed by three questions that ask you to *identify, analyze*, and *evaluate* each text. **Identify** questions ask for basic information about a document. **Analyze** questions ask you to draw appropriate inferences and logical conclusions about a document. **Evaluate** questions require you to make an informed judgment about a document.

When you answer these three questions, you will think about the following topics:

Identify
What is being said or depicted?

When was this person or item historically significant?

What other significant events took place around this item or individual?

Analyze
What is the speaker's or writer's intent or purpose? What does it tell us about its creator?

Who is the audience?

Why was an item made a certain way?

What biases or interests went into its creation?

Evaluate
How valuable is this text as a source of information?

What circumstances influenced the creation of this text?

What does it tell us about its time and place of creation?

How does it compare to other primary sources from the same period?

How fully does this text represent a larger period?

4. Applying AP® Historical Thinking Skill Exercises

Each chapter features a series of **historical thinking skill** exercises that encourage you to think about the documents in the development of a historical argument. You will get a lot of practice in learning and applying historical thinking skills. Each historical thinking skill is introduced in a step-by-step process and is reinforced throughout the textbook. Here is part of an applying AP® Historical Thinking Skills exercise for the period 1607 to 1754 from Chapter 2:

The historical thinking skill called comparison can be used to answer the following prompt:

Compare the Spanish, English, and French policies toward Native Americans. To what extent were these policies shaped by economic considerations?

In the first few chapters, you will find a number of steps to guide you through your response to the prompt. For example:

STEP 1   Use the documents from Topics 1 and 2 above (and if you have time, Documents 1.6–1.9 and 1.11–1.12 from Chapter 1) to characterize Spanish, English, and French policies toward Native Americans. Consider the ways in which these policies were shaped by economic considerations. One is already done for you.

European colonizers	Policies toward natives	Ways in which these policies were shaped by economic considerations
Spanish	Philip IV tried to prevent further uprisings by ordering Governor Don Luis de Valdés to treat natives less cruelly (Doc. 2.7).	The Spanish depended on native laborers, especially through the encomienda system.
English		
French		

When a historical thinking skill is introduced for the first time, the skill is identified as a new skill. The purpose of these exercises is to introduce you to how historians apply a particular skill to primary documents.

The historical thinking skills build on the primary documents that you have already read. Sometimes you need to combine documents, as you can see in the example above, where you are asked to use documents that you read earlier in the chapter.

If the historical thinking skill is reintroduced, especially in a more complex format, then the exercise is labeled as review.

As your historical thinking skills develop while working with this book, so too does your overall body of knowledge. You might be undertaking the historical thinking skill exercise in a particular chapter, but you may refer to documents in prior chapters.

These historical thinking skill exercises often culminate with practice paragraphs where you combine your reading, thinking, and writing. This is in preparation for the chapter's end focus on developing a full historical argument, which you must display on the AP® exam.

By the time that you complete Periods One through Four (Chapters 1–9 in this book), you will have been introduced to all of the historical thinking skills. In Periods Five through Nine (Chapters 10–22 in this book), you will learn effective and creative combinations of these historical thinking skills, so that by the time you finish this book, you will have a full range of historical thinking skills to apply to any given task.

5. Using Outside Sources

Outside sources include your classroom notes, secondary source readings, and other primary documents that you discover on your own. They all play an important role in your study of AP® US History, and you are encouraged to use this book along with your other sources.

The first time that you are asked to incorporate outside knowledge is in the Applying AP® Historical Thinking Skills exercises. At the end of each chapter, the "Building AP® Writing Skills" question requires you to use outside information as well.

6. Post-reading Thematic Questions

The reading sections conclude with AP®-based thematic prompts that focus on the key themes presented in a chapter. Answering these "Putting It All Together: Revisiting the Main Point" prompts requires you to combine various sources from the chapter, just as you must do on the AP® exam. These prompts are more specific versions of the prereading "Seeking the Main Point" questions and help you to monitor your understanding of the key concepts of the chapter.

These prompts also build on the **identify**, **analyze**, and **evaluate** questions that follow the documents. Here is an example of one of these post-reading thematic prompts:

> In what ways did the religious and economic interests of the British, French, and Spanish influence their relations with the native peoples they encountered?

This question might seem intimidating now, but it will seem easier after you have learned about this material in class and read Chapter 2 in this book. Then you will be able to use historical themes to think about the *religion* and *economics* of the

British, French, and Spanish and the ways in which these themes influenced their relations with native peoples.

7. Building AP® Writing Skills

The chapters in this textbook end with a feature that will teach you how to write historical argument by integrating historical thinking skills and useful writing strategies to form clear, coherent arguments. "Building AP® Writing Skills" will enable you to pull together the *skills*, *concepts*, and *themes* in each chapter into a coherent essay.

These lessons are arranged sequentially, beginning with prewriting (Lesson 1) and organization (Lesson 2) and moving into increasingly sophisticated aspects of writing, such as creative synthesis of sources, inclusion of multiple perspectives, and effective approaches to logical argument. Each "Building AP® Writing Skills" segment

- offers its own AP®-style prompt, which represents the thematic focus and primary documents of the given chapter;
- provides a step-by-step approach to build your abilities and confidence in tackling such questions;
- provides opportunities to practice developing your argument—because the more you practice, the more natural it feels

These writing units are developed sequentially, beginning with fundamental building blocks to writing historical argument, moving toward effective ways of using and organizing evidence, and concluding with different ways of approaching historical argument.

8. Working with Secondary Sources: Short Answer Questions for the AP® Exam

One important skill of AP® US History is interpreting and analyzing historical writing by professional historians. For each of the nine time periods, you will find sections titled "Working with Secondary Sources: AP® Short Answer Questions," which include two short readings by prominent historians. These readings are followed by questions that ask you to construct short answer responses like those needed for the AP® US History exam.

These Skills Will Help in Other Classes Too!

The skills developed in this textbook are transferable to many of your other classes. For example, you will be able to apply what you learn here in your AP® English language and composition classroom. The ability to read a piece critically, synthesize multiple sources, and develop an original argument is featured prominently in the AP® English Language and Composition curriculum.

Acknowledgments

We appreciate the combined efforts of the editorial, production, and marketing departments at Bedford/St. Martin's and BFW Publishers. This was a significant undertaking that required the support and persistence of all involved. We especially would like to thank the instructors and colleagues who graciously provided helpful and constructive feedback for improving this text:

Scott Birrell, Lone Peak High School, UT

Christine Bond-Curtright, Edmond Memorial High School, OK

Gwendolyn Cash, Clear Creek High School, TX

Paul Dickler, Neshaminy School District, PA

Dana Duenzen, Woodbridge High School, CA

Todd Feldman, Canandaigua Academy, NY

Jason George, Bryn Mawr School, MD

James Glinski, Xaverian Brothers High School, MA

Eric Hahn, Ladue Horton Watkins High School, MO

Barbara Harbour, Cass Technical School, MI

Geri Hastings, Catonsville High School, MD

Warren Hierl, Career Center, NC

Fred Jordan, Woodberry Forest School, VA

Michael Kim, Schurr High School, CA

Mary Lopez, Schaumburg High School, IL

Jackie McHargue, Duncanville High School, TX, retired

Timothy Mitchell, Shaker Heights High School, OH

Louisa Moffitt, Marist School, GA

Ron Olson, Governor John R. Rogers High School, WA

Bill Polasky, Stillman Valley High School, IL

Susan Reeder, Winter Springs High School, FL

Dave Rider, Bellows Free Academy, VT

Penny Rosas, Mayde Creek High School, TX

Nancy Schick, Los Alamos High School, NM

Bill Shelton, Trinity Valley School, TX

Thomas F. Sleete, Thomas Jefferson High School, VA

Michael Smith, San Gorgonio High School, CA

John Struck, Floyd Central High School, NY

Matt Tassinari, Palmdale High School, CA

Keith Wood, Murray High School, UT

Also from Jason Stacy: I would like to thank my colleagues in the Department of Historical Studies at Southern Illinois University Edwardsville for their support and good cheer during the creation of this book, especially Robert Paulett and Jeffrey Manuel, who offered a sympathetic ear throughout, and Mark Neels, who proved to be the best of research assistants. Thanks also to my good friends James Sabathne, Bill Polasky, and Robin Wanosky, who witnessed many ups and downs along the way for one week each year at the AP® US Reading; and thanks, finally, to the good people at Bedford, Freeman & Worth: Janie Pierce-Bratcher, Rachel Chlebowski, and especially Dan McDonough, who were unwavering advocates of this project. And to Michelle, Abigail, and Margaret Stacy, my joy; I've not enough space to thank you properly here.

Also from Steve Heller: To my dearest Lauren, for your unending support and love. To my little women, Carrie, Tina, Alex, and Olivia, for all you've given us. To my parents, Frances and Maurice Heller, for your deep commitment to education, and to my brother, Geoffrey, for your love of history. And to the Communication Arts and Social Studies Divisions at Adlai E. Stevenson High School, whose collegiality, scholarship, professionalism, and love for teaching is embedded within these pages. And to Bedford, Freeman & Worth for its unflinching support of this project and the work of high school teachers.

BRIEF CONTENTS

CONTENTS

> **PERIOD TWO   1607–1754**

CHAPTER 2 | Colonial North America   27

CHAPTER 3 | **Awakening, Enlightenment, and Empire in British North America**   57

PERIOD THREE   1754–1800

CHAPTER 4 | An Atlantic Empire   85

CHAPTER 5 | **A Republic Envisioned and Revised** 115

PERIOD FOUR   1800–1848

CHAPTER 7 | **Reform and Reaction**   169

CHAPTER 13 | **A Gilded Age**

CHAPTER 14 | The Throes of Assimilation   327

PERIOD SEVEN   1890–1945

CHAPTER 17 | **Challenges to the Status Quo**   381

CHAPTER 18 | **Isolated No More**

CHAPTER 21 | **Discontinuities**   473

PERIOD NINE   1980 TO THE PRESENT

CHAPTER 22 | **A Conservative Tenor**   489

CHAPTER 1

First Contacts

The Western Hemisphere is often referred to as the New World, but for the Native Americans who lived there, it was an ancient and diverse land. Although Spanish, Portuguese, and later English, French, and Dutch colonists often perceived native peoples in simplistic ways—as savages to be suppressed or as pagans to be converted—the lives of North and South Americans before European contact were varied and complex. North American Indians lived both nomadic and agricultural lives in forests and deserts. They lived in towns in the Southwest, as nomads in the Great Plains, and in villages in the vast forests in the East. In Central and South America, Native Americans lived in enormous cities and tiny villages, in mountains, in jungles, and on the plains. Native America was a place of vast cultures, societies, religions, and histories. It was a very old world before it was the New World. It is also a world for which few written sources remain, and so historians must rely on material culture—artifacts and other visual sources—in analyzing the history of the continents.

Christopher Columbus's "discovery" of the Western Hemisphere in 1492 began a time of dislocation and destruction for Native Americans, but this era also inaugurated an era of exchange for both peoples. Europeans brought goods (like onions, olives, wheat, barley, and oats) and livestock (like cattle, sheep, pigs, and horses) to the Western Hemisphere from Europe, and vanilla, beans, cacao, pineapples, tobacco, maize, potatoes, cassava, and turkeys entered the European economy from the New World. The exchange was not wholly positive, however, because Europeans introduced diseases (like smallpox, influenza, and measles) that decimated Native American populations and brought syphilis back from the Western Hemisphere to Europe. Because this exchange of plants, animals, and microbes began with Columbus's arrival in 1492, historians call it the *Columbian exchange*.

In Central and South America, where Spanish and Portuguese colonies ruled after Hernán Cortés's destruction of the Aztec empire between 1519 and 1521, native populations were reduced to a subservient class and converted to Christianity. Although Europeans believed in their own superiority to native populations and often used this belief to justify their conquests, some Europeans protested against the oppression of Southern American Indians. Largely grounded in theological arguments, these debates revolved around whether native peoples were capable of religious conversion and salvation and, if so, whether they deserved European benevolence and perhaps, on conversion, equality with fellow Christians.

Native Americans often proved ambivalent or hostile to attempts to change their beliefs, cultural mores, and economic and social practices. To capture the spirit of this vast and often unrecorded resistance, this chapter offers a document from the revolt of a single native town in what is now modern New Mexico (Doc. 1.9). This revolt was one of many forms of resistance to European conquest that took place across the continent and throughout this era.

Europeans also supplemented a need for labor in the Western Hemisphere by opening a transatlantic trade economy in slaves from West Africa. Many enslaved Africans resisted the horrors of slavery by maintaining belief systems and languages that they brought from West Africa to the Western Hemisphere. These traditions often mixed easily with those of Europeans and Native Americans, beginning a heritage of cultural blending and exchange throughout the region.

Seeking the Main Point

As you read the documents that follow, keep these broad questions in mind. These questions will help you understand the relationship between the documents in this chapter and the historical changes that they represent. As you reflect on these questions, determine which themes and which documents best address them.

- Why did Europeans travel to the Western Hemisphere? How did first contact between Europeans, Africans, and Native Americans affect each group of people?
- What environmental factors shaped Native American and European contact?
- After first contact, what factors—economic, religious, political, environmental—most shaped European actions in the Western Hemisphere?
- Why do historians rely on artifacts in analyzing the native cultures of the Americas? What are the strengths and limitations of these kinds of sources?
- Consider the costs and benefits of the Columbian exchange to both Europeans and Native Americans. How did each group perceive the other and themselves in light of first contact?
- To what extent did an increasingly global society broaden the Europeans' and native peoples' worldview?

The Diverse Societies
of Native America

DOCUMENT 1.1 | Gold Frog Ornaments
Mixtec, Southern Mexico, 15th to 16th century

A member of the Mixtec people, who lived within the Aztec empire, made this necklace for an Aztec aristocrat. Mixtec and Aztec peoples associated frogs with rain and fertility, which were important factors for survival in civilizations with large cities and complex societies that depended on stable crop yields of maize and other products.

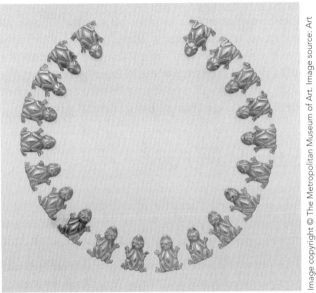

Image copyright © The Metropolitan Museum of Art. Image source: Art Resource, NY.

PRACTICING Historical Thinking

What does it mean to **read closely**? Three questions accompany each document in this textbook. They ask you to examine the text—either written or visual—a second or third time to develop your critical reading and thinking skills.

The most fundamental task of close reading is to identify the visible, concrete, or literal features of the text, as in this question:

Identify: When historians examine documents or artifacts, they need to identify details that may be relevant to their research. Describe this necklace, taking care to identify details that you think are relevant to events of this era.

After identification comes analysis, which is the process of rereading the text to determine key features of the text's creation, organization, and style. You also may take into account what you know about the writer or artist and the intended audience. Historians must do more than just identify details. They must offer some analysis of the item within the context of the time and place in which it originated, as in this next question:

Analyze: If frogs represented fertility for the Aztecs, why might a high-status Aztec want to wear these symbolic objects?

Finally, a historian must consider the meaning of the object or document and assess its historical significance. In this process, called *evaluation*, the reader makes an informed judgment about the text. Evaluation often depends on additional reading experiences, which you used in your assessment of the text, as in this question:

Evaluate: How did the natural environment contribute to the development of this artifact?

DOCUMENT 1.2 | ## Ruins of the Pueblo Town of Cicuique
New Mexico, 16th century

The pueblo of Cicuique, whose ruins are photographed below, housed two thousand residents who grew corn, beans, and squash and traded goods with neighboring towns. The residents lived in an arid climate and practiced a type of farming that required very little water. The town was fortified and contained five hundred warriors who defended the town from the nomadic tribes of the Great Plains. The ruins are located in New Mexico.

Library of Congress Prints and Photographs Division, HABS, Reproduction number HABS NM,24-PECO,1--2.

DOCUMENT 1.3 | Chief Powhatan's Deerskin Cloak

Virginia, 1608

Chief Powhatan, who ruled the Pamunkey in present-day Virginia, wore this deerskin cloak for tribal ceremonies. Powhatan's tribe was part of the Algonquin peoples who inhabited the southeastern region of North America. The objects in this cloak are made of shells, which were considered items of value by the Pamunkey people. The circles could represent regions under Powhatan's control, the animals probably represent deer, and the individual in the center represents Chief Powhatan.

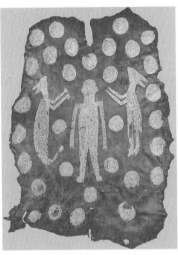

Ashmolean Museum, University of Oxford, UK/Bridgeman Images.

Change and Exchange

DOCUMENT 1.4 | CHRISTOPHER COLUMBUS, Journal
1492

Italian explorer Christopher Columbus (1451–1506) sought a westerly route to Asia but landed in the Western Hemisphere in October 1492. The sovereigns of Spain, Ferdinand and Isabella, funded Columbus's voyages in hopes of expanding Spanish trade routes to Asia. This excerpt from his journal is the first recorded contact between Europeans and native peoples.

They are very well made, with very handsome bodies, and very good countenances. Their hair is short and coarse, almost like hairs of a horse's tail. They wear the hairs brought down to the eyebrows, except a few locks behind, which they wear long and never cut. They paint themselves black, and they are the colour of the Canarians, neither black nor white. Some paint themselves white, others red, and others of what colour they find. Some paint their faces, others the whole body, some only round the eyes, others only on the nose. They neither carry nor know anything of arms, for I showed them swords, and they took them by the blade and cut themselves through ignorance. They have no iron, their darts being wands without iron, some of them having a fish's tooth at the end, and others being pointed in various ways. They are all of fair stature and size, with good faces, and well made. I saw some with marks of wounds on their bodies, and I made signs to ask what it was, and they gave me to understand that people from other adjacent islands came with the intention of seizing them, and that they defended themselves. I believed, and still believe, that they come here from the mainland to take them prisoners. They should be good servants and intelligent, for I observed that they quickly took in what was said to them, and I believe that they would easily be made Christians, as it appeared to me that they had no religion. . . .

Christopher Columbus, John Cabot, and Gaspar Corte Real, *The Journal of Christopher Columbus (during His First Voyage, 1492–93) and Documents Relating the Voyages of John Cabot and Gaspar Corte Real*, ed. and trans. Clements R. Markham (London: Hakluyt Society, 1893), 38.

DOCUMENT 1.5 | **Images of Hernán Cortés Assisted by the Tlaxcalan People of Mexico**
1560

The Tlaxcalan people of central Mexico assisted Hernán Cortés (1485–1547) in the conquest of the Aztec empire after the death of Moctezuma in 1520. The two images below portray Spanish and Tlaxcalan armies under the command of Cristóbal de Olid, a lieutenant of Cortés, as they battle against the Aztecs. These images appear in the *Lienzo de Tlaxcala*, an illustrated manuscript, but were copies of murals painted for Tlaxcalan nobles to commemorate the part that they played in the conquest of the Aztec empire.

LAM. NUM. 48.

Jal-ixco, (hoy Guadalajara). En la superficie de la arena.

Courtesy of the Bancroft Library, University of California, Berkeley.

LAM. NUM. 49.

Totothán. (Pueblo). Lugar donde abundan los pájaros.

PRACTICING Historical Thinking

Identify: According to these images, who were the victors? How is their victory portrayed?

Analyze: How might the fact that the Tlaxcalans were enemies of the Aztecs have influenced the way they portrayed themselves in this battle?

Evaluate: Observe the weaponry shown in these two panels. Assess the influence of Spanish technology on these Native Americans.

NEW SKILL | Patterns of Continuity and Change over Time

When historians draw conclusions about time periods, they look for **patterns of continuity and change over time**. That means they are looking at the ways that some things changed and other things stayed the same during the same period.

Usually when we analyze patterns of continuity and change, we do so in **thematic** terms. For example, the theme of **politics and power** refers to the ways that different groups compete for influence over society and government. With that theme in mind, consider the following prompt, which focuses on different groups of people and their ensuing struggles for power:

> To what extent did competition and cooperation among different societies in North America change with the coming of Europeans in the late fifteenth and early sixteenth centuries?

In this prompt, words such as "competition and cooperation" relate to the larger theme (politics and power), and your understanding of these ideas stems from the analysis and evaluation questions above. Even though this question uses only the word "change," you must consider the extent of that change, which allows you to consider both the extent to which things changed and the extent to which they stayed the same.

In this case, you need to consider the ways in which Native Americans competed and cooperated with each other before and after the arrival of the Spanish. How did their competition and cooperation with each other change after the Spanish arrived? How did they remain the same? Answering these questions means focusing on specific aspects (competition and cooperation) of a larger theme (politics and power).

Note: You are creating what is called a **historical argument**. When we use the word *argument*, we refer to an original **claim** (or position) that is supported by clear **evidence** and explanations. Historians use arguments not to express conflicts and debates but to explain the past. A historical argument is an original statement in which you put forth a plausible interpretation of some aspect of past events and support and defend that argument with primary-source evidence.

STEP 1 To answer this question, organize your response visually. Copy this chart into your notebook.

	Continuity	Change
Competition		
Evidence		
Cooperation		
Evidence		

Complete the chart using the preceding documents and your answers to these documents' questions. Notice that there can be both continuity and change (or one in particular) under each category of the question. For example, your response could include the following information:

	Continuity	Change
Competition	Before and after conquest, native peoples often competed with each other for resources and power.	The Spanish invasion changed the dynamic of these conflicts and often tipped the balance in favor of one native group over another.
Evidence	Aztecs and Tlaxcalans were in competition before and after the Spanish arrived (Doc. 1.5, see Analysis question).	The Spanish allied with the Tlaxcalans; the Tlaxcalans used Spanish weapons (Doc. 1.5, see Evaluate question).

Cooperation		Before conquest, natives traded exclusively with other native peoples (Doc. 1.1). After conquest, agricultural and craft production shifted to reflect the interests of Spanish consumers.
Evidence		Natives produced new agricultural products like cattle and Spanish-influenced crafts, like Catholic icons (consult textbook or class lecture).

Notice that the findings here claim that competition between natives both changed and remained the same in particular ways. According to the chart, however, cooperation between natives in agriculture and crafts changed after the conquest to reflect Spanish exploitation of native economies. This is why the continuity spaces in the chart remain blank under the category of cooperation.

STEP 2 Use your chart above to write the **claim** (or original position) that describes patterns of continuity and change over time for each category. Then support each claim with **support** that refers to the **evidence** you have gathered in your chart. By the word *evidence*, we mean examples of events, people, or ideas from the documents above and from your outside readings. For example:

> **Claim (competition):** The Spanish invasion of the Aztec empire transformed conflicts **[change]** that already existed **[continuity]** among native peoples in this part of the world.
> **Support:** For example, the Aztecs and Tlaxcalans had long been enemies, and the Tlaxcalans had been under the control of the Aztecs before the Spanish conquest **[evidence of continuity]**. During the conquest, however, the Tlaxcalans allied with the Spanish and took advantage of superior Spanish weapons and mounted cavalry **[evidence of change]** (Doc. 1.5). This contributed to the Aztec defeat.

Based on what you know about this period, what additional documents not provided here might you look at to find appropriate support for the claim and complete the paragraph?

> **Claim (cooperation):** Cooperation in trade between native peoples existed before the conquest, but after the conquest, natives produced overwhelmingly for Spanish consumption **[change]**.
> **Support (cooperation):** For example, trade networks that required a degree of cooperation between different peoples within the Aztec empire produced the Mixtec gold necklace above (Doc. 1.1). After the Spanish conquest, however, Native Americans increasingly produced goods for the European market. The production of cattle and Catholic icons by native farmers and artisans mark this change **[evidence for change]**.

What additional documents can you think of that would provide appropriate support for the claim and complete the paragraph?

Historians also use the term **argument** to describe primary-source documents because these documents put forth an original statement that is grounded in the writer's interpretation of contemporary events. A fully developed argument represents a series of claims that are supported by appropriate evidence and explanations. The following document, for example, represents Pope Paul III's argument—or position—on the conversion of native peoples to Christianity.

Transatlantic Conquest

DOCUMENT 1.6 | **POPE PAUL III, Papal Bull:** *Sublimis Deus*
| 1537

A papal bull is a statement or decree by the Roman Catholic Pope and is meant to represent the Catholic Church's position on a particular issue. Pope Paul III (1468–1549) issued the following papal bull in 1537 to forbid the enslavement of native peoples. Under the encomienda system, the Spanish Crown granted conquistadors and colonists a right to control a number of natives, ostensibly to protect, educate, and convert them to Christianity but in effect to use them as forced labor for mining and agriculture.

The sublime God so loved the human race that He created man in such wise that he might participate, not only in the good that other creatures enjoy, but endowed him with capacity to attain to the inaccessible and invisible Supreme Good and behold it face to face; and since man, according to the testimony of the sacred scriptures, has been created to enjoy eternal life and happiness, which none may obtain save through faith in our Lord Jesus Christ, it is necessary that he should possess the nature and faculties enabling him to receive that faith; and that whoever is thus endowed should be capable of receiving that same faith. Nor is it credible that any one should possess so little understanding as to desire the faith and yet be destitute of the most necessary faculty to enable him to receive it. Hence Christ, who is the Truth itself, that has never failed and can never fail, said to the preachers of the faith whom He chose for that office "Go ye and teach all nations." He said all, without exception, for all are capable of receiving the doctrines of the faith. . . .

We, who, though unworthy, exercise on earth the power of our Lord and seek with all our might to bring those sheep of His flock who are outside, into the fold committed to our charge, consider, however, that the Indians are truly men and that they are not only capable of understanding the catholic faith but, according to our information, they desire exceedingly to receive it. Desiring to provide ample remedy for these evils, we define and declare by these our letters . . . the said Indians and all other people who may later be discovered by Christians, are by no means to be deprived of their liberty or the possession of their property, even though they be outside the faith of Jesus Christ; and that they may and should, freely and legitimately, enjoy their liberty and the possession of their property; nor should they be in any way enslaved; should the contrary happen, it shall be null and of no effect.

Francis Augustus MacNutt, *Bartholomew de las Casas: His Life, Apostolate, and Writings* (New York: G.P. Putnam's Sons, 1909), 427, 429.

DOCUMENT 1.7	BARTOLOMÉ DE LAS CASAS, *Brief Account of the Destruction of the Indies*
	1542

Dominican priest Bartolomé de las Casas (1484–1566), one of the first settlers in New Spain, protested the treatment of Indians by the Spanish in this address to Prince Philip, the future king of Spain. In this passage, Las Casas advocates for the rights of native peoples and rejects the encomienda system.

They are by nature the most humble, patient, and peaceable, holding no grudges, free from embroilments, neither excitable nor quarrelsome. . . . They are also poor people, for they not only possess little but have no desire to possess worldly goods. For this reason they are not arrogant, embittered, or greedy. . . . They are very clean in their persons, with alert, intelligent minds, docile and open to doctrine, very apt to receive our holy Catholic faith, to be endowed with virtuous customs, and to behave in a godly fashion. And once they begin to hear the tidings of the Faith, they are so insistent on knowing more and on taking the sacraments of the Church and on observing the divine cult that, truly, the missionaries who are here need to be endowed by God with great patience in order to cope with such eagerness. . . .

Yet into this sheepfold, into this land of meek outcasts there came some Spaniards who immediately behaved like ravening wild beasts, wolves, tigers, or lions that had been starved for many days. . . .

Bartolomé de las Casas, *The Devastation of the Indies: A Brief Account*, ed. Bill M. Donavan (Baltimore, MD: Johns Hopkins University Press, 1992), 28.

DOCUMENT 1.8 | **JUAN GINÉS DE SEPÚLVEDA,** *Concerning the Just Causes of the War against the Indians*
1547

Juan Ginés de Sepúlveda (1489–1573), a Spanish theologian and philosopher, was tasked by Charles V, grandson of Ferdinand and Isabella, to respond to Bartolomé de las Casas's assertions that the Spaniards were unjustly treating Native Americans. Below is an excerpt from his book, *Concerning the Just Causes of the War against the Indians.*

. . . [T]he Spanish have a perfect right to rule these barbarians of the New World and the adjacent islands, who in prudence, skill, virtues, and humanity are as inferior to the Spanish as children to adults, or women to men, for there exists between the two as great a difference as between savage and cruel races and the most merciful, between the most intemperate and the moderate and temperate and, I might even say, between apes and men. . . .

Compare, then, these gifts of prudence, talent, magnanimity, temperance, humanity, and religion with those possessed by these half-men . . . , in whom you will barely find the vestiges of humanity, who not only do not possess any learning at all, but are not even literate or in possession of any monument to their history except for some obscure and vague reminiscences of several things put down in various paintings; nor do they have written laws, but barbarian institutions and customs. Well, then, if we are dealing with virtue, what temperance or mercy can you expect from men who are committed to all types of intemperance and base frivolity, and eat human flesh? And do not believe that before the arrival of the Christians they lived in that pacific kingdom of Saturn which the poets have invented; for, on the contrary, they waged continual and ferocious war upon one another with such fierceness that they did not consider a victory at all worthwhile unless they sated their monstrous hunger with the flesh of their enemies. . . .

Columbia University, "*Democrates Alter;* Or, On the Just Causes for War against the Indians," in *Introduction to Contemporary Civilization in the West,* 3rd ed. (New York: Columbia University Press, 1960), 526–527.

Identify: What elements of Native American society and culture does Sepúlveda highlight to support his argument?

Analyze: Another analytical tool for historians is **comparison**—looking for similarities or differences among different types of evidence to gain a better understanding of them. Compare Sepúlveda's assessment of the Native Americans with that of Bartolomé de las Casas (Doc. 1.7). In what way does Sepúlveda use arguments that are similar to those of Las Casas?

Evaluate: Using your analysis of Sepúlveda's and Las Casas's arguments from the Analyze question above, what can you infer about the ways that the Spanish perceived themselves in relation to the Native Americans?

DOCUMENT 1.9 | **Transcript of the Spanish Trial in the Aftermath of a Pueblo Revolt**
1598

In 1598, Spanish authorities sent a force of four hundred soldiers into modern New Mexico in search of gold and met resistance at the pueblo of Acoma. The following document is the testimony of a Spanish survivor of the violence, which was often widespread in northern Mexico.

By this time the Indians had given them some flour and maize, although not so much as was needed. For this reason, and because the Indians themselves suggested it, the maese de campo [commanding general of the royal troops in New Mexico] sent Captain Diego Núñez de Chaves with six men to get the rest of the provisions at the places indicated by the Indians. He went, and a short time later the maese de campo asked this witness to find out what the captain was doing. This witness went to Captain Diego Núñez, who told him that the Indians would not give anything, and told him to return to the maese de campo for more men to finish the task quickly as it was getting very late. This witness did so, and the maese de campo gave him six more men to gather flour in other places and to finish quickly. When he went to ask for some at a house not far from there, he heard shouting at that moment from the direction of Captain Diego Núñez. What had happened was that the Indians, as soon as they saw that the forces were divided, began to attack and kill. So this witness fell back immediately with his soldiers to rejoin the maese de campo, followed by the Indians who had hitherto accompanied this witness. They pursued the Spaniards in large groups, and began to hurl countless stones, arrows, and clubs, not only from the ground but from the terraces, both men and women participating in the attack. This witness is certain that this was done treacherously and with premeditation, as they waited until the Spaniards were divided, as he has stated. This witness saw Captain Diego Núñez and his soldiers fall back toward the maese de campo, who at that very moment received an arrow wound in the leg, and other soldiers were killed and wounded. The Indians were so numerous, threw so many stones, and shot so many arrows that they forced the Spaniards to a high cliff where they killed the maese de campo, Captains Felipe de Escalante and Diego Núñez, other soldiers and two Indian servants. . . .

George P. Hammond and Agapito Rey, eds. and trans., *Don Juan de Oñate, Colonizer of New Mexico, 1595–1628*, vol. 5 (Albuquerque: University of New Mexico Press, 1953), 434–435.

PRACTICING Historical Thinking

Identify: What details does this speaker highlight as important? What evidence does the author give for charging that the incident at Acoma was a premeditated attack?

Analyze: How might the speaker's audience have influenced the details that he chose to highlight?

Evaluate: What details of the violence at Acoma might this speaker have left out, either intentionally or otherwise?

APPLYING AP® Historical Thinking Skills

NEW SKILL | Periodization

We use the skill of **periodization** all the time. When we talk about the 1960s as being an era of rebellion or the 1980s as an era of conformity, we organize a set of dates into a block of time (a period) when certain common themes or trends existed. When you ask someone about her experiences in the 1980s, you are asking her to periodize this era of her life. You want her to tell you what the 1980s were like.

For historians, a **time period** is a technical term for the arrangement of past events and processes into discrete—or specifically defined—blocks of time that are often characterized thematically. Time periods begin and end with **turning points**—key moments that mark a change in the course of events. Some turning points are visible (such as a discovery, a death, a speech, or an event), and some turning points are conceptual (such as the announcement of a new theory, the beginning or end of a movement, or the pronouncement of a policy).

For example, historians characterize Cortés's conquest of the Aztec empire between 1519 and 1521 as a **turning point** between two periods of Native American history. Below is an example of what that **claim** might look like as it relates to Native American society:

Claim: "The first eighty years of Native American history after Hernán Cortés's conquest **[turning point]** were a time period of great social upheaval **[periodization]**, especially in Central America."

A historian could support this **claim** with **evidence statements** that are drawn from historical documents. This evidence may reflect your understanding of a historical thinking skill that has already been looked at, such as recognizing patterns of continuity and change over time (see Applying AP® Historical Thinking Skills, p. 9).

Here is an example of an evidence statement that is related to the claim above:

Evidence statement: "For example, during Cortés's conquest, peoples within the Aztec empire fought with Spanish troops and weapons to overthrow their Aztec overlords (Doc. 1.5) and destabilized the social order that had existed before the conquest. The Spanish also brought diseases that decimated native populations (Doc. 1.7), the encomienda system that forced them to work for the Spanish (Docs. 1.7 and 1.8), and a new religion that undermined their traditional religious hierarchy (Docs. 1.6 and 1.8)."

Using the sentences above as a model, write two more evidence statements of your own to support the following claim:

> The first eighty years of Native American history after Hernán Cortés's conquest were a time period of great social upheaval, especially in Central America.

DOCUMENT 1.10 | AFONSO I (MVEMBA A NZINGA), Letter to John III, King of Portugal
1526

Afonso I (Mvemba a Nzinga) (1460–1542), the West African king of Kongo, converted to Christianity, westernized his name, and adopted a European-style coat of arms after opening trade with the Portuguese. In this letter, Afonso writes to the king of Portugal, John III, on the growth of the slave trade in Kongo.

. . . Sir, in our Kingdoms there is another great inconvenience which is of little service to God, and this is that many of our people, keenly desirous as they are of the wares and things of your Kingdoms, which are brought here by your people, and in order to satisfy their voracious appetite, seize many of our people, freed and exempt men, and very often it happens that they kidnap even noblemen and the sons of noblemen, and our relatives, and take them to be sold to the white men who are in our Kingdoms; and for this purpose they have concealed them; and others are brought during the night so that they might not be recognized.

And as soon as they are taken by the white men they are immediately ironed and branded with fire, and when they are carried to be embarked, if they are caught by our guards' men the whites allege that they have bought them but they cannot say from whom, so that it is our duty to do justice and to restore to the freemen their freedom, but it cannot be done if your subjects feel offended, as they claim to be.

And to avoid such a great evil we passed a law so that any white man living in our Kingdoms and wanting to purchase goods in any way should first inform three of our noblemen and officials of our court whom we rely upon in this matter. . . . But if the white men do not comply with it they will lose the aforementioned goods. And if we do them this favor and concession it is for the part Your Highness has in it, since we know that it is in your service too that these goods are taken from our Kingdom, otherwise we should not consent to this. . . .

Basil Davidson, *The African Past: Chronicles from Antiquity to Modern Times* (Boston, MA: Atlantic Monthly Press, 1964), 192–193.

PRACTICING Historical Thinking

Identify: According to this letter, King Afonso was upset that some of his people were selling certain subjects of his kingdom into slavery. Which of his subjects did he wish to protect from the European slave trade?

Analyze: Why might Europeans be less concerned with these subjects than Afonso was?

Evaluate: Compare Afonso's perception of Africans to Pope Paul III's perception of Native Americans (Doc. 1.6). What are the similarities and differences?

DOCUMENT 1.11 | **JACQUES CARTIER, Voyage to the St. Lawrence**

| 1534

French explorer Jacques Cartier (1491–1557) was the first European to traverse the region of the Gulf of St. Lawrence, which he named the "Land of the Canadas." In his memoir, he described the following interaction with native peoples in modern Quebec.

. . . And we navigated with weather at will until the second day of October, . . . during which time and on the way we found many folks of the country, . . . [who] brought us fish and other victuals, dancing and showing great joy at our coming. And to attract and hold them in amity [friendship] with us, the said captain gave them for recompense some knives, paternosters [rosaries], and other trivial goods, with which they were much content. And we having arrived at the said Hochelaga [an Iroquois village], more than a thousand persons presented themselves before us, men, women, and children alike, . . . [who] gave us as good reception as ever father did to child, showing marvelous joy; for the men in one band danced, the women on their side and the children on the other, . . . [who] brought us store of fish and of their bread made of coarse millet, which they cast into our said boats in a way that it seemed as if it tumbled from the air. Seeing this, our said captain landed with a number of his men, and as soon as he was landed they gathered all about him, and about all the others, giving them an unrestrained welcome.

And the women brought their children in their arms to make them touch the said captain and others, making a rejoicing which lasted more than half an hour. And our captain, witnessing their liberality and good will, caused all the women to be seated and ranged in order, and gave them certain paternosters of tin and other trifling things, and to a part of the men knives. Then he retired on board the said boats to sup and pass the night, while these people remained on the shore of the said river nearest the said boats all night, making fires and dancing, crying all the time "Aguyaze!" which is their expression of mirth and joy. . . .

. . . [W]e marched farther on, and about a half-league from there we began to find the land cultivated, and fair, large fields full of grain of their country, which is like Brazil millet, as big or bigger than peas, on which they live just as we do on wheat; and in the midst of these fields is located and seated the town of Hochelaga, near to and adjoining a mountain, which is cultivated round about it and highly fertile, from the summit of which one sees a very great distance. We named the said mountain Mont Royal. . . .

Jacques Cartier, *A Memoir of Jacques Cartier, Sieur de Limoilou, His Voyages to the St. Lawrence; a Bibliography and a Facsimile of the Manuscript of 1534, with Annotations, Etc.*, ed. and trans. James Phinney Baxter (New York: Dodd, Mead, 1906), 161–162.

PRACTICING Historical Thinking

Identify: Identify the details of this encounter that were significant to Cartier.

Analyze: Cartier's memoir was published soon after his exploration of the St. Lawrence River. What impressions did Cartier hope to make on his audience regarding natives and resources in the Western Hemisphere?

Evaluate: Reread the excerpts in this chapter from Christopher Columbus's journal (Doc. 1.4) and Cartier's memoir (Doc. 1.11). To what extent do these documents present the relationship between natives and Europeans in similar ways?

DOCUMENT 1.12 | JOHN SMITH, *The Generall Historie of Virginia*
1624

Captain John Smith (1580–1631) was commissioned by the British Crown to oversee "all things abroad." Here he reflects on an encounter with native peoples in the Virginia Colony, Great Britain's earliest successful settlement in North America. This excerpt is from Smith's book *The Generall Historie of Virginia*.

The new president and Martin, being little beloved, of weak judgment in dangers, and less industry in peace, committed the managing of all things abroad to Captain Smith: who by his own example, good words, and fair promises, set some to mow, others to bind thatch, some to build houses, others to thatch them, himself always bearing the greatest task for his own share, so that in short time, he provided most of them lodgings, neglecting any for himself. . . . [Smith] shipped himself in the shallop to search the country for trade. The want [lack] of the language, knowledge to manage his boat without sails, the want [lack] of a sufficient power (knowing the multitude of the savages), apparel for his men, and other necessaries, were infinite impediments, yet no discouragement. Being but six or seven in company he went down the river to Kecoughtan, where at first they [the natives] scorned him, as a famished man, and would in derision offer him a handful of corn, a piece of bread, for their swords and muskets, and such like proportions also for their apparel. But seeing by trade and courtesy there was nothing to be had, he . . . [l]et fly his muskets, ran his boat on shore, whereat they all fled into the woods. So marching toward their houses, they might see great heaps of corn: much ado he had to restrain his hungry soldiers from present taking of it, expecting as it happened that the savages would assault them, as not long after they did with a most hideous noise. Sixty or seventy of them, some black, some red, some white, some party-colored, came in a square order, singing and dancing out of the woods, with their okee (which was an idol made of skins, stuffed with moss, all painted and hung with chains and copper) borne before them: and in this manner being well armed, with clubs, targets, bows and arrows, they charged the English, that so kindly received them with their muskets loaded with pistol shot, that down fell their God, and divers lay sprawling on the ground; the rest fled again to the woods, and ere long sent one of their . . . [own] to offer peace, and redeem their okee. Smith told them, if only six of them would come unarmed and load his boat, he would not only be their friend, but restore them their okee, and give them beads, copper, and hatchets besides: which on both sides was to their contents performed: and then they brought him venison, turkeys, wild fowl, bread, and what they had, singing and dancing in sign of friendship till they departed. . . .

John Smith, *The Generall Historie of Virginia, New-England, and the Summer Isles* (Bedford, MA: Applewood Books, 2006), 93–94, originally printed in 1629, transcribed into modern English by Jason Stacy.

PRACTICING Historical Thinking

Identify: What economic activities does Smith describe? What impediments did Smith list that interfered with his attempts to trade?

Analyze: Is Smith's account more favorable or unfavorable to the native peoples? Explain. In what ways are Smith's descriptions of native peoples similar to those of both Spanish and French colonizers (Docs. 1.4, 1.5, 1.7, 1.9, 1.11)?

Evaluate: In what ways might this document be a useful primary source for historians? In what ways might this document pose challenges for historians?

NEW SKILL | Causation

When we think about change over time, we think about **causation**—the relationship between cause and effect. In other words, things change over time because there is a cause (an event or a process) that leads to one or more effects. Historians use the term **proximate causes** to refer to **short-term causes** that are set into motion by one or more immediate events. But change usually is also the result of **long-term causes** that are affected by events and changes that have occurred over a long period of time. Many historical events and processes are the result of both long-term and proximate causes. An ability to determine causes rests on a logical relationship between cause and effect.

For example, consider Smith's description of his encounter with Native Americans in Document 1.12. Some **long-term causes** of this encounter might include Columbus's first landing in the Western Hemisphere, the Spanish and Portuguese discovery of gold and silver in Central and South America, and the advent of the encomienda system. **Proximate causes** might include the English arrival in what is now modern Virginia in the early seventeenth century and the native peoples' unfamiliarity with European weapons.

Review the documents from this chapter, and choose two documents for which you can identify long-term and proximate causes of the events described in them. Create a chart in your notebook similar to the one below for the documents you select.

	Long-term causes	Proximate (short-term) causes
Event 1 Example: Smith's description of his encounter with Native Americans (Doc. 1.12)	• Columbus's first landing in the Western Hemisphere • The Spanish and Portuguese discovery of gold and silver in Central and South America • The advent of the encomienda system (Doc. 1.7)	• The English arrival in what is now modern Virginia • A desperation for food during early years of settlement • The natives' unfamiliarity with European weapons (Doc. 1.12)
Event 2		
Event 3		

PUTTING IT ALL TOGETHER

Revisiting the Main Point

- To what extent did European migration to the Western Hemisphere foster assimilation and cooperation among Europeans, Africans, and Native Americans?
- How did the natural environment of the New World figure prominently into the economic, political, and social conflicts of this period? How did colonization of the Western Hemisphere shape European society? How did ongoing colonization shape the societies of the Western Hemisphere (both colonial and native)?
- After European contact, what economic considerations influenced both native and colonial societies? What elements of native, African, and European work, exchange, and technology were transformed by the Columbian exchange? What elements remained the same for each?
- Which of the following factors (economics, politics, environment, religion, and social interactions) was most important in the struggle for power during this time period? Why?
- What were the competing points of view of Europeans toward the treatment of native peoples? What do these different points of view reveal about the European mind-set toward colonization?

BUILDING AP® WRITING SKILLS **Prewriting**

There are three main steps to take prior to writing a historical essay that uses documents.

STEP 1 *Understand the prompt, and identify the key words*

Writing a response to a prompt depends on your ability to understand what you have been asked to write about. For example, consider this prompt:

> Using the documents above and your knowledge of the historical period, analyze the extent to which economics, religion, and politics shaped the earliest contacts between Europeans and native peoples in the Western Hemisphere.

Although you may feel strongly that religion, for example, had the most influence in shaping contact between European and native peoples, the prompt asks you to identify economic, religious, and political factors. Your answer therefore needs to address all three of these factors and not just religious ones.

Note also how the question asks you to use "the documents above and your knowledge of the historical period." This means that your answer needs to draw on evidence beyond the documents to be complete. Knowledge of the historical period may come from your understanding of the textbook, classroom lectures, and any outside books and sources that you have read that pertain to this period. If you do not include "your knowledge of the historical period," your answer will be incomplete.

You also need to identify the key words within each prompt that carry significant weight so that you can be certain to address each word in your essay. Here is a simple brainstorming activity to help you make sure that you always understand a prompt completely.

1. Draw a box around "earliest contacts between Europeans and native peoples in the Western Hemisphere." This is your **topic**.

2. Underline the word "analyze." This is your **task**.

3. Circle "economics," "religion," and "politics." These are the **categories** of your essay.

For the prompt above, your annotations may look like this:

> Using the documents above and your knowledge of the historical period,
> analyze the extent to which economics, religion, and politics shaped the
> earliest contacts between European and native peoples in the Western
> Hemisphere.

STEP 2 *Generate a working thesis*

A thesis statement is your response to the prompt. It is usually no more than two sentences. Your thesis statement includes your main argument in response to a prompt.

Review the prompt's **topic**, and create a list of important information that comes to mind, such as the following:

1. The Spanish brought diseases to the Aztecs.

2. The Aztecs had gold that the Spanish wanted.

3. The Spanish wanted to convert the Native Americans to Christianity.

4. There were many different kinds of Native American cultures.

After you have finished your list, think of at least eight to ten pieces of information that are not included in the documents above. Then go back to the prompt, and begin to organize some of this information loosely into the **categories** of your question (economics, religion, politics).

Because this prompt asks you to analyze how economics, religion, and politics shaped contact, it makes sense to group items in your list according to these categories. Label these "E," "R," and "P" for economics, religion, and politics. You can even categorize these items under the headings that you created as part of your brainstorming activity.

Next, generate a **thesis statement** based on the information that you have brainstormed. What you have created is a **working thesis** (which may change) based on **secondary sources** (namely, the information that you remember from your text or from class). This brainstormed information will also function as some of the **outside information** that the prompt requires you to incorporate into your response.

STEP 3 Categorize and connect historical information and documents

Review the documents in this chapter, and create a chart that allows you to connect your brainstorming of outside information to the documents. Your review of the documents allows you to understand the ways in which they fit into the prompt itself. For example, a document might apply to multiple categories of the prompt, or a document might be viewed differently by another source.

Below, some of the documents of this chapter have been aligned to outside information that is not found in this chapter but might be found in your textbook or your class notes.

Outside information or knowledge	Documents	Categories: Economic, religious, political
Columbus arrived in the Western Hemisphere (1492).	Doc. 1.4, Christopher Columbus	Political
The Aztec emperor Moctezuma was assassinated (1520); Pizzaro conquered the Incan empire (similar to defeat of Aztecs).	Doc. 1.5, Hernán Cortés	Political and economic
The Spanish tried to convert native peoples to Christianity (16th century).	Doc. 1.6, Pope Paul III	Economic and religious
Disease played a large role (enormous native population losses and loss of labor).	Doc. 1.7, Bartolomé de las Casas	Economic, religious, and political
The French began to colonize North America (16th century).	Doc. 1.11, Jacques Cartier	Economic
The English began to colonize North America (16th century).	Doc. 1.12, John Smith	Political

STEP 4 *Organize your response through an outline*

Organizing your ideas and evidence is the most important step when creating a **coherent** and **logical** historical argument. First, write your working thesis. Second, outline your body paragraphs based on the following outline. Your chart of outside information, documents, and categories above will help you to create this outline.

Economics

1. Compose a **claim** that answers the prompt in terms of economics.
2. Compose one or two **evidence statements** that prove your claim about economics. These evidence statements should use the historical information and documents that you gathered in your brainstorming.

Religion

1. Compose a **claim** that answers the prompt in terms of religion.
2. Compose one or two **evidence statements** that prove your claim about religion. These evidence statements should use the historical information and documents that you gathered in your brainstorming.

Politics

1. Compose a **claim** that answers the prompt in terms of politics.
2. Compose one or two **evidence statements** that prove your claim about politics. These evidence statements should use the historical information and documents that you gathered in your brainstorming.

Native Americans, Europeans, and the Exchange of Misconceptions

From 1492 to 1754, profound changes took place on the North American continent. Over this period, diverse Native American societies that had existed for hundreds of years encountered and interacted with Europeans. The effects of the interactions between Europeans and Native Americans are the subject of intense study by historians. You already have had the opportunity to study a variety of sources that deal with both Native American and European perspectives on these interactions. Now read the two passages below, and consider how different historians have sought to explain the encounter of these two cultures.

> The soldiers of Christ were entering a world of deeply held religious beliefs every bit as complex and sophisticated as their own, but one they would rarely fathom or even try to understand. Native religions did not possess a specific theology; nor did they require that "believers" give verbal confessions of faith and live in obedience to a set of religious tenets stipulated by the church. Nevertheless, religion and ritual permeated the everyday lives of Indian peoples. European missionaries, convinced that there was only one true religion and it was theirs, tended to see things as black or white, good or evil. Indians who converted to Christianity must demonstrate unquestioning faith; Indians who resisted were clinging to heathen ways. For Christian missionaries, conversion was a simple matter: Indian people who had been living in darkness and sin would receive the light and accept salvation. It proved to be not that simple.

—Colin G. Galloway, *New Worlds for All: Indians, Europeans, and the Remaking of Early America* (Baltimore, MD: Johns Hopkins University Press, 1997), 69.

> Before the arrival of the French, it is unlikely that there was an Indian market for scalps, for the practice of scalping seems to have been linked to rites of passage rather than to commerce. One eighteenth-century visitor recalled that among the neighboring Creeks, boys took their first scalps to establish their manhood. . . . Later in life, men took scalps to establish their bravery and to rise in the estimation of their families and communities. . . . [B]y the 1730s[,] scalps had become commodities. Responding to market incentive . . . , Choctaws adopted the practice of cutting enemy scalps into several pieces so as to receive more than one payment for a single scalp. . . . For a brief period, French officers closely inspected their grisly purchases, paying for pieces in proportion to the whole, but this cost-saving measure soon had to be abandoned when Choctaws objected to such market regulation.

—Claudio Saunt, "'Our Indians': European Empires and the History of the Native American South," in Jorge Cañizares-Esguerra and Eric R. Seeman, eds., *The Atlantic in Global History, 1500–2000* (Upper Saddle River, NJ: Pearson/Prentice Hall, 2007), 70.

Based on the two interpretations above, complete the following three tasks:

1. Briefly explain the main point made by the first passage.
2. Briefly explain the main point made by the second passage.
3. Provide one document from Chapter 1, 2, or 3, and explain how it supports the interpretation of either passage.

CHAPTER 2

Colonial North America

England and France began to challenge Spanish dominance of the Western Hemisphere in the early seventeenth century. Although these three kingdoms struggled with one another militarily, economically, and socially, each also consolidated power on the North American continent. Each engaged in shifting patterns of cooperation and competition with native populations in ways that reflected their cultural, social, religious, and economic interests.

For example, the French steadily established trade networks with native peoples in Canada, and the Spanish in the Southwest sought to convert natives to Catholicism while at the same time exploiting their labor. The English colony at Jamestown tried to replicate the success of the Spanish in finding easy profits in gold and silver mines, but the climate and geography of Virginia were radically different from the Central American regions that Hernán Cortés conquered nearly a hundred years before. The early Jamestown settlers were technically under the control of the Crown, but they built a colony that differed from the ordered and authoritarian encomienda system of the Spanish, where native peoples worked under close Spanish supervision. Instead, a labor system where English-born indentured servants agreed to a set time of labor in return for passage to the English colony gave way to a racial caste system where enslaved Africans made up the bulk of the labor force on large cash-crop plantations. In the western backcountry regions of Virginia, the majority of the population was made up of independent, semisubsistence farmers, many of whom were former

servants themselves. These backcountry settlers encountered native agricultural-
ists along a shifting borderland of conflict and trade.

By the late 1600s, Great Britain dominated the North American Atlantic
seaboard, and its colonies were populated with diverse British populations.
Although the British colonists came from a loosely homogeneous culture, the
diversity throughout the North American British colonies led to great diversity
in economic and social structures.

Seeking the Main Point

As you read the documents in this chapter, keep the following broad questions
in mind. They will help you understand the relationship between the documents
in this chapter and the historical changes that they represent. As you reflect on
these questions, determine which themes and which documents best address
them.

- In what ways did colonization stimulate conflicts between native peoples
  and European colonists?
- What were the effects of these conflicts on European colonists? On native
  peoples?
- Compare the interests of Europeans, colonists, and native peoples during
  this era of expansion. In what ways were these interests similar? In what
  ways did they diverge?
- What documents here signified the development of a slave-based economy
  in North America?
- What regional differences began to become apparent in North America during this period?

TOPIC I

Settling Atlantic North America

DOCUMENT 2.1 | **SAMUEL DE CHAMPLAIN, "Description of the French Fur Trade"**
| 1608

Samuel de Champlain (1574–1635) founded the French colony of Quebec in 1608. In this document, he describes the beginnings of the fur trade between the French and the native peoples of modern Canada. Although Champlain refers to himself in the third person in this document, he is its author.

Near the spot which had thus been selected for a future settlement, Champlain discovered a deposit of excellent clay, and, by way of experiment, had a quantity of it manufactured into bricks, of which he made a wall on the brink of the river. . . . In the mean time, Champlain had been followed to his rendezvous by a herd of adventurers from the maritime towns of France, who, stimulated by the freedom of the trade, had flocked after him in numbers all out of proportion to the amount of furs which they could hope to obtain from the wandering bands of savages that might chance to visit the St. Lawrence [River]. The river was lined with . . . [Frenchmen] anxiously watching the coming of the savages, all impatient and eager to secure as large a share as possible of the uncertain and meager booty for which they had crossed the Atlantic. Fifteen or twenty barques [sailing vessels with three masts] were moored along the shore, all seeking the best opportunity for the display of the worthless trinkets for which they had avariciously [greedily] hoped to obtain a valuable cargo of furs.

Samuel de Champlain, *Voyages of Samuel de Champlain: 1567–1635*, trans. Charles Pomeroy Otis, vol. 11 (Boston, MA: Prince Society, 1880), 107–108.

PRACTICING Historical Thinking

Identify: How does Champlain portray the Frenchmen who join him on his journey?

Analyze: In what ways were the interests of Champlain and his fellow Frenchmen the same? In what ways were they different?

Evaluate: Compare Champlain's perceptions of natives with those of the Spanish, as seen in Documents 1.4, 1.7, and 1.8.

DOCUMENT 2.2 | JOHN ROLFE, Letter on Jamestown Settlement
1618

John Rolfe (1585–1622), one of the first British colonists in Jamestown, Virginia, perfected a mild strain of tobacco that proved so popular among European consumers that by the 1620s, tobacco became Jamestown's primary export. This letter was recorded in Captain John Smith's *The Generall Historie of Virginia* (Doc. 1.12).

. . . [A]n industrious man not other ways employed, may well tend four acres of corn, and 1,000 plants of tobacco, and where they say an acre will yield but three or four barrels, we have ordinarily four or five, but of new ground six, seven, and eight, and a barrel of peas and beans, which we esteem as good as two of corn, . . . so that one man may provide corn for five [people], and apparel for two [people] by the profit of his tobacco . . . had we but carpenters to build and make carts and ploughs, and skillful men that know how to use them, and train up our cattle to draw them, . . . yet our want of experience brings but little to perfection but planting tobacco, and yet of that many are so covetous to have much, they make little good. . . .

John Smith, *The Generall Historie of Virginia* (London: Printed by I. Dawson and I. Haviland for Michael Sparkes, 1632), 125–126, transcribed into modern English by Jason Stacy.

PRACTICING Historical Thinking

Identify: According to Rolfe, what economic advantages and social problems did tobacco pose for the colony?

Analyze: Rolfe wanted "skillful men" who could grow corn and wheat and build carts and ploughs. What does Rolfe's vision of ideal colonists tell us about the reality of the colonists who settled there?

Evaluate: Compare this document to Samuel de Champlain's description of the French fur trade (Doc. 2.1). What were some similarities and some differences between these French and English enterprises?

DOCUMENT 2.3 | The Mayflower Compact
1620

William Bradford (1590–1657) joined a group of Separatists who left the Church of England and escaped with them to Leiden, Holland, where they lived in self-imposed exile for over ten years. After receiving permission to settle in British North America, members of the group set sail from Plymouth, England. The Mayflower Compact, signed aboard the ship *Mayflower* after it was anchored in waters off Cape Cod in what is now Massachusetts, was an unofficial agreement for governance made by these English migrants.

We whose names are underwritten, the loyal subjects of our dread sovereign lord, King James, by the grace of God, of Great Britain, France, and Ireland King, Defender of the Faith, etc., having undertaken, for the glory of God, and advancement of the Christian faith, and honor of our king and country, a voyage to plant the first colony in the northern parts of Virginia, do by these presents solemnly and mutually, in the presence of God and one of another, *covenant and combine ourselves together into a civil body politic*, for our better ordering and preservation, and furtherance of the ends aforesaid; and by virtue hereof, to enact, constitute, and frame such *just and equal laws*, ordinances, Acts, constitutions, and offices, from time to time, as shall be thought most *meet and convenient for the general good* of the colony; *unto which we promise all due submission and obedience*. In witness whereof we have hereunder subscribed our names, at Cape Cod, the 11th day of November, in the year of the reign of our sovereign lord, King James, of England, France, and Ireland the eighteenth, and of Scotland the fifty-fourth, Anno Domini, 1620.

Albert Stickney, *Democratic Government: A Study of Politics* (New York: Harper & Brothers, 1885), 162.

PRACTICING Historical Thinking

Identify: What justification does Bradford provide for the formation of this government?

Analyze: In what ways is this document a declaration of independence, and in what ways does it declare its allegiance to Great Britain?

Evaluate: What does the organization of this document tell us about the values of the signatories?

DOCUMENT 2.4 | **JOHN WINTHROP, "A Model of Christian Charity"**
1630

John Winthrop (1587–1649) led the first wave of English Protestant "Puritans" to New England a decade after William Bradford and his Separatists. On board the ship *Arbella*, Winthrop, who served as the first governor of New England, gave this sermon as a way to situate Puritan New England within the framework of God's plan.

Now the only way to . . . provide for our posterity . . . is to follow the counsel of Micah, to do justly, to love mercy, to walk humbly with our God. For this end, we must be knit together, in this work, as one man. . . . We must be willing to abridge ourselves of our superfluities, for the supply of others' necessities. We must uphold a familiar commerce together in all meekness, gentleness, patience and liberality. We must delight in each other; make others' conditions our own; rejoice together, mourn together, labor and suffer together, always having before our eyes our commission and community in the work, as members of the same body. . . . We shall find that the God of Israel is among us, when ten of us shall be able to resist a thousand of our enemies; when he shall make us a praise and glory that men shall say of succeeding plantations, "The Lord make it likely that of New England." For we must consider that we shall be as a city upon a hill. The eyes of all people are upon us. So that if we shall deal falsely with our God in this work we have undertaken, and so cause him to withdraw his present help from us, we shall be made a story and a by-word through the world. We shall open the mouths of enemies to speak evil of the ways of God, and all professors for God's sake. We shall shame the faces of many of God's worthy servants, and cause their prayers to be turned into curses upon us till we be consumed out of the good land whither we are agoing. . . .

Edmund Clarence Stedman and Ellen Mackay Cortissoz, eds., *A Library of American Literature from the Earliest Settlement to the Present Time*, vols. 1–2, *Colonial Literature, 1607–1764* (New York: Charles Webster and Co., 1891), 306–307.

PRACTICING Historical Thinking

Identify: What kind of society does Winthrop envision? What will be the result if that society fails to come to pass?

Analyze: Winthrop presents his social vision in religious terms. What secular advantages also might underlie his appeal to build a society "knit together . . . as one man"?

Evaluate: Compare this document to William Bradford's (Doc. 2.3). Describe the similarities and differences between them. How were the societies that they sought to create different from the one that John Rolfe describes in Jamestown (Doc. 2.2)?

APPLYING AP® Historical Thinking Skills

REVIEW | Causation

As you'll recall from Chapter 1, **causation** refers to the relationship between cause and effect—the ways that things change over time and the causes that precede those changes. Historians are concerned with both long-term causes and proximate (short-term) causes. Using your textbook and your class notes, determine and explain two long-term and two proximate causes of the events described in one of the documents above. Use the graphic organizer identified in Chapter 1 if it is helpful.

The Conquest of Native North America

DOCUMENT 2.5 | Native Attack on Jamestown
1622

Matthaeus Merian (1593–1650), a Swiss engraver, created this image of Opechankanough's attack on a Virginian settlement. A simultaneous attack on Jamestown is pictured in the background. Opechankanough's brother, Chief Powhatan (Doc. 1.3), had established an uneasy peace with the colonists of Jamestown. However, the English expansion into native territories in pursuit of land forced Opechankanough to lead a series of raids against the Virginia colonists. After Opechankanough's raids, the Virginia colony was placed under a governor appointed by the king.

The Granger Collection, New York.

Identify: Consider the upper left quadrant, the upper right quadrant, the lower left quadrant, and the lower right quadrant in this picture. Write a sentence that describes each. What is happening in the background and foreground of this picture?

Analyze: When historians make an inference, they make an educated guess based on available evidence. Based on this image, infer what the artist intended us to think happened before and after the attack.

Evaluate: How are these images different from the information conveyed in John Smith's and John Rolfe's descriptions of the Virginia colony (Docs. 1.12 and 2.2)?

DOCUMENT 2.6 | JOHN MARTIN, "Proposal for Subjugating Native Americans"
1622

John Martin (1560–1632), a Jamestown councilman, suggested the strategy below for subjugating the Pamunkey after the attacks by Opechankanough depicted in Document 2.5 above.

The manner how to bring in the Indians into subjugation [under control of the English] without making an utter extirpation of them together with the reasons.

First, by disabling the main body of the enemy from having . . . [all necessities]. As namely corn and all manner of victuals of any worth.

This is to be acted two manner of ways.—First by keeping them from setting corn at home and fishing. Secondly by keeping them from their accustomed trading for corn.

For the first it is performed by having some 200 soldiers on foot, continually harrowing and burning all their Towns in winter, and spoiling their wares. . . .

For the second there must [be] provided some 10 ships, that in May, June, July and August may scour the bay and keep the rivers yet are belonging to Opichankanoe [Opechancanough].

By this arises two happy ends.—First the assured taking of great purchases in skins and prisoners. Secondly in keeping them from trading for corn on the Eastern shore and from the southward from whence they have five times more than they set themselves.

This course being taken they have no means, but must yield to obedience, or fly to bordering neighbors who neither will receive them nor indeed are able, for they have but ground cleared for their own use.

Susan Myra Kingsbury, ed., *The Records of the Virginia Company of London, 1607–26*, vol. 3, *Miscellaneous Records* (Washington, DC: Government Printing Office, 1906–1935), 740, transcribed into modern English by Jason Stacy.

PRACTICING Historical Thinking

Identify: What is Martin's plan for subjugating the natives around Jamestown?

Analyze: In what ways does this plan play to the colonists' strengths?

Evaluate: Martin's plan took place before the advent of widespread slavery in Jamestown. To what extent does this plan reflect certain British attitudes toward non-Europeans?

DOCUMENT 2.7 | **PHILIP IV, Letter to Don Luis de Valdés**
1647

Philip IV (1605–1665) ruled the Spanish empire at a time when Spain claimed much of modern North, Central, and South America. However, Spanish magistrates faced conflicts with the tribes of northern Mexico (Doc. 1.9). In this letter to Governor Luis Valdés, Philip sought to stabilize this region.

To my governor and captain-general of the province of Nueva Vizcaya: It has been learned in my royal Council of the Indies that that province adjoins the barbarous nations . . . who are now at war, though they are usually at peace; that while they were so at peace, there went among them to trade certain *alcaldes mayores* [magistrates] and religious instructors who carried off and sold their children to serve in the mines and elsewhere, disposing of them as slaves or giving them as presents, which amounts to the same thing. As a result they became disquieted, and the governor, Don Luis de Valdés, began to punish them immoderately and without regard for the public faith, for, after calling them to attend religious instruction, he seized and shot some of them. Thereupon they revolted, took up their arms and arrows, and made some raids; they broke into my treasury, and it has cost me over 50,000 pesos to pacify them, although they are not entirely quieted yet. It is very fitting to my service and to their peace to command strictly that the barbarous Indians shall not be made slaves nor sent as presents to anyone, nor made to serve anywhere against their will when they are at peace and are not taken in open war.

Charles W. Hackett, Adolph Francis Alphonse Bandelier, and Fanny Bandelier, eds., *Historical Documents Relating to New Mexico, Nueva Vizcaya and Approaches Thereto, to 1773* (Washington, DC: Carnegie Institution of Washington, 1923), 161.

PRACTICING Historical Thinking

Identify: What is the cause of the king's dissatisfaction with Governor Don Luis de Valdés? What is the king's proposed solution?

Analyze: What does Philip hope will result from this letter?

DOCUMENT 2.8 | JOHN EASTON, *A Relation of the Indian War*
1675

John Easton (1624–1705) was governor of Rhode Island during King Philip's War (1675–1678), a series of attacks on New England settlements by the leader of the Wampanoag Confederacy, Metacomet (who was called King Philip by the English). Below, Easton describes how the Narragansett and Rhode Islanders were pulled into the war after forces from the Puritan colonies of Massachusetts and Connecticut attacked the Narragansett people in Rhode Island on suspicion of harboring Wampanoag warriors.

. . . I having often informed the Indians that English men would not begin a war, otherwise it was brutish so to do. I am sorry so the Indians have case to think me deceitful for the English thus began the war with the Narogansets [Narragansetts], we having sent off our island [Rhode Island] many Indians and informed them if they kept by the water side and did not meddle that . . . the English would do them no harm. . . . The war [began] without proclamation, and some of our people did not know the English had begun mischief to [conflict with the] Indians. . . . They [the forces from New England] sold the Indians that they had taken . . . for slaves, . . . and now the English army is out to seek after the Indians, but it is most likely that such most able to do mischief will escape, and women and children and impotent may be destroyed. . . .

J. Franklin Jameson and Charles H. Lincoln, eds., *Original Narratives of Early American History: Narratives of the Indian Wars, 1675–1699* (New York: Charles Scribner's Sons, 1913), 15–16, transcribed into modern English by Jason Stacy.

PRACTICING Historical Thinking

Identify: According to Easton, what were the origins of this conflict? How far has it progressed?

Analyze: What was Easton's attitude toward the Narragansetts of Rhode Island?

Evaluate: What conflicting relations between natives and New Englanders does this document portray?

| **EDWARD RANDOLPH, Assessment of the Causes of King Philip's War**

1675

Edward Randolph (1632–1703), a prominent British colonial administrator, assessed the causes of King Philip's War for the British government. His critical report led Charles II to revoke the charter of the Massachusetts Bay Colony and place it under a governor who was appointed by the king.

Various are the reports and conjectures of the causes of the present Indian war. Some impute it to an imprudent zeal in the magistrates of Boston . . . for that while the magistrates, for their profit, put the laws severely in execution against the Indians, the people, on the other side, for lucre [profit] and gain, entice and provoke the Indians to the breach thereof, especially to drunkenness, to which those people are so generally addicted that they will strip themselves to their skin to have their fill of rum and brandy. . . .

Some believe there have been vagrant and Jesuitical priests [missionaries of the Society of Jesus, who were converting natives to Catholicism], who have made it their business, for some years past, to go from Sachem to Sachem [sachems were native leaders], to exasperate the Indians against the English and to bring them into a confederacy, and that they were promised supplies from France and other parts to extirpate the English nation out of the continent of America. Others impute the cause to some injuries offered to the Sachem Philip; for he being possessed of a tract of land called Mount Hope, . . . some English had a mind to dispossess him thereof, who never wanting one pretense or other to attain their end, complained of injuries done by Philip and his Indians to their stock and cattle, whereupon Philip was often summoned before the magistrate, sometimes imprisoned, and never released but upon parting with a considerable part of his land.

But the government of the Massachusetts (to give it in their own words) do declare these are the great evils for which God hath given the heathen commission to rise against them: The woeful breach of the 5th commandment, in contempt of their authority, which is a sin highly provoking to the Lord: For men wearing long hair and periwigs made of women's hair; for women wearing borders of hair and for cutting, curling and laying out the hair, and disguising themselves by following strange fashions in their apparel: For profaneness in the people not frequenting their meetings, and others going away before the blessing be pronounced. . . .

With many such reasons, but whatever be the cause, the English have contributed much to their misfortunes, for they first taught the Indians the use of arms, and admitted them to be present at all their musters and trainings, and showed them how to handle, mend and fix their muskets, and have been furnished with all sorts of arms by permission of the government, so that the Indians are become excellent firemen. . . .

Albert B. Hart, ed., *American History Told by Contemporaries*, vol. 1, *Era of Colonization, 1492–1689* (New York: Macmillan, 1897), 458–460, transcribed into modern English by Jason Stacy.

PRACTICING Historical Thinking

Identify: Randolph offers a number of causes of the conflict. List those that stem from factors in North America. List those that stem from factors tied to European conflicts. Who did Randolph accuse of stirring up the Indians against the English?

Analyze: What do the causes of the war according to "the government of . . . Massachusetts" tell you about the values of the leaders of the Massachusetts Bay Colony? How do they differ from those of Randolph and the British government?

Evaluate: In what ways was King Philip's War a product of both local and global forces?

DOCUMENT 2.10 | NATHANIEL BACON, "Declaration against Governor William Berkeley"
| 1676

Virginia colonist Nathaniel Bacon (1647–1676) wrote the following declaration to justify his revolt and temporary overthrow of Virginia governor William Berkeley (1605–1677) in 1676. Bacon's Rebellion was put down after Bacon died of dysentery and Governor Berkeley conquered Jamestown with armed naval vessels.

FIRST. For having upon specious pretences of public works raised great unjust taxes upon the Commonalty for the advancement of private favorites and other sinister ends, but no visible effects in any measure adequate. For not having during this long time of his government, in any measure advanced this hopeful Colony, either by fortifications, towns or trade.

2. For having abused and rendered contemptible the Magistrates of Justice, by advancing to places of judicature scandalous and ignorant favorites.

3. For having wronged his Majesty's prerogative and interest by assuming monopoly of the beaver trade, and for having in that unjust gain betrayed and sold his Majesty's Country and the lives of his loyal subjects to the barbarous heathen.

4. For having protected, favored, and emboldened the Indians against his Majesty's loyal subjects; never contriving, requiring, or appointing any due or proper means of satisfaction for their many invasions, robberies, and murders committed upon us.

5. For having, when the army of English was just upon the track of those Indians, who now in all places burn, spoil, murder, and when we might with ease have destroyed them who then were in open hostility, for then having expressly countermanded and sent back our army, by passing his word for the peaceable demeanor of the said Indians, who immediately prosecuted their evil intentions, committing horrid murders and robberies in all places, being protected by the said engagement and word past of him the said Sir William Berkeley; having ruined and laid desolate a great part of his Majesty's Country, and have now drawn themselves into such obscure and remote places, and are by their success so emboldened and confirmed, by their confederacy so strengthened, that the cries of blood are in all places, and the terror and consternation of the people so great, are now become, not only a difficult, but a very formidable enemy, who might at first with ease have been destroyed.

Edmund Clarence Stedman and Ellen Mackay Hutchinson, eds., *A Library of American Literature from the Earliest Settlement to the Present Time*, vol. 3, *Literature of the Revolutionary Period, 1765–1787* (New York: Charles L. Webster, 1888), 448–449.

PRACTICING Historical Thinking

Identify: Who, according to Bacon and his rebels, was the cause of their complaints? In what ways does he implicate local Native Americans in these complaints?

Analyze: Why did Bacon appeal to both the king and his fellow countrymen in his charges against the governor?

Evaluate: What does this document tell us about the relations between natives and the English in the Virginia backcountry and the ways in which this relationship played into rivalries within Jamestown society?

DOCUMENT 2.11 | **EXPERIENCE MAYHEW and THOMAS PRINCE,** *Indian Converts: or, Some Account of the Lives and Dying Speeches of a Considerable Number of the Christianized Indians of Martha's Vineyard, in New-England*
1727

Experience Mayhew (1673–1758) and Thomas Prince (1687–1758), two New England missionaries, provided testimony of the conversion of Wampanoag natives in this excerpt from their book *Indian Converts*, although New Englanders still felt animosity toward the Wampanoag in the aftermath of King Philip's War. In this excerpt, Mayhew describes a native woman whom he converted to Puritan-style Christianity.

I observed at this time, that she appeared to be unhealthy, and I heard a while after that her friends feared she was falling into a consumption: however, I did not see and speak with her again, till at least a year after I had my first discourse with her; but hearing that she was grown worse, and was like to die, I again visited her, and I shall here set down the substance of what she said to me, chiefly in answer to such questions as I then put to her.

She said she remembered the discourse which I formerly had with her, and said she had been thereby encouraged to seek after God, and she manifested a desire that I would further instruct her.

I then put many questions to her for the trial of her understanding, and found she well understood the principles of the Christian faith; as the doctrine of original sin, the guilt which it brought on all mankind, and the depravation of the humane nature by it, by which man is now naturally inclined to that which is evil only, and that continually. She owned, that from this corrupt fountain all those actual sins do flow, which mankind commit, and said, her own sins had been very many and great.

I found also that she had a distinct understanding of the doctrine of redemption by Jesus Christ. I put several questions to her concerning his person, offices, and the righteousness he fulfilled in his obedience and sufferings for sinners; all which she answered well, and declared her belief of his resurrection from the dead, and ascension into Heaven, &c.

I likewise found she understood the doctrine of regeneration, and the absolute necessity of it, in order to the eternal salvation of sinners. She owned, that without holiness of heart and life, none could have any saving benefit by Jesus Christ, or ever enter into the kingdom of God.

Experience Mayhew and Thomas Prince, *Indian Converts: or, Some Account of the Lives and Dying Speeches of a Considerable Number of the Christianized Indians of Martha's Vineyard, in New-England* (London: S. Gerrish, 1727), 273, transcribed into modern English by Jason Stacy.

PRACTICING Historical Thinking

Identify: What evidence do Mayhew and Prince provide for their claim to have converted this native woman to Christianity?

Analyze: What interests do Mayhew and Prince have in presenting this conversion in this fashion?

Evaluate: In Chapter 1, Pope Paul III sought the conversion of native peoples in New Spain a little over ten years after the Spanish conquest of Central America (Doc. 1.6). Likewise, Bartolomé de las Casas portrayed natives as ideal Catholics around twenty years after Hernán Cortés's conquest (Doc. 1.7). This document, on the other hand, was written nearly a hundred years after Puritans first settled New England (Doc. 2.4). What in these four documents accounts for the difference between Spanish Catholic and English Puritan conceptions of native peoples and their possibility of salvation?

NEW SKILL | Comparison

Sometimes we **compare** two things to understand each one better. For example, if you want to understand the weather today, it often helps to compare it to yesterday's weather: "Today is warmer than yesterday." If your listener knows what the weather was yesterday, she will understand what the weather is today. Historians use comparison to illuminate the similarities and differences between two or more historical events, individuals, or concepts.

The historical thinking skill called **comparison** can be used to answer the following prompt:

> Compare the Spanish, English, and French policies toward Native Americans. To what extent were these policies shaped by economic considerations?

STEP 1 Use the documents from Topics 1 and 2 above (and if you have time, Docs. 1.6–1.9 and 1.11–1.12 from Chapter 1) to characterize Spanish, English, and French policies toward Native Americans. Consider the ways in which these policies were shaped by economic considerations. One is already done for you.

European colonizers	Policies toward natives	Ways in which these policies were shaped by economic considerations
Spanish	Philip IV tried to prevent further uprisings by ordering Governor Don Luis de Valdés to treat natives less cruelly (Doc. 2.7).	The Spanish depended on native laborers, especially through the encomienda system.
English		
French		

STEP 2 Now that you have characterized each nation's policies and economic relations with Native Americans, you're ready to compare them. Compile the similarities and the differences between the Spanish, the English, and the French using the chart below. (Note: Your similarities will be **generalizations**, or common statements, about all three nations. Your differences also will be generalizations but about each nation in particular.) Try to come up with three for each. One similarity and one difference are already completed for you.

Similarities: Policies and economics	Differences: Policies and economics
1. All three European nations needed some form of cooperation from natives to fulfill their economic goals in North America.	**Spanish:** The Spanish used natives as labor and needed to maintain their subservient social and economics status to fulfill this goal.
2.	**French:**
3.	**English:**

STEP 3 You're now ready to create a thesis statement that compares these three nations and the ways that their policies affected economic relations with Native Americans. Your thesis statement should include both your similarities and differences. For example, it could begin with a similarity:

Although Spain, England, and France all instituted policies that sought to exploit native peoples, . . .

and could end with a statement of differences:

. . . Spain overwhelmingly sought to convert natives to Catholicism and treat them as economic dependents, England traded with native peoples but primarily pursued cultivation of Native American land, and France sought to trade raw materials with Native Americans.

After you have written your own thesis statement, create between three and five claim statements that incorporate evidence for your thesis statement based on the documents above. Each claim statement should correspond to your claims in your thesis statement.

Slavery in the British Colonies

DOCUMENT 2.12 | RICHARD LIGON, Map of Barbados
1657

Richard Ligon (1585–1662) made this map of the British colony of Barbados to portray the economic and social conditions on this Caribbean island for his British readers. Most of the writing on the map (particularly the small labels along the coastline) delineates individual plantation holdings by British sugar planters. Near the center of the island are these words: "The ten thousand acres of land which belong to the merchants of London."

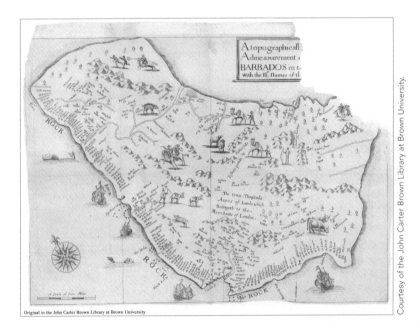

Courtesy of the John Carter Brown Library at Brown University.

Original in the John Carter Brown Library at Brown University

PRACTICING Historical Thinking

Identify: List five types of details that the mapmaker has illustrated on the map.

Analyze: Based on these images of people, what can we infer about the social hierarchy of Barbados? What images allow you to make these inferences?

Evaluate: Based on details that the mapmaker has chosen to illuminate, what are the interests and concerns of the British colonists on Barbados?

| **Virginia Slave Laws**
1662–1669

Throughout the 1660s, the Virginia House of Burgesses passed a series of statutes for the purpose of socially separating white settlers from black slaves. Below are some of those statutes.

December, 1662

Whereas some doubts have arisen whether children got by any Englishman upon a negro woman should be slave or free, *Be it therefore enacted and declared by this present grand assembly*, that all children borne in this country shalbe held bond or free only according to the condition of the mother, *And* that if any christian shall commit fornication with a negro man or woman, hee or shee soe offending shall pay double the fines imposed by the former act. . . .

September, 1667

Whereas some doubts have risen whether children that are slaves by birth, and by the charity and piety of their owners made partakers of the blessed sacrament of baptisme, should by virtue of their baptisme be made free; *It is enacted and declared by this grand assembly, and the authority thereof*, that the conferring of baptisme doth not alter the condition of the person as to his bondage or freedom; that diverse masters, freed from this doubt, may more carefully endeavour the propagation of christianity by permitting children, though slaves, or those of greater growth if capable to be admitted to that sacrament. . . .

September, 1668

Whereas it has been questioned whether servants running away may be punished with corporall punishment by their master or magistrate since the act already made gives the master satisfaction by prolonging their time by service, *It is declared and enacted by this assembly* that moderate corporall punishment inflicted by master or magistrate upon a runaway servant, shall not deprive the master of the satisfaction allowed by the law, the one being as necessary to reclayme them from persisting in that idle course, as the other is just to repair the damages susteyned by the master. . . .

October, 1669

Whereas the only law in force for the punishment of refractory [resistant] servants (*a*) resisting their master, mistress or overseer cannot be inflicted upon negroes, nor the obstinacy of many of them by other than violent means suppresst, *Be it enacted and declared by this grand assembly*, if any slave resist his master (or other by his masters order correcting him) and by the extremity of the correction should chance to die, that his death shall not be accounted felony, but the master (or that other person appointed by the master to punish him) be acquit from molestation, since it cannot be presumed that prepensed [premeditated] malice (which alone makes murder felony) should induce any man to destroy his own estate.

William Waller Hening, ed., *The Statutes at Large; Being a Collection of All the Laws of Virginia*, vol. 11 (New York: R. & W. & G. Bartow, 1809–1823), 170, 260, 266, 270.

PRACTICING Historical Thinking

Identify: Describe in one sentence each of what these four laws sought to do.

Analyze: What interest would Virginian colonists have in ensuring that children born of a white father and an enslaved African mother remained enslaved?

Evaluate: How might these laws influence the self-identity of white residents of the colony, both rich and poor?

DOCUMENT 2.14 | Enslaved Africans to the Western Hemisphere
1450–1900

An estimated eleven million Africans were brought to the Western Hemisphere as slaves during nearly five hundred years of European colonialism. The chart below traces the growth of the slave trade over these years.

Period	Number of people	Percentage of total number of slaves who traveled to the Western Hemisphere
1450–1600	367,000	3.1%
1601–1700	1,868,000	16%
1701–1800	6,133,000	52.4%
1801–1900	3,330,000	28.5%
Total	11,698,000	100%

Paul E. Lovejoy, "The Volume of the Atlantic Slave Trade: A Synthesis," *Journal of African History* 23, no. 4 (1982): 473–501.

PRACTICING Historical Thinking

Identify: What was the greatest period of growth in the number of slaves who traveled to the Western Hemisphere between 1450 and 1900?

Analyze: What economic and political factors could have accounted for this growth?

Evaluate: How might the expansion of the slave economy in colonial North America have influenced colonies like Virginia and Barbados?

| GEORGE CATO, "Account of the Stono Rebellion"

1739

The Stono Rebellion of 1739, which took place in the British colony of South Carolina, was led by enslaved Africans who were captured in the Kongo region of West Africa and forcibly transported to the Western Hemisphere. This excerpt was taken from a recording made in 1937 as part of the Works Progress Administration's Federal Writers' Project. The speaker is George Cato, great-great-grandson of the Stono Rebellion leader, Cato.

How it all start? Dat what I ask but nobody ever tell me how 100 slaves between de Combahee and Edisto rivers come to meet in de woods not far from de Stono River on September 9, 1739. And how they elect a leader, my kinsman, Cato, and late dat day march to Stono town, break in a warehouse, kill two white men in charge, and take all de guns and ammunition they wants. But they do it. Wid dis start, they turn south and march on.

They work fast, coverin' 15 miles, passin' many fine plantations, and in every single case, stop, and break in de house and kill men, women, and children. Then they take what they want, 'cludin' arms, clothes, liquor and food. Near de Combahee swamp, Lieutenant Governor Bull, drivin' from Beaufort to Charleston, see them and he smell a rat. Befo' he was seen by de army he detour into de big woods and stay 'til de slave rebels pass.

Governor Bull and some planters, between de Combahee and Edisto [rivers], ride fast and spread de alarm and it wasn't long 'til de militiamen was on de trail in pursuit of de slave army. When found, many of de slaves was singin' and dancin' and Cap. Cato and some of de other leaders was cussin' at them sumpin awful. From dat day to dis, no Cato has tasted whiskey, 'less he go 'gainst his daddy's warnin'. Dis war last less than two days but it sho' was pow'ful hot while it last.

I reckons it was hot, 'cause in less than two days, 21 white men, women, and chillun, and 44 Negroes, was slain. My granddaddy say dat in de woods and at Stono, where de war start, dere was more than 100 Negroes in line. When de militia come in sight of them at Combahee swamp, de drinkin' dancin' Negroes scatter in de brush and only 44 stand deir ground.

Commander Cato speak for de crowd. He say: "We don't lak slavery. We start to jine de Spanish in Florida. We surrender but we not whipped yet and we 'is not converted.'" De other 43 say: "Amen." They was taken, unarmed, and hanged by de militia. Long befo' dis uprisin', de Cato slave wrote passes for slaves and do all he can to send them to freedom. He die but he die for doin' de right, as he see it.

Mark M. Smith, *Stono: Documenting and Interpreting a Southern Slave Revolt* (Columbia: University of South Carolina Press, 2005), 56.

DOCUMENT 2.16 | South Carolina Slave Code
1740

The colonial legislature of South Carolina instituted these laws in the aftermath of the Stono Rebellion. Note that the term *mulatto* referred to a person of European and African descent and that *mustizo* was used to describe a person of Indian and African descent.

And be it enacted, . . . That all negroes and Indians, (free Indians in amity with this government, and negroes, mulattoes and mustizoes, who are now free, excepted), mulattoes or mustizoes who now are, or shall hereafter be, in this Province, and all their issue and offspring, born or to be born, shall be, and they are hereby declared to be, and remain forever hereafter, absolute slaves, and shall follow the condition of the mother, and shall be deemed, held, taken, reputed and adjudged in law, to be chattels personal, in the hands of their owners and possessors, and their executors, administrators and assigns, to all intents, constructions and purposes whatsoever. . . .

. . . Be it further enacted by the authority aforesaid, That no person whatsoever shall permit or suffer any slave under his or their care or management, and who lives or is employed in Charlestown, or any other town in this Province, to go out of the limits of the said town, or any such slave who lives in the country, to go out of the plantation to which such slave belongs, or in which plantation such slave is usually employed, without a letter . . . which . . . shall be signed by the master or other person having the care or charge of such slave, or by some other [person] by his or their order, directions and consent; and every slave who shall be found out of Charlestown, or any other town, (if such slave lives or is usually employed there,) or out of the plantation to which such slave belongs, or in which [such] slave is usually employed, if such slave lives in this country, without such letter . . . , or without a white person in his company, shall be punished with whipping on the bare back, not exceeding twenty lashes. . . .

... And be it further enacted by the authority aforesaid, That if any slave who shall be out of the house or plantation where such slave shall live, or shall be usually employed, or without some white person in company with such slave, shall refuse to submit to or undergo the examination of any white person, it shall be lawful for any such white person to pursue, apprehend, and moderately correct such slave; and if any such slave shall assault and strike such white person, such slave may be lawfully killed.

The Statutes at Large of South Carolina, vol. 7, Containing the Acts Relating to Charleston, Courts, Slaves, and Rivers, ed. Thomas Cooper and David James McCord (Columbia, SC: A. S. Johnson, 1840), 397–399.

PRACTICING Historical Thinking

Identify: What parts of this statute strengthen social controls over enslaved Africans?

Analyze: How does this document seek to regulate the ambiguities of racial differences in the colony?

Evaluate: Compare this document to the Virginia slave laws excerpted in Document 2.13. What do the similarities and differences between them tell us about slave-based economies of Virginia and South Carolina?

APPLYING AP® Historical Thinking Skills

REVIEW | Causation

Using your knowledge of the time period and relevant documents from this chapter and Chapter 1, in what ways did European colonialism give rise to the racial caste system in the colonies?

NEW SKILL | Contextualization

When historians practice **contextualization**, they consider the ways in which particular historical events connect to broader regional or global processes or changes. For example, if your friend is anxious about applying for college one weekend, her anxiety fits into the broader context of a high school career that is coming to an end and a new phase of her life that is relatively unknown.

Contextualization helps historians analyze a particular event by giving them a broader view of forces that frame an event. In Document 2.9, the author fears that Catholic priests encourage natives to attack the English population. This fear fits within the broader context of the religious wars between Protestant and Catholic nations in Europe during the seventeenth century. Likewise, a historian might connect an event like Opechankanough's war on Jamestown in 1622 (Docs. 2.5 and 2.6) to the growing English population in the Virginia colony and the relative success of tobacco as a cash crop (Doc. 2.2) and then contextualize Opechankanough's attacks within these broader processes of European peopling of North America.

The **historical context** of a document may incorporate other contexts, such as economic, political, social, and religious.

Use the following **thesis statement** to write a series of claims that situate the Stono Rebellion within its historical context:

> The economic and social context of late seventeenth- and early eighteenth-century colonial North America shaped the events that came to be known as the Stono Rebellion of 1739.

STEP 1 Using your textbook, connect the Stono Rebellion (Doc. 2.15) to at least three broader economic and social processes of late seventeenth- and early eighteenth-century colonial North America. The chart below will help you organize your thoughts. One has already been done for you.

Thesis statement	Economic processes (claim)	Social processes (claim)
The economic and social context of late seventeenth- and early eighteenth-century colonial North America shaped the events that came to be known as the Stono Rebellion of 1739.		Since the seventeenth century, slaves were assumed to be nonwhite, as is shown in the Virginia Slave Laws (Doc. 2.13). A racial caste system was already in place.

STEP 2 Use the chart above to turn the economic and social processes that you have determined into at least one **claim** for each. Your statements of **evidence** should explain why your **claim** proves a portion of your **thesis statement**.

STEP 3 Now **analyze** one of your claims for the economic or social process that created the context for the Stono Rebellion. Your **evidence** explains to the reader how your **claim** helps prove your **thesis statement**. For example:

Thesis statement: The economic and social context of late seventeenth- and early eighteenth-century colonial North America shaped the events that came to be known as the Stono Rebellion of 1739.

Claim: Since the seventeenth century, slaves were assumed to be nonwhite, as is shown in the Virginia Slave Laws (Doc. 2.13). A racial caste system was already in place.

Evidence: A racial caste system that gave enslaved Africans or their children little hope of freedom or equality created a social context where violent rebellion against the entire society offered the only hope for many enslaved Africans.

PUTTING IT ALL TOGETHER

Revisiting the Main Point

- How did imperial competitions and exchanges of goods across the Atlantic Ocean influence the development of the British North American colonies?
- Compare and contrast the goals of the New England and Virginia colonists. How were their relations with native peoples both similar and different?
- How did the British system of slavery in North America grow from economic, social, and geographic factors?
- How did conflict with native peoples shape European conceptions of them?
- In what ways did regional identities begin to emerge in British North America during this period? How did these regional identities shape regional policies regarding race and power?

BUILDING AP® WRITING SKILLS

Comparison When Assembling Multiple Body Paragraphs

When historians practice comparison, they also incorporate ideas of continuity and change over time, which you learned about in Chapter 1. For example, below is a response that compares different British colonies within an economic context. It incorporates the chronological reasoning skills of causation and patterns of continuity and change over time.

> Since the early seventeenth century, the needs of Great Britain shaped colonial economies [long-term cause], which fostered an ongoing colonial dependence on England [continuity]. However, the colonies also developed relatively diverse economies [change] under this single economic system. For example, the agricultural colonies of Virginia, the Carolinas, and Barbados (Docs. 2.2 and 2.12) were land rich and in need of laborers. They produced a radically different social system than the religious utopias of New England (Docs. 2.3 and 2.4), which had an inhospitable climate and theological governments and never codified slavery to the extent that Southern colonies did [comparison].

Practice blending comparison with patterns of continuity and change and of causation by prewriting a response to this prompt:

> The pursuit of economic gain and the spread of religious fervor drove the early settlement in North America. To what extent did economics and religion remain important between 1650 and 1750?

STEP 1 *Understand the prompt, and identify the key words*

As you remember from Chapter 1, you must first understand your question. Draw a square around your topic ("early settlement in North America"), draw a line underneath your task ("To what extent did economics and religion remain important between 1650 and 1750?"), and draw a circle around the categories of the question ("economic gain" and "religious fervor").

For the prompt above, your annotations may look like this:

> The pursuit of ⟨economic gain⟩ and the spread of ⟨religious fervor⟩ drove the
>
> [early settlement in North America.] To what extent did economics and
>
> religion remain important between 1650 and 1750?

STEP 2 *Generate a working thesis*

As you learned in Chapter 1, you can generate a **working thesis statement** to a historical prompt by asking questions that use your historical thinking skills. Remember that your thesis statement is both your answer to the prompt and also a hypothesis that needs to be proven by your analysis of historical evidence and documents in your essay itself.

To help you generate your thesis statement, consider the following questions:

1. How do two **factors** (or specified aspects of a particular context)—in this case economic gain and religious fervor—**compare** in promoting early colonization?

2. What **turning points** (key moments that mark a change in the course of events) characterized a shift in these factors? What **events or trends**, both proximate (short-term) and long-term, contributed to changes in economic gain and religious fervor? (See Chapter 1 for a review of these terms.)

3. In what ways did the economic and religious reasons for colonization change or remain the same (**continuity**)?

Examine when these points of comparison show **similarities** and **differences**.

As you learned in Chapter 1, taking time to **brainstorm** answers to these questions will provide you with a working thesis, based on the documents above and secondary sources (namely, the information you remember from your text or from class). This brainstormed information also will function as some of the outside information that the prompt requires you to incorporate into your response.

STEP 3 *Identify your evidence, and categorize your documents*

Using your knowledge of the time period, brainstorm a list of facts that you remember about this topic, including any of the documents from this chapter. These facts are the evidence that you will present to support your argument.

Categorize the evidence by completing the chart below:

Event	Document	Category(ies)
Tobacco becoming a cash crop (1610s)	Doc. 2.2, John Rolfe, Letter on Jamestown Settlement	Economic
Attack by Pamunkey chief, Opechankanough (1622)	Doc. 2.6, John Martin, "Proposal for Subjugating Native Americans"	Economic, religious
Growth of slave trade and rise of slavery in the South (seventeenth to eighteenth centuries)	Doc. 2.13, Virginia Slave Laws	Economic
Stono Rebellion (1739)	Doc. 2.15, George Cato, "Account of the Stono Rebellion"	Economic
Separatists' departure from Leiden, Holland, for North America (1620)	Doc. 2.3, The Mayflower Compact	Religious
John Winthrop's arrival in New England (1630)	Doc. 2.4, John Winthrop, "A Model of Christian Charity"	Religious
British exploitation of Caribbean sugar (seventeenth century)	Doc. 2.12, Richard Ligon, Map of Barbados	Economic
Other events?		

STEP 4 *Outline a multiple-paragraph essay*

As you may recall from the previous chapter, **body paragraphs** serve one primary purpose—to prove a part of an author's thesis. When outlining an essay, view each body paragraph as a subargument of the larger argument that you made in your thesis statement. Each body paragraph begins with a claim that is followed by analyses that prove the claim.

The basic structure of a comparison essay is a categorical outline. With the categorical outline, you explain two (or more) distinct categories that are determined by the prompt and your own interpretation of the task. In this sample prompt, the two areas have been generated for you:

- Economic gain
- Religious fervor

A categorical outline that compares the degree of consistency in these two causes of early settlements would look like this:

> Claim for category 1: Economic gain
>> Supporting evidence circa 1650
>>
>> Supporting evidence circa 1750
>
> Claim for category 2: Religious fervor
>> Supporting evidence circa 1650
>>
>> Supporting evidence circa 1750

Use your working thesis as a rough version of your answer to the question, and organize your body paragraphs around this working thesis. Use your claims and analyses to create body paragraphs that do the following:

Body paragraph 1

Write a **claim** that describes economic gain during early colonization and that considers the following questions:

1. What trends, both proximate and long-term, contributed to changes in economic gain?
2. What turning points contributed to these changes?
3. Overall, was there more change or more continuity between first settlements and later practices?

Your response to these questions will be the **evidence** that proves the claim at the beginning of the paragraph.

Body paragraph 2

Write a **claim** that describes religious fervor during early colonization and that considers the following questions:

1. What trends, both proximate and long-term, contributed to changes in religious fervor?
2. Were these trends similar to those that influenced economic gain?
3. What turning points contributed to this change?
4. Were these turning points similar to those that contributed to economic gain?
5. Overall, was there more change or more continuity between first settlements and later practices?

Your response to these questions will be the **evidence** that proves the claim at the beginning of the paragraph.

Conclusion

Effective conclusions move beyond a summary of the body paragraphs into more global statements about the issue at hand. When you conclude a comparison-and-contrast essay, the conclusion should answer one (or more) of these questions:

1. Why is this particular comparison important to understanding this topic? In this case, how does comparing the economic and religious aspects of early colonization enhance our understanding of this era?

2. What allowed these competing forces of economics and religion to endure?

3. To what extent does this comparison resemble earlier eras of history? Why?

Compose a concluding statement to this outline. In a future revision, this concluding statement may actually be closer to your revised final thesis.

CHAPTER 3

Awakening, Enlightenment, and Empire in British North America

European settlements in the New World led to the development of a transatlantic world in which Europeans, Native Americans, and Africans traded, competed, and interacted along networks that stretched from the foothills of the Appalachian Mountains to the cities of London, Paris, and Madrid to the villages of West Africa and back to the islands of the Caribbean.

Great Britain's colonies in North America formed an integral part of this transatlantic world. With the passage of the Navigation Acts, Britain formalized a mercantilist policy that sought to monopolize trade with its colonies and protect British economic interests. Starting in the late seventeenth century, the British fought a series of colonial wars with other European powers, most prominently the French, to establish English hegemony—meaning cultural, ideological, and economic dominance—in the North Atlantic and the North American interior.

Despite the consolidation of British power in North America, colonists used European models to shape a distinctly British North American culture. For example, the Enlightenment, a European intellectual movement that embraced science and reason as the hallmarks of human progress, manifested itself among elites. Likewise, the First Great Awakening, a wave of religious revivalism, swept North America during the 1740s with a spiritual fervor that touched all classes, thereby challenging England's tradition of strict class differentiation.

Seeking the Main Point

As you read the documents in this chapter, keep in mind the following broad questions. These questions will help you understand the relationship between the documents in this chapter and the historical changes that they represent. As you reflect on these questions, determine which themes and which documents best address them.

- In what ways were the North American colonies influenced by both contact with and distance from Europe?
- What were the geographic boundaries of the transatlantic world? How did those boundaries shape the economics of the transatlantic world?
- In what ways did the transatlantic world shape societies of Africans, Native North Americans, and Europeans?
- How did changes in thought and belief strengthen the bonds between the colonies and Europe? At the same time, how did they also weaken those bonds?

Strengthening Empire

DOCUMENT 3.1 | First Navigation Act of 1660

The Navigation Act of 1660 regulated British exports to and imports from North America, which allowed the colonial power to monopolize trade with its colonies and thereby create a commercial empire. The economic theory behind government regulation of the economy to promote its own power is called *mercantilism*. This act raised significant revenue for the Crown, which used the funds to expand the navy and strengthen the empire.

Be it enacted, etc., that no commodity [economic product or raw material] of the growth, production, or manufacture of Europe, shall be imported into any land, island, plantation, colony, territory, or place, to his Majesty belonging, or which shall hereafter belong unto or be in possession of his Majesty, his heirs and successors, in Asia, Africa, or America (Tangiers only excepted), but which shall be bona fide [made in good faith], and without fraud, laden and shipped in England, Wales, or the town of Berwick-upon-Tweed, and in English-built shipping, and which were bona fide bought before the 1st of October, 1662, and had such a certificate thereof as is directed in one act, passed the last session of the present Parliament, entitled, "An act for preventing frauds and regulating abuses in his Majesty's customs"; and whereof the master and three fourths of the mariners, at least, are English, and which shall be carried directly thence to the said lands, islands, plantations, colonies, territories, or places, and from no other place or places whatsoever; any law, statute, or usage to the contrary notwithstanding; under the penalty of the loss of all such commodities of the growth, production, or manufacture of Europe, as shall be imported into any of them, from any other place whatsoever, by land or water; and if by water, of the ship or vessel, also, in which they were imported, with all her guns, tackle, furniture, ammunition, and apparel; one third part to his Majesty, his heirs and successors; one third part to the governor of such land, island, plantation, colony, territory, or place into which such goods were imported, if the said ship, vessel, or goods, be there seized, or informed against and sued for; or, otherwise, that third part, also, to his Majesty, his heirs and successors; and the other third part to him or them who shall seize, inform, or sue for the same in any of his Majesty's courts in such of the said lands, islands, colonies, plantations, territories, or places where the offence was committed, or in any court of record in England, by bill, information, plaint, or other action, wherein no essoin [excuse for not appearing in court], protection, or wager of law shall be allowed.

Judson Stuart Landon, *The Constitutional History and Government of the United States* (New York: Houghton, Mifflin, 1889), 317.

PRACTICING Historical Thinking

Identify: Describe three of the rules that regulated exports to the colonies.

Analyze: What interest did Great Britain have in establishing these rules? What interests might the colonies have had in these rules? In what ways did these rules undermine colonial interests?

Evaluate: How might Parliament justify passing legislation that benefited Great Britain but undermined colonial interests?

DOCUMENT 3.2 | Charter of the Royal African Company
1662

Charles II (1630–1685) granted a charter for the creation of the British Company of Royal Adventurers Trading to Africa in 1662 to foster trade in Africa. The Royal African Company served British economic interests along the west coast of Africa for almost a hundred years and helped establish British power in the transatlantic world.

The Royal African Compa[ny]'s Limits for Trade granted them by His Ma[jes]ty's Charter. . . .

In the River Gambia, upon James Island, the Compa[ny] have built a Fort, where seventy men, at least, are kept. And there is a Factory from whence Elephants' Teeth, Bees-wax, and Cowhides are exported in very considerable quantities. The River Gambia is very large, and runs up very high (much higher than any discovery hath bin made) and it is supposed the Gold comes most from places, at the head of this River.

The Company have several small factory in this River, . . . at Rio Noones, Riopongo, and Calsamança, and doe trade by their Sloops, to Rio Grande and Catchao, for those Commodities, and also for Negro's. . . .

Thence they sail into another River called Sherbero, where alsoe a factory is setled, and the Trade there is chiefly for Red-wood, useful in dying; of which sometimes Three hundred Tonns per ann [year], may bee got, and some Elephants' Teeth. . . .

The Slaves they purchas[e]d are sent, for a Supply of Servants, to all His Ma[jes]tie's American Plantations which cannot subsist without them.

The Gold and Elephants' Teeth, and other Commodities, which are procured in Africa, are all brought into England. The Gold is always coined in His Ma[jes]ty's Mint. And the Elephants Teeth, and all other goods, which the Company receives, either from Africa or the Plantations, in returne for their Negros, are always sold publicly. . . .

"The Royal African Company Trades for Commodities along the West African Coast CO 268/1, ff. 5–6," *Black Presence: Asian and Black History in Britain 1500–1850*, National Archives, www.nationalarchives.gov.uk.

PRACTICING Historical Thinking

Identify: What goods did the Royal African Company acquire along the coast of West Africa?

Analyze: How might Africa's incorporation into the British mercantilist system have shaped the economies of British North America?

Evaluate: Who were the beneficiaries of this charter?

DOCUMENT 3.3 | ## Commission for the Dominion of New England
1688

James II (1633–1701) created the Dominion of New England in 1688 to place the New England colonies under royal control as part of the British mercantile policy that included the First Navigation Act of 1660 (Doc. 3.1) and the Charter of the Royal African Company (Doc. 3.2). James II made Sir Edmund Andros, former governor of New York, governor of the Dominion, which encompassed the New England colonies of Plymouth, Rhode Island, Connecticut, and Massachusetts Bay. James II was toppled by Parliament during the Glorious Revolution of 1689 and the Dominion of New England was dissolved.

James the Second by the Grace of God King of England, Scotland, France and Ireland Defender of the Faith &c. To our trusty and well beloved Sr. Edmund Andros Knt. Greeting: Whereas by our Commission under our Great Seal of England, bearing date the third day of June in the second year of our reign wee have constituted and appointed you to be our Captain General and Governor in Chief in and over all that part of our territory and dominion of New England in America known by the names of our Colony of the Massachusetts Bay, our Colony of New Plymouth, our Provinces of New Hampshire and Main and the Narraganset Country or King's Province. And whereas since that time Wee have thought it necessary for our service and for the better protection and security of our subjects in those parts to join and annex to our said Government the neighboring Colonies of Road Island and Connecticutt, our Province of New York and East and West Jersey, with the territories thereunto belonging, as wee do hereby join annex and unite the same to our said government and dominion of New England. Wee therefore reposing especiall trust and confidence in the prudence courage and loyalty of you the said Sir Edmund Andros, out of our especiall grace certain knowledge and mere motion, have thought fit to constitute and appoint as wee do by these presents constitute and appoint you the said Sr. Edmund Andros to be our Captain Generall and Governor in Chief in and over our Colonies of the Massachusetts Bay and New Plymouth, our Provinces of New Hampshire and Main, the Narraganset country or King's Province, our Colonys of Road Island and Connecticutt our Province of New York and East and West Jersey, and of all that tract of land circuit continent precincts and limits in America lying and being in breadth from forty degrees of Northern latitude from the Equinoctiall Line to the River of St. Croix Eastward, and from thence directly Northward to the river of Canada, and in length and longitude by all the breadth aforesaid and throughout the main land from the Atlantick or Western Sea or Ocean on the East part, to the South Sea on the West part, with all the Islands, Seas, Rivers, waters, rights, . . . thereunto belonging (our province of Pensilvania and country of Delaware only excepted), to be called and known as formerly by the name and title of our territory and dominion of New England in America. . . .

The Federal and State Constitutions, Colonial Charters, and Other Organic Laws of the States, Territories, and Colonies Now or Heretofore Forming the United States of America, vol. 3, ed. Francis Newton Thorpe (Washington, DC: Government Printing Office, 1909), 1863.

PRACTICING Historical Thinking

Identify: A writer's or speaker's **audience** may include some people who agree with his point of view and others who disagree with his point of view. Who is James II's intended audience? What colonies would be affected by this new policy?

Analyze: Describe the society and values of the original English settlers of New England (Docs. 2.9 and 2.10). What might their response have been to this policy?

Evaluate: The Dominion of New England did not survive James II's rule. With his overthrow in the Glorious Revolution of 1689, what precedent was set for legislative power in Great Britain? (You may need to check your textbook to answer this question.) How might this precedent also have affected the British North American colonies?

| # Map of North America, Eastern Seaboard

1701

By the beginning of the eighteenth century, Great Britain, Spain, and France began to compete for territory in North America, as shown in the map below. Native Americans increasingly found themselves forced to choose sides among Europeans in these colonial conflicts.

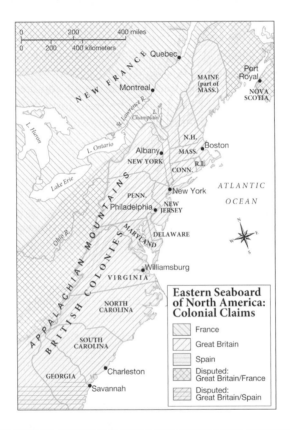

PRACTICING Historical Thinking

Identify: Locate the North American territories of the three primary colonial powers in this map, and note the economic advantages of each location.

Analyze: You will recall from previous chapters that an **inference** is an educated guess based on available evidence. Looking at this map, what potential areas of conflict do you see? What can you infer will be the causes of these conflicts?

Evaluate: Based on this map, what geographic and political factors could foster competition and exchanges between native peoples and Europeans?

DOCUMENT 3.5 | THOMAS OLIVER, Letter to Queen Anne
1708

Thomas Oliver, writing on behalf of the colonial government of Massachusetts, composed this letter to Queen Anne of Great Britain to describe native attacks on British colonists during Queen Anne's War (1702–1713). Throughout the war, the French were allied with the Algonquin, and the British allied with the Iroquois.

And they are Animated & Encouraged to such Barbarity's by the french setting the heads of your Ma:tys [Majesty's] Subjects, at a price upon bringing in their Scalps, and they kill many in cold blood after they have received them to Quarter, They have the advantage of Retiring for shelter, to the Obscured Recesses of a Vast rude Wilderness, full of Woods, Lakes, Rivers, ponds, Swamps, Rocks and Mountains, whereto they make an Easy and quick Passage, by means of their Wherry's [shallow river barges] or burchen [birch] Canoes of great Swiftness and light of Carriage; The matter whereof they are made being to be found almost every where, and their skill and dexterity for the making and Using of them is very extraordinary, which renders our Tiresome marches after them Ineffectual. These Rebels have no fixt Settlements, but are Ambulatory, & make frequent removes . . . , having no other Houses, but Tents or hutts made of Barque or Kinds of Trees, Matts &c. which they soon provide in all places where they come, So that it is Impracticable to pursue or follow them with any Body of Regular Troops, they are supported and Encouraged by the french, who make them yearly Presents Gratis [for free], of Clothing, Armes and Ammunition, Besides the Supply they Afford them for the Beaver and Furrs, which they take in hunting, and Constantly keep their Priests & Emissaries among them, to steady them in their Interests, and the bigotries w:ch [which] they have Instilled into them. The French also oft times join them in their Marches on our Frontiers. We humbly Conceive w.th [within] Submission, That the most probable Method of doing Execution upon them & Reduceing them, is by men of their own Colour, way & manner of living. And if yor Majesty shall be Graciously pleased to Command the Service of the Mohawks, and other Nations of the Western Indians that are in friendship and Covenant with your Ma.tys [Majesty's] Several Governments, against these Eastern Indian Rebels, for which they Express themselves to stand ready, and to whom they are a Terrour. They would with the Blessing of God in Short time Extirpate [destroy] or Reclaim them, and prevent the Incursions made upon us from Canada or the East. . . .

Thomas Oliver, "A Memorial of the State of the Province of Massachusetts Bay in New England to Queene Anne during Queen Anne's War," Boston, MA, October 20, 1708, Gilda Lehrman Institute of American History, collection #GLC04891, www.gilderlehrman.org.

PRACTICING Historical Thinking

Identify: Describe the attacks that take place. What does Oliver propose as a solution to these attacks?

Analyze: Why might native peoples ally with a European power against other native peoples?

Evaluate: Why might Queen Anne, three thousand miles away in England, find Oliver's request to ally with natives compelling?

DOCUMENT 3.6 | **Treaty of Utrecht**
| 1713

Below is an excerpt from the Treaty of Utrecht, which ended Queen Anne's War in 1713.

The subjects of France inhabiting Canada, and others, shall hereafter give no hinderance or molestation to the five nations or cantons of Indians, subject to the domination of Great Britain, nor to the other natives of America, who are friends to the same. In like manner, the subjects of Great Britain shall behave themselves peaceably towards the Americans who are subjects or friends to France; and on both sides they shall enjoy full liberty of going and coming on account of trade. As also the natives of those countries shall, with the same liberty, resort, as they please, to the British and French colonies, for promoting trade on one side and the other, without any molestation or hinderance, either on the part of the British subjects or of the French. But it is to be exactly and distinctly settled by commissaries [government officials], who are, and who ought to be accounted the subjects and friends of Britain or of France.

William MacDonald, *Select Charters and Other Documents Illustrative of American History, 1606–1775* (London: Macmillan, 1899), 232.

PRACTICING Historical Thinking

Identify: Identify at least four North American actors in this conflict.

Analyze: What causes of conflict does this section of the treaty seek to overcome?

Evaluate: What interests do the signatories of this treaty have in relations between natives and colonists?

REVIEW | ## Causation

The late seventeenth and early eighteenth centuries represented a time of confrontation between the French, the English, and their Native American allies in North America. Choose two long-term and two proximate causes for these conflicts (use your textbook or class notes as necessary). How did all of these short- and long-term causes play a role in the creation of at least four of the documents above? Copy the chart below into your notebook to help you organize your thoughts:

Confrontation between the French, the English, and their native allies (seventeenth and early eighteenth centuries)	
Proximate causes	Long-term causes

Transatlantic Ideas in a North American Context

DOCUMENT 3.7 | **WILLIAM PENN, Preface to "Frame of Government"**
| 1682

William Penn (1644–1718) founded the colony of Pennsylvania in 1681 as a haven for religious dissidents, especially Quakers. Below is an excerpt from his "Frame of Government," which established the political structure of the colony.

. . . I know what is said by the several admirers of monarchy, aristocracy and democracy, which are the rule of one, a few, and many, and are the three common ideas of government, when men discourse on that subject. But I chuse to solve the controversy with this small distinction, and it belongs to all three: any government is free to the people under it (whatever be the frame) where the laws rule, and the people are a party to those laws, and more than this [anything else] is tyranny, oligarchy [government by a small, powerful group], or confusion.

. . . [W]hen all is said, there is hardly one frame of government in the world so ill designed by its first founders, that, in good hands, would not do well enough; and story tells us, the best, in ill ones, can do nothing that is great or good; witness the Jewish and Roman states. Governments, like clocks, go from the motion men give them; and as governments are made and moved by men, so by them they are ruined too. Wherefore governments rather depend upon men, than men upon governments. Let men be good, and the government cannot be bad; if it be ill, they will cure it. But if men be bad, let the government be never so good, they will endeavor to warp and spoil it to their turn.

The Federal and State Constitutions, Colonial Charters, and Other Organic Laws of the United States (Washington, DC: Government Printing Office, 1878), 1519.

PRACTICING Historical Thinking

Identify: What European kinds of government does Penn draw on to make his case? What does Penn propose that men must do to create good government?

Analyze: How does Penn propose to solve the controversy between supporters of these European forms of government?

Evaluate: In what ways are Penn's and John Winthrop's (Doc. 2.4) visions of government similar? In what ways are they different? How do both reflect European models of religion and government?

Letter from a Gentleman of the City of New York on Leisler's Rebellion

1689

After the dissolution of the Dominion of New England in 1689 and the overthrow of James II (Doc. 3.3), Jacob Leisler (1640–1691), a German-born colonist living in the Province of New York, claimed that royal power no longer ruled in the New York colony. Leisler's rebellion managed to control New York for two years, but in 1691, Leisler's rebels were expelled by British troops, and Leisler was sentenced to be executed for treason.

. . . [A]gainst Expectation it soon happened, that on the last day of said Month of May, Capt. Leisler having a Vessel with some Wines in the Road, for which he refused to pay the Duty, did in a Seditious manner stir up the meanest sort of the Inhabitants (affirming, That King James being fled the Kingdom, all manner of Government was fallen in this Province) to rise in Arms, and forcibly possess themselves of the Fort and Stores, which accordingly was effected whilst the Lieut. Governor and Council, with the Convention, were met at the City Hall to consult what might be proper for the common Good and Safety; where a party of Armed Men came from the Fort, and forced the Lieut. Governor to deliver them the Keys; and seized also in his Chamber a Chest with Seven Hundred Seventy Three Pounds, Twelve Shillings, in Money of the Government. . . .

About a week after, Reports came from Boston, That their Royal Highnesses, the Prince and Princess of Orange were proclaimed King and Queen of England. . . . Capt. Leisler . . . did proclaim the same, though very disorderly, after which he went with his Accomplices to the Fort . . . and drank the Health and Prosperity of King William and Queen Mary with great Expressions of Joy.

Two days after, a printed Proclamation was procured by some of the Council, . . . appointed to collect the Revenue until Orders should arrive from England. . . .

But as soon as those Gentlemen entered upon the Office, Capt. Leisler with a party of his Men in Arms, and Drink, fell upon them at the Custom-House, and with Naked Swords beat them thence, endeavoring to Massacre some of them, which were Rescued by Providence. Whereupon said Leisler beat an Alarm, crying about the City, "Treason, Treason." . . .

The said Capt. Leisler, finding almost every man of Sense, Reputation, or Estate in the place to oppose and discourage his Irregularities, caused frequent false Alarms to be made, and sent several parties of his armed Men out of the Fort, drag'd into nasty . . . [Jails]. . . . Gentlemen, and others, . . . without any Process, or allowing them to Bail. . . .

In this manner he the said Leisler, with his Accomplices, did force, pillage, rob and steal from their Majesties good Subjects within this Province, almost to their utter Ruin, vast Sums of Money, and other Effects, the estimation of the Damages done only within this City of New-York amounting, as by Account may appear, to the Sum of Thirteen Thousand Nine Hundred and Fifty Nine Pounds, besides the Rapines, Spoils and Violences done at Coll. Willets on Nassau-Island, and to many others in several parts of the Province.

Charles McLean Andrews, ed., *Narratives of the Insurrections, 1675–1690* (New York: Charles Scribner's Sons, 1915), 363–369, transcribed into modern English by Jason Stacy.

PRACTICING Historical Thinking

Identify: What actions did Leisler take after receiving word of the overthrow of James II? Did Leisler's actions change after hearing that the prince and princess of Orange were proclaimed king and queen of England? Explain what actions followed.

Analyze: What is the author's attitude toward Leisler's Rebellion? What details of this description communicate this attitude?

Evaluate: Characterize the range of attitudes toward the British government portrayed in this document.

DOCUMENT 3.9 | **JOHN LOCKE, "Second Treatise on Civil Government"**
| 1690

John Locke (1632–1704), an English political philosopher, wrote primarily in support of the Glorious Revolution, the peaceful, parliamentary overthrow of James II in 1689. Locke's "Two Treatises on Civil Government" proved influential with North American British colonists in the eighteenth century.

If man in the state of nature be so free, as has been said; if he be absolute lord of his own person and possessions, equal to the greatest, and subject to no body, why will he part with his freedom? Why will he give up this empire, and subject himself to the dominion and control of any other power? To which 'tis obvious to answer, that though in the state of nature he hath such a right, yet the enjoyment of it is very uncertain, and constantly exposed to the invasion of others; for all being kings as much as he, every man his equal, and the greater part no strict observers of equity and justice; the enjoyment of the property he has in this state is very unsafe, very unsecure. This makes him willing to quit this condition, which however free, is full of fears and continual dangers: And 'tis not without reason, that he seeks out, and is willing to join in society with others who are already united, or have a mind to unite for the mutual preservation of their lives, liberties and estates, which I call by the general name, property.

The great and chief end, therefore, of men's uniting into commonwealths, and putting themselves under government, is the preservation of their property. . . .

John Locke, *Two Treatises on Civil Government* (London: Printed for Awnsham and John Churchill, at the Black Swan in Pater-Noster-Row, 1698), 261, transcribed into modern English by Jason Stacy.

PRACTICING Historical Thinking

Identify: According to Locke, why do governments exist?

Analyze: Compare Locke's arguments here to William Penn's in Document 3.7. What contextual factors might have influenced both? (For a review of contextualization, see Chapter 2.)

Evaluate: In what ways could Locke's conception of freedom as natural be used to undermine royal authority? In answering this question, consider this quote from Locke: "If man in the state of nature be so free, as has been said; if he be absolute lord of his own person and possessions, equal to the greatest, and subject to no body, why will he part with his freedom?"

DOCUMENT 3.10 | ## Image of John Winthrop IV
| 1773

John Winthrop IV (1714–1779), professor of mathematics and natural philosophy, was the great-great-grandson of the first governor of Massachusetts, John Winthrop (Doc. 2.4).

Photo by Universal History Archive/Getty Images.

DOCUMENT 3.11 | **BENJAMIN FRANKLIN,** *Poor Richard's Almanack*
1739

Benjamin Franklin (1706–1790), printer and prominent leader of the American Revolution, published the first best-selling series in the British North American colonies, *Poor Richard's Almanack*. Below is the introduction from the 1739 edition. Franklin published under the pseudonym "Richard Saunders" and was both the author and the publisher of the book.

Kind Reader,

Encouraged by thy former Generosity, I once more present thee with an Almanack, which is the 7th of my Publication. While thou art putting Pence in my Pocket, and furnishing my Cottage with necessaries, Poor Dick is not unmindful to do something for thy Benefit. The Stars are watch'd as narrowly as old Bess watch'd her Daughter, that thou mayst be acquainted with their Motions, and told a Tale of their Influences and Effects, which may do thee more good than a Dream of last Year's Snow.

Ignorant Men wonder how we Astrologers foretell the Weather so exactly, unless we deal with the old black Devil. Alas! . . . For Instance; The Stargazer peeps at the Heavens thro' a long Glass: He sees perhaps TAURUS, or the great Bull, in a mighty Chase, stamping on the Floor of his House, swinging his Tail about, stretching out his Neck, and opening wide his Mouth. 'Tis natural from these Appearances to judge that this furious Bull is puffing, blowing and roaring. Distance being consider'd, and Time allow'd for all this to come down, there you have Wind and Thunder. He spies perhaps VIRGO (or the Virgin;) she turns her Head round as it were to see if any body observ'd her; then crouching down gently, with her Hands on her Knees, she looks wistfully for a while right forward. He judges rightly what she's about: And having calculated the Distance and allow'd Time for its Falling, finds that next Spring we shall have a fine April shower. What can be more natural and easy than this? I might instance the like in many other particulars; but this may be sufficient to prevent our being taken for Conjurors. O the wonderful Knowledge to be found in the Stars! Even the smallest Things are written there, if you had but Skill to read. . . .

Besides the usual Things expected in an Almanack, I hope the profess'd Teachers of Mankind will excuse my scattering here and there some instructive Hints in Matters of Morality and Religion. And be not thou disturbed, O grave and sober Reader, if among the many serious Sentences in my Book, thou findest me trifling now and then, and talking idly. In all the Dishes I have hitherto cook'd for thee, there is solid Meat enough for thy Money. There are Scraps from the Table of Wisdom, that will if well digested, yield strong Nourishment to thy Mind. . . .

Some People observing the great Yearly Demand for my Almanack, imagine I must by this Time have become rich, and consequently ought to call myself Poor Dick no longer. But, the Case is this,

When I first begun to publish, the Printer made a fair Agreement with me for my Copies, by Virtue of which he runs away with the greatest Part of the Profit.—However, much good may't do him; I do not grudge it him; he is a Man I have a great Regard for, and I wish his Profit ten times greater than it is. For I am, dear Reader, his, as well as thy

Affectionate Friend,

R. SAUNDERS.

Benjamin Franklin, *The Writings of Benjamin Franklin*, vol. 2, ed. Albert Henry Smyth (London: Macmillan, 1907), 216–218.

PRACTICING Historical Thinking

Identify: *Poor Richard's Almanack* is considered to be the first secular best seller in British North America. In what ways does Franklin acknowledge the growing market in consumable goods like books?

Analyze: How does Franklin poke fun at any of the following—wealth, youth, and religious devotion?

Evaluate: By poking fun at important topics like wealth, youth, and religious devotion, Franklin subtly comments on humanity and human nature. How would you characterize Franklin's commentary?

DOCUMENT 3.12 | GEORGE WHITEFIELD, "Marks of a True Conversion"
1739

George Whitefield (1714–1770) was an English theologian who visited British North America in the 1730s and 1740s, and he inspired, like Jonathan Edwards (Doc. 3.13), a wave of religiosity in the colonies that is known as the First Great Awakening. In this excerpt from the sermon "Marks of a True Conversion," Whitefield encourages his listeners to communicate with God in a personal, informal manner.

Are ye God's children? Are ye converted, and become like little children? Then deal with God as your little children do with you; as soon as ever they want any thing, or if any body hurts them, I appeal to yourselves if they do not directly run to their parent. Well, are ye God's children? Doth the devil trouble you? Doth the world trouble you? Go tell your Father of it, go directly and complain to God. Perhaps you may say, I cannot utter fine words: but do any of you expect fine words from your children? If they come crying, and can speak but half words, do not your hearts yearn over them? And has not God unspeakably more pity to you? If ye can only make signs to him; "As a father pitieth his children, so will the Lord pity them that fear him." I pray you therefore be bold with your Father, saying, "Abba, Father! Satan troubles me, the world troubles me, my own mother's children are angry with me; heavenly Father, plead my cause!" The Lord will then speak for you some way or other.

George Whitefield, *Sermons on Important Subjects* (London: Henry Fisher and P. Jackson, 1832), 277.

PRACTICING Historical Thinking

Identify: What topics does Whitefield encourage his listeners to discuss with God?

Analyze: How might a discussion with God in this manner influence a worshipper's understanding of her place in the universe?

Evaluate: Compare Whitefield's tone to Benjamin Franklin's (Doc. 3.11). How are they both similar in their informality and appeal to the individual? How do they differ?

DOCUMENT 3.13 | JONATHAN EDWARDS, "Sinners in the Hands of an Angry God"
| 1741

Jonathan Edwards wrote the sermon "Sinners in the Hands of an Angry God" to proclaim the horrors of damnation in terms that were more personal and visceral than the language used by his Puritan forebearers. Edwards's rhetoric and tone reflect the emphasis on individual salvation that marked the First Great Awakening, the British North American religious movement of the 1740s.

So that thus it is that natural men are held in the hand of God over the pit of hell; they have deserved the fiery pit, and are already sentenced to it; and God is dreadfully provoked, his anger is as great towards them as to those that are actually suffering the executions of the fierceness of his wrath in hell, and they have done nothing in the least to appease or abate that anger, neither is God in the least bound by any promise to hold them up one moment: the devil is waiting for them, hell is gaping for them, the flames gather and flash about them, and would fain lay hold on them, and swallow them up; the fire pent up in their own hearts is struggling to break out; and they have no interest in any Mediator, there are no means within reach that can be any security to them. In short, they have no refuge, nothing to take hold of; all that preserves them every moment is the mere arbitrary will, and uncovenanted, unobliged forbearance of an incensed God. . . .

The use of this awful subject may be for awakening unconverted persons in this congregation. This that you have heard is the case of every one of you that are out of Christ.—That world of misery, that lake of burning brimstone, is extended abroad under you. There is the dreadful pit of the glowing flames of the wrath of God; there is hell's wide gaping mouth open; and you have nothing to stand upon, nor any thing to take hold of; there is nothing between you and hell but the air; it is only the power and mere pleasure of God that holds you up. . . .

The God that holds you over the pit of hell, much as one holds a spider, or some loathsome insect, over the fire, abhors you, and is dreadfully provoked: his wrath towards you burns like fire; he looks upon you as worthy of nothing else, but to be cast into the fire; he is of purer eyes than to bear to have you in his sight; you are ten thousand times more abominable in his eyes, than the most hateful venomous serpent is in ours. You have offended him infinitely more than ever a stubborn rebel did his prince: and yet, it is nothing but his hand that holds you from falling into the fire every moment. It is to be ascribed to nothing else, that you did not go to hell the last night; that you was suffered to awake again in this world, after you closed your eyes to sleep. And there is no other reason to be given, why you have not dropped into hell since you arose in the morning, but that God's hand has held you up. There is no other reason to be given why you have not gone to hell, since you have sat here in the house of God, provoking his pure eyes by your sinful wicked manner of attending his solemn worship. Yea, there is nothing else that is to be given as a reason why you do not this very moment drop down into hell.

Jonathan Edwards, *The Works of Jonathan Edwards*, ed. Sereno Edwards Dwight and Edward Hickman (New York: Daniel Appleton, 1835), 9–10.

PRACTICING Historical Thinking

Identify: What is Edwards's primary argument in this sermon? To whom is the sermon directed?

Analyze: To what extent does the image of John Winthrop IV (Doc 3.10) communicate values that are similar to those expressed in Edwards's sermon? Explain.

Evaluate: Compare Edwards's understanding of God to George Whitefield's in Document 3.12. What are key similarities between the two? What are key differences?

| # Interior of St. James Anglican Church

1711–1719

The interior of St. James Anglican Church, built between 1711–1719 in Goose Creek, South Carolina, represents a traditional Anglican pulpit of the early eighteenth century. Anglicanism was the official and recognized Church of England, whose leader was the king or queen.

Library of Congress Prints and Photographs Division, LC-DIG-csas-03828.

PRACTICING Historical Thinking

Identify: What is the **focal point** of this image—that is, to what image is the viewer's eye drawn?

Analyze: What does the focal point tell us about the social structures and values of this Anglican congregation?

Evaluate: How did this pulpit translate secular English conceptions of social hierarchy into religious ones in the North American colonies?

DOCUMENT 3.15 | # Interior of Mt. Shiloh Baptist Church

1700s

Mt. Shiloh Baptist Church in rural Virginia fell under the classification of "dissenting" churches according to the British government. Dissenting churches were not officially recognized forms of Christianity, and Dissenters were prevented from attending certain universities and undertaking certain professions, especially those connected to the government.

Virginia Baptist Historical Society.

PRACTICING Historical Thinking

Identify: What is the focal point of this image?

Analyze: What does the focal point tell us about the social structures and values of this Baptist congregation?

Evaluate: Compare this pulpit to the image in Document 3.14. What are the similarities? What are the differences? What differences might each represent in their parishioners' ideas about social hierarchy?

APPLYING AP® Historical Thinking Skills

COMBINING SKILLS REVIEW | Comparison and Contextualization

As you'll recall from the previous chapters, when you **compare** or **contextualize**, you think broadly about historical events. These two skills complement each other because when you determine a broad context, you invite comparisons. Consider the following prompt:

> Although Benjamin Franklin (Doc. 3.11), George Whitefield (Doc. 3.12), and Jonathan Edwards (Doc. 3.13) wrote these documents within two years of each other, each presented seemingly different views of human nature. Characterize the context in which British subjects in North America produced these views and the extent to which they conflicted with each other. Refer to the documents above and your knowledge of the time period to make your case.

STEP 1 *Rereading and Analyzing*

Reread the documents by Benjamin Franklin (Doc. 3.11), George Whitefield (Doc. 3.12), and Jonathan Edwards (Doc. 3.13). Determine at least four similarities, and list them in the chart below regarding human nature:

	Similarity 1	Similarity 2	Similarity 3	Similarity 4
Franklin, Whitefield, and Edwards				

Now consider at least four differences between the three documents:

	Difference 1	Difference 2	Difference 3	Difference 4
Franklin, Whitefield, and Edwards				

STEP 2 *Incorporating Contextualization*

After you have completed the chart, provide two claims, and follow each claim with at least three evidence statements that answer the prompt. (For definitions of *claim* and *evidence*, see Chapter 1.) Your claims should include the context in which all three authors wrote. Your evidence statements should incorporate similarities and differences from your chart as well as references to the documents themselves. You will use a categorical outline to organize your paragraphs.

    I. Claim of similarities and their context

Evidence statements:

    A. Franklin

    B. Whitefield

    C. Edwards

    II. Claim of differences and their context

Evidence statements:

    A. Franklin

    B. Whitefield

    C. Edwards

Now write a thesis statement that summarizes both of your claims above. For a review of a thesis statement, see Chapter 1.

PUTTING IT ALL TOGETHER

Revisiting the Main Point

- How did transatlantic interactions solidify as well as challenge traditional British conceptions of power and hierarchy?
- What effects did the First Great Awakening and the Enlightenment in colonial North America have on British imperial policy and colonists' conception of their place within the empire?
- Discuss three ways in which geography helped shape the transatlantic world.
- To what extent were the First Great Awakening and the Enlightenment products of British mercantilist policies?
- How did the geography of North America fuel conflicts between Europeans and between Europeans and natives?
- To what extent were the social hierarchies created in the New World a holdover from European hierarchies?

BUILDING AP® WRITING SKILLS **The Subordinated Thesis Statement**

Rarely does a thesis statement provide a simple answer. As you may have noticed in the third Applying AP® Historical Thinking Skills exercise in Chapter 1 (on causation), questions about cause and effect (such as "What are the causes of the Revolutionary War?") provide room for ambiguity, complexity, and counterargument.

When historians combine historical thinking skills, they are able to **subordinate**, or weigh several arguments within a single statement. A subordinated thesis statement offers more than one point to make an argument. Here is an example of such a statement:

> Although ideological values initiated the First Great Awakening and British Enlightenment [claim 1], economic motives were the primary force in spreading this new way of thinking [claim 2].

Practice blending comparison, contextualization, and causation by preparing a subordinated thesis to the following prompt:

> Consider which had a greater influence over British colonial thinking by 1754—religious thought or secular thought. Explain your reasoning.

STEP 1 *Understand the prompt, and identify the key words*

As you remember from Chapter 1, you must first understand your question. Draw a square around your topic ("colonial thinking"). Draw a line underneath your task ("Consider which had a greater influence"). Draw a circle around the events in the question ("religious thought" or "secular thought").

STEP 2 *Generate a working thesis*

To generate a working thesis to a historical prompt, begin by brainstorming what you know. Review the prompt's topic above, and create a list of potential questions, such as this one:

- Causation: What were the influences on colonial thinking?
- Comparison: How do the religious and secular ideas of this era compare?
- Contextualization: What were the key contexts that shaped colonial life during each period?

Your thesis statement to this question will benefit from subordination. For example, if you write, "Colonial thinking was influenced more by religious thought than secular thought," you need to acknowledge the many contexts (economic, political, religious, and social) that shape a group's mind-set.

If you write, "Religious thought and secular thought had an equal degree of influence over colonial thinking," you still need to acknowledge the complexities of colonial mind-sets.

The following flowchart may help you determine a subordinated thesis:

Determine your initial claim here:
Example: Politically, by 1754, colonists were . . .

↓

Determine your initial claim here:
Example: Socially, by 1743, colonists were . . .

↓

THESIS

STEP 3 *Identify your evidence, and categorize your documents*

Using your knowledge of the time period, brainstorm a list of facts that you remember about this topic. The following chart may assist you in developing your comparison:

Document	Type of thought	Key context(s)
Letter from a Gentleman of the City of New York on Leisler's Rebellion, 1689 (Doc. 3.8)	Secular	Economic, political
Benjamin Franklin, *Poor Richard's Almanack*, 1739 (Doc. 3.11)	Secular	Social, cultural
Jonathan Edwards, "Sinners in the Hands of an Angry God," 1741 (Doc. 3.13)	Religious	Religious, political

STEP 4 *Outline your response*

A **subordinated thesis statement** often is determined after the essay has been planned. When you outline an essay with a subordinated thesis, it can be useful to organize your response using a point-by-point outline. Unlike the categorical outline, which outlines an essay according to categories provided by the prompt, a point-by-point outline organizes an essay by **claims** that you generate as part of your argument.

Given the comparative nature of this task, consider the following point-by-point outline as a way to structure your response:

Point 1: Economic influences (claim)

    Evidence:

    Religious thought (proximate and long-term causes)

    Secular thought (proximate and long-term causes)

Point 2: Political influences (claim)

    Evidence:

    Religious thought (proximate and long-term causes)

    Secular thought (proximate and long-term causes)

Point 3: Social influences (claim)

    Evidence:

    Religious thought (proximate and long-term causes)

    Secular thought (proximate and long-term causes)

Notice how the topic (economic, political, and social influences) of each paragraph's claim is not from the prompt. Each is, instead, a point *determined by the author* of the essay based on her understanding of the time period.

After you have composed your outline, you are in a position to make a clear thesis about this era. You can write, for example, "Colonial thought was shaped by religious influences X and Y, although the secular influence of Z was also prominent." This approach allows you to achieve greater complexity in your thesis.

Although you might determine your thesis after you have organized your essay, this thesis statement generally will appear in your introductory paragraph.

When you subordinate one of the points in your thesis, you use words that evaluate competing ideas, such as the following:

However

Still

While

Although

Since

Despite

Even though

Nevertheless

But

Using these terms, your subordinated thesis might look something like this:

Although secular social and political influences shaped English colonial thinking during the eighteenth century, most British North Americans lived within a religious mind-set.

or like this:

After 1700, a religious mind-set remained important for British North Americans. **Nevertheless**, throughout the eighteenth century, colonial thinking became increasingly influenced by secular social and political ideas from the European continent.

Conclusion

Effective conclusions move beyond a summary of the body paragraphs or a restatement of the thesis and make global statements about the issue at hand. In concluding a comparison-and-contrast essay, consider the conclusion as answering one (or more) of these questions:

1. Why is this particular comparison important to understanding this topic? In this case, how does comparing two modes of thought enhance our understanding of this era?

2. What made these competing modes of thinking endure?

3. To what extent does this comparison invite an understanding of additional modes of thinking that influenced the American identity?

Complete the process with a concluding paragraph to your outline.

How Puritan Were the Puritans?

Competing views of the Puritans have emerged, with some historians viewing the Puritans—and their beliefs—as the beginnings of the American desire to break free of rigid, institutionalized belief systems. For others, the Puritans' shared beliefs and commitments to community provided the moral foundation for a new experiment in democracy that protected the inalienable rights of man. Perhaps at the core of these different views is the extent to which the new colonists could successfully assume greater control over their own lives in the enormous uncertainties of the New World. You already have studied various perspectives of the belief systems of the colonists. As you read the two passages below, consider how different historians promote different perspectives on the Puritans.

Thus Puritanism appears, from the social and economic point of view, to have been a philosophy of social stratification, placing the command in the hands of the properly qualified and demanding implicit obedience from the uneducated; from the religious point of view it was the dogged assertion of the unity of intellect and spirit in the face of a rising tide of democratic sentiment suspicious of the intellect and intoxicated with the spirit. It was autocratic, hierarchical, and authoritarian. It held that in the intellectual realm holy writ was to be expounded by right reason, that in the social realm the expounders of holy writ were to be mentors of farmers and merchants. Yet in so far as Puritanism involved such ideals it was simply adapting to its own purposes and ideals of the age. Catholics in Spain and in Spanish America pursued the same objectives, and the Puritans were no more rigorous in their application of an autocratic standard than King Charles himself endeavored to be—and would have been had he not been balked in the attempt.

—Perry Miller and Thomas H. Johnson, eds., *The Puritans* (New York: American Book Company, 1938).

. . . We have no way of knowing how many of the colonists were devout Calvinists, for no one took a census of beliefs. Yet common sense instructs us that religion (or the church) attracts not only a committed core, but also others who, like "horse-shed" Christians, limit their commitment. . . . From her childhood experiences as the daughter of a New England minister, Harriet Beecher Stowe [the author of *Uncle Tom's Cabin*] remembered that in winters when the farm people were satisfied with their minister, they honored their contract to supply him with his firewood by bringing logs that were "of the best: none of your old makeshifts,—loads made out with crooked sticks and snapping chestnut logs, most noisy, and destructive to good wives' aprons." I wish to insist, therefore, on acknowledging variety and change, and accepting "horse-shed" Christians as part of my story.

—David D. Hall, *Worlds of Wonder, Days of Judgment: Popular Religious Belief in Early New England* (New York: Knopf, 1989).

Using the above two excerpts, respond to the following prompts:

1. Briefly explain one major difference between Miller and Johnson's and Hall's historical interpretations.
2. Briefly explain how you could support one of the excerpts by using one document that is from the same time period but is not mentioned in the excerpts.
3. Briefly explain how one document from Chapter 2 could be used to support the excerpt that you did not choose in the second prompt.

An Atlantic Empire

B y the mid-eighteenth century, conflict in North America between the colonial empires of Great Britain and France came to a head. During the French and Indian War (or the Seven Years' War, as it became known in Europe), colonists fought alongside imperial troops, while native peoples often found themselves caught between the two imperial powers.

When the war ended in 1763, the victorious British empire was in control of the North American continent but also saddled with debt beyond what any had imagined possible at the beginning of the conflict. To offset the costs of defeating the French, the British Parliament instituted a series of revenue-raising measures (including new taxes like the Stamp Act) that sparked colonial anger and set the path toward conflict between Great Britain and the British colonists in North America.

After American independence, George Washington's administration continued its expansion into native territory in the West and sought neutrality in the renewed wars between France and Great Britain in the late 1700s. Support for and against France's democratic revolution, especially when it turned violent after 1793, divided Washington's cabinet and, ultimately, divided the United States into two broad factions whose conflict threatened to undermine the new nation.

Seeking the Main Point

As you examine the documents in this chapter, keep in mind the following broad questions. These questions will help you understand the relationship between the documents in this chapter and the historical changes that they represent. As you reflect on these questions, determine which themes and which documents best address them.

- Describe the ways in which environmental factors contributed to economic and political conflicts throughout this period.
- How did British economic policy shape the colonists' drive for independence?
- What objectives were behind British and later American territorial expansion?
- What ideas shaped the drive for American independence?
- How did international events shape politics during the early years of independence?
- What events helped Americans begin to define themselves as uniquely American during this period?

Challenging an Empire

DOCUMENT 4.1 | **North America before and after the French and Indian War**
1754 and 1763

Competition between the French and the English over control of North America came to a head in the French and Indian War (1754–1763) (known as the Seven Years' War in Europe). The British victory in this conflict guaranteed British control over much of North America. The two maps below show European colonies in North America at the beginning of the French and Indian War and at the end.

North America
1763

- Spanish
- French
- British

PACIFIC OCEAN

NEW SPAIN

ATLANTIC OCEAN

Proclamation Line of 1763

PRACTICING Historical Thinking

Identify: Describe the changes in territorial holdings in the two maps.

Analyze: Analyze how the changing territorial holdings could influence the European relationships with Native Americans. (Consult your textbook or class notes if needed.)

Evaluate: Using your textbook and classroom notes and lessons, determine whether Native Americans gained advantages from the war. Explain your response.

DOCUMENT 4.2 | **The Diary of William Trent**
1763

William Trent (1715–1787) was a British merchant who served as an officer for the Virginia militia during the French and Indian War (1754–1763). This excerpt from Trent's journal describes the siege of Fort Pitt (in what is now Pittsburgh, Pennsylvania), during Pontiac's Rebellion, when native peoples west of the Appalachian Mountains revolted against British settlement in territories formerly held by the French.

[July 27, 1763]

Fifty-seven Indians all on horseback were seen from the fort, going down the road and some on foot. Soon after some were seen returning, some appeared in Hulings field cutting some wheat with their knives and a scythe[.] [W]e imagine they are hungry.

A gun was fired according to agreement to call them over to get their answer, soon after they appeared on the other side; as soon as they came over, Captain Ecuyer's answer to this speech was delivered . . . , letting them know that we took this place from the French, that this was our home and we would defend it to the last, that we were able to defend it against all the Indians in the woods, that we had ammunition and provisions for three years (I wish we had for three months), that we paid no regard to the Ottawas and Chippawas, that we knew that if they were not already attacked, that they would be in a short time in their own country which would find enough for them to do.

That they had pretended to be our friends, at the same time they murdered our traders in their towns and took their goods, that they stole our horses and cows from here, and killed some of our people, and every three or four days we hear the death halloo [a war cry], which we know must be some of their people who have been down the country and murdered some of the country people. That if they intended to be friends with us to go home to their towns and sit quietly till they heard from us. . . .

The Yellow Bird, a Shawnee chief, asked for the four rifle guns we had taken from the four Indians the 25th[.] [T]hey were answered, if it appeared that their nation had done us no harm, and that they continued to behave well, when we were convinced of it that they should either have their guns or pay for them. He was very much enraged. . . . White Eyes and Wingenum seemed to be very much irritated and would not shake hands with our people at parting.

Mary C. Darlington, Pierre Joseph Céloron de Blainville, Simeon Ecuyer, and William M. Darlington, *Fort Pitt and Letters from the Frontier* (Pittsburgh, PA: J. R. Weldin, 1892), 103–104.

PRACTICING Historical Thinking

Identify: List three key features of the relationship between Trent's army and the native peoples.

Analyze: Does Trent's attitude appear more sympathetic or more critical of the native peoples? Explain your response with textual support.

Evaluate: In the aftermath of the French and Indian War, what advantage might the British have seen in maintaining good relations with western natives?

DOCUMENT 4.3 | Stamp Act
March 22, 1765

The Stamp Act was one of many ways in which the British government tried to recoup some of its losses from the French and Indian War. This tax on paper products and other common goods was the first British tax on goods that were produced and used exclusively in the colonies.

Whereas, by an act made in the last session of Parliament, several duties were granted, continued and appropriated toward defraying the expenses of defending, protecting, and securing the British colonies and plantations in America; and whereas it is first necessary, that provision be made for raising a further revenue within your majesty's dominions in America, towards defraying the said expenses; we, your majesty's most dutiful and loyal subjects, *the Commons of Great Britain*, in parliament assembled, have therefore resolved to give and grant unto your majesty the rights and duties hereinafter mentioned. . . . That from and after the first day of November, one thousand seven hundred and sixty-five, there shall be raised, levied, collected, and paid unto his majesty. . . :

. . . For every skin or piece of vellum or parchment, or sheet or piece of paper, on which shall be engrossed, written, or printed, any declaration, plea, replication, rejoinder, demurrer, or other pleading, or any copy thereof, in any court of law within the British colonies and plantations in America, a stamp duty of *three pence*. . . .

Charles Botta, *History of the United States of America: War of Independence*, vol. 2 (London: A. Fullarton & Co.), 29–33.

PRACTICING Historical Thinking

Identify: Summarize the purpose of the Stamp Act as described in the first paragraph above.

Analyze: Why might a North American colonist see the Stamp Act as unfair? Why might a British policy maker see it as fair?

Evaluate: Compare the British treatment of the colonists as outlined in the Stamp Act with William Trent's treatment of the native peoples in Document 4.2.

DOCUMENT 4.4 | PATRICK HENRY, Virginia Resolves
1765

Patrick Henry (1736–1799), a Virginia attorney and planter, shocked his fellow members of the Virginia House of Burgesses with his heated speeches against the Stamp Act. Henry's arguments proved increasingly popular as relations between the British government and the colonies soured throughout the 1760s and 1770s.

Whereas, the honorable House of Commons in England have of late drawn into question how far the General Assembly of this colony hath power to enact laws for laying of taxes and imposing duties, payable by the people of this, his majesty's most ancient colony: for settling and ascertaining the same to all future times, the House of Burgesses of this present General Assembly have come to the following resolves:—

. . . *Resolved*, That the first adventurers and settlers of this, his majesty's colony and dominion, brought with them and transmitted to their posterity, and all other his majesty's subjects, since inhabiting in this, his majesty's colony, all the privileges, franchises, and immunities that have at any time been held, enjoyed, and possessed, by the people of Great Britain. . . .

. . . *Resolved*, That his majesty's liege people of this most ancient colony have uninterruptedly enjoyed the right of being thus governed by their own Assembly in the article of their taxes and internal police, and that the same hath never been forfeited, or any other way given up, but hath been constantly recognized by the kings and people of Great Britain.

. . . *Resolved*, therefore, That the General Assembly of this colony have the only and sole exclusive right and power to lay taxes and impositions upon the inhabitants of this colony; and that every attempt to vest such power in any person or persons whatsoever, other than the General Assembly aforesaid, has a manifest tendency to destroy British as well as American freedom.

Moses Coit Tyler, *Patrick Henry* (New York: Houghton, Mifflin, 1898), 69–70.

PRACTICING Historical Thinking

Identify: Describe the problem and proposed solution to the injustices that Henry describes.

Analyze: Determine two opposing audiences that Henry has in mind, and explain why you chose them.

Evaluate: In what ways does Henry's resolution echo documents like John Locke's "Second Treatise on Civil Government" (Doc. 3.9)?

DOCUMENT 4.5 | **JOHN DICKINSON, Letter from a Farmer in Pennsylvania**
1767

John Dickinson (1732–1808) was a prominent Pennsylvania lawyer and essayist who published the series *Letters from a Farmer in Pennsylvania* to protest British imperial policies in the aftermath of the Stamp Act crisis of 1765. Here he is referring to the Townshend Duties, which were a series of taxes placed on imported goods in the aftermath of the Stamp Act crisis.

The assembly of that government [New York] complied with a former act of parliament, requiring certain provisions to be made for the troops in *America*, in every particular, I think, except the articles of salt, pepper and vinegar. . . .

If the *British* parliament has legal authority to issue an order, that we shall furnish a single article for the troops here, and to compel obedience to *that* order, they have the same right to issue an order for us to supply those troops with arms, cloths, and every necessary; and to compel obedience to *that* order also; in short, to lay *any burthens* they please upon us. What is this but *taxing* us at a *certain sum*, and leaving to us only the *manner* of raising it? How is this mode more tolerable than the Stamp-Act? Would that act have appeared more pleasing to *Americans*, if being ordered thereby to raise the sum total of the taxes, the mighty privilege had been left to them, of saying how much should be paid for an instrument of writing on paper, and how much for another on parchment? . . .

The matter being thus stated, the assembly of *New-York* either had, or had not, a right to refuse submission to that act. If they had, and I imagine no *American* will say they had not, then the parliament had *no right* to compel them to execute it. If they had not *that right*, they had *no right* to punish them for not executing it; and therefore *no right* to suspend their legislation, which is a punishment. In fact, if the people of *New-York* cannot be legally taxed but by their own representatives, they cannot be legally deprived of the privilege of legislation, only for insisting on that exclusive privilege of taxation. If they may be legally deprived in such a case, of the privilege of legislation, why may they not, with equal reason, be deprived of every other privilege? Or why may not every colony be treated in the same manner, when any of them shall dare to deny their assent to any impositions, that shall be directed? Or what signifies the repeal of the *Stamp-Act*, if these colonies are to lose their *other* privileges, by not tamely surrendering *that* of taxation?

John Dickinson, *The Writings of John Dickinson*, vol. 1, *Political Writings, 1764–1774*, ed. Paul Leicester Ford (Philadelphia: Historical Society of Pennsylvania, 1895), 308–309.

PRACTICING Historical Thinking

Identify: Is Dickinson for or against paying taxes to the British? Explain.

Analyze: What are Dickinson's chief concerns?

Evaluate: Based on Dickinson's letter and your outside knowledge, evaluate the pros and cons of the colonists' obedience to the Stamp Act.

DOCUMENT 4.6 | Testimony in the Trial of the British Soldiers of the Nineteenth Regiment of Foot
1770

In March 1770, tensions between colonists and British soldiers erupted in Boston, Massachusetts, when British soldiers fired into an angry crowd of protesters, killing five and injuring six. Called the Boston Massacre by anti-British forces throughout the colonies, six accused soldiers were acquitted by a jury of colonists, and two were convicted of the lesser charge of manslaughter and given relatively light punishments. John Adams (1735–1826), a Boston lawyer who later served in the Continental Congress and eventually became the second president of the United States, defended the accused British soldiers. In this passage from court transcripts, Adams questions a citizen of Boston who witnessed the event.

Q. Do you know any of the prisoners at the bar?

A. I particularly saw that tall man (pointing to Warren, one of the prisoners). Next day after the firing in King street, I saw more of them whom I cannot particularly swear to now.

Q. Did you see the soldiers before the justices on examination?

A. Yes.

Q. Did you then observe you had seen any of them the night before in King street?

A. I was well persuaded next day in my own mind, that I saw that tall one; but a few days after, I saw another man belonging to the same regiment, so very like him, that I doubt whether I am not mistaken with regard to him.

Q. Were there any other of the party you knew?

A. I am well satisfied I saw the corporal there.

Q. Did you see White there?

A. I do not remember.

Q. What was the situation of the corporal?

A. He was the corner man at the left of the party.

Q. Did you see either of the persons, you think you know, discharge their guns?

A. Yes; the man I take to be the tall man, discharged his piece as it was upon a level.

Q. Did you see the corporal discharge his gun?

A. I did not.

Q. Where did you stand?

A. I was behind them in the circle.

Q. What part of the circle did the tall man stand in?

A. He stood next but one to the corporal. The tall man, whoever he was, was the man I saw discharge his piece.

Q. Was any thing thrown at the soldiers?

A. Yes, there were many things thrown, what they were I cannot say.

Q. How did the soldiers stand?

A. They stood with their pieces before them to defend themselves; and as soon as they had placed themselves, a party, about twelve in number, with sticks in their hands, who stood in the middle of the street, gave three cheers, and immediately surrounded the soldiers, and struck upon their guns with their sticks, and passed along the front of the soldiers, towards Royal Exchange lane, striking the soldiers' guns as they passed; numbers were continually coming down the street.

Frederic Kidder, *History of the Boston Massacre, March 5, 1770; Consisting of the Narrative of the Town, the Trial of the Soldiers: and a Historical Introduction, Containing Unpublished Documents of John Adams, and Explanatory Notes* (Albany, NY: Joel Munsell, 1870), 17–18.

PRACTICING Historical Thinking

Identify: Summarize the testimony of this witness.

Analyze: Does this testimony paint the British soldiers in a sympathetic light? Explain your response.

Evaluate: To what extent was the Boston Massacre a culmination of economic, geographic, and political concerns? Explain your response with evidence from the first six documents of this chapter and information from your textbook and classroom lessons.

DOCUMENT 4.7 | ## "Account of the Boston Tea Party," *Massachusetts Gazette*
1773

By the early 1700s, secret Patriot organizations like the Sons of Liberty actively resisted British economic policies throughout the colonies and encouraged fellow colonists to boycott British goods. The Boston Tea Party, organized by the Sons of Liberty, is the most famous of these protests and led Parliament to pass the Coercive Acts, which closed the port of Boston and suspended the Massachusetts legislative assembly in favor of a military governor.

"Just before the dissolution of the meeting" [discussing the new Tea Act], . . . a number of brave and resolute men, dressed in the Indian manner, approached near the door of the assembly, gave the war-whoop, which rang through the house, and was answered by some in the galleries, but silence was commanded, and a peaceable deportment enjoined until the dissolution. The Indians, as they were then called, repaired to the wharf, where the ships lay that had the tea on board, and were followed by hundreds of people, to see the event of the transactions of those who made so grotesque an appearance. The Indians immediately repaired on board Captain Hall's ship, where they hoisted out the chests of tea, and when on deck stove the chests and emptied the tea overboard. Having cleared this ship, they proceeded to Captain Bruce's, and then to Captain Coffin's brig. They applied themselves so dexterously to the destruction of this commodity, that in the space of three hours they broke up three hundred and forty-two chests, which was the whole number in these vessels, and discharged the contents into the dock. When the tide rose it floated the broken chests and the tea insomuch that the surface of the water was filled therewith a considerable way from the south part of the town to Dorchester Neck, and lodged on the shores. There was the greatest care taken to prevent the tea from being purloined by the populace; one or two being detected in endeavoring to pocket a small quantity were stripped of their acquisitions and very roughly handled. . . .

Francis S. Drake, *Tea Leaves: Being a Collection of Letters and Documents Relating to the Shipment of Tea to the American Colonies in the Year 1773, by the East India Tea Company* (Boston, MA: A. O. Crane, 1884), lxviii.

PRACTICING Historical Thinking

Identify: Describe the events of the Boston Tea Party as recounted by the *Massachusetts Gazette.*

Analyze: What do you think the rebels intended by dressing as Indians?

Evaluate: A writer's **bias** reveals his attitude about an event or a phenomenon. What is the article's bias? Is it more sympathetic to the British or to the colonists? Support your response with references to statements in the document.

DOCUMENT 4.8 | **"Memory of a British Officer Stationed at Lexington and Concord,"** *Atlantic Monthly*
| April 19, 1775

Military Governor Thomas Gage (1720–1787), following the requirements of the Coercive Acts, ordered British regulars into the Massachusetts countryside in April 1775 to retrieve weapons that he believed were stored by Patriot forces in an arsenal in the town of Concord. The British met stiff resistance from the Massachusetts militia, as recalled by a British officer in this contemporary diary entry, which was published over a hundred years after the events it describes.

We set out upon our return; before the whole had quitted the Town we were fired on from Houses and behind Trees, and before we had gone ½ a mile we were fired on from all sides, but mostly from the Rear, where People had hid themselves in houses till we had passed, and then fired; the Country was an amazing strong one, full of Hills, Woods, stone Walls, &c., which the Rebels did not fail to take advantage of, for they were all lined with People who kept an incessant fire upon us, as we did too upon them, but not with the same advantage, for they were so concealed there was hardly any seeing them: in this way we marched between 9 and 10 miles, their numbers increasing from all parts, while ours was reducing by deaths, wounds, and fatigue; and we were totally surrounded with such an incessant fire as it's impossible to conceive; our ammunition was likewise near expended. . . .

"A British Officer in Boston in 1775," *The Atlantic Monthly* 39, no. 234 (April 1877): 400.

PRACTICING Historical Thinking

Identify: List the key details that the British officer remembers.

Analyze: Compare the attitude of the speaker with the writer from the *Massachusetts Gazette* (Doc. 4.7). Who is more hostile to the Patriot cause? What statements in the documents support your answer?

Evaluate: This passage was found in a diary. Who might have been the intended audience? How does the intended audience affect the trustworthiness of the document in your opinion?

APPLYING AP® Historical Thinking Skills

SKILL REVIEW | Patterns of Continuity and Change over Time

Consider the following protests (and their corresponding documents in this book) that took place in the British North American colonies during the seventeenth and eighteenth centuries:

Bacon's Rebellion, 1676 (Doc. 2.10)

Leisler's Rebellion, 1689–1691 (Doc. 3.8)

British North American protests of the 1770s (Docs. 4.4–4.8)

What patterns of continuity do you notice among these rebellions? What are some of the changes that you trace between 1676 and the 1770s? To what extent are these continuities a product of recurring issues between colonists and those in power? To what extent are the changes that you traced a product of changes within the colonies themselves?

Construct two paragraphs that answer these questions—one paragraph for continuities and one paragraph for changes. Each paragraph must begin with a **claim** that is followed by supporting **evidence**. To write your paragraphs, be sure to consult your textbook, your class notes, and the documents mentioned above.

NEW SKILL | Analyzing Evidence: Content and Sourcing

When historians use primary sources, they are careful to know something about those sources before they use them. This is called **analyzing and using evidence appropriately**. There are many factors that a historian must consider to use a source appropriately, including the following:

Audience: Who did the author or speaker have in mind when she or he created this source? An audience is more than a demographic (such as the British or the Americans). An audience is comprised of people who share certain beliefs with the speaker, oppose the speaker's beliefs, or are undecided and need convincing.

Attitude: What are the author's biases?

Purpose: What is the author's intent in creating this source? What is the source for?

Point of view: Which perspective(s) does the author employ?

Format: How has the author presented her or his source? (For example, is it handwritten or printed? Is it a picture, a cartoon, or an artifact?)

Argument: Aligned with purpose is **argument**, a term that is introduced in Chapter 1. A source's argument seeks to fulfill its purpose.

Context: What events, ideas, and people surrounded the author when this source was created? Where did this source appear, and how credible was the source?

Limitations: Based on all of the above, what are some limitations of this source? What additional information is needed to know more about the argument, purpose, or point of view?

When considering these factors, historians also must be able to make supportable inferences and draw appropriate conclusions based on these factors. Recall from Chapter 2 that when historians **infer**, they make an educated guess that is based on available evidence. The terms listed above also depend on inference. For example, your understanding of a writer's **attitude** or **purpose** will help you infer his point of view and audience. Appropriate conclusions depend on your ability to infer these key features of historical documents and combine these documents to develop your own argument.

This might seem like a lot of things to keep in mind, but don't worry. Rather than memorize this list, when you approach a source, you should be ready to analyze its meaning beyond what it says. Believe it or not, we do this sort of thing all the time.

Let's say that you are thinking of seeing a movie and want to read some reviews of the movie before you go to see it. The movie is called *The Dead Who Walk Around*. The first review that you find online is called "Evil Movies for Evil People," and this paragraph jumps out at you:

> *The Dead Who Walk Around* is a perfect example of all that is wrong with Hollywood. The film industry is more interested in profits than it is in the future of our children. So for short-term financial gain, Hollywood produces splatterfests like this movie, where the shambling hordes from the grave feast on human brains without consideration of how these images might affect the nation's children. The fact that this movie is rated PG-13 is proof that the ratings industry is not doing its job. If you have a child who is between thirteen and seventeen, you should not let him or her see this movie.

To understand this review, you begin to analyze it and consider the factors listed above. This review appears to have been written for an audience of people who are thinking of letting children see *The Dead Who Walk Around*. When you consider the purpose of this review, it also appears that the author is trying to convince you not to see the film. However, the author's purpose is tied to her or his audience, who are parents of children between ages thirteen and seventeen.

When you consider the point of view of this review, you start to suspect that the opinion of this author was formed before seeing the movie because he or she writes for a website called "Evil Movies for Evil People." The website and the author of this review want you to believe that scary movies ("evil movies") are seen by bad people ("evil people").

The format is that of a traditional movie review, which requires a reviewer who usually knows movies better than most people and therefore can offer an informed opinion of a film. This makes the review appear to be more reliable than a flame war between two people on a comments section of a blog.

However, the argument in this review does not balance the good and bad elements of the film. Instead, the author is biased against the whole genre of scary movies (consider the website on which the review was published), and this makes the argument weaker. If a reviewer automatically does not like scary movies, why would his or her reaction to this one be any different? This fact points to the limitations of this piece of writing as a movie review. You wanted to learn about the movie and perhaps read about some of its good and bad points to help you decide whether to see it. Because the author published this review in a context that disapproves of this kind of movie, however, his or her arguments cannot be taken seriously.

From this review, you are able to infer that this author has a bias against scary movies. You therefore draw the appropriate conclusion (based on all prior inferences about audience, purpose, point of view, format, argument, context, and limitations) that this reviewer did not give the movie a fair viewing and that you cannot really trust the author about whether the film is any good.

So should you see the film? It is almost impossible for you to decide based on this one review. You should read a few more before you make any judgments about *The Dead Who Walk Around*.

STEP 1 Consider the following three documents:

Document 4.6, Testimony in the Trial of the British Soldiers of the Nineteenth Regiment of Foot, 1770

Document 4.7, "Account of the Boston Tea Party," *Massachusetts Gazette*, 1773

Document 4.8, "Memory of a British Officer Stationed at Lexington and Concord," *Atlantic Monthly*, 1775

All three documents relate stories of protests that were made against imperial power in British North America. Complete the following chart regarding their audience, purpose, point of view and attitude, format, argument, context, and limitations. Some of the items have been completed for you.

	Doc. 4.6, Testimony in the Trial of the British Soldiers of the Nineteenth Regiment of Foot, 1770	Doc. 4.7, "Account of the Boston Tea Party," *Massachusetts Gazette*, 1773	Doc. 4.8, "Memory of a British Officer Stationed at Lexington and Concord," 1775
Audience: Who did the author have in mind when she or he created this source?	The judge and jury		
Purpose: What is the author's intent in creating this source? What is it for?		To relate event and encourage support for the Patriot cause	
Point of view and **attitude:** Which perspective(s) does the author consider? What are the author's biases?			This British soldier was at the Battle of Lexington and Concord and wants to present a view that is sympathetic to soldiers.
Format: How has the author presented her or his source? Is it handwritten, printed, a picture or cartoon, or an artifact?			Diary; handwritten
Argument: A source often reflects a writer's argument. What might this source be arguing for?	That the British soldiers were being attacked by the mob		
Context: What events, ideas, and people surrounded the author when this source was created? Where did the source appear? How credible is the source?			Growing conflicts between the British and Patriot colonists; the background included the Stamp Act, Boston Massacre, Tea Act, Boston Tea Party, Coercive Acts, etc.
Limitations: Based on all of the above, what are some limitations of this source? What can it not do or be because of its audience, purpose, point of view, etc.?		Biased in support of Patriot cause; unable to present both sides of the debate between the Patriots and British	

STEP 2 Review your results. Now you're ready to make some inferences and draw appropriate conclusions.

Based on these documents about colonial protests and the British reactions to them, offer three inferences of your own that communicate the author's **purpose**. (Review the inference made about the movie review above if you aren't sure what it means to infer something.) What evidence do you have to support these inferences?

Doc. 4.6 _____

Evidence: _____

Doc. 4.7 _____

Evidence: _____

Doc. 4.8 _____

Evidence: _____

STEP 3 Based on these three inferences, what appropriate conclusion(s) can you draw about colonial protests and British reactions to them? Treat this conclusion like a claim in a paragraph. It should be a statement that you need to support with evidence and explanations to convince your reader.

Conclusion(s) (claim): _____

Supporting evidence and explanations: _____

Entangling Alliances

DOCUMENT 4.9 | **Treaty of Alliance between the United States and France**
| 1778

The alliance between France and the United States forced Great Britain to face the prospect of a worldwide war with France over its colonial holdings. It also offered the United States international recognition and material and military support, which culminated in the American victory at the Siege of Yorktown (1781) with the assistance of the French fleet.

The most Christian king and the United States of North-America, . . . for the reciprocal advantage of their subjects and citizens, have thought it necessary to take into consideration the means of strengthening those engagements, and of rendering them useful to the safety and tranquillity of the two parties. . . . [H]is majesty and the said United States having resolved in that case to join their councils and efforts against the enterprizes of their common enemy, . . . have, after the most mature deliberation, concluded and determined on the following articles:

Art. 1. If war should break out between France and Great-Britain, during the continuance of the present war between the United States and England, his majesty and the said United States, shall make it a common cause, and aid each other mutually with their good offices, their counsels and their forces, . . . as becomes good and faithful allies.

Art. 2. The essential and direct end of the present defensive alliance, is, to maintain effectually the liberty, sovereignty and independence, absolute and unlimited, of the said United States, as well in matters of government as of commerce.

Art. 3. The two contracting parties shall, each on its own part, and in the manner it may judge most proper, make all the efforts in its power against their common enemy, in order to attain the end proposed.

Journals of the American Congress: From 1774 to 1788, vol. 3 (Washington, DC: Way and Gideon, 1823), 485–486.

PRACTICING Historical Thinking

Identify: According to the French, why are they creating this alliance with the United States?

Analyze: How might France's recognition of the United States affect other countries' perception of British North America?

Evaluate: Based on this document and your knowledge of other sources, which is the strongest motivation for the French to form this alliance—political, economic, or military? Explain your response.

DOCUMENT 4.10 | **COLONEL DANIEL BRODHEAD, Letter to General George Washington on an American Expedition into Pro-British Iroquois Territory**
1779

Daniel Brodhead (1736–1809) served as an officer in the Continental Army during the first years of the American Revolution and as commander of the Western Reserve between 1779 and the end of the war. As commander of the Western Reserve, Brodhead was ordered by General George Washington to subdue Native American tribes in northwestern Pennsylvania that allied with the British. Most prominent were tribes that were part of the Iroquois Confederacy, a loose alliance of mostly Algonquin peoples in the northwest region of British America. In this document, Brodhead provides an update of his progress and mentions a parallel offensive under Major John Sullivan against a coalition of Loyalists and Iroquois in western New York.

I had only six hundred & five Rank & File, including volunteers & Militia; with those I marched to the upper town on the River, called the Yahrungwago, I met with no opposition from the enemy after killing six or seven, & wounding a number out of a party of warriors consisting of Forty, that were coming against the settlements—this was done in a few minutes by the advanced Guard—composed of fifteen Light Infantry & eight Delaware Indians, without any loss on our side, except three men very slightly wounded—we destroyed in the whole, one hundred & sixty-five Cabins, 130 of which were deserted on the approach of the troops; & the most of them were new & large enough for accommodation of three or four Indian families. . . .

I congratulate you on your success against the Indians and the more savage tories, & am quite happy in the reflection that our efforts promise a lasting tranquility to the Frontiers we have covered. Something still remains to be done to the westward, which I expect leave to execute, & then I conceive the wolves of the forest will have sufficient cause to howl as they will be quite destitute of food. . . .

Samuel Hazard, ed., *Pennsylvania Archives Selected and Arranged from Original Documents in the Office of Secretary of the Commonwealth Conformably to Acts of the General Assembly, February 15, 1851, & March 1, 1852*, vol. 12 (Philadelphia, PA: Joseph Severns, 1854), 165–166.

DOCUMENT 4.11 | **Treaty of Paris**
| 1783

After the siege at Yorktown, where General George Washington, with the help of the French fleet, bottled up British General Charles Cornwallis in October 1781, the United States, France, Great Britain, Spain, and Holland took nearly two years to negotiate the Treaty of Paris (1783), which recognized the independence of the United States.

Article I

His Brittanic Majesty acknowledges the said United States . . . to be free, sovereign and independent States; that he treats with them as such; and for himself, his heirs and successors, relinquishes all claims to the gouvernment, propriety and territorial rights of the same, and every part thereof. . . .

Article V

It is agreed that Congress shall earnestly recommend it to the legislatures of the respective states, to provide for the restitution of all estates, rights and properties, which have been confiscated, belonging to real British subjects, and also of the estates, rights and properties of persons resident in districts in the possession of his Majesty's arms, and who have not borne arms against the said United States. And that persons of any other description shall have free liberty to go to any part or parts of any of the thirteen United States, and therein to remain twelve months, unmolested in their endeavours to obtain the restitution of such of their estates, rights and properties, as may have been confiscated; and that Congress shall also earnestly recommend to the several states a reconsideration and revision of all acts or laws regarding the premises, so as to render the said laws or acts perfectly consistent, not only with justice and equity, but with that spirit of conciliation, which on the return of the blessings of peace should universally prevail. And that Congress shall also earnestly recommend to the several states, that the estates, rights and properties of such last mentioned persons, shall be restored to them, they refunding to any persons who may be now in possession, the bona fide price (where any has been given) which such persons may have paid on purchasing any of the said lands, rights and properties, since the confiscation. . . .

Richard Peters, ed., *The Public Statutes at Large of the United States of America from the Organization of the Government in 1789, to March 3, 1845* (Boston, MA: Little, Brown, 1867), 55–56.

PRACTICING Historical Thinking

Identify: Identify the key provisions of this treaty.

Analyze: Who are the intended audiences of this treaty? Explain.

Evaluate: In what ways do you detect the influence of John Locke's philosophy (Doc. 3.9) in this document? What are some other possible influences on this treaty?

DOCUMENT 4.12 | **THOMAS JEFFERSON, Letter to Thomas Pinckney**
| 1793

Thomas Jefferson (1743–1826) served as secretary of state in George Washington's first presidential administration. In this letter to Thomas Pinckney (1750–1828), minister to Great Britain, Jefferson discusses negotiations with native peoples in the northwestern frontier and the efforts of Edmond-Charles Genet (1763–1834), who had been sent by France to enlist US support for the French revolutionary government. When this letter was written, Great Britain was at war with revolutionary France.

Our negotiations with the North-Western Indians have completely failed, so that war must settle our difference. We expected nothing else, and had gone into negotiations only to prove to all our citizens that peace was unattainable on terms which any one of them would admit.

You have probably heard of a great misunderstanding between Mr. Genet and us. On the meeting of Congress it will be made public. . . . We have kept it merely personal, convinced his nation [France] will disapprove him. To them [the French] we have with the utmost assiduity given every proof of inviolate attachment. We wish to hear from you on the subject of Marquis de La Fayette, though we know that circumstances [the increasing violence of the French Revolution, which put the lives of moderates like Lafayette in danger] do not admit sanguine [optimistic] hopes.

H. A. Washington, ed., *The Writings of Thomas Jefferson: Being His Autobiography, Correspondence, Reports, Messages, Addresses, and Other Writings, Official and Private*, vol. 4 (New York: Taylor & Maury, 1854), 85–86.

DOCUMENT 4.13 | THOMAS JEFFERSON, Letter to James Monroe
1795

Thomas Jefferson wrote the following letter to political ally James Monroe (1758–1831) regarding the public reaction to Jay's Treaty. The treaty was intended to maintain US neutrality between France and Great Britain but was perceived by many Americans to be a pro-British treaty.

. . . Mr. Jay's treaty has at length been made public. So general a burst of dissatisfaction never before appeared against any transaction. Those who understand the particular articles of it, condemn these articles. Those who do not understand them minutely, condemn it generally as wearing a hostile face to France. This last is the most numerous class, comprehending the whole body of the people, who have taken a greater interest in this transaction than they were ever known to do in any other. It has in my opinion completely demolished the monarchial party here. The Chamber of Commerce in New York, against the body of the town, the merchants in Philadelphia, against the body of their town, also, and our town of Alexandria have come forward in . . . [its] support. Some individual champions also appear. *Marshall, Carrington, Harvey, Bushrod Washington, Doctor Stewart.* A more powerful one is *Hamilton,* under the signature of *Camillas. Adams* holds his tongue with an address above his character. We do not know whether the President has signed it or not. If he has it is much believed the H. of representatives will oppose it as constitutionally void, and thus bring on an embarrassing and critical state in our government.—

Thomas Jefferson, *The Works of Thomas Jefferson,* vol. 7, ed. Paul Leicester Ford (New York: G. P. Putnam's, 1896), 27–28.

DOCUMENT 4.14	Anti-Jefferson Cartoon, "The Providential Detection"
	1797

In 1793, Jefferson left the Washington administration after his debate with Alexander Hamilton over the creation of the National Bank, which for Jefferson signaled a shift in Washington's policies toward pro-British monarchism. "The Providential Detection" appeared during the height of the debate between Federalists, who supported Hamilton and Washington, and Jeffersonian Republicans over the direction of national and international policy, specifically regarding the ongoing war between Great Britain and the revolutionary French Republic. In this image, the American eagle takes the Constitution away from Jefferson before he can burn it on the "Altar to Gallic [French] Despotism." Fueling the flames are the works of Thomas Paine and French philosophers, whom Federalists saw as threats to order. In Jefferson's right hand is a letter from Jefferson to the Italian Philip Mazzei (1730–1816), also a supporter of the French Revolution. The letter supposedly criticized George Washington.

Universal History Archive/UIG via Getty Images.

APPLYING AP® Historical Thinking Skills

COMBINING SKILLS | Causation and Argumentation

Documents 4.9 through 4.14 relate to the relations between the United States and France. The documents begin with a treaty between the two countries and end with a document in which the author of the Declaration of Independence is portrayed as an enemy to the United States because of his worship of "Gallic (French) Despotism."

Consider the following prompt:

> Between 1778 and 1798, the relations between France and the United States rapidly deteriorated, but the origins of this deterioration lay in the century-old hostilities between British Americans and the French. Accept, modify, or refute this statement.

This prompt presents a thesis without proving it. It then asks you to agree with the thesis, reject the thesis, or modify the thesis in the form of a historical argument.

STEP 1 First, review your textbook, your class notes, and the documents in this book on the subject of British-American and French relations between 1700 and 1798. Here are documents that will help you:

Document 3.5, Thomas Oliver, Letter to Queen Anne, 1708

Document 3.6, Treaty of Utrecht, 1713

Document 4.1, North America before and after the French and Indian War, 1754 and 1763

Document 4.9, Treaty of Alliance between the United States and France, 1778

Document 4.11, Treaty of Paris, 1783

Document 4.12, Thomas Jefferson, Letter to Thomas Pinckney, 1793

Document 4.13, Thomas Jefferson, Letter to James Monroe, 1795

Document 4.14, Anti-Jefferson Cartoon, "The Providential Detection," 1797

After you have reviewed these documents and your classroom sources, complete the following table. For each category, brainstorm at least three causes with documentary evidence for each cause. One example in each category has been provided.

Long-term causes for French and British-American hostilities	Proximate causes for French and British-American hostilities
Long-term cause 1: French and British colonial wars (eighteenth century)	**Proximate cause 1:** Jay's Treaty (1795)
Documentary evidence: Doc. 3.5, Thomas Oliver, Letter to Queen Anne, 1708	**Documentary evidence:** Doc. 4.13, Thomas Jefferson, Letter to James Monroe, 1795
Long-term cause 2:	**Proximate cause 2:**
Documentary evidence:	**Documentary evidence:**
Long-term cause 3:	**Proximate cause 3:**
Documentary evidence:	**Documentary evidence:**

STEP 2 Now you're ready to write a thesis that accepts, refutes, or modifies the statement in the prompt. You will prove your thesis with a historical argument that analyzes the causes of British-American and French hostilities, both long-term and proximate.

An example might look like this:

> British-American and French relations were mixed before 1778, with both sides sometimes working together and sometimes fighting with each other. After 1778, France and the United States formed a firm alliance that was later destroyed by Federalists and Jeffersonian Republicans who were competing with each other for political power.

This thesis rejects the prompt's claim that the origins of British-American and French hostilities lay in the early eighteenth century. Instead, it claims that the relations between these two groups were mixed and became hostile during the 1790s because of domestic American politics.

STEP 3 After you've written your own thesis, revisit the table that you brainstormed above. Turn your brainstorm into a historical argument by organizing the information into two main claims for the causes of the hostilities between the French and British-Americans.

For the sample thesis above, a historical argument table might look like this:

Historical Argument	
Long-term causes of hostility (claims)	**Proximate causes of hostility (claims)**
Claim: The parties engaged in off and on hostilities and were sometimes at peace and sometimes at war. **Evidence:** French and British colonial wars (eighteenth century)	**Claim:** The parties experienced a steady decline in relations from the end of the Revolutionary War through the split in Washington's administration caused by competition between Federalists and Jeffersonian Republicans.

Evidence: French colonies in North America caused conflicts (Doc. 3.5, Thomas Oliver, Letter to Queen Anne, 1708).

Evidence: Peace treaties were signed between Britain and France (Doc. 3.6, Treaty of Utrecht, 1713).

Evidence: Hostilities broke out again during the French and Indian War (Doc. 4.1, North America before and after the French and Indian War, 1754 and 1763).

Evidence: But Americans were willing to make an alliance with the French (Doc. 4.9, Treaty of Alliance between the United States and France, 1778).

Evidence: The high point of French-American relations occurred in 1783 (Doc. 4.11, Treaty of Paris, 1783).

Evidence: Jefferson (still in Washington's cabinet) acknowledged that the French Revolution was an issue for the Washington administration (Doc. 4.12, Thomas Jefferson, Letter to Thomas Pinckney, 1793).

Evidence: Jefferson rejected Washington's treaty with Britain and called Hamilton and others members of a "monarchial party" (Doc. 4.13, Thomas Jefferson, Letter to James Monroe, 1795).

Evidence: Federalists connected their political enemy, Jefferson, to the French Revolution (Doc. 4.14, Anti-Jefferson Cartoon, "The Providential Detection," 1797).

Using your completed table, turn your historical argument into two body paragraphs under your thesis from Step 2.

PUTTING IT ALL TOGETHER

Revisiting the Main Point

* In what ways did the pursuit of natural resources and political domination lead to conflicts among the French, English, Americans, and Native Americans in North America between 1754 and 1800?

* What motivated British-American expansion into the territory west of the Appalachian Mountains? To what extent was this motivation a product of British imperial policy?

* In what ways did Europe shape domestic politics in British North America and the United States?

* To what extent did British-Americans form a group identity that was distinct from Great Britain between 1754 and 1800?

* To what extent did the ideals of the Enlightenment influence the anti-British revolts of the 1770s? How might Native Americans and African Americans have viewed these ideals and their influence on these anti-British revolts?

BUILDING AP® WRITING SKILLS | ## The Subordinated Thesis Statement and Appropriate Organization

As you learned from Chapter 3, the point-by-point comparison analyzes key factors, concepts, issues, or ideas for their similarities and differences. Rarely are thesis statements simple answers. The first historical thinking skill discussed in Chapter 1—causation—appears to promise a direct answer to questions about cause and effect. Yet even these questions—such as "What are the causes of the Revolutionary War?"—provide room for ambiguity, complexity, and counterargument.

When historians combine historical thinking skills, they are able to **subordinate**, or analyze several categories, within a single statement by making some categories of a question depend on others. When you use a subordinated thesis statement, one point will be dominant and one will be subordinate.

For example, consider the following prompt:

> To what extent did the pursuit of natural resources and political domination lead to conflicts among the French, English, Americans, and Native Americans in North America between 1754 and 1800?

Notice that there are two broad topics in this prompt—"pursuit of natural resources and political domination" and "conflicts among the French, English, Americans, and Native Americans"—and four categories. Both topics are related, but a subordinated thesis statement allows you to give one of the topics greater significance than the other while still acknowledging their interrelatedness. In your subordinated thesis, you will subordinate either the topics to the categories, or vice versa.

STEP 1 *Understand the prompt, and identify the key words*

As you remember from Chapter 1, you must first understand your question. Draw a square around your topic ("pursuit of natural resources and political domination"), draw a line underneath your task (analyze "To what extent"), and draw a circle around the categories in the question ("conflicts among the French, English, Americans, and Native Americans in North America between 1754 and 1800").

STEP 2 *Brainstorm and organize your evidence*

To generate a working thesis from a historical prompt, begin by brainstorming what you know. Review the prompt's topic and categories above, and create a list of facts that fit under the topics and the categories. A few have been done for you:

> "pursuit of natural resources and political domination"

The British and French used their colonies for raw materials.
>   British: tobacco, shipbuilding materials, hemp, fish, etc.
>   French: furs
>   Stamp Act

> "conflicts among the French, English, Americans, and Native Americans"

The French and English fought throughout the seventeenth and eighteenth centuries.
>   French and Indian War
>   Pontiac's Rebellion
>   American Revolution

With this information, you have two choices to subordinate:

1. Pursuit of natural resources
2. Political domination

When you subordinate, you often use words such as these:

> However
> Still
> While
> Although

Since

Despite

Even though

Nevertheless

But

A possible thesis statement that subordinates the pursuit of natural resources might read as follows:

> Although the pursuit of natural resources was an important factor in conflicts among the French, English, Americans, and Native Americans [subordinate], the quest for political domination of North America proved to be the primary source of conflict among these groups [dominant].

Notice how in this thesis, the word "Although" cues the reader that the first part is the subordinate portion of the thesis; it depends on the second part. After the comma, the words "primary source of conflict" tell the reader that this part of the thesis is dominant. It is more important.

A possible thesis statement that subordinates political domination might read as follows:

> Even though political domination was the stated goal of the competing parties in eighteenth-century North America [subordinate], the quest for natural resources proved to be the underlying cause of all conflicts among the French, English, Americans, and Native Americans [dominant].

In this thesis, "Even though" cues the reader that "political domination" is subordinate. The words "proved to be the underlying cause" tell the reader that underneath the goal of political domination was the quest for natural resources. So "political domination" is dependent on, or subordinate to, "natural resources."

STEP 3 *Outline your response*

A point-by-point comparison provides a more streamlined approach to this prompt, as seen with the outlines below. The first is partially completed for you.

I. Thesis: Although the pursuit of natural resources was an important factor in conflicts among the French, English, Americans, and Native Americans, the quest for political domination of North America proved to be the primary source of conflict among these groups.

II. Claim: The pursuit of natural resources was an important factor in conflicts.

Evidence:

A. French/English conflict

1. French and Indian War

B. English/American conflict

C. English/Native American conflict

D. American/Native American conflict

    1. Pontiac's Rebellion, Diary of William Trent (Doc. 4.2)

III. Claim: The quest for political domination proved to be the primary source of conflict.

    Evidence:

    A. French/English conflict

        1. Treaty of Alliance (Doc. 4.9)

    B. English/American conflict

        1. Stamp Act (Doc. 4.3)

    C. English/Native American conflict

    D. American/Native American conflict

        1. Battle against the Iroquois Confederacy during the Revolutionary War, Brodhead's letter (Doc. 4.10)

IV. Conclusion

or

I. Thesis: Even though political domination was the stated goal of the competing parties in eighteenth-century North America, the quest for natural resources proved to be the underlying cause of all conflicts among the French, English, Americans, and Native Americans.

II. Claim: Political domination was the stated goal.

    Evidence:

    A. French pursuit of political domination

    B. English pursuit of political domination

    C. Native American pursuit of political domination

    D. American pursuit of political domination

III. Claim: Natural resources were the underlying cause of conflict.

    Evidence:

    A. French/English conflict

    B. English/American conflict

    C. English/Native American conflict

    D. American/Native American conflict

IV. Conclusion

A Republic Envisioned and Revised

T he economic protests of the 1760s drew inspiration from the religious fervor of the First Great Awakening and the theories of natural rights of the European Enlightenment. The democratic forces that were unleashed by the American Revolution also depended on religious and intellectual ideas and ultimately forced Americans to confront issues that were larger than independence.

With independence achieved, Americans wrestled with the degree of liberty that was promised by their self-proclaimed ideals: How much power should be given to a national government? How much power lay in the hands of the democratic majority? What rights of the minority were to be protected, and how would they be protected? Within ten years of independence, the United States scrapped one national constitution, the Articles of Confederation, and instituted another, the Constitution—in some cases over the protests of Americans who had supported independence.

The ideals of the Revolution forced Americans to confront the legacies of oppression that remained in the former colonies. Women and African Americans, whose subjugation was taken for granted, drew on the language of the Revolution to demand recognition of their natural rights—exposing some of the shortcomings of the Revolution and establishing the parameters of struggles to come.

Seeking the Main Point

As you read the documents that follow, keep these broad questions in mind. These questions will help you understand the relationship between the documents in this chapter and the historical changes that they represent. As you reflect on these questions, determine which themes and which documents best address them.

- How did European ideas shape American debates about the future of the new republic?
- In what ways did economic concerns shape American debates about the future of the new republic?
- How did debates over the new Constitution shape political debates after its ratification?
- In what ways did the American Revolution mirror similar revolutions in Europe and in the Western Hemisphere?
- Individuals or groups often use their public and private writings and speeches to present their purposes. In what ways do the writings of women and African Americans, who were marginalized in the eighteenth century, present similar purposes during and after the Revolution?

Rights-Based Government

DOCUMENT 5.1 | **JOHN LOCKE, *Two Treatises of Government***
| 1690

English political philosopher John Locke (1632–1704) first articulated the political theory of republican government and civil society that influenced many European Enlightenment thinkers and prominent American revolutionaries, like Thomas Jefferson. In his *Second Treatise on Civil Government* (1690), Locke articulated his social contract theory, which viewed society as an agreement among citizens. Below, Locke calls this "civil society."

89. Whereever therefore any number of Men are so united into one Society, as to quit every one his executive power of the Law of Nature, and to resign it to the publick, there and there only is a *political, or civil Society*. And this is done, whereever any number of Men, in the state of Nature, enter into Society to make one People, one Body politick, under one supream Government; or else when any one joyns himself to, and incorporates with any Government already made. For hereby he authorizes the Society, or which is all one, the Legislative thereof, to make Laws for him, as the publick good of the Society shall require; to the Execution whereof, his own Assistance (as to his own Decrees) is due. And this *puts Men* out of a state of Nature *into* that of a *Commonwealth*, by setting up a Judge on Earth, with Authority to determine all the Controversies, and redress [correct] the Injuries, that may happen to any Member of the Commonwealth; which Judge is the Legislative, or Magistrates appointed by it. And whereever there are any number of Men, however associated, that have no such decisive Power to appeal to, there they are still in *the state of Nature*.

90. Hence it is evident, that *absolute Monarchy*, which by some Men is counted the only Government in the World, is indeed *inconsistent with civil Society*, and so can be no form of Civil-Government at all. . . .

John Locke, *The Works of John Locke*, vol. V (London: Printed for J. Johnson, 1801), 389–390.

PRACTICING Historical Thinking

Identify: When you **paraphrase**, you restate another idea in your own words. Paraphrase the first full sentence of this document.

Analyze: According to Locke, what is the relationship between a "state of Nature" and "civil Society"?

Evaluate: Why, according to Locke, is absolute monarchy "inconsistent with civil Society"?

| **JONATHAN MAYHEW, "Discourse Concerning Unlimited Submission and Non-Resistance to the Higher Powers"**
1750

Jonathan Mayhew (1720–1766), a prominent Boston Congregational minister, gave the following sermon on the anniversary of the execution of Charles I (1649). Charles I (1600–1649) was executed during the English Civil War (1642–1651), when Puritan Parliamentary forces overthrew the king and instituted the Commonwealth of England, Scotland, and Ireland (1649–1660).

The essence of government, I mean good government, and this is the government the apostle [Paul] treats of, consists in making good laws, and in the wise and just execution of them—laws attempered [formed] to the common welfare of the governed. And if this be in fact done, it is evidently, in itself, a thing of no consequence what the particular form of government is; whether the legislative and executive power be lodged in one and the same person, or in different persons; whether in one person, which is called a monarchy; whether in a few—whether in many, so as to constitute a republic; or in three co-ordinate branches, in such manner as to make the government partake of each of these forms, and to be, at the same time, essentially different from them all. If the end be attained, it is enough. But no form of government seems to be so unlikely to accomplish this end as absolute monarchy; nor is there any one which has so little pretence to a *divine* original, unless it be in this sense, that God first permitted it into, and thereby overturned, the commonwealth of Israel, as a curse or punishment on that people, for their folly and wickedness particularly, in desiring such a government.

Alden Bradford, ed., *Memoir of the Life and Writings of Rev. Jonathan Mayhew, D.C.: Pastor of the West Church and Society in Boston, from June, 1747, to July, 1766* (Boston, MA: C. C. Little, 1838), 110.

PRACTICING Historical Thinking

Identify: According to Mayhew, what is the relationship between legislative and executive powers?

Analyze: Why would Mayhew claim that an absolute monarchy is "unlikely" to accomplish the aim of government?

Evaluate: How does Mayhew's vision of government build on John Locke's view (Doc. 5.1)?

| PHILLIS WHEATLEY, "On Being Brought from Africa to America"
1770

Phillis Wheatley (1753–1784) was born in Africa, transported as a girl to slavery in North America, and eventually bought by John Wheatley of Boston, who taught her to read and write. Wheatley was freed after her master's death in 1778. She was the first African American poet published in America. Most of her work is on religious topics.

> 'Twas mercy brought me from my *Pagan* land,
> Taught my benighted soul to understand
> That there's a God, that there's a *Saviour* too;
> Once I redemption neither sought nor knew.
> Some view our sable race with scornful eye,
> "Their colour is a diabolic dye."
> Remember, *Christians*, negroes, black as *Cain*,
> May be refin'd, and join th' angelic train.

Phillis Wheatley, *Poems on Various Subjects, Religious and Moral* (Denver, CO: W. H. Lawrence, 1887), 17.

PRACTICING Historical Thinking

Identify: According to Wheatley, what is God's role in this poem?

Analyze: As you may recall from Chapter 4, a writer's **attitude** is her attitude toward a subject. One word that often describes an attitude is **tone**, which usually is discerned through an analysis of the writer's language or **diction**. Is Wheatley's tone at the end of the poem hopeful or cynical? What might explain her tone?

Evaluate: Redemption, in this poem, means to be saved from sin and become Christian. Based on this poem, determine the extent to which God determines redemption.

| THOMAS PAINE, *Common Sense*
1776

Thomas Paine (1737–1809) arrived in Philadelphia from England on the eve of the American Revolution. Paine wrote for Pennsylvania periodicals before anonymously publishing *Common Sense* (1776), a pamphlet that eventually sold 100,000 copies and helped solidify popular support for American independence.

But there is another and greater distinction, for which no truly natural or religious reason can be assigned, and that is, the distinction of men into KINGS and SUBJECTS.

Male and female are the distinctions of nature, good and bad, the distinction of heaven; but how a race of men came into the world so exalted above the rest, and distinguished like some new species, is worth enquiring into, and whether they are the means of happiness or of misery to mankind.

In the early ages of the world, according to the scripture chronology, there were no kings; the consequence of which was, there were no wars: it is the pride of kings which throws mankind into confusion. Holland without a king hath enjoyed more peace for this last century than any of the monarchical governments in Europe. . . .

Government by kings was first introduced into the world by the Heathens, from whom the children of Israel copied the custom. It was the most prosperous invention the Devil ever set on foot for the promotion of idolatry. The Heathens paid divine honors to their deceased kings, and the Christian world hath improved on the plan, by doing the same to their living ones. How impious is the title of *sacred majesty* applied to a worm who in the midst of his splendor is crumbling into dust!

Thomas Paine, *Common Sense: Addressed to the Inhabitants of America* (New York: Peter Eckler, 1918), 8–9.

PRACTICING Historical Thinking

Identify: What is the influence of the arrival of kings in history, according to Paine?

Analyze: What is the role of religion in Paine's argument?

Evaluate: How does this document represent both the religious thinking of the First Great Awakening and the secular thinking of the Enlightenment?

DOCUMENT 5.5 | ABIGAIL ADAMS, Letter to John Adams
| 1776

In this letter to her husband, John Adams, Abigail Adams expresses support for American independence but asks her husband to improve women's traditionally subordinate role to men.

I long to hear that you have declared an independence. And by the way, in the new code of laws which I suppose it will be necessary for you to make, I desire you would remember the ladies, and be more generous and favorable to them than your ancestors. Do not put such unlimited power into the hands of the husbands! Remember, all men would be tyrants if they could! If particular care and attention is not paid to the ladies, we are determined to foment a rebellion, and will not hold ourselves bound by any laws in which we have no voice or representation. That your sex are naturally tyrannical is a truth so thoroughly established as to admit of no dispute. . . .

Library of the World's Best Literature, Ancient and Modern, ed. Charles Dudley Warner, vol. 1 (New York: International Society, 1896), 87–88.

PRACTICING Historical Thinking

Identify: What request does Adams make of her husband? What result does she foresee if this request is not met?

Analyze: In what ways does Adams's request echo the ideas of Thomas Paine (Doc. 5.4) and John Locke (Doc. 5.1)?

Evaluate: In what ways do Adams's arguments foreshadow future debates in American politics and society?

DOCUMENT 5.6 | THOMAS JEFFERSON, Declaration of Independence
1776

When, Thomas Jefferson (1743–1826), Virginia planter and delegate to the Continental Congress, was asked to write a justification for American independence, he drew from Enlightenment ideas that were familiar to many British Americans. Congress adopted Jefferson's declaration on July 4, 1776.

When, in the course of human events, it becomes necessary for one people to dissolve the political bands which have connected them with another, and to assume, among the powers of the Earth, the separate and equal station to which the laws of nature and of nature's God entitle them, a decent respect to the opinions of mankind requires that they should declare the causes which impel them to the separation.

We hold these truths to be self-evident; that all men are created equal; that they are endowed, by their Creator, with certain unalienable rights; that among these are life, liberty, and the pursuit of happiness.—That to secure these rights, governments are instituted among men, deriving their just powers from the consent of the governed; that whenever any form of government becomes destructive of these ends, it is the right of the people to alter or to abolish it, and to institute new government, laying its foundation on such principles, and organizing its powers in such form, as to them shall seem most likely to effect their safety and happiness. Prudence, indeed, will dictate, that governments long established, should not be changed for light and transient causes; and accordingly all experience hath shewn, that mankind are more disposed to suffer, while evils are sufferable, than to right themselves by abolishing the forms to which they are accustomed. But when a long train of abuses and usurpations, pursuing invariably the same object, evinces a design to reduce them under absolute despotism, it is their right, it is their duty, to throw off such government, and to provide new guards for their future security. . . .

The Constitution of the United States of America, Established March 4, 1789: To Which Is Added the Declaration of Their Reasons for Separating from This Country, Made in Congress, July 4, 1776. And a Resolution of Congress Expressive of Their High Sense of the Services of Mr. Thomas Paine (London: D. I. Eaton, 1794), 23.

PRACTICING Historical Thinking

Identify: Identify the five most significant words in this document. Explain your choices.

Analyze: Based on this document, what is the relationship between government and human beings' inalienable rights?

Evaluate: In what ways does this document build on Jonathan Mayhew's (Doc. 5.2)?

DOCUMENT 5.7 | ABIGAIL ADAMS, Letter to John Quincy Adams
1780

Abigail Adams wrote the letter excerpted below to her thirteen-year-old son, John Quincy Adams, while he accompanied his father, John Adams, on his diplomatic duties as special envoy to Europe during the American Revolution.

. . . It will be expected of you my son that as you are favour'd with superiour advantages under the instructive Eye of a tender parent, that your improvements should bear some proportion to your advantages. Nothing is wanting with you, but attention, diligence and steady application, Nature has not been deficient.

. . . The Habits of a vigorous mind are formed in contending with difficulties. All History will convince you of this, and that wisdom and penetration are the fruits of experience, not the Lessons of retirement and leisure.

Great necessities call out great virtues. When a mind is raised, and animated by scenes that engage the Heart, then those qualities which would otherways lay dormant, wake into Life, and form the Character of the Hero and the Statesman.

War, Tyrrany, and Desolation are the Scourges of the Almighty, and ought no doubt to be deprecated. Yet it is your Lot my Son to be an Eye witness of these Calimities in your own Native land, and at the same time to owe your existance among a people who have made a glorious defence of their invaded Liberties, and who, aided by a generous and powerful Ally, with the blessing of heaven will transmit this inheritance to ages yet unborn. . . .

The strict and invoilable regard you have ever paid to truth, gives me pleasing hopes that you will not swerve from her dictates, but add justice, fortitude, and every Manly Virtue which can adorn a good citizen, do Honour to your Country, and render your parents supreemly happy, particuliarly your ever affectionate Mother,

AA

"Abigail Adams to John Quincy Adams, 19 January 1780," Founders Online, National Archives, http://founders.archives.gov/volumes/Adams/04-03. Reprinted by permission of the publisher from *The Adams Papers: Adams Family Correspondence*, vol. 3, *April 1778–September 1782*, ed. L. H. Butterfield and Marc Friedlaender (Cambridge, MA: Harvard University Press, 1973), 268–269. Copyright © 1973 by the Massachusetts Historical Society

---

PRACTICING Historical Thinking

Identify: List Adams's main reasons for writing to her son.

Analyze: What does Adams mean when she states, "War, Tyrrany and Desolation are the Scourges of the Almighty, and ought no doubt to be deprecated"?

Evaluate: To what extent does Adams's letter reinforce traditional views of women in late eighteenth-century America?

DOCUMENT 5.8 | Franchise Restrictions in the Georgia State Constitution
1777

During the American Revolution, British-American colonies reorganized themselves into sovereign (or self-governing) states and composed constitutions to frame the boundaries of government power. These constitutions often limited voting rights, as seen in this excerpt from Georgia's first state constitution.

ART. IX. All male white inhabitants, of the age of twenty-one years, and possessed in his own right of ten pounds value, and liable to pay tax in this State, or being of any mechanic trade, and shall have been resident six months in this State, shall have a right to vote at all elections for representatives, or any other officers, herein agreed to be chosen by the people at large; and every person having a right to vote at any election shall vote by ballot personally.

ART. X. No officer whatever shall serve any process, or give any other hinderances to any person entitled to vote, either in going to the place of election, or during the time of the said election, or on their returning home from such election; nor shall any military officer, or soldier, appear at any election in a military character, to the intent that all elections may be free and open.

ART. XI. No person shall be entitled to more than one vote, which shall be given in the county where such person resides, except as before excepted; nor shall any person who holds any title of nobility be entitled to a vote, or be capable of serving as a representative, or hold any post of honor, profit, or trust in this State, whilst such person claims his title of nobility; but if the person shall give up such distinction, in the manner as may be directed by any future legislation, then, and in such case, he shall be entitled to a vote, and represent, as before directed, and enjoy all the other benefits of a free citizen.

Francis Newton Thorpe, ed., *The Federal and State Constitutions, Colonial Charters, and Other Organic Laws of the States, Territories, and Colonies Now or Heretofore Forming the United States of America*, vol. 2 (Washington, DC: Government Printing Office, 1909), 779–780.

PRACTICING Historical Thinking

Identify: According to this document, who gets to vote? Who does not get to vote?

Analyze: Why is a claim to a "title of nobility" (Article XI) included in this document?

Evaluate: What are the origins of these restrictions on who gets to vote and which titles cannot be used? Use outside knowledge from your textbook and class work in your response.

DOCUMENT 5.9 | Articles of Confederation and Perpetual Union
1781–1789

The Articles of Confederation and Perpetual Union, drafted by the Continental Congress in 1776, were an attempt to create a government of the United States that would be incapable of wielding the kind of power that Parliament and the king had formerly held over British America.

Art. 2. Each state retains its sovereignty, freedom, and independence, and every power, jurisdiction, and right which is not by this Confederation expressly delegated to the United States in Congress assembled.

Art. 3. The said states hereby severally enter into a firm league of friendship with each other for their common defence, the security of their liberties, and their mutual and general welfare; binding themselves to assist each other against all force offered to or attacks made upon them on account of religion, sovereignty, trade, or any other pretence whatever. . . .

Art. 9. . . . The United States in Congress assembled shall never engage in a war nor grant letters of marque or reprisal in time of peace, nor enter into any treaties or alliances, nor coin money nor regulate the value thereof, nor ascertain the sums and expenses necessary for the defence and welfare of the United States, or any of them; nor emit bills, nor borrow money on the credit of the United States, nor appropriate money, nor agree upon the number of vessels of war to be built or purchased, or the number of land or sea forces to be raised, nor appoint a commander-in-chief of the army or navy, unless nine states assent to the same; nor shall a question on any other point, except for adjourning from day to day, be determined, unless by the votes of a majority of the United States in Congress assembled. . . .

Art. 13. Every state shall abide by the determinations of the United States in Congress assembled on all questions which by this Confederation are submitted to them. And the Articles of this Confederation shall be inviolably observed by every state, and the Union shall be perpetual; nor shall any alteration at any time hereafter be made in any of them; unless such alteration be agreed to in a Congress of the United States, and be afterwards confirmed by the legislatures of every state.

George Ticknor Curtis, *Constitutional History of the United States*, vol. 1 (New York: Harper & Brothers, 1897), 713–719.

PRACTICING Historical Thinking

Identify: List the powers of the new national government that are described in this document. List the powers that are guaranteed to the states.

Analyze: Using Article 9, infer how past injustices led the writers to include the specific statutes of this article.

Evaluate: In what ways does this document attempt to apply John Locke's theories from Document 5.1?

SKILL REVIEW | Contextualization and Argumentation

Consider the following claim:

> The First Great Awakening proved to be a greater influence than the Enlightenment on American political identity between 1754 and 1787. Accept, refute, or modify this statement, and support your position with appropriate evidence.

For a review of the historical thinking skills of contextualization and argumentation, revisit your work in the Applying AP® Historical Thinking Skills exercises on pages 49–50, 77–78, and 108–110.

Debating Liberty and Security

DOCUMENT 5.10 | "The Address and Reasons of Dissent of the Minority of the Convention of Pennsylvania to Their Constituents"
| December 12, 1787

Throughout the summer of 1787, delegates from the states met in Philadelphia, Pennsylvania, to revise the Articles of Confederation, but they ultimately wrote an entirely new constitution for the republic. In late 1787, a minority of delegates to the Pennsylvania constitutional convention offered this dissent regarding elements of the new constitution.

We dissent, first, because it is the opinion of the most celebrated writers on government, and confirmed by uniform experience, that a very extensive territory cannot be governed on the principles of freedom, otherwise than by a confederation of republics, possessing all the powers of internal government; but united in the management of their general, and foreign concerns.

We dissent, secondly, because the powers vested in congress by this constitution, must necessarily annihilate and absorb the legislative, executive, and judicial powers of the several states; and produce, from their ruins, one consolidated government, which, from the nature of things, will be an iron-handed despotism, as nothing short of the supremacy of despotic sway could connect and govern these United States under one government. . . .

The powers of congress, under the new constitution, are complete and unlimited over the purse and the sword; and are perfectly independent of, and supreme over, the state governments, whose intervention in these great points, is entirely destroyed. By virtue of their power of taxation, congress may command the whole, or any part of the properties of the people. They may impose what imposts upon commerce—they may impose what land-taxes and taxes, excises, duties on all the instruments, and duties on every fine article that they may judge proper. In short, every species of taxation whether of an external or internal nature, is comprised in section the 8th, of article the first [of the Constitution], . . . "the congress shall have power to lay and collect taxes, duties, imposts, and excises, to pay the debts, and provide for the common defence and general welfare of the united states."

The American Museum, or, Repository of Ancient and Modern Fugitive Pieces, &c. Prose and Poetical (Philadelphia, PA: Matthew Carey, 1787), 542–544.

> **PRACTICING Historical Thinking**
>
> *Identify:* What are the chief concerns of the dissenters?
>
> *Analyze:* How are these concerns justified in this document?
>
> *Evaluate:* Using your knowledge of the history of the relationship between Great Britain and the North American British colonies, determine whether the dissenters' claims are justified. Explain.

DOCUMENT 5.11 | ## James Madison, Federalist No. 10
November 22, 1787

James Madison (1751–1836), Virginian and delegate to the Constitutional Convention in Philadelphia in the summer of 1787, composed the first draft of the new constitution. Along with Alexander Hamilton (1757–1804) and John Jay (1745–1829), he argued for its ratification in a series of essays entitled *The Federalist Papers* (1787–1788). Here, in Federalist No. 10, Madison argues that the new constitution will prevent factionalism, or divisions between groups, which many Americans feared would ultimately destroy the young republic.

The latent causes of faction are thus sown in the nature of man; and we see them everywhere brought into different degrees of activity, according to the different circumstances of civil society. A zeal for different opinions concerning religion, concerning government, and many other points, as well of speculation as of practice; an attachment to different leaders, ambitiously contending for pre-eminence and power; or to persons of other descriptions, whose fortunes have been interesting to the human passions, have, in turn, divided mankind into parties, inflamed them with mutual animosity, and rendered them much more disposed to vex and oppress each other, than to cooperate for their common good. So strong is this propensity of mankind, to fall into mutual animosities, that where no substantial occasion presents itself, the most frivolous and fanciful distinctions have been sufficient to kindle their unfriendly passions, and excite their most violent conflicts. But the most common and durable source of factions, has been the various and unequal distribution of property. Those who hold, and those who are without property, have ever formed distinct interests in society. Those who are creditors, and those who are debtors, fall under a like discrimination. A landed interest, a manufacturing interest, a mercantile interest, a moneyed interest, with many lesser interests, grow up of necessity in civilized nations and divide them into different classes, actuated by different sentiments and views. The regulation of these various and interfering interests forms the principal task of modern legislation, and involves the spirit of party and faction in the necessary and ordinary operations of the government. . . .

It is in vain to say, that enlightened statesmen will be able to adjust these clashing interests, and render them all subservient to the public good. Enlightened statesmen will not always be at the helm: nor in many cases, can such an adjustment be made at all, without taking into view indirect and remote considerations, which will rarely prevail over the immediate interest which one party may find in disregarding the rights of another, or the good of the whole.

The inference to which we are brought is, that the *causes* of faction cannot be removed; and that relief is only to be sought in the means of controlling its *effects*. . . .

By what means is this object attainable? . . . Either the existence of the same passion or interest in a majority, at the same time, must be prevented; or the majority, having such coexistent passion or interest, must be rendered, by their number and local situation, unable to concert and carry into effect schemes of oppression. . . .

Hence, it clearly appears, that the same advantage, which a republic has over a democracy, in controlling the effects of faction, is enjoyed by a large over a small republic—is enjoyed by the union over the states composing it. Does this advantage consist in the substitution of representatives, whose enlightened views and virtuous sentiments render them superior to local prejudices, and to schemes of injustice? It will not be denied, that the representation of the union will be most likely to possess these requisite endowments. Does it consist in the greater security afforded by a greater variety of parties, against the event of any one party being able to outnumber and oppress the rest? In an equal degree does the increased variety of parties, comprised within the union, increase this security. Does it, in fine, consist in the greater obstacles opposed to the concert and accomplishment of the secret wishes of an unjust and interested majority? Here, again, the extent of the union gives it the most palpable advantage.

The Federalist, on the New Constitution, Written in 1788, by Mr. Hamilton, Mr. Madison, and Mr. Jay (Hallowell, ME: Masters, Smith, 1852), 43–48.

PRACTICING Historical Thinking

Identify: What are the sources of factionalism, according to Madison?

Analyze: What does he say are the best ways to address factionalism?

Evaluate: To what extent does this document address the concerns presented in Document 5.10?

DOCUMENT 5.12 | ## Political Cartoon on Virginia's Ratification of the Constitution, *Boston Independent Chronicle*
June 12, 1788

This political cartoon appeared in the *Boston Independent Chronicle* in 1788. According to the proposed US Constitution, nine of the thirteen states were required for ratification. In this cartoon, the Virginian "pillar" is being erected by a hand reaching out from a cloud. New Hampshire ratified the new constitution before Virginia, on June 21, 1788, and became the ninth state to do so.

PRACTICING Historical Thinking

Identify: Whose hand is present at the top of the cartoon?

Analyze: Based on the imagery in this cartoon, what is the cartoonist's attitude toward the ratification of the US Constitution?

Evaluate: Why would some colonies not ratify the Constitution? Consult your textbook or class notes as needed.

APPLYING AP® Historical Thinking Skills

SKILL REVIEW | Comparison and Argumentation

STEP 1 Review the following three documents. What are similar beliefs of all three? Write down your ideas in your notebook.

> Document 5.1, John Locke, *Two Treatises of Government*, 1690
>
> Document 5.2, Jonathan Mayhew, "Discourse Concerning Unlimited Submission and Non-Resistance to the Higher Powers," 1750
>
> Document 5.6, Thomas Jefferson, Declaration of Independence, 1776

STEP 2 Now compare the following two documents. Which of the two seems closer to the common beliefs of the above three documents? Write down these ideas too.

> Document 5.10, "The Address and Reasons of Dissent of the Minority of the Convention of Pennsylvania to Their Constituents," December 12, 1787
>
> Document 5.11, James Madison, Federalist No. 10, November 22, 1787

STEP 3 Now construct a historical argument that accepts, refutes, or modifies the following claim:

> In their debates over the new constitution, the Antifederalists used arguments that were closer to the ideals of the American Revolution than did the Federalists. Support your response with appropriate evidence.

Write your answer with a thesis statement and two body paragraphs, each of which begins with a main point and has supporting points that use the documents above and outside information from your textbook and your class notes.

*For a review of comparison and argumentation, revisit your work from the Applying AP®
Historical Thinking Skills exercises on pages 42–43, 49–50, 77–78, 108–110, and 127.*

Reverberations

DOCUMENT 5.13 | Pennsylvania Act for the Gradual Abolition of Slavery
1780

In 1780, Pennsylvania enacted provisions for the abolition of slavery within its borders. Below is an excerpt from this statute.

And whereas the condition of those persons who have heretofore been denominated negro and mulatto slaves, has been attended with circumstances which not only deprived them of the common blessings that they were by nature entitled to, but has cast them into the deepest afflictions by an unnatural separation and sale of husband and wife from each other, and from their children, an injury the greatness of which can only be conceived by supposing that we were in the same unhappy case. In justice, therefore, to persons so unhappily circumstanced, and who, having no prospect before them whereon they may rest their sorrows and their hopes, have no reasonable inducement to render that service to society which they otherwise might, and also in grateful commemoration of our own happy deliverance from that state of unconditional submission to which we were doomed by the tyranny of Britain:

Be it enacted and it is hereby enacted by the Representatives of the Freemen of the Commonwealth of Pennsylvania in General Assembly met, and by the authority of the same, That all persons, as well negroes and mulattoes as others who shall be born within this state, from and after the passing of this act, shall not be deemed and considered as servants for life or slaves; and that all servitude for life or slavery of children in consequence of the slavery of their mothers, in the case of all children born within this state from and after the passing of this act as aforesaid, shall be and hereby is utterly taken away, extinguished and forever abolished.

Statutes at Large of Pennsylvania from 1682–1801, vol. 10 (Philadelphia, PA: Wm. Stanley Ray, 1904), 68.

PRACTICING Historical Thinking

Identify: List the grievances that are presented in this act.

Analyze: What are the connections between the effects of tyranny and slavery?

Evaluate: Compare this document to Phillis Wheatley's poem (Doc. 5.3). To what extent do these documents reveal religious values in the law?

US Constitution, Preamble

1787

The following preamble to the US Constitution was written during the Constitutional Convention in 1787 to justify the scrapping of the Articles of Confederation and the creation of an entirely new government.

We the People of the United States, in Order to form a more perfect Union, establish Justice, insure domestic Tranquility, provide for the common defence, promote the general Welfare, and secure the Blessings of Liberty to ourselves and our Posterity, do ordain and establish this Constitution for the United States of America.

National Archives, *Charters of Freedom* exhibit, www.archives.gov/exhibits/charters /constitution_transcript.html.

PRACTICING Historical Thinking

Identify: List the verbs that appear in this document. What kinds of actions do they describe? What role do they lay out for the new government?

Analyze: Consider the sequence of causes for developing the preamble, beginning with "in order to form" and ending with "to ourselves and our Posterity." Why compose the preamble in this order?

Evaluate: What gaps in the Articles of Confederation does this preamble address?

DOCUMENT 5.15

US Constitution, Article I, Sections 2 and 9

1787

The institution of slavery proved to be a sticking point for delegates to the Constitutional Convention. The so-called three-fifths compromise and the extension of the slave trade until 1808 were compromises between proslavery and antislavery delegates at the Convention.

Representatives and direct Taxes shall be apportioned among the several States which may be included within this Union, according to their respective Numbers, which shall be determined by adding to the whole Number of free Persons, including those bound to Service for a Term of Years, and excluding Indians not taxed, three fifths of all other Persons. . . .

The Migration or Importation of such Persons as any of the States now existing shall think proper to admit, shall not be prohibited by the Congress prior to the Year one thousand eight hundred and eight, but a Tax or duty may be imposed on such Importation, not exceeding ten dollars for each Person.

National Archives, *Charters of Freedom* exhibit, www.archives.gov/exhibits/charters /constitution_transcript.html.

PRACTICING Historical Thinking

Identify: What is the actual compromise?

Analyze: Explain the thinking behind this compromise.

Evaluate: To what extent does this compromise address the concerns presented in Document 5.11?

DOCUMENT 5.16 | Declaration of the Rights of Man
1789

The Declaration of the Rights of Man was adopted by the French National Assembly a little over one month after the storming of the Bastille prison in Paris on July 14, 1789. Inspired by the ideas of John Locke, Montesquieu, and Voltaire, this declaration echoed the sentiments of the American Declaration of Independence and the US Constitution.

1. Men are born and remain free and equal in rights. Social distinctions may only be founded upon the general good.

2. The aim of all political association is the preservation of the natural and imprescriptible rights of man. These rights are liberty, property, security and resistance to oppression.

3. The principle of all sovereignty resides essentially in the nation. No body nor individual may exercise any authority which does not proceed directly from the nation.

4. Liberty consists in the freedom to do everything which injures no one else; hence the exercise of the natural rights of each man has no limits except those which assure to the other members of the society the enjoyment of the same rights. These limits can only be determined by law.

5. Law can only prohibit such actions as are hurtful to society. Nothing may be prevented which is not forbidden by law, and no one may be forced to do anything not provided for by law.

6. Law is the expression of the general will. Every citizen has a right to participate personally or through his representative in its foundation. It

must be the same for all, whether it protects or punishes. All citizens, being equal in the eyes of the law, are equally eligible to all dignities and to all public positions and occupations, according to their abilities, and without distinction except that of their virtues and talents.

James Harvey Robinson, ed., *Translations and Reprints from the Original Sources of European History*, vol. 1, no. 5 (Philadelphia: University of Pennsylvania Press, 1897), 6–7.

PRACTICING Historical Thinking

Identify: Determine five significant points that are made in this declaration. Explain your choices.

Analyze: In what ways does this document borrow from the American Declaration of Independence (Doc. 5.6)?

Evaluate: In what ways does this document express concerns or interests that differed from those of British North Americans?

DOCUMENT 5.17 | **TOUSSAINT L'OUVERTURE, Letter to the Directory**
1797

Toussaint L'Ouverture (1743–1803) was the leader of Haitian revolutionary forces in the island colony of Saint Domingue that led to the liberation of the slaves there. In 1797, he faced an attempt by former slaveholders to recover their lost property. In this letter, L'Ouverture warns the French revolutionary government not to attempt to reestablish slavery on the island.

. . . They [the former slaveholders on the island on Saint Domingue] cannot see how this odious conduct on their part can become the signal of new disasters and irreparable misfortunes, and that far from making them regain what in their eyes liberty for all has made them lose, they expose themselves to a total ruin and the colony to its inevitable destruction. Do they think that men who have been able to enjoy the blessing of liberty will calmly see it snatched away? They supported their chains only so long as they did not know any condition of life more happy than that of slavery. But to-day when they have left it, if they had a thousand lives they would sacrifice them all rather than be forced into slavery again. But no, the same hand which has broken our chains will not enslave us anew. France will not revoke her principles, she will not withdraw from us the greatest of her benefits. She will protect us against all our enemies; she will not permit her sublime morality to be perverted, those principles which do her most honor to be destroyed, her most beautiful achievement to be degraded, her Decree of 16 Pluviose [which abolished slavery in French colonies] which so honors humanity to be revoked.

But if . . . this was done, then I declare to you it would be to attempt the impossible: we have known how to face dangers to obtain our liberty, we shall know how to brave death to maintain it.

C. L. R. James, *A History of Negro Revolt* (New York: Haskell House, 1938), 19.

PRACTICING Historical Thinking

Identify: What are L'Ouverture's main concerns?

Analyze: What is L'Ouverture's tone? Review your response regarding Phillis Wheatley's tone in Document 5.3. Are the two tones similar? Explain.

Evaluate: To what extent does race influence L'Ouverture's message? To what extent does race influence the Declaration of Independence (Doc. 5.6)? What accounts for the difference?

DOCUMENT 5.18 | ## Sedition Act
| 1798

The Sedition Act was passed by the Federalist-dominated Congress in 1798 during the Quasi-War with France. It made illegal any writings and statements that were considered destabilizing to the power of the federal government and was used primarily against Jeffersonian Republicans for the benefit of Federalists.

SECTION 2. *And be it further enacted,* That if any person shall write, print, utter, or publish, or shall cause or procure to be written, printed, uttered, or published, or shall knowingly and willingly assist or aid in writing, printing, uttering, or publishing any false, scandalous and malicious writing or writings against the government of the United States, with intent to defame the said government, or either house of the said Congress, or the said President, or to bring them or either of them into disrepute; or to excite against them, or either, or any of them, the hatred of the good people of the United States, or to stir up sedition within the United States, or to excite any unlawful combinations therein, for opposing or resisting any law of the United States, or any act of the President of the United States, and one in pursuance of any such law, or of the powers in him vested by the Constitution of the United States, or to resist, oppose or defeat any such law or act, or to aid, encourage or abet any hostile designs of any foreign nation against the United States, their people or government, then such person, being thereof convicted before any court of the United States having jurisdiction thereof, shall be punished by a fine not exceeding ten thousand dollars, and by imprisonment not exceeding two years.

Albion Woodbury Small, *The Growth of American Nationality: An Introduction to the Constitutional History of the United States* (Waterville, ME: Colby University, 1888), 74.

DOCUMENT 5.19 | # Kentucky Resolution
1799

The Kentucky Resolution (1799) represented the Jeffersonian Republicans' public rejection of the Sedition Act (Doc. 5.18). Although the resolution was not binding on the federal government, it was a symbolic affirmation of the Republicans' dedication to states' rights and a weak federal government.

Resolved, That this Commonwealth considers the Federal Union, upon the terms and for the purposes specified in the late compact, as conducive to the liberty and happiness of the several states; that it does now unequivocally declare its attachment to the Union, and to that compact, agreeable to its obvious and real intention, and will be among the last to seek its dissolution: That if those who administer the General Government be permitted to transgress the limits fixed by that compact, by a total disregard to the special delegations of power therein contained, an annihilation of the State Governments, and the erection upon their ruins of a general consolidated government, will be the inevitable consequence: That the principle and construction contended for by sundry [various types] of the State Legislatures, that the General Government is the exclusive judge of the extent of the powers delegated to it, stop nothing short of despotism, since the *discretion* of those who administer the government, and not the *Constitution*, would be the measure of their powers. That the several states who formed that instrument, being sovereign and independent, have the unquestionable right to judge of its infraction, and *that a nullification by those sovereignties, of all unauthorized acts done under color of that instrument, is the rightful remedy*: That this Commonwealth does, upon the most deliberate reconsideration, declare that the said Alien and Sedition Laws are, in their opinion, palpable violations of the said Constitution; and, however cheerfully it may be disposed to surrender its opinion to a majority of its sister states in matters of ordinary or doubtful policy, yet, in momentous regulations like the present, which so vitally wound the best rights of the citizen, it would consider a silent acquiesecence as highly criminal: That although this Commonwealth, as a party to the Federal Compact, will bow to the laws of the Union, yet it does at the same time declare that it will not now, nor ever hereafter, cease to oppose in a constitutional manner, every attempt, from what quarter soever offered, to violate that compact. . . .

Edwin Williams, *The Book of the Constitution: Containing the Constitution of the United States; A Synopsis of the Several State Constitutions; with Various Other Important Documents and Useful Information* (New York: Peter Hill, 1833), 85.

PRACTICING Historical Thinking

Identify: What is the role of government, according to this document?

Analyze: According to this document, how does the Sedition Act (Doc. 5.18) undermine the proper role of government?

Evaluate: If this document is a threat, who or what is being threatened? And with what are they being threatened?

APPLYING AP® Historical Thinking Skills

SKILL REVIEW | Analyzing Evidence: Content and Sourcing

In this chapter, many documents use the ideas of the Enlightenment to justify different ends. Here are three that you read:

Document 5.11, James Madison, Federalist No. 10, November 22, 1787
Document 5.17, Toussaint L'Ouverture, Letter to the Directory, 1797
Document 5.19, Kentucky Resolution, 1799

STEP 1 Analyze these documents using the chart below (first introduced in Chapter 4):

	Doc. 5.11, James Madison, Federalist No. 10, November 22, 1787	Doc. 5.17, Toussaint L'Ouverture, Letter to the Directory, 1797	Doc. 5.19, Kentucky Resolution, 1799
Audience: Who did the author have in mind when she or he created this source?			
Purpose: What is the author's intent in creating this source? What is it for?			

Point of view and **attitude:** Which perspective(s) does the author consider? What are the author's biases?			
Format: How has the author presented her or his source? Is it hand-written, printed, a picture or cartoon, or an artifact?			
Argument: A source often reflects a writer's argument. What might this source be arguing for?			
Context: What events, ideas, and people surrounded the author when this source was created? Where did the source appear? How credible is the source?			
Limitations: Based on all of the above, what are some limitations of this source? What can it not do or be because of its audience, purpose, point of view, etc.?			

STEP 2 Now consider the following prompt:

> To what extent were Enlightenment ideals used to promote greater freedoms throughout the late eighteenth century?

In responding to this prompt, be sure to write a working thesis that answers the prompt and body paragraphs that prove your thesis. Each body paragraph should begin with a claim that is supported by multiple evidence.

For a review of analyzing evidence, its content, and its sourcing, see the Applying AP®️ Historical Thinking Skills exercise on pages 98–101.

PUTTING IT ALL TOGETHER

Revisiting the Main Point

- In what ways did the new language of human rights shape economic policies during the eighteenth century?
- As seen in the prereading theme questions, the **rhetoric** of an individual or a group refers to the language used in public or private discourse. How was the rhetoric of marginalized groups like women and African Americans similar in the eighteenth century?
- How did European ideas fuel the rhetoric, or public discourse, of the American Revolution? How did the rhetoric of the American Revolution influence revolutionary idealism in other parts of the world?
- Characterize the Federalist and Antifederalist positions in the debates over the Constitution during the 1780s. Characterize the Federalist and Jeffersonian Republican positions in the debates over government power during the 1790s. What is one similarity and one difference between the debates of the 1780s and the 1790s?

BUILDING AP® WRITING SKILLS | Avoiding the Either/Or Fallacy in Historical Argument

Any argument that is worth making has at least two credible sides. Although you may firmly believe one side, fully addressing both sides makes a more complete argument.

Acknowledging the other side's validity is called a **concession**. An appropriate use of historical evidence will acknowledge the opposing views of any argument. Even after acknowledging a second side, however, you must be careful to avoid the **either/or fallacy**, which artificially reduces an argument to only two choices.

For example, consider the following prompt:

> Review two of the major sides in the political debates of the 1780s and 1790s—the Antifederalists/Jeffersonian Republicans on one side and the Federalists on the other. Determine the extent to which one had a greater claim to fulfilling the ideals of the Declaration of Independence.

STEP 1 *Understand the prompt, and identify the key words*

As you remember from Chapter 1, you must first understand your question. Draw a square around your topic ("two of the major sides in the political debates of the 1780s and 1790s"), draw a line underneath your task ("Determine the extent to which one had a greater claim to fulfilling the ideals of the Declaration of Independence"), and draw a circle around the categories in the question ("Antifederalists/Jeffersonian Republicans" and "Federalists").

STEP 2 *Brainstorm and organize your evidence*

In debate, a good starting point is to organize your evidence by two sides. The following graphic organizer will help you to identify the reasons that each side believes its position.

Document	Federalists	Reasons	Antifederalists/ Jeffersonian Republicans	Reasons
Doc. 5.11, Federalist No. 10	For greater national power	A stronger national government will lead to greater security and prosperity		
Doc. 5.10, "The Address and Reasons of Dissent of the Minority of the Convention of Pennsylvania to Their Constituents"			Suspicious of federal power	The "iron-handed despotism" of a single government

Review the historical thinking skills exercises in this chapter that provide other reasons that influenced both sides of the debate.

STEP 3 *Outline your response*

As you will recall from earlier chapters, a **working thesis** provides a starting point. With a prompt that lends itself to two sides, it is helpful to use a **point-by-point** comparison, with the first point being the first side (in favor of a strong central government) and the second point being the opposite side (in favor of states' rights).

Working thesis: One side had a greater claim to fulfilling the Declaration.

   I. Point 1 (claim): Antifederalists/Jeffersonian Republicans

      A. Supporting evidence

      B. Supporting evidence

II. Point 2 (claim): Federalists

    A. Supporting evidence

    B. Supporting evidence

A review of the reasons, however, allows your argument to move beyond just two sides—and beyond the either/or fallacy. A more complex point-by-point comparison may look like this:

Working thesis: Both sides had some claim to the Declaration's legacy.

  I. Point 1 (claim): Antifederalists/Jeffersonian Republicans

    A. Evidence from the supporting side

    B. Evidence from the opposing side

  II. Point 2 (claim): Federalists

    A. Evidence from the supporting side

    B. Evidence from the opposing side

  III. Point 3 (claim), etc.

  IV. Conclusion

Such an approach acknowledges that there are two sides to the debate but also allows you to avoid oversimplifying the debate into two sides, especially as not all reasons will favor the same side.

Two body paragraphs for point 1 might look like this:

The Antifederalists and the Jeffersonian Republicans claimed to hold many of the ideals of the Declaration of Independence. However, many of those ideals undermined the nation's ability to foster a stable government and therefore protect many of the rights celebrated by the Declaration itself. [claim] For example, the Antifederalists, echoing the Declaration's criticism of a tyrannical government, were suspicious of the power of the new federal government to tax without the unanimous support of the legislature. Likewise, the Jeffersonian Republicans, harkening back to the Declaration's attack on the Crown's admiralty courts, believed that the Federalist government of John Adams overstepped its bounds with the Sedition Act. [evidence of supporting side]

However, the Articles of Confederation's weak taxation powers had left the government perpetually unable to secure loans or guarantee payment of debts. The new Constitution solved this problem with stronger taxation powers. Also, although the Sedition Act was harshly criticized by the Jeffersonians, it was symbolic of a newly robust government that was able to quell the kinds of internal rebellions that plagued the Articles of Confederation. [evidence of opposing side]

Although Americans marked the creation of the United States and the political upheaval of its first twenty years of independence as a new era in North American history, continuities with the colonial era remained. Westward expansion from the Atlantic seaboard and the backcountry of the original colonies continued steadily throughout the period, often causing conflicts with Native Americans and settlers in the West and wealthy, established communities in the East. Likewise, Spanish settlements spread up the western coast of North America through the mission system, which offered opportunities for Spanish colonists, often at the expense of the native peoples there.

The United States also built westward migration into its national policy. One of the few successful pieces of legislation under the Articles of Confederation government was the institution of the Northwest Ordinances of 1785 and 1787, by which new territories were incorporated as states within the United States.

Throughout this period, tensions arose between regional, national, social, and ethnic identities as Americans wrestled with the meaning of their revolution and the ways that they would apply the ideals of the Declaration of Independence and the Bill of Rights to a vast, diverse, and expanding republic.

Seeking the Main Point

As you read the documents that follow, keep these broad questions in mind. These questions will help you understand the relationship between the documents in this chapter and the historical changes that they represent. As you reflect on these questions, determine which themes and which documents best address them.

- What were the effects of westward migration within North America, both on Native Americans and the descendants of Europeans?
- In what ways did the environment contribute to economic and political identities throughout North America during this period? In what ways did the environment contribute to different systems of labor?
- How did political conflicts between the new settlers in the West and more established communities in the East change during this period? How did they remain the same?
- Describe the various identities that Americans embraced (regional, economic, social, and gender or a combination of these) during this period. What contexts shaped these identities?

The Perils and Possibilities of Expansion

DOCUMENT 6.1 | **WILLIAM HENRY, Letter Regarding Attacks of Paxton Boys on Conestoga Indians in Lancaster, Pennsylvania**
| 1763

After the evacuation of French forces from North America, British colonists and Native Americans struggled for control of the western backcountry, best exemplified by Pontiac's Rebellion (1763) against British settlers in formerly French territories (Doc. 4.2). The "Paxton Boys" (named for the town of Paxtang) attacked local Conestoga Indians, whom they unfairly blamed for plotting an uprising against colonists in the region. The following letter describes a massacre of Conestoga Indians by the Paxton Boys in central Pennsylvania in the aftermath of the French and Indian War (1754–1763).

There are few, if any murders to be compared with the cruel murder committed on the Conestoga Indians in the jail of Lancaster, in 1763, by the Paxton boys, as they were then called. . . . The first notice I had of this affair was, that while at my father's store, near the court house, I saw a number of people running down street towards the jail, which enticed me and other lads to follow them. At about six or eight yards from the jail, we met from twenty-five to thirty men, well mounted on horses, and with rifles, tomahawks, and scalping knives, equipped for murder. I ran into the prison yard, and there, oh what a horrid sight presented itself to my view! Near the back door of the prison lay an old Indian and his squaw, particularly well known and esteemed by the people of the town on account of his placid and friendly conduct. His name was Will Soc; across him and squaw lay two children, of about the age of three years, whose heads were split with the tomahawk, and their scalps taken off. Towards the middle of the jail yard, along the west side of the wall, lay a stout Indian, whom I particularly noticed to have been shot in his breast; his legs were chopped with the tomahawk, his hands cut off, and finally a rifle ball discharged in his mouth, so that his head was blown to atoms, and the brains were splashed against and yet hanging to the wall, for three or four feet around. This man's hands and feet had also been chopped off with a tomahawk.—In this manner lay the whole of them, men, women, and children, spread about the prison yard; shot—scalped—hacked and cut to pieces.

Israel Daniel Rupp, *History of Lancaster County* (Lancaster, PA: Gilbert Hills, 1844), 359–360.

Identify: What makes this murder especially cruel, according to Henry?

Analyze: With whom does Henry sympathize? Provide evidence from the letter to support your position.

Evaluate: Compare Henry's description of the treatment of Native Americans to descriptions of European interactions with Native Americans in the 1500s and 1600s, as seen in Chapter 1 of this text. Are these descriptions more alike or different? Explain. Refer to specific documents to support your response.

DOCUMENT 6.2 | ## A Declaration and Remonstrance of the Distressed and Bleeding Frontier Inhabitants of the Province of Pennsylvania (Paxton Boys' Declaration)
1764

In January 1764, after being charged with murder for the massacre of native peoples by Governor John Penn, around 250 "Paxton Boys" marched from Lancaster to Philadelphia to charge the colonial government with not protecting them from native attacks. When a delegation of colonial leaders, led by Benjamin Franklin, agreed to read their "Declaration and Remonstrance" to the colonial legislature, the Paxton Boys disbanded and returned to their homes.

Inasmuch as the killing those Indians at Conestogoe Manor and Lancaster has been, and may be, the subject of much Conversation, and by invidious [unfair] Representations of it, which some, we doubt not, will industriously spread, many unacquainted with the true state of Affairs may be led to pass a Severe Censure on the Authors of those Facts, and any others of the like nature, which may hereafter happen, than we are persuaded they would if matters were duly understood and deliberated. We think it, therefore, proper thus openly to declare ourselves, and render some brief hints of the reasons of our Conduct, which we must, and frankly do, confess, nothing but necessity itself could induce us to, or justify us in, as it bears an appearance of flying in the face of Authority, and is attended with much labour, fatigue, and expence.

Ourselves, then, to a Man, we profess to be loyal Subjects to the best of Kings, our rightful Sovereign George the third, firmly attached to his Royal Person, Interest, and Government, & of consequence, equally opposite to the Enemies of His Throne & Dignity, whether openly avowed, or more dangerously concealed under a mask of falsely pretended Friendship, and cheerfully willing to offer our Substance & Lives in his Cause.

These Indians, known to be firmly connected in Friendship with our openly avowed embittered Enemies, and some of whom have, by several Oaths, been proved to be murderers, and who, by their better acquaintance with the Situation and State of our Frontier, were more capable of doing us mischief, we saw, with indignation, cherished and caressed as dearest Friends; But this, alas! is but a part, a small part, of that excessive regard manifested to Indians, beyond His Majesty's loyal Subjects, whereof we complain, and which, together with various other Grievances, have not only enflamed with resentment the Breasts of a number, and urged them to the disagreeable Evidence of it they have been constrained to give, but have heavily displeased by far the greatest part of the good Inhabitants of this Province.

Minutes of the Provincial Councilor of Pennsylvania, from the Organization to the Termination of the Proprietary Government, vol. 9 (Harrisburg, PA: Theo. Fenn, 1852), 142–143.

PRACTICING Historical Thinking

Identify: In addition to the Conestoga who are the "openly avowed embittered Enemies" of the Paxton Boys?

Analyze: Why do the Paxton Boys declare their loyalty to King George?

Evaluate: How do the Paxton Boys identify themselves in regard to Native Americans, the citizens of Philadelphia, and the king of England?

DOCUMENT 6.3 | **FATHER JUNIPERO SERRA, Letter to Father Palóu Regarding the Founding of Mission San Diego de Alcala in California**
1769

Junipero Serra (1713–1784), a Franciscan monk, founded the first Spanish mission in California in 1769. In this letter, he writes to Father Francisco Palóu (1723–1789), a fellow Spanish missionary in New Spain, and mentions the missionary activities of Father Joseph Soler in northern Mexico.

My Dearest Friend and Sir. On the 31st day of May, by the favor of God, after rather a painful voyage of a month and a half, this packet, San Antonio [the name of the vessel], commanded by Don Juan Perez, arrived and anchored in this horrible port of Monterey, which is unaltered in any degree from what it was when visited by the expedition of Don Sebastian Vizcaino in the year 1603. . . . On the 3d June, being the holy day of Pentecost, the whole of the officers of sea and land, and all the people, assembled on a bank at the foot of an oak, where we caused an altar to be raised, and the bells to be rung: we then chaunted [chanted] the *Veni Creator*, blessed the water, erected and blessed a grand cross, hoisted the royal standard, and chaunted the first mass that was ever performed in this place. . . . Tell me also if it is true, that the Indians have killed Father Joseph Soler in Sonora, and how it happened; and if there are any other friends defunct, in order that I may commend them to God, with anything else that your reverence may think fit to communicate to a few poor hermits separated from human society. We proceed to-morrow to celebrate the feast, and make the procession of *Corpus Christi*, . . . in order to scare away whatever little devils there possibly may be in this land. . . .

George Simpson, *Overland Journey round the World during the Years 1841 and 1842* (Philadelphia, PA: Lea and Blanchard, 1847), 201–202.

PRACTICING Historical Thinking

Identify: What are two purposes of Serra's letter?

Analyze: Based on your knowledge of the time period, what political or social factors contributed to the westward expansion of missionary work?

Evaluate: Compare the behaviors of Spanish missionaries in this era with those of the original Spanish colonizers, as described in Chapters 1 and 2 of this book and in your other reading. To what extent have the behaviors of the Spanish changed or remained the same? Explain your answer. Consult your history textbook for additional information.

DOCUMENT 6.4 | **Correspondence between Daniel Shays and Benjamin Lincoln**
1787

In the winter of 1786–1787, Daniel Shays (1747–1825), a former Continental Army officer, led a large contingent of Revolutionary War veterans in protest against the tax policies and debt-collection laws of the state of Massachusetts. A coalition of state militias stopped Shays and his rebels when they marched on the arsenal in Springfield in southwestern Massachusetts. The following letters are part of an exchange between Daniel Shays and Benjamin Lincoln (1733–1810), general of the militia force that defeated Shays's rebels. Shays was pardoned in 1788.

January 30th, 1787.

To General Lincoln, commanding the government troops at *Hadley.*

. . . We are sensible of the embarrassments the people are under; but that virtue which truly characterizes the citizens of a republican government, hath hitherto marked our paths with a degree of innocence. . . . At the same time, the people are willing to lay down their arms, on the condition of a general pardon, and return to their respective homes, as they are unwilling to stain the land, which we in the late war purchased at so dear a rate, with the blood of our brethren and neighbours. Therefore, we pray that hostilities may cease . . . until our united prayers may be presented to the General Court, and we receive an answer, as a person is gone for that purpose. . . .

DANIEL SHAYS, CAPTAIN.

The Honorable General Lincoln.

As the officers of the people, now convened in defence of their rights and privileges, have sent a petition to the General Court, for the sole purpose of accommodating our present unhappy affairs, we justly expect that hostilities may cease on both sides, until we have a return from our legislature. . . .

FRANCIS STONE, CHAIRMAN.

DANIEL SHAYS, CAPTAIN.

ADAM WHEELER.

January 31st, 1787

Gentlemen,

Your request is totally inadmissible, as no powers are delegated to me which would justify a delay of my operations. Hostilities I have not commenced.

I have again to warn the people in arms against the government, immediately to disband, as they would avoid the ill consequences which may ensue, should they be inattentive to this caution.

B. LINCOLN.

George Richards Minot, *The History of the Insurrections in Massachusetts, in the Year MDCCLXXXVI, and the Rebellion Consequent Thereon* (Worcester, MA: Isaiah Thomas, 1788), 120–122, transcribed into modern English by Jason Stacy.

PRACTICING Historical Thinking

Identify: What are Shays's demands? What is Lincoln's response?

Analyze: Why does Lincoln have to "warn the people in arms against the government . . . to disband"?

Evaluate: To what extent does Shays's Rebellion mirror other armed conflicts that preceded the Revolutionary War?

SKILL REVIEW | Causation and Argumentation

Answer the following prompt using the four documents above and your knowledge of the time period between 1763 and 1787. Consult your textbook and class notes to help you answer the question.

> To what extent did internal migration in North America stimulate conflicts between migrants and the established societies that they left?

Your response should include an introductory paragraph with a thesis (see Chapter 1) and at least two body paragraphs, each of which must include a main point and supporting points. (See Building AP® Writing Skills, p. 25, for examples of *claims* and *evidence*.) Be sure to decide which organizational format will be better for your response—subject-by-subject (see Building AP® Writing Skills, p. 51) or point-by-point (see Building AP® Writing Skills, p. 81).

For a review of causation and argumentation, see the Applying AP® Historical Thinking Skills features on pages 21 and 108.

Securing Borders

DOCUMENT 6.5 | Northwest Ordinance, Key Sections
1787

The Northwest Ordinance of 1787 was passed under the Articles of Confederation government and helped establish the process for creating new state governments west of the Appalachian Mountains and around the Great Lakes. The United States acquired these territories in the Treaty of Paris (1783), which also recognized American independence.

Sec. 13. And for extending the fundamental principles of civil and religious liberty, which form the basis whereon these republics, their laws, and constitutions are erected; to fix and establish those principles as the basis of all laws, constitutions, and governments, which for ever hereafter shall be formed in the said territory; to provide, also, for the establishment of States, and permanent government therein, and for . . . [their] admission to a share in the federal councils on an equal footing with the original States, at as early periods as may be consistent with the general interest: . . .

Article III. Religion, morality, and knowledge, being necessary to good government, and the happiness of mankind, schools and the means of education shall forever be encouraged. The utmost good faith shall always be observed towards the Indians; their lands and property shall never be taken from them without their consent; and in their property, rights, and liberty, they shall never be invaded or disturbed, unless in just and lawful wars authorized by Congress; but laws founded in justice and humanity shall, from time to time, be made, for preventing wrongs being done to them, and for preserving peace and friendship with them. . . .

Article VI. There shall be neither slavery nor involuntary servitude in the said territory, otherwise than in the punishment of crimes, whereof the party shall have been duly convicted: Provided, always, That any person escaping into the same, from whom labor or service is lawfully claimed in any one of the original States, such fugitive may be lawfully reclaimed, and conveyed to the person claiming his or her labor or service as aforesaid.

"The Ordinance of 1787," *Marietta Times*, 1888, 8–9, 11–12.

DOCUMENT 6.6 | Treaty of Greenville, Article 9

1795

The Treaty of Greenville was signed between the United States and the Algonquin-speaking Shawnee and Lenape tribes of the Northwest Territories after the Battle of Fallen Timbers in 1794. This battle ended a long-term strategy by George Washington's administration to force the tribes of the Northwest Territories into submission.

Lest the firm peace and friendship now established should be interrupted by the misconduct of individuals, the United States, and the said Indian tribes agree, that for injuries done by individuals on either side, no private revenge or retaliation shall take place; but instead thereof, complaint shall be made by the party injured, to the other: By the said Indian tribes, or any of them, to the President of the United States, or the superintendant by him appointed; and by the superintendant or other person appointed by the President, to the principal chiefs of the said Indian tribes, or of the tribe to which the offender belongs; and such prudent measures shall then be pursued as shall be necessary to preserve the said peace and friendship unbroken, until the Legislature (or Great Council) of the United States, shall make other equitable provision in the case, to the satisfaction of both parties. Should any Indian tribes meditate a war against the United States or either of them, and the same shall come to the knowledge of the before-mentioned tribes, or either of them, they do hereby engage to give immediate notice thereof to the general or officer commanding the troops of the United States, at the nearest post. And should any tribe, with hostile intentions against the United States, or either of them, attempt to pass through their country, they will endeavour to prevent the same, and in like manner give information of such attempt, to the general or officer commanding, as soon as possible, that all causes of mistrust and suspicion may be avoided between them and the United States. In like manner the United States shall give notice to the said Indian tribes of any harm that may be meditated against them, or either of them, that shall come to their knowledge; and do all in their power to hinder and prevent the same, that the friendship between them may be uninterrupted.

Richard Peters, ed., *The Public Statutes at Large of the United States of America*, vol. 7 (Boston, MA: Little, James Brown, 1846), 52–53.

PRACTICING Historical Thinking

Identify: Paraphrase the main provisions of the Treaty of Greenville.

Analyze: How does this treaty represent a change in relations between Native Americans and the United States government?

Evaluate: Was this treaty advantageous to the Shawnee and Lenape? Why or why not?

DOCUMENT 6.7 | **Pinckney's Treaty, Article IV**
| 1795

Pinckney's Treaty, named after its chief negotiator and the US ambassador to Great Britain, Thomas Pinckney, established the right of the United States to navigate the Mississippi River, an important transportation source for farmers in the Northwest Territories. The treaty was negotiated between the United States and Spain.

It is . . . agreed that the western boundary of the United States which separates them from the Spanish colony of Louisiana, is in the middle of the channel or bed of the river Mississippi, from the northern boundary of the said states to the completion of the thirty-first degree of latitude north of the equator. And his Catholic Majesty has likewise agreed that the navigation of the said river, in its whole breadth from its source to the ocean, shall be free only to his subjects and the citizens of the United States, unless he should extend this privilege to the subjects of other powers by special convention.

Richard Peters, ed., *The Public Statutes at Large of the United States of America*, vol. 8 (Boston, MA: Little, Brown, 1867), 140.

PRACTICING Historical Thinking

Identify: What was the western boundary of the United States in 1795?

Analyze: How did this boundary provide significant geographic and economic power to United States citizens?

Evaluate: How does Pinckney's letter signal a shift in the United States' international relations with both Great Britain and Spain?

SKILL REVIEW | # Comparison and Analyzing Evidence: Content and Sourcing

Answer the following prompt using the three documents above and your knowledge of the time period between 1785 and 1795. Consult your textbook and class notes to help you answer the question.

> The following three pieces of diplomatic legislation were approved by the US legislature between 1785 and 1795, and each guaranteed individual, states', or national rights. How did each define *rights* differently? In what ways were these differences produced by each document's particular goal?
>
> Document 6.5, Northwest Ordinance, Key Sections, 1787
> Document 6.6, Treaty of Greenville, Article 9, 1795
> Document 6.7, Pinckney's Treaty, Article IV, 1795

Your response should include an introductory paragraph that states a thesis and at least two body paragraphs, each of which includes a main point and supporting points. (See Building AP® Writing Skills, p. 25, for examples of *claims* and *evidence*.) Be sure to decide which organizational format will be better for your response—subject-by-subject (see Building AP® Writing Skills, p. 51) or point-by-point (see Building AP® Writing Skills, p. 81).

Regional and National Identities

DOCUMENT 6.8 | **JAMES PEALE,** *The Artist and His Family*
| 1795

James Peale (1749–1831) and his brother Charles Willson Peale (1741–1827) painted members of the American elite, including George Washington, in the late eighteenth and early nineteenth centuries. This painting portrays James Peale and his family.

Courtesy of the Pennsylvania Academy of the Fine Arts, Philadelphia.
Gift of John Frederick Lewis.

PRACTICING Historical Thinking

Identify: Identify the key details of the adults and children in this painting.

Analyze: Compare the rendition of Peale's wife and daughters with Peale himself. Who is in the foreground? Background? What might be the significance of these positions in the painting?

Evaluate: In what ways does the presentation of Mrs. Peale represent an ideal of Republican motherhood? Consult your history textbook for additional information.

DOCUMENT 6.9 | THOMAS JEFFERSON, Letter to Philip Mazzei
1796

In this letter to Philip Mazzei (1730–1816), an Italian physician and prominent supporter of the American Revolution, Thomas Jefferson (1743–1826) laments the rise of the Federalist faction during President George Washington's second administration (1793–1796). After the letter became public, the Federalists used it to claim that Jefferson was unpatriotic (Doc. 4.14).

. . . In place of that noble love of liberty and republican government which carried us triumphantly through the war, an Anglican, monarchical, and aristocratical party has sprung up, whose avowed object is to draw over us the substance, as they have already done the forms of the British government. The main body of our citizens, however, remain true to their republican principles; the whole landed interest is republican, and so is a great mass of talents. Against us are the executive, the judiciary, two out of three branches of the legislature, all the officers of the government, all who want to be officers, all timid men who prefer the calm of despotism to the boisterous sea of liberty, British merchants, and Americans trading on British capitals, speculators, and holders in the banks and public funds, a contrivance invented for purposes of corruption, and for assimilating us in all things to the rotten as well as the sound parts of the British model. It would give you a fever were I to name to you the apostates who have gone over to these heresies, men who were Samsons [the Israelite leader known for his strength] in the field, and Solomons [the Israelite king known for his wisdom] in the council, but who have had their heads shorn by the harlot of England [a reference to Samson's loss of physical strength when his hair was cut by Delilah]. In short, we are likely to preserve the liberty we have gained only by unremitting labours and perils. But we shall preserve it; and our mass of weight and wealth on the good side is so great as to leave no danger that force will ever be attempted against us. We have only to awake and snap the Lilliputian cords with which they have been entangling us during the first sleep which succeeded our labours.

Charles Carter Lee, ed., *Observations on the Writings of Thomas Jefferson* (Philadelphia, PA: J. Dobson; Thomas, Cowperthwait; Carey & Hart, 1839), 81.

PRACTICING Historical Thinking

Identify: Identify the reasons that Jefferson believes that two-thirds of the legislature is corrupt.

Analyze: Given that Jefferson claims that the "landed interest" maintains "republican principles," that the landowners include the southern and western farmers, and that the "aristocratical party" has the support of the merchants and banking classes, what inferences can you make about the regional conflicts?

Evaluate: Why would Jefferson perceive the mercantile class to be pro-British? To what extent is this perception based on economic, social, or regional factors?

| ISAAC WELD, *Travels throughout the States of North America*
1797

Isaac Weld (1774–1856) traveled from Great Britain to North America in 1795. His *Travels*, published two years later, is an early account of North America in the first decade after Independence.

The number of the slaves increases most rapidly, so that there is scarcely any estate but what is overstocked. This is a circumstance complained of by every planter, as the maintenance of more than are requisite for the culture of the estate is attended with great expence. Motives of humanity deter them from selling the poor creatures, or turning them adrift from the spot where they have been born and brought up, in the midst of friends and relations.

What I have here said, respecting the condition and treatment of slaves, appertains, it must be remembered, to those only who are upon the large plantations in Virginia; the lot of such as are unfortunate enough to fall into the hands of the lower class of white people, and of hard task-masters in the towns, is very different. In the Carolinas and Georgia again, slavery presents itself in very different colors from what it does even in its worst form in Virginia. I am told, that it is no uncommon thing there, to see gangs of negroes staked at a horse race, and to see these unfortunate beings bandied about from one set of drunken gamblers to another for days together. How much to be deprecated [disapproved of] are the laws which suffer such abuses to exist! yet these are laws enacted by people who boast of their love of liberty and independence, and who presume to say, that it is in the breasts of Americans alone that the blessings of freedom are held in just estimation.

Isaac Weld, *Travels through the States of North America and the Provinces of Upper and Lower Canada,* vol. 1 (London: John Stockdale, 1799), 150–151, transcribed into modern English by Jason Stacy.

PRACTICING Historical Thinking

Identify: Describe Weld's observations.

Analyze: Determine Weld's attitude toward slavery.

Evaluate: Compare Weld's observations to the regional divisions that Thomas Jefferson mentions in his letter to Philip Mazzei (Doc. 6.9).

SKILL REVIEW | **Contextualization and Analyzing Evidence: Content and Sourcing**

Answer the following prompt using the three documents above and your knowledge of the time period between 1787 and 1797. Consult your textbook and class notes to help you answer the question.

> The three documents above (Docs. 6.8, 6.9, and 6.10) exhibit examples of American gender, political, and economic identities in the ten years after the election of George Washington as first president of the United States. Analyze how the value systems in each document reflected an emerging national identity.

Your response should include an introductory paragraph with a thesis and at least two body paragraphs, each of which must include a claim and evidence. (See Building AP® Writing Skills, p. 25, for examples of *claims* and *evidence*.) Be sure to decide which organizational format will be better for your response—subject-by-subject (see Building AP® Writing Skills, p. 51) or point-by-point (see Building AP® Writing Skills, p. 81).

When writing about a national identity, combine those factors that influenced the creation of that identity. For example, in the previous Applying AP® Historical Thinking Skills exercise, you examined the *legislation* that developed during this time period. This exercise asks you to combine (or synthesize) the gender, political, and economic issues that also contributed to this national identity.

PUTTING IT ALL TOGETHER

Revisiting the Main Point

- To what extent did the end of the French and Indian War in 1763 represent a turning point for Native American and British North American relations? For a review of turning points, see Applying AP® Historical Thinking Skills (pp. 51–55).
- To what extent were emerging regional identities in the United States shaped by environmental factors in the late eighteenth century?
- In what ways did technology and transportation contribute to emergent regional identities?
- In what ways did economic and environmental factors give rise to political identities in the United States between 1781 and 1797?
- Characterize the motives behind US expansion of power in North America between 1781 and 1797.
- Review James Peale's *The Artist and His Family* (Doc. 6.8). How does this image portray gender identities in the new republic?

BUILDING AP® WRITING SKILLS | **Causation: The Linear Argument**

As you'll recall, **historical arguments** are original interpretations of statements about historical events. When making arguments about **causation**, it is crucial to present a clear cause-and-effect relationship between events. One way to do that is with a **linear argument** in which one idea follows another in a progression from one point to the next, working toward a concluding statement. One hallmark of a linear argument is that the summary becomes the clearest articulation of the **thesis**. In a linear argument, the essay *justifies* the arrangement of evidence, the development of ideas, and the significance of the closing statement.

First, it is useful to think of the overall progression of your essay. Below is the prompt from Chapter 5, followed by general models that illustrate a sample thesis statement for the prompt:

> Consider two of the major sides in the political debates of the 1780s and 1790s—the Antifederalists/Jeffersonian Republicans on one side and the Federalists on the other. Determine the extent to which one had a greater claim to fulfilling the ideals of the Declaration of Independence.

- *Cause and effect:* This model looks at a series of phenomena that occur in consequence of preceding phenomena.

Sample

> *As a result* of increased tensions with unstable regimes in France and England, the Jeffersonian Republicans, who emphasized states' rights against the pro-British Federalists, more closely fulfilled the ideals of the Declaration of Independence.

- *Comparison and contrast:* This model invites a comparison or contrast between competing phenomena.

Sample

> *Although* Jeffersonian Republicans and Federalists *both* acknowledged the importance of an independent, American economy and government, the Jeffersonians' suspicions of a strong central government put them closer to the ideals of the Declaration of Independence.

- *Concession and refutation:* This model anticipates the counterargument and then addresses it.

Sample

> *Admittedly,* the Jeffersonian Republicans advocated states' rights in the spirit of independence and support of the common man's labor; *however,* such support countered the efforts of the Federalists to create a strong federal government that ultimately upheld the goals of the Declaration of Independence.

Second, it is useful to develop a working vocabulary of transitional terms that help create a linear argument. The transitional words appear in boldface in the above sample thesis statements.

Cause and effect
> As a result,
> Consequently,
> Therefore,
> Thus,

Comparison and contrast
> Although
> Both
> Like

Similar to

Unlike

Concession and refutation

Admittedly,

Despite

Even though

However,

These words also can appear within a body paragraph, especially as you look at the ways in which cause and effect may complement comparison and contrast or concession and refutation. The following body paragraph illustrates multiple uses of these words in support of a single claim from the sample prompt above.

> The Federalists' argument may appear to support monarchical rule, but their principles were based on a more enlightened approach to the rights of man. [claim] *As a result* of John Locke's *Second Treatise*, the Federalists pursued the practice of "the public good of society" (1690), which meant creating laws to bring people into a state of civilization. *Admittedly*, Jeffersonians advocated the pursuit of individual rights, *but* such pursuits led to discriminatory practices, such as the restrictive voting rights introduced by the state of Georgia in 1777. *Both* parties valued the passions of individual rights, and *both* feared the oppressive nature of a strong controlling government; *yet* the Federalists more actively sought to avoid "schemes of oppression," as described in Madison's Federalist No. 10.

Consider the following prompt in developing a linear argument:

> In what ways did economic and environmental factors give rise to political identities in the United States between 1781 and 1797?

STEP 1 *Understand the prompt, and identify the key words*

Draw a square around your topic ("political identities in the United States between 1781 and 1797"), draw a line underneath your task ("give rise to"), and draw a circle around the categories ("economic and environmental factors").

STEP 2 *Brainstorm*

The nature of this prompt invites three distinct categories for your evidence, as shown in the table below. Complete the table, using all the available sources as well as outside knowledge from your textbook. Some are completed for you.

Source	Economic factors	Environmental factors	Political identities
Doc. 6.2, A Declaration and Remonstrance of the Distressed and Bleeding Frontier Inhabitants of the Province of Pennsylvania			
Doc 6.3, Father Junipero Serra, Letter to Father Palóu Regarding the Founding of Mission San Diego de Alcala in California	Native Americans as economic allies		
Doc. 6.4, Correspondence between Daniel Shays and Benjamin Lincoln			More equal taxation across all citizens
Doc. 6.5, Northwest Ordinance, Key Sections	Omission of slavery; greater distribution of wealth	Territories as potential states	

STEP 3 *Outline your response*

Although there is a clear cause-and-effect relationship built into the prompt, there is also an implied comparison-contrast and concession-refutation. You could, for example, weigh the economic and environmental factors against each other and, in so doing, would create an even more linear outline.

Adequate model

    I. Introduction

    II. Economic factors

    III. Environmental factors

    IV. Political identity

    V. Conclusion

Effective model

      I. Introduction

  II–III. Linear progression between economic and environmental factors

     IV. Political identity

     V. Conclusion

Complete your outline, adding the information from Step 3.

STEP 4 *Write your essay*

As you draft your main points and supporting points for the body paragraphs, use the transitional terms that are presented earlier in this section.

Rationales for Revolution

Although American history celebrates the contributions of almost mythical figures in the American Revolution, the role that was played by the common person is less clear. For average people, especially colonists who remained loyal to Great Britain, the process of coming to see their "natural rights" as something worth sacrificing their lives for was complicated. The early republic had wide gaps between the ruling elite and the ordinary citizen, so how the common man came to lay down his life for the Revolution is a subject that historians study. You have already read various sources that reflect competing views of the common man toward Britain. As you read the two passages below, consider how different historians interpret the role and motivations of the common man in the American Revolution.

> [In England,] [o]rdinary people—laboring men and women as well as members of a self-confident middling group—who bellowed out the words to the newly composed "Rule Britannia" and who responded positively to the emotional appeal of "God Save the King" gave voice to the common aspirations of a militantly Protestant culture. Or, stated negatively, they proclaimed their utter contempt for Catholicism and their rejection of everything associated with contemporary France. . . .
>
> . . . For most English people, the expression of national identity seems to be been quite genuine. Indeed, by noisy participation in patriotic rituals, the middling and working classes thrust themselves into a public sphere of national politics. . . .
>
> . . . Within an empire strained by the heightened nationalist sentiment of the metropolitan center [of London], natural rights acquired unusual persuasive force [for the American colonists]. Threatened from the outside by a self-confident military power, one that seemed intent on marginalizing the colonists within the empire, Americans countered with the universalist vocabulary of natural rights, in other words, with a language of political resistance that stressed a bundle of God-given rights. . . .
>
> —T. H. Breen, "Ideology and Nationalism on the Eve of the American Revolution: Revisions *Once More* in Need of Revising," *Journal of American History* 84 (June 1997), 13–39.

Many of the figures we will encounter were from the middle and lower ranks of American society, and many of them did not have pale complexions. From these ranks, few heroes have emerged to enter the national pantheon. For the most part, they remain anonymous. Partly this is because they faded in and out of the picture, rarely achieving the tenure and status of men such as John Adams and John Hancock of Boston, Robert Morris and Benjamin Franklin of Philadelphia, Alexander Hamilton and John Jay of New York, or Thomas Jefferson, Patrick Henry, and George Washington of Virginia, all of whom remained on the scene from the Revolution's beginning to the very end. But, although they never rose to the top of society, where they could trumpet their own achievements and claim their place in the pages of history, many other men and women counted greatly at the time. . . . The shortness of their lives also explains the anonymity of ordinary people. It is safer to conduct a revolution from the legislative chamber than fight for it on the battlefield, healthier to be free than enslaved, and one is more likely to reach old age with money than with crumbs.

—Gary B. Nash, *The Unknown American Revolution: The Unruly Birth of Democracy and the Struggle to Create America* (New York: Viking, 2005), 15–24.

Based on the two interpretations above, complete the following three tasks:

1. Briefly explain the main point that the first passage makes about the common man.
2. Briefly explain the main point that the second passage makes about the common man.
3. Choose one document from Chapter 4, 5, or 6, and explain how it supports the interpretation of either passage.

CHAPTER 7

Reform and Reaction

PERIOD
FOUR

1800–1848

D ebates regarding the rightful powers of the federal government over the state government and of the state over the individual continued in the early nineteenth century. These debates manifested themselves in varied and unexpected ways as Americans attempted to align the ideals of the Enlightenment with their political institutions and society.

Although the words of the Declaration of Independence claimed to speak for "all men," Americans in the late eighteenth century increasingly encountered tensions within a unified nation that nonetheless contained diverse, often conflicting voices. These tensions, coupled with the reality that not all Americans equally shared the promise of the Declaration, fueled the struggle to fulfill the ideals of the Revolution against forces that would halt progress toward freedom.

Seeking the Main Point

As you read the documents that follow, keep these broad questions in mind. These questions will help you understand the relationship between the documents in this chapter and the historical changes that they represent. As you reflect on these questions, determine which themes and which documents best address them.

* How did different interpretations of the legacy of the Revolution shape economic, political, and social debates in the early nineteenth century? In what ways did these debates divide along regional lines?
* How did Americans' ideals about themselves as a people shape their values and their culture?
* How did the ideals of the Revolution continue to shape reform movements during this period?

Factions and Federal Power

DOCUMENT 7.1 | **JAMES MONROE, Second Inaugural Address**
| 1821

James Monroe (1758–1831) was elected president as a Jeffersonian Republican. During Monroe's two terms, the opposing Federalist Party all but disappeared.

If we turn our attention, fellow-citizens, more immediately to the internal concerns of our country, and more especially to those on which its future welfare depends, we have every reason to anticipate the happiest results. It is now rather more than forty-four years since we declared our independence, and thirty-seven since it was acknowledged. The talents and virtues which were displayed in that great struggle were a sure presage of all that has since followed. A people who were able to surmount in their infant state such great perils would be more competent as they rose into manhood to repel any which they might meet in their progress. Their physical strength would be more adequate to foreign danger, and the practice of self-government, aided by the light of experience, could not fail to produce an effect equally salutary on all those questions connected with the internal organization. These favorable anticipations have been realized.

In our whole system, National and State, we have shunned all the defects which unceasingly preyed on the vitals and destroyed the ancient Republics. In them there were distinct orders, a nobility and a people, or the people governed in one assembly. Thus, in the one instance there was a perpetual conflict between the orders in society for the ascendency, in which the victory of either terminated in the overthrow of the government and the ruin of the state; in the other, in which the people governed in a body, and whose dominions seldom exceeded the dimensions of a county in one of our States, a tumultuous and disorderly movement permitted only a transitory existence. In this great nation there is but one order, that of the people, whose power, by a peculiarly happy improvement of the representative principle, is transferred from them, without impairing in the slightest degree their sovereignty, to bodies of their own creation, and to persons elected by themselves, in the full extent necessary for all the purposes of free, enlightened, and efficient government. The whole system is elective, the complete sovereignty being in the people, and every officer in every department deriving his authority from and being responsible to them for his conduct.

Our career has corresponded with this great outline. Perfection in our organization could not have been expected in the outset either in the National or State Governments or in tracing the line between their respective powers. But no serious conflict has arisen, nor any contest but such as are managed by argument and by a fair appeal to the good sense of the people, and many of the defects which experience had clearly demonstrated in both Governments have been remedied. By steadily pursuing this course in this spirit there is every reason to believe that our system will soon attain the highest degree of perfection of which human institutions are capable, and that the movement in all its branches will exhibit such a degree of order and harmony as to command the admiration and respect of the civilized world.

James Monroe, "Second Inaugural Address," *The Writings of James Monroe*, vol. 6, ed. Stanislaus Murray Hamilton (New York: Putnam's Sons, 1902), 172–174.

PRACTICING Historical Thinking

Identify: What, according to Monroe, will "command the admiration and respect of the civilized world"?

Analyze: According to Monroe, why did ancient republics fail, and why would America avoid this same fate?

Evaluate: How does Monroe's Second Inaugural Address signal a shift in the relationship between the federal government and states' rights from the arguments of the Kentucky Resolution (Doc. 5.19)?

DOCUMENT 7.2 | JOHN C. CALHOUN, **Address to the Southern States**
1831

In this address, John C. Calhoun (1782–1850), former vice president and senator from South Carolina, argues that states can "nullify" (and therefore make void within their borders) federal laws that are deemed dangerous to a state's interest.

The great and leading principle is, that the General Government emanated from the people of the several states, forming distinct political communities, and acting in their separate and sovereign capacity, and not from all the people forming one aggregate political community; that the Constitution of the United States is, in fact, a compact, to which each state is a Party, . . . and that the several states, or parties, have the right to judge of its infractions; . . . be it called what it may— State-right, veto, nullification, or by any other name—I conceive to be the fundamental principle of our system, resting on facts as certain as our revolution itself,

. . . and I firmly believe that on its recognition depend the stability and safety of our political institutions. . . .

. . . Whenever separate and dissimilar interests have been separately represented in government; whenever the sovereign power has been divided in its exercise, the experience and wisdom of ages have devised but one mode by which such political organization can be preserved—the mode adopted in England, and by all governments, ancient and modern, blessed with constitutions deserving to be called free—to give each co-estate the right to judge of its powers, with a negative or veto on the acts of the others, in order to protect against encroachments the interests it particularly represents. . . . So essential is the principle, that to withhold this right from either, where the sovereign power is divided, is, in fact, *to annul the division* itself, and to *consolidate* in the one left in the exclusive possession of the right *all* powers of government. . . .

John C. Calhoun, *Speeches of John C. Calhoun: Delivered in the Congress of the United States from 1811 to the Present* (New York: Harper & Brothers, 1848), 28, 30–31.

PRACTICING Historical Thinking

Identify: Paraphrase Calhoun's message.

Analyze: Calhoun uses the word *compact* to mean the union of states under the Constitution. In what ways does Calhoun's understanding of the word *compact* differ from James Monroe's in his Second Inaugural Address?

Evaluate: To what extent does Calhoun's message invoke Thomas Jefferson's concept of "unalienable rights" (Doc. 5.6)?

DOCUMENT 7.3 | JAMES MADISON, **Letter to Mathew Carey**
| 1831

Former president and author of the US Constitution, James Madison (1751–1836), described his aversion to the theory of nullification in this letter to printer and entrepreneur Mathew Carey (1760–1839). Madison's letter was written in response to the growing tensions between the state of South Carolina and the federal government regarding the Tariff of 1828, which some South Carolinians, most prominently Senator John C. Calhoun, claimed that the state could "nullify" within its borders and therefore not follow the law.

Dear Sir

. . . To trace the great causes of this state of things out of which these unhappy aberrations have sprung, in the effect of markets glutted with the products of the land, and with the land itself; to appeal to the nature of the Constitutional compact, as precluding a right in any one of the parties to renounce it at will, by giving to all an equal right to judge of its obligations; and, as the obligations are mutual, a right to enforce correlative with a right to dissolve them; to make manifest the impossibility as well as injustice, of executing the laws of the Union, particularly the laws of commerce, if even a single State be exempt from their operation; to lay open the effects of a withdrawal of a Single State from the Union on the *practical* conditions & relations of the others; thrown apart by the intervention of a foreign nation; to expose the obvious, inevitable & disastrous consequences of a separation of the States, whether into alien confederacies or individual nations; these are topics which present a task well worthy the best efforts of the best friends of their country, and I hope you will have all the success, which your extensive information and disinterested views merit. If the States cannot live together in harmony, under the auspices of such a Government as exists, and in the midst of blessings, such as have been the fruits of it, what is the prospect threatened by the abolition of a Common Government, with all the rivalships collisions and animosities, inseparable from such an event. The entanglements & conflicts of commercial regulations, especially as affecting the inland and other non-importing States, & a protection of fugitive slaves, substituted for the present obligatory surrender of them, would of themselves quickly kindle the passions which are the forerunners of war.

James Madison, *The Writings of James Madison 1819–1836*, vol. 9, ed. Gaillard Hunt (New York: Putnam and Sons, 1910), 462–463.

PRACTICING Historical Thinking

Identify: Identify the causes of conflict between the North and the South, as stated by Madison.

Analyze: How does Madison contextualize slavery as an economic factor? Is this a threat? Explain.

Evaluate: To what extent does Madison's argument call for a uniform economic policy? Is this a reasonable request, based on your knowledge of the time period? Consult your history textbook for additional information.

DOCUMENT 7.4 | JUSTICE JOHN MARSHALL, *Worcester v. Georgia*
| 1832

In the case *Worcester v. Georgia*, the US Supreme Court had to determine whether the federal government could use its commerce powers to remove Native Americans from the southeastern United States. Chief Justice John Marshall (1755–1835) wrote the majority opinion.

In the regulation of commerce with the Indians, congress have exercised a more limited power than has been exercised in reference to foreign countries. The law acts upon our own citizens, and not upon the Indians, the same as the laws referred to act upon our own citizens in their foreign commercial intercourse.

It will scarcely be doubted by any one, that, so far as the Indians, as distinct communities, have formed a connection with the federal government, by treaties; that such connection is political, and is equally binding on both parties. This cannot be questioned, except upon the ground that, in making these treaties, the federal government has transcended the treaty-making power. Such an objection, it is true, has been stated; but it is one of modern invention, which arises out of local circumstances; and is not only opposed to the uniform practice of the government, but also to the letter and spirit of the constitution.

But the inquiry may be made, is there no end to the exercise of this power over Indians within the limits of a State, by the general government? The answer is, that, in its nature, it must be limited by circumstances.

If a tribe of Indians shall become so degraded or reduced in numbers, as to lose the power of self-government, the protection of the local law, of necessity, must be extended over them. The point at which this exercise of power by a State would be proper, need not now be considered; if indeed it be a judicial question. Such a question does not seem to arise in this case. So long as treaties and laws remain in full force, and apply to Indian nations exercising the right of self-government, within the limits of a State, the judicial power can exercise no discretion in refusing to give effect to those laws, when questions arise under them, unless they shall be deemed unconstitutional.

B. R. Curtis, *Reports of Decisions in the Supreme Court of the United States* (Boston: Little, Brown, 1881), 270–271.

PRACTICING Historical Thinking

Identify: How does Marshall justify legal protection for the Cherokee?

Analyze: Does the Court's decision favor the expansion or reduction of Native American freedom within the United States? Explain.

Evaluate: What are some similarities and some differences between the arguments in this document and those of James Madison's letter to Mathew Carey (Doc. 7.3)?

NEW SKILL | Interpretation

In addition to reading primary documents, historians also read secondary documents that are written by other historians. As you probably have guessed from the kinds of questions that you have answered so far in this book, historians have different opinions about the same historical events. Therefore, historians also have to know how to **interpret** other historians' arguments. Historians practice **interpretation** to help them understand how other historians understand events from the past.

Below are two historians' interpretations of the origins of the nullification crisis of the 1830s. In addition to Documents 7.1 through 7.4 of this chapter, consult your textbook or class notes for additional details.

STEP 1 Read David F. Ericson's interpretation below.

Interpretation 1

> On the surface, the nullification crisis revolved around the question of sovereignty: Which level of government has the last say on such matters as the tariff rates? Does the federal government, the state governments, or really neither (because the governmental system was set up in such a way that there is no locus of "last say")? Here, of course, the participants in the crisis had recourse to the Constitution, and their conflict was defined by opposing constitutional philosophies. Another question, though, emerged beneath the sovereignty question during the course of the crisis: What is the nature of the American republic? Is it a federation of smaller, state republics, a national republic, or both, in roughly equal proportions? Answering this question seemed to be the only conclusive way of answering the sovereignty question, and, since the Constitution did not provide an answer, the participants had to appeal to some deeper political standard or theory to try to do so.

David F. Ericson, "The Nullification Crisis, American Republicanism, and the Force Bill Debate," *Journal of Southern History* 61, no. 2 (May 1995): 249–270, 251.

What is Ericson's main point in the first interpretation?

STEP 2 Read Jane H. Pease and William H. Pease's interpretation below.

Interpretation 2

> Intensifying Charleston's nullification experience was anxiety over the city's stagnant economy in the 1820s. Between 1820 and 1830 her imports had diminished every year but one. In 1825 the international cotton market collapsed, and the dramatic growth in the city's cotton exports earlier in the decade leveled off. In the wake of that collapse, general economic depression followed. Unemployment and inflation plagued Charleston's inhabitants. Up-country legislators threatened to reduce the

city's representation in a state government which already taxed city property and commercial income more heavily than agricultural land and produce. Charleston's appeals for aid to internal improvements went unheard in the rest of the state. Then, in 1828, her languishing economy seemed further threatened by the new federal tariff.

Jane H. Pease and William H. Pease, "The Economics and Politics of Charleston's Nullification Crisis," *Journal of Southern History* 47, no. 3 (August 1981): 335–362, 336.

What is Pease and Pease's main point in the second interpretation?

STEP 3 Which document or documents above (Docs. 7.1–7.4) best support Ericson's argument in his passage above? Which document or documents best support Pease and Pease's argument in their passage above? Explain your answers.

STEP 4 Answer the following in two paragraphs, each with a claim and evidence. In your response, provide one piece of information from the nullification crisis that is not included in these passages.

Which of these interpretations analyzes the nullification crisis through an *economic* lens? Which of these interpretations analyzes the nullification crisis through a political and *ideological* lens? How do these respective lenses shape each of the arguments in each interpretation?

Debating the Identity of America

DOCUMENT 7.5 | LYMAN BEECHER, "The Evils of Intemperance"
1827

Lyman Beecher (1775–1863), a prominent theologian in the early nineteenth century, cofounded the American Temperance Society, an organization that was devoted to social reforms, including the abolition of slavery and the expansion of women's rights. Beecher was the father of Harriet Beecher Stowe (1811–1896), who wrote the influential abolition-ist novel *Uncle Tom's Cabin* (1852) (Doc. 11.2).

When we behold an individual cut off in youth or in middle age, or witness the waning energies, improvidence, and unfaithfulness of a neighbor, it is but a single instance, and we become accustomed to it; but such instances are multi-plying in our land in every direction, and are to be found in every department of labor, and the amount of earnings prevented or squandered is incalculable: to all which must be added the accumulating and frightful expense incurred for the support of those and their families whom intemperance has made pau-pers. In every city and town the poor-tax, created chiefly by intemperance, is augmenting. The receptacles for the poor are becoming too strait for their accommodation. We must pull them down and build greater to provide accom-modations for the votaries of inebriation; for the frequency of going upon the town has taken away the reluctance of pride, and destroyed the motives to prov-idence which the fear of poverty and suffering once supplied. The prospect of a destitute old-age, or of a suffering family, no longer troubles the vicious portion of our community. They drink up their daily earnings, and bless God for the poor-house, and begin to look upon it as, of right, the drunkard's home, and contrive to arrive thither as early as idleness and excess will give them a pass-port to this sinecure of vice. Thus is the insatiable destroyer of industry march-ing through the land, rearing poor-houses, and augmenting taxation: night and day, with sleepless activity, squandering property, cutting the sinews of industry, undermining vigor, engendering disease, paralyzing intellect, impairing moral principle, cutting short the date of life, and rolling up a national debt, invisible, but real and terrific as the debt of England; continually transferring larger and larger bodies of men from the class of contributors to the national income to the class of worthless consumers.

Lyman Beecher, *Six Sermons on the Nature, Occasion, Signs, Evils and Remedy of Intemperance* (New York: American Tract Society, 1827), 54–55.

DOCUMENT 7.6 | DAVID WALKER, "Walker's Appeal . . . to the Coloured Citizens of the World"
1830

David Walker (1796–1830) was a prominent African American printer who was born in North Carolina and eventually settled in Boston, Massachusetts, where he was an early participant in the abolitionist movement.

Men of colour, who are also of sense, for you particularly is my APPEAL designed. Our more ignorant brethren are not able to penetrate its value. I call upon you therefore to cast your eyes upon the wretchedness of your brethren, and to do your utmost to enlighten them—*go to work and enlighten your brethren!*—Let the Lord see you doing what you can to rescue them and yourselves from degradation. Do any of you say that you and your family are free and happy, and what have you to do with the wretched slaves and other people? So can I say, for I enjoy as much freedom as any of you, if I am not quite as well off as the best of you. Look into our freedom and happiness, and see of what kind they are composed!! They are of the very lowest kind—they are the very *dregs*!—they are the most servile and abject kind, that ever a people was in possession of! If any of you wish to know how FREE you are, let one of you start and go through the southern and western States of this country, and unless you travel as a slave to a white man (a servant is a *slave* to the man whom he serves) or have your free papers, (which if you are not careful they will get from you) if they do not take you up and put you in jail, and if you cannot give good evidence of your freedom, sell you into eternal slavery, I am not a living man: or any man of colour, immaterial who he is, or where he came from, if he is not *the fourth from the negro race*!! (as we are called) the white Christians of America will serve him the same they will sink him into wretchedness and degradation for ever while he lives. And yet some of you have the hardihood to say that you are free and happy! . . .

David Walker, *David Walker's Appeal* (New York: Hill and Wang, 1995), 28–29.

DOCUMENT 7.7 | **WILLIAM LLOYD GARRISON,** *The Liberator*
| 1831

William Lloyd Garrison (1805–1879) started the abolitionist newspaper *The Liberator* in 1831. Frederick Douglass's *North Star* and Garrison's *The Liberator* were the leading abolitionist newspapers until the abolition of slavery in 1865.

During my recent tour for the purpose of exciting the minds of the people by a series of discourses on the subject of slavery, every place that I visited gave fresh evidence of the fact, that a greater revolution in public sentiment was to be effected in the free States—*and particularly in New-England*—than at the South. I found contempt more bitter, opposition more active, detraction more relentless, prejudice more stubborn, and apathy more frozen, than among slave-owners themselves. Of course, there were individual exceptions to the contrary. This state of things afflicted, but did not dishearten me. I determined, at every hazard, to lift up the standard of emancipation in the eyes of the nation, *within sight of Bunker Hill and in the birthplace of liberty.* That standard is now unfurled; and long may it float, unhurt by the spoliations of time or the missiles of a desperate foe—yea, till every chain be broken, and every bondman set free! Let Southern oppressors tremble—let their secret abettors tremble—let their Northern apologists tremble—let all the enemies of the persecuted blacks tremble.

Wendell Phillips Garrison and Francis Jackson Garrison, *William Lloyd Garrison, 1805–1879* (Boston, MA: Houghton, Mifflin, 1894), 224.

DOCUMENT 7.8 | JOHN C. CALHOUN, "Slavery a Positive Good"
1837

In this selection, John C. Calhoun advocates the rights of individual states as part of a broader defense of the institution of slavery, which he claims is good for slaveholders, for slaves, and for society.

. . . I hold that in the present state of civilization, where two races of different origin, and distinguished by color, and other physical differences, as well as intellectual, are brought together, the relation now existing in the slave-holding States between the two, is, instead of an evil, a good—a positive good. I feel myself called upon to speak freely upon the subject where the honor and interests of those I represent are involved. I hold then, that there never has yet existed a wealthy and civilized society in which one portion of the community did not, in point of fact, live on the labor of the other. Broad and general as is this assertion, it is fully borne out by history. This is not the proper occasion, but if it were, it would not be difficult to trace the various devices by which the wealth of all civilized communities has been so unequally divided, and to show by what means so small a share has been allotted to those by whose labor it was produced, and so large a share given to the non-producing classes. The devices are almost innumerable, from the brute force and gross superstition of ancient times, to the subtle and artful fiscal contrivances of modern. I might well challenge a comparison between them and the more direct, simple, and patriarchal mode by which the labor of the African race is, among us, commanded by the European. I may say with truth, that in few countries so much is left to the share of the laborer, and so little exacted from him, or where there is more kind attention paid to him in sickness or infirmities of age. Compare his condition with the tenants of the poor houses in the most civilized portions of Europe—look at the sick, and the old and infirm slave, on one hand, in the midst of his family and friends, under the kind superintending care of his master and mistress, and compare it with the forlorn and wretched condition of the pauper in the poor house. But I will not dwell on this aspect of the question; I turn to the political; and here I fearlessly assert that the existing relation between the two races in the South, against which these blind fanatics are waging war, forms the most solid and durable foundation on which to rear free and stable political institutions. It is useless to disguise the fact. There is and always has been in an advanced stage of wealth and civilization, a conflict between labor and capital. The condition of society in the South exempts us from the disorders and dangers resulting from this conflict; and which explains why it is that the political condition of the slave-holding States has been so much more stable and quiet than those of the North. . . .

Surrounded as the slave-holding States are with such imminent perils, I rejoice to think that our means of defence are ample, if we shall prove to have the intelligence and spirit to see and apply them before it is too late. All we want is concert, to lay aside all party differences, and unite with zeal and energy in repelling approaching dangers. Let there be concert of action, and we shall find ample means of security without resorting to secession or disunion. I speak with full knowledge and a thorough examination of the subject, and for one see my way clearly. . . . I dare not hope that any thing I can say will arouse the South to a due sense of danger; I fear it is beyond the power of mortal voice to awaken it in time from the fatal security into which it has fallen.

John Calhoun, *Speeches of Mr. Calhoun of S. Carolina, on the Bill for the Admission of Michigan: Delivered in the Senate of the United States, January, 1837* (Washington, DC: Duff Green, 1837), 6–7.

PRACTICING Historical Thinking

Identify: What are Calhoun's moral and economic arguments?

Analyze: How does Calhoun's comparison to Europe or ancient times further his argument?

Evaluate: Compare this document to those by Lyman Beecher (Doc. 7.5), David Walker (Doc. 7.6), and William Lloyd Garrison (Doc. 7.7) above.

DOCUMENT 7.9 | **FREDERICK DOUGLASS,** *Narrative of the Life of Frederick Douglass, an American Slave, Written by Himself*
1845

Frederick Douglass (1818–1895) was the best-known African American abolitionist of his day. His *Narrative of the Life of Frederick Douglass, an American Slave, Written by Himself* served as a template for similar narratives of escaped slaves and sought to prove to skeptical readers that enslaved African Americans were capable of demanding freedom and enjoying equal rights with white Americans.

Very soon after I went to live with Mr. and Mrs. Auld, she very kindly commenced to teach me the A, B, C. After I had learned this, she assisted me in learning to spell words of three or four letters. Just at this point of my progress, Mr. Auld found out what was going on, and at once forbade Mrs. Auld to instruct me further, telling her, among other things, that it was unlawful, as well as unsafe, to teach a slave to read. To use his own words, further, he said, "If you give a nigger an inch, he will take an ell. A nigger should know nothing but to obey his master—to do as he is told to do. Learning would *spoil* the best nigger in the world. Now," said he, "if you teach that nigger (speaking of myself) how to read, there would be no keeping him. It would forever unfit him to be a slave. He would at once become unmanageable, and of no value to his master. As to himself, it could do him no good, but a great deal of harm. It would make him discontented and unhappy." These words sank deep into my heart, stirred up sentiments within that lay slumbering, and called into existence an entirely new train of thought. It was a new and special revelation, explaining dark and mysterious things, with which my youthful understanding had struggled, but struggled in vain. I now understood what had been to me a most perplexing difficulty—to wit, the white man's power to enslave the black man. It was a grand achievement, and I prized it highly. From that moment, I understood the pathway from slavery to freedom. It was just what I wanted, and I got it at a time when I the least expected it. Whilst I was saddened by the thought of losing the aid of my kind mistress, I was gladdened by the invaluable instruction which, by the merest accident, I had gained from my master. Though conscious of the difficulty of learning without a teacher, I set out with high hope, and a fixed purpose, at whatever cost of trouble, to learn how to read. The very decided manner with which he spoke, and strove to impress his wife with the evil consequences of giving me instruction, served to convince me that he was deeply sensible of the truths he was uttering. It gave me the best assurance that I might rely with the utmost confidence on the results which, he said, would flow from teaching me to read. What he most dreaded, that I most desired. What he most loved, that I most hated. That which to him was a great evil, to be carefully shunned, was to me a great good, to be diligently sought; and the argument which he so warmly urged against my learning to read, only served to inspire me with a desire and determination to learn. In learning to read, I owe almost as much to the bitter opposition of my master, as to the kindly aid of my mistress. I acknowledge the benefit of both.

Frederick Douglass, *Narrative of the Life of Frederick Douglass, an American Slave, Written by Himself* (Boston: Anti-Slavery Office, 1845), 36–37.

PRACTICING Historical Thinking

Identify: According to Douglass, what is at the core of a white man's ability to enslave a black man?

Analyze: Compare and contrast the portrayals of Mr. and Mrs. Auld. Which portrayal elicits greater sympathy? Explain.

Evaluate: Why, according to Douglass, did Mr. Auld feel that educating a slave was a great evil?

| ## ELIZABETH CADY STANTON, Declaration of Sentiments and Resolutions

1848

The Declaration of Sentiments and Resolutions was written by Elizabeth Cady Stanton and presented at the first Woman's Rights Convention, which met in Seneca Falls, New York, in 1848. After changes made by attendees, it became the official statement of the convention.

When, in the course of human events, it becomes necessary for one portion of the family of man to assume among the people of the earth a position different from that which they have hitherto occupied, but one to which the laws of nature and of nature's God entitle them, a decent respect to the opinions of mankind requires that they should declare the causes that impel them to such a course.

We hold these truths to be self-evident: that all men and women are created equal; that they are endowed by their Creator with certain inalienable rights; that among these are life, liberty, and the pursuit of happiness; that to secure these rights governments are instituted, deriving their just powers from the consent of the governed. Whenever any form of government becomes destructive of these ends, it is the right of those who suffer from it to refuse allegiance to it, and to insist upon the institution of a new government, laying its foundation on such principles, and organizing its powers in such form, as to them shall seem most likely to effect their safety and happiness. Prudence, indeed, will dictate that governments long established should not be changed for light and transient causes; and accordingly all experience hath shown that mankind are more disposed to suffer, while evils are sufferable, than to right themselves by abolishing the forms to which they were accustomed. But when a long train of abuses and usurpations, pursuing invariably the same object evinces a design to reduce them under absolute despotism, it is their duty to throw off such government, and to provide new guards for their future security. Such has been the patient sufferance of the women under this government, and such is now the necessity which constrains them to demand the equal station to which they are entitled.

The history of mankind is a history of repeated injuries and usurpations on the part of man toward woman, having in direct object the establishment of an absolute tyranny over her. To prove this, let facts be submitted to a candid world.

He has never permitted her to exercise her inalienable right to the elective franchise.

He has compelled her to submit to laws, in the formation of which she had no voice.

He has withheld from her rights which are given to the most ignorant and degraded men—both natives and foreigners.

Having deprived her of this first right of a citizen, the elective franchise, thereby leaving her without representation in the halls of legislation, he has oppressed her on all sides.

He has made her, if married, in the eye of the law, civilly dead.

He has taken from her all right in property, even to the wages she earns.

He has made her, morally, an irresponsible being, as she can commit many crimes with impunity, provided they be done in the presence of her husband. In the covenant of marriage, she is compelled to promise obedience to her husband, he becoming, to all intents and purposes, her master—the law giving him power to deprive her of her liberty, and to administer chastisement.

He has so framed the laws of divorce, as to what shall be the proper causes, and in case of separation, to whom the guardianship of the children shall be given, as to be wholly regardless of the happiness of women—the law, in all cases, going upon the false supposition of the supremacy of man, and giving all power into his hands.

After depriving her of all rights as a married woman, if single, and the owner of property, he has taxed her to support a government which recognizes her only when her property can be made profitable to it.

He has monopolized nearly all the profitable employments, and from those she is permitted to follow, she receives but a scanty remuneration.

Elizabeth Cady Stanton et al., *History of Woman Suffrage* (Rochester, NY: Charles Mann, 1889), 70–71.

PRACTICING Historical Thinking

Identify: Summarize the main points of the Declaration.

Analyze: Compare Stanton's tone in this document to Frederick Douglass's tone in Document 7.9. Where are they similar, and where are they different? Explain your response.

Evaluate: Compare this document to the Declaration of Independence (Doc. 5.6). In what ways does this document differ from the Declaration? In what ways is this document similar to the Declaration?

DOCUMENT 7.11 | ASHER DURAND, *Dover Plains*
1850

Asher Durand (1796–1886) was one of the artists who made up the Hudson River School, a group of artists named for the Hudson River region that was often featured in the artists' work. The European Romantics, who sought mystery and transcendence in nature, inspired the Hudson River School. This lithograph of Durand's *Dover Plains* depicts a group of people who are exploring the Hudson River Valley in New York State.

Smithsonian American Art Museum, Washington, DC/
Art Resource, NY.

PRACTICING Historical Thinking

Identify: Describe the images in the foreground and background. Which images are most prominent?

Analyze: What kind of people are featured here? What is omitted from this picture? What might Durand's purpose be in omitting these things?

Evaluate: Turn Durand's picture into a statement about the relationship between nature and people. Explain your response.

APPLYING AP® Historical Thinking Skills

NEW SKILL | Synthesis

One of a historian's most important skills is the ability to synthesize complex and often contradictory evidence in a way that will be clear and informative to a reader. **Synthesis** is the skill that turns separate pieces of information into a cohesive, sensible statement that teaches and informs.

The title of Topic II is "Debating the Identity of America," which is a broad topic, and the seven documents in this section (Docs. 7.5–7.11) cannot capture all of the arguments about what it meant to be an American between 1800 and 1848. Using a secondary source like a textbook or classroom notes, however, you can draw some broad conclusions about the debates regarding the identity of America during this time period. To do so, you need to practice synthesis.

STEP 1 Organize Documents 7.5 through 7.11 into two to four categories. For example, you could arrange them into "proslavery," "antislavery," and "other." This method of arrangement focuses on the appropriate use of historical evidence, which may be limiting because not all of these documents fall neatly into a pro and con argument about slavery.

You could take a further step back, however, and contextualize the documents according to the way that their authors conceive of America. For John C. Calhoun (Doc. 7.2) and Lyman Beecher (Doc. 7.5), for example, America is a place where ideologies about class differences are made manifest. Both envision America as a place where some people are superior to others. You could call this category "Unequal America," where class differences still exist. Another category might be "Equal America" and could include abolitionists such as William Lloyd Garrison (Doc. 7.7) and Frederick Douglass (Doc. 7.9), who conceive of enslaved African Americans as being naturally equal to white Americans and demand that they be treated accordingly. The Declaration of Sentiments and Resolutions (Doc. 7.10) also fits in this category. But where does Asher Durand's *Dover Plains* (Doc. 7.11) belong? To evaluate the painting, you might focus on how the subject matter is portrayed. For example, consider the relative insignificance that Durand gives to individuals compared to the natural beauty that surrounds them and the ways that this might reflect the artist's ideas. Review your response to the "evaluate" question that follows Document 7.11.

Whether your synthesis occurs at a concrete level (such as analysis of evidence) or a conceptual level (such as contextualization), the most effective syntheses will purposefully and accurately use as many documents as possible.

STEP 2   After you have organized the documents, consult your textbook and class notes for additional background on the time period (1800–1848) and on the subjects who are prominent in these documents. For example, if you use the category "Equal America," find chapters that cover the abolitionist movement and the early women's rights movement. Read the relevant sections. While you read them, take notes from the textbook and your class notes under the category where you have organized your documents. You should now have a list of primary sources and secondary information that is organized by the categories that fall under the subtheme "Debating the Identity of America." For example:

Debating the Identity of America

Equal America	Unequal America
Doc. 7.6, David Walker, "Walker's Appeal . . . to the Coloured Citizens of the World"	Doc. 7.5, Lyman Beecher, "The Evils of Intemperance"
Notes: Free African Americans in the North lived segregated and impoverished lives.	Notes: The temperance movement was overwhelmingly middle class and aimed at reforming working class.

STEP 3   Turn your organized notes into a statement that synthesizes this information by answering the following prompt:

> Throughout the early nineteenth century, Americans debated their identity as a people. Using the seven documents in this section and information from your textbook and class notes, define some of the major contemporary debates about the identity of the United States in the early nineteenth century.

PUTTING IT ALL TOGETHER

Revisiting the Main Point

* Characterize the social debates in the early nineteenth century as featured in this chapter. To what extent did political ideology, economic necessity, and sectional interests drive these debates?
* In what ways did groups that were left out of the liberties granted to Americans during the Revolution use the language of the Revolution to demand those rights?
* Establish and analyze the changing definitions of freedom following the Revolutionary War.

BUILDING AP® WRITING SKILLS | Patterns in Historical Argument

One challenge of writing historical arguments is using **evidence** and **explanations** as effective support. Chapters 1 through 6 focus on organizing evidence and developing a **thesis,** and Chapters 7 through 12 provide instruction on how to use evidence to support your thesis.

Perhaps the strongest use of evidence from history is the discovery of **patterns**—repetitions among events or phenomena that reinforce your point. For example, both Frederick Douglass (Doc. 7.9) and Elizabeth Cady Stanton (Doc. 7.10) argue for greater liberties, and although the people involved in each document differ (African Americans and women), the reinforcement of similar circumstances allows your evidence to form a stronger case about the Second Great Awakening, a period of religious revival in the United States that ran from the 1820s to the 1850s, as a time of social reform as well. Review your textbook or class notes on the Second Great Awakening if you need a reminder about this important religious movement.

Although historical themes build on each other (as in the example about liberties that is cited above), attempting to force evidence into a single, limited framework might lead you to fall into the **either/or fallacy**. Also known as the **black-or-white fallacy**, this logical error ignores the gray area of facts and ideas that do not fit into a predetermined category. For example, Lyman Beecher's (Doc. 7.5) call for the end of debtors' prisons is primarily an economic one, but it echoes other reformers' pleas for sympathy and condemnation of the moral aspects of inequality. Also, effective combinations of evidence invite a fuller **evaluation** of the evidence.

When you discover **breaks** in the pattern, you are able to discover a gray area and look for evidence and explanations that provide a different perspective or point of view. In some cases, it may be an opposing point of view, but be wary about trying to fit all evidence into just two sides.

Patterns and **synthesis** go hand in hand. Your ability to combine evidence into available frameworks or processes predicts your ability to present patterns in your use of evidence and explanations.

Consider the following prompt to illustrate the effective use of patterns in historical evidence and explanations:

> Characterize the social debates that occurred in the early nineteenth century as featured in this chapter. To what extent did political ideology, economic necessity, and sectional interests drive these debates?

STEP 1 *Understand the prompt, and identify the key words*

For a review of this step, see Building AP® Writing Skills in Chapter 1 (p. 22).

STEP 2 *Brainstorm*

For a review of this step, see Building AP® Writing Skills in Chapter 4 (p. 111).

STEP 3 *Identify and organize your evidence*

Complete the graphic organizer below to help you uncover patterns in historical evidence. The columns allow you to evaluate the sources in terms of their effectiveness in supporting your position. The columns also give you a head start with your **explanations**, which are as important as the evidence you provide.

Note, too, that some examples (such as Doc. 7.5) may be used more than once, especially if their arguments apply to multiple factors.

Political ideology evidence (ranked in terms of importance)	Economic necessity evidence (ranked in terms of importance)	Sectional interests evidence (ranked in terms of importance)
Doc. 7.2, John C. Calhoun, Address to the Southern States	Doc. 7.5, Lyman Beecher, "The Evils of Intemperance"	Doc. 7.8, John C. Calhoun, "Slavery a Positive Good"
Doc. 7.5, Lyman Beecher, "The Evils of Intemperance"		Doc. 7.11, Asher Durand, *Dover Plains*

STEP 4 *Outline your response*

When you organize your evidence, a good rule of thumb is to save the best for last. For example, your outline may feature a section on political ideology, as shown here:

Body paragraph: Main point (on political ideology)

   A. Supporting point: Evidence and explanation for example 1 (such as John C. Calhoun)

   B. Supporting point: Evidence and explanation for example 2 (such as Lyman Beecher)

To make your supporting statements more persuasive, use language that evaluates:

To show similarities

   Like

   Similar to

   In the same way,

To show differences

   Even more important,

   Less noteworthy was

   The greatest example is

Breaks in patterns become useful transitions to other categories, which you will likely discover in your explanations of the evidence. For example, Lyman Beecher's argument—used twice—introduces a new factor to consider in the development of social debates.

Even supporting categories may be evaluated to provide coherence to the skeleton of your outline. What categories do you provide first? Last? By prioritizing your categories, you answer the language of the prompt "To what extent" and assess the degree to which one factor influences a larger argument.

For example, your broad outline may appear this way:

   I. Introduction with thesis

   II. Main point 1: Economic necessity

   III. Main point 2: Sectional interests

   IV. Main point 3: Political ideology

   V. Conclusion

Such an organization suggests an essay that defends how and why political ideology compares with the other two factors. If you save the best for last, then political ideology is the most important. If you begin with your strongest point, then you will explain why economic necessity is the most important.

Remember too that in a **linear argument** the working thesis culminates in a final position that presents a strong statement of the thesis. There are natural and logical progressions among the body paragraphs. In the example presented above, you would present a clear rationale for why economic necessity is first, sectional interests are second, and political ideology is last.

The Market Revolution

During the first half of the nineteenth century, innovations in technology and infrastructure transformed the economic landscape of the United States. These changes allowed goods to be produced more efficiently and to be traded more easily between the various regions of the United States and between the nation and the world. These changes also affected where and how Americans lived, reshaped regional and national identities, and influenced how citizens interacted with each other at home, in the marketplace, and at work. These economic changes and their social effects are often called "the Market Revolution" by historians.

Technological changes made the mass production of goods like textiles more efficient, and transportation innovations like canals and steam-powered water travel allowed a wider movement of people and goods. In this newly integrated economy, certain regions could specialize in the production of particular goods for trade with other regions in the young nation. This regional specialization led to greater economic integration through trade but also to starker economic and social differences between different regions.

The changes brought about by the Market Revolution transformed the lives of Americans in ways that shaped where they lived, how they understood gender and family, and what they expected from American politics and politicians. The Market Revolution ultimately proved to be as socially important as the American Revolution itself.

Seeking the Main Point

As you read the documents that follow, keep these broad questions in mind. These questions will help you understand the relationship between the documents in this chapter and the historical changes that they represent. As you reflect on these questions, determine which themes and which documents best address them.

- In what ways did technological and economic changes in the United States between 1800 and 1848 shape US regions differently? How did these changes transform labor relations?
- How did ideas about individuals and economics shape economic policies during this period?

A Market Economy

DOCUMENT 8.1 | **ELI WHITNEY, Petition for Renewal of Patent on Cotton Gin**
1812

The inventor Eli Whitney (1765–1825) is best known for creating the cotton gin, a mechanical device that removed seeds from raw cotton. The mechanization of this formerly labor-intensive process made the crop exponentially more profitable and transformed cotton into a cash crop. It also solidified and strengthened the economic viability of slavery in the South and contributed to its spread west to the Mississippi River. Whitney presented his April 16, 1812, petition to the US Congress.

So alluring were the advantages developed by this invention that in a short time the whole attention of the planters of the middle and upper country of the Southern States was turned to planting green seed cotton. The means furnished by this discovery of cleaning that species of cotton were at once so cheap and expeditious and the prospects of advantage so alluring that it suddenly became the general crop of the country.

Little or no regard, however, was paid to the claims of your memorialist, and the infringements of his rights became almost as extensive as the cultivation of cotton. He was soon reduced to the disagreeable necessity of resorting to courts of justice for the protection of his property.

After the unavoidable delays which usually attend prosecutions of this kind and a laboured trial, it was discovered that the defendants had only *used*—and that as the law then stood they must both *make* and *use* the machine, or they could not be liable. The court decided that it was a fatal though inadvertent defect in the law, and gave judgment for the defendant.

It was not until the year 1800 that this defect in the law was amended. Immediately after the amendment of the law your memorialist commenced a number of suits; but so effectual were the means of procrastination and delay resorted to by the defendants that he was unable to obtain any decision on the merits of his claim until the year 1807—not until he had been eleven years in the law, and thirteen years of his patent term had expired. . . .

Permit your memorialist further to remark that . . . before the invention of your memorialist, the value of this species of cotton, after it was cleaned, was not equal to the expence of cleaning it—that since; the cultivation of this species has been a great source of wealth to the community & of riches to thousands of her citizens—That as a labour-saving machine it is an invention which enables *one man* to perform in a given time *that* which would require a *thousand men*, without its aid, to perform in the same time—in short that it furnishes to the whole family of mankind the means of procuring the article of cotton, that important raw material, which constitutes a great part of their cloathing at a much cheaper rate.

William Phipps Blake, *History of the Town of Hamden, Connecticut: With an Account of the Centennial Celebration, June 15th, 1886* (New Haven, CT: Price, Lee, 1888), 287–288.

PRACTICING Historical Thinking

Identify: What is Whitney's chief complaint?

Analyze: What is the cause of Whitney's complaint in this excerpt?

Evaluate: In what ways could Whitney's invention transform the American labor market?

DOCUMENT 8.2	**Election Ticket: Agriculture, Trade, Manufactures**
	1828

This election ticket for Andrew Jackson allowed the holder to vote easily by placing it in a ballot box. These kinds of election tickets became popular throughout the early nineteenth century as enfranchisement spread to all white men regardless of wealth or literacy. Preprinted ballots were printed by the candidates' campaigns or political parties themselves. This ballot lists a vote for two Jackson supporters underneath an image of an anchor, bales, barrels, a ship, and the words "Agriculture, Commerce and Manufactures." The words "Edes Print" on the trunk could be the name of the printer of the ballot.

Library of Congress Prints and Photographs Division, LC-USZ61-1446.

DOCUMENT 8.3 | THOMAS GRIGGS, Advertisement of a South Carolina Slave Dealer

1835

As cotton production and export grew throughout the early nineteenth century, the institution of slavery spread throughout the southern United States. The international slave trade ended in 1808, but the slave population in the United States continued to grow throughout the first half of the nineteenth century.

Library of Congress Prints and Photographs Division, LC-USZ62-62799.

| **JOSEPH H. DAVIS,** Family Portraits

1832–1837

Joseph H. Davis (1811–1865) painted portraits for middle-class families to display in their homes. He traveled throughout New England and made a modest living as a painter, creating watercolor portraits of families and married couples that featured their favorite household items and articles of clothing.

Image copyright © The Metropolitan Museum of Art. Image source: Art Resource, NY.

The Azariah Caverly Family, 1836, attributed to Joseph H. Davis, N0061.1961. Gift of Stephen C. Clark, Fenimore Art Museum, Cooperstown, New York.

PRACTICING Historical Thinking

Identify: What details do Davis's paintings share?

Analyze: In what ways do these images portray the roles that were played by men and women in the middle-class households of this era?

Evaluate: What objects in these portraits define those roles? In what ways are these objects a product of the economic changes represented in Docs. 8.1–8.3?

| MIKE WALSH, "Meeting: Democratic Mechanics and Working Men of New York"
1842

Mike Walsh was a prominent New York Democrat and labor leader in the 1840s and 1850s. Starting out as a labor activist, Walsh formed the Spartan Association in New York City to rival the political machine in Tammany Hall. He eventually became a successful politician in New York and served as a legislator in the state assembly in Albany and as a representative for New York State in the US Congress. In this excerpt from a speech to New York working men, the bracketed audience responses appeared in the original newspaper accounts.

When I look back upon the past history of the world and see how many of the working classes have shed oceans of each other's blood for the elevation and aggrandizement of tyrants, the reflection causes deep feelings of pity and sorrow—to think that these noble classes have suffered themselves to be used solely for the advancement of their oppressors, without ever attempting to throw off their shackles and redeem themselves. [Loud cheers.] . . .

There are two great principles in the moral, social, material and political world; yes, in every thing. Life and death, heat and cold, light and darkness, sickness and health, freedom and despotism! [Tremendous cheering, which continued some minutes.] Which of these do you choose—slavery or liberty? [Loud cries of "Liberty! liberty!"] Then why not make some exertions to carry out your choice. Don't stand with folded arms, and silently look on, while a reckless gang of conspiring traitors [turning round and pointing to the men on the stand] are using you and your best exertions for their own selfish purposes. [Loud cheers.] Don't stand by and see them do this and grumble for a year afterwards. [Cheers and laughter.] I've seen men on this stand talk about advancing the interests of the working classes, and decrying monopolies in the most unqualified terms, who, when they got to Albany, voted for the incorporation of old Allaire's works, making his shinplasters legal tender among his workmen. [Cheers.] I say these things shall not be tolerated any longer! [Cries of "No; no!—three cheers for Mike Walsh"—and nine loud cheers were given, which shook the walls of the building.] You will find such men receive nominations at Tammany Hall, while men who have sacrificed every thing to elevate the working portion of the community are rejected. This is not our fault; and yet again it is, because we don't attend primary meetings; or, when we do attend primary meetings, we select men merely on account of their miscalled respectability, who have succeeded in raising a few thousand dollars by robbing the community; who afterwards prove recreant to their trust. [Cheers.] . . .

Spartan Association, *Michael Walsh: Sketches of Speeches and Writing Including His Poems and Correspondence* (New York: Thomas McSpedon, 1843), 13–14.

PRACTICING Historical Thinking

Identify: What does Walsh mean when he uses the phrase "miscalled respectability"?

Analyze: Based on this reading, what might be the values or beliefs of Walsh's audience regarding American society and politics?

Evaluate: To what extent does this document represent conflicts that are similar to those expressed in Eli Whitney's petition (Doc. 8.1)?

DOCUMENT 8.6 | HARRIET ROBINSON, *Loom and Spindle: or, Life among the Early Mill Girls*
1898

Harriet Robinson worked in the textile mills of Lowell, Massachusetts, from 1835 to 1848, when she was between the ages of ten and twenty-three. Robinson submitted this report to the Massachusetts Bureau of Statistics of Labor in 1883. The Lowell mills perfected the water-powered production of textiles in the United States.

In 1831 Lowell was little more than a factory village. Several corporations were started, and the cotton-mills belonging to them were building. Help was in great demand; and stories were told all over the country of the new factory town, and the high wages that were offered to all classes of work-people,—stories that reached the ears of mechanics' and farmers' sons, and gave new life to lonely and dependent women in distant towns and farmhouses. . . .

. . . Troops of young girls came by stages and baggage-wagons, men often being employed to go to other States and to Canada, to collect them at so much a head, and deliver them at the factories. . . .

At the time the Lowell cotton-mills were started, the factory girl was the lowest among women. In England, and in France particularly, great injustice had been done to her real character; she was represented as subjected to influences that could not fail to destroy her purity and self-respect. In the eyes of her over-seer she was but a brute, a slave, to be beaten, pinched, and pushed about. It was to overcome this prejudice that such high wages had been offered to women that they might be induced to become mill-girls, in spite of the opprobrium that still clung to this "degrading occupation." . . .

. . . I worked first in the spinning-room as a "doffer." The doffers were the very youngest girls, whose work was to doff, or take off, the full bobbins, and replace them with the empty ones. . . .

. . . These mites had to be very swift in their movements, so as not to keep the spinning-frames stopped long, and they worked only about fifteen minutes in every hour. The rest of the time was their own, and when the overseer was kind they were allowed to read, knit, or go outside the mill-yard to play. . . .

We were paid two dollars a week. . . .

The working-hours of all the girls extended from five o'clock in the morning until seven in the evening, with one-half hour for breakfast and dinner. Even the doffers were forced to be on duty nearly fourteen hours a day, and this was the greatest hardship in the lives of these children. For it was not until 1842 that the hours of labor for children under twelve years of age were limited to ten per day; but the "ten-hour law" itself was not passed until long after some of these little doffers were old enough to appear before the legislative committee on the subject, and plead, by their presence, for a reduction of the hours of labor.

Harriet H. Robinson, *Loom and Spindle or Life among the Early Mill Girls* (Boston: Thomas Y. Crowell & Company, 1898), 62–63, 61, 30–31.

PRACTICING Historical Thinking

Identify: According to Robinson, what distinguished the mill girls of Lowell from the factory girls in Europe?

Analyze: What is Robinson's attitude toward the experience of working in the mills? Cite details to support your response.

Evaluate: Compare this document with Elizabeth Cady Stanton's statement at the Seneca Falls Convention (Doc. 7.10). What differences do you see? What similarities?

APPLYING AP® Historical Thinking Skills

SKILL REVIEW | **Patterns of Continuity and Change over Time and Interpretation**

Below are two interpretations of the origins of the Market Revolution. In addition to Documents 8.1 through 8.6 of this chapter, consult your textbook and class notes for further details on the Market Revolution. After reading each interpretation, complete the steps that follow.

Commercial boom touched off industrialization, as expansive capital engrossed the desperate rural labor set adrift by the northeastern agrarian crisis. Large scale production started with textiles and shoes, articles of potentially enormous demand that promised high returns to capital and entrepreneurship. When shoemakers in Lynn and other towns discovered distant markets for cheap, mass-produced shoes, the more resourceful masters, usually backed by merchant capital, began putting-out various steps of the process to rural families in the surrounding countryside. Increasingly they assembled unskilled labor in central workshops to perform the steps under supervision. Long before shoemaking machinery was developed, manufacturers in many Yankee towns were mass-producing cheap shoes for a national market through the putting-out and central shop systems. . . .

These early manufacturers succeeded by exploiting efficiently the most vulnerable workers forced into the labor market by agrarian crisis. To utilize the cheapest female and child labor, they hired large families, housing them in company-owned villages or compounds and feeding and clothing them from company stores. Hired by contract for terms up to a year, workers saw cash wages at the end of a term only if their earnings exceeded their charges at the company store. Constrained by debt peonage, repetitiously tending the relentless machinery twelve to fourteen hours a day, isolated from the surrounding rural culture, and frequently moving from mill to mill in search of better conditions, mill workers began to be regarded as a separate and inferior class.

Charles Sellers, *The Market Revolution: Jacksonian America, 1815–1846* (New York: Oxford University Press, 1991), 27–28.

In 1813, Francis Cabot Lowell formed a business association with Patrick T. Jackson and Nathan Appleton, subsequently incorporated as the Boston Manufacturing Company with other investors. The purpose was to construct a water-powered loom for the manufacture of cotton textiles. Lowell had recently returned from one of the most successful of all enterprises of industrial espionage, conceived even before the war [of 1812] began. He had spent two years in Britain, where he meticulously observed the textile mills of Manchester. The technology of the power loom invented by Edmund Cartwright remained a scrupulously guarded British national secret. When Lowell left Britain just before war broke out, customs officers searched his luggage twice. They did not realize that the sharp-eyed Lowell had carefully memorized the structure of the loom well enough to replicate it once he got back to the United States. By 1814, Lowell and his brilliant mechanic, Paul Moody, could proudly demonstrate to the company directors an operational water-powered loom in Waltham, Massachusetts. . . .

Farm women had long supplemented the family income by weaving woolen yarn and cloth, using spinning wheels and hand looms at home. Now cotton from the South provided raw material much more plentiful than local sheep. So young women left home, recruited by company-owned boardinghouses in Lowell. There they put in long hours under unhealthy conditions and contracted not to leave until they had worked at least a year. But twelve to fourteen dollars a month was a good wage, and the new town had attractive shops, social activities, churches, lending libraries, and evening lectures. The "mill girls," as they called themselves, wrote and published a magazine, the *Lowell Offering*. Americans had feared industrialization, lest it create an oppressed, depraved, and turbulent proletariat. But because these women typically worked for only a few years prior to marriage, and did so in a morally protected environment, they did not seem to constitute a permanent separate working class. To observers, the community looked like an industrial utopia, more successful than the Scottish models that Francis Lowell and Nathan Appleton had toured years before. Lowell, Massachusetts, boasted the largest concentration of industry in the United States before the Civil War.

Daniel Walker Howe, *What Hath God Wrought: The Transformation of America, 1815–1848* (New York: Oxford University Press, 2007), 132–134.

STEP 1

What is Sellers's main point in the first interpretation?

What is Howe's main point in the second interpretation?

STEP 2

Which of Documents 8.1 through 8.6 best support Sellers's argument in his passage above? Explain your answer.

Which of Documents 8.1 through 8.6 best support Howe's argument in his passage above? Explain your answer.

STEP 3   Provide one piece of outside information about the Market Revolution that is not included in these passages and one piece of evidence from Documents 8.1 through 8.6. In one paragraph, explain how these two pieces of information support the interpretation provided in one of the two passages.

The Politics of Growth

DOCUMENT 8.7 | **JOHN C. CALHOUN, "South Carolina Exposition and Protest"**
1828

In this excerpt, John C. Calhoun (1782–1850), vice president under Andrew Jackson and senator from South Carolina, justifies state nullification of federal law. President Jackson vehemently rejected Calhoun's reasoning and helped pass the Force Bill through Congress to counteract the theory that states could "nullify" federal law. When Calhoun refers to "they" and "their" in this passage, he is referring to New England textile manufacturers and their supporters in Congress.

We cultivate certain great staples for the supply of the general market of the world; and they manufacture almost exclusively for the home market. Their object in the Tariff is to keep down foreign competition, in order to obtain a monopoly of the domestic market. The effect on us is to compel us to purchase at a higher price, both what we purchase from them and from others, without receiving a corresponding increase of price for what we sell. The price at which we can afford to cultivate, must depend on the price at which we receive our supplies. The lower the latter, the lower we may dispose of our products with profit; and in the same degree our capacity of meeting competition is increased; on the contrary, the higher the price of our supplies, the less the profit at the same price, and the less consequently the capacity for meeting competition. . . .

Statutes at Large of South Carolina, ed. Thomas Cooper, vol. 1 (Columbia, SC: A. S. Johnston, 1836), 252.

PRACTICING Historical Thinking

Identify: What is Calhoun's argument against high tariffs for American exports?

Analyze: How does Calhoun's argument represent a conflict between the development of technology and larger economic concerns?

Evaluate: In what ways does Calhoun's argument reflect the United States' changing and continuing role in the world economy?

"General Jackson Slaying the Many-Headed Monster"

1836

The cartoon below represents Andrew Jackson's conflict with the Bank of the United States during his second presidential term (1833–1837). The cartoonist depicts Jackson (left), Vice President Martin Van Buren (center), and Major Jack Downing (right), a popular fictional character at the time, as they struggle against a serpent whose heads represent the states. The largest head (with top hat) is that of Nicholas Biddle of Pennsylvania, director of the bank.

GENERAL JACKSON SLAYING THE MANY HEADED MONSTER.

Library of Congress Prints and Photographs Division, LC-USZ62-1575.

Summary of the cartoon by the Library of Congress

A satire on Andrew Jackson's campaign to destroy the Bank of the United States and its support among state banks. Jackson, Martin Van Buren, and Jack Downing struggle against a snake with heads representing the states.

Jackson (on the left) raises a cane marked "Veto" and says, "Biddle thou Monster Avaunt!! avaount I say! or by the Great Eternal I'll cleave thee to the earth, aye thee and thy four and twenty satellites. Matty if thou art true . . . come on. if thou art false, may the venomous monster turn his dire fang upon thee . . ."

Van Buren (center): "Well done General, Major Jack Downing, Adams, Clay, well done all. I dislike dissentions beyond every thing, for it often compels a man to play a double part, were it only for his own safety. Policy, policy is my motto, but intrigues I cannot countenance."

Downing (dropping his axe): "Now now you nasty varmint, be you imperishable? I swan Gineral that are beats all I reckon, that's the horrible wiper wot wommits wenemous heads I guess . . ."

The largest of the heads is president of the Bank Nicholas Biddle's, which wears a top hat labeled "Penn" (i.e., Pennsylvania) and "$35,000,000." This refers to the rechartering of the Bank by the Pennsylvania legislature in defiance of the adminstration's efforts to destroy it.

_____

"General Jackson Slaying the Many-Headed Monster" printed by H. R. Robinson, New York, 1836, in *American Political Prints, 1766–1876*, ed. Bernard F. Reilly (Boston, MA: G. K. Hall, 1991), entry 1836–7, Library of Congress.

PRACTICING Historical Thinking

Identify: Describe the heads of the monster that General Jackson is slaying. Who or what do these heads represent?

Analyze: How does this image represent the conflict between class and politics in the new market economy? What "weapons" does Jackson have at his disposal?

Evaluate: To what extent are Jackson's concerns the same as John C. Calhoun's in Document 8.7?

DOCUMENT 8.9 | JOHN L. O'SULLIVAN, "The Great Nation of Futurity," *United States Democratic Review*
1839

John L. O'Sullivan (1813–1895), a prominent Democratic journalist and editor, argued for American expansion in terms of the nation's "Manifest Destiny," or the claim that the United States was destined to spread from the Atlantic to the Pacific and beyond.

The American people having derived their origin from many other nations, and the Declaration of National Independence being entirely based on the great principle of human equality, these facts demonstrate at once our disconnected position as regards any other nation; that we have, in reality, but little connection with the past history of any of them, and still less with all antiquity, its glories, or its crimes. On the contrary, our national birth was the beginning of a new history, the formation and progress of an untried political system, which separates us from the past and connects us with the future only; and so far as regards the entire development of the natural rights of man, in moral, political, and national life, we may confidently assume that our country is destined to be *the great nation* of futurity. . . .

America is destined for better deeds. It is our unparalleled glory that we have no reminiscences of battle fields, but in defence of humanity, of the oppressed of all nations, of the rights of conscience, the rights of personal enfranchisement. Our annals describe no scenes of horrid carnage, where men were led on by hundreds of thousands to slay one another, dupes and victims to emperors, kings, nobles, demons in the human form called heroes. We have had patriots to defend our homes, our liberties, but no aspirants to crowns or thrones; nor have the American people ever suffered themselves to be led on by wicked ambition to depopulate the land, to spread desolation far and wide, that a human being might be placed on a seat of supremacy.

We have no interest in the scenes of antiquity, only as lessons of avoidance of nearly all their examples. The expansive future is our arena, and for our history. We are entering on its untrodden space, with the truths of God in our minds, beneficent objects in our hearts, and with a clear conscience unsullied by the past. We are the nation of human progress, and who will, what can, set limits to our onward march? Providence is with us, and no earthly power can. We point to the everlasting truth on the first page of our national declaration, and we proclaim to the millions of other lands, that "the gates of hell"—the powers of aristocracy and monarchy—"shall not prevail against it."

The far-reaching, the boundless future will be the era of American greatness. In its magnificent domain of space and time, the nation of many nations is destined to manifest to mankind the excellence of divine principles. . . .

John L. O'Sullivan, "The Great Nation of Futurity," *United States Democratic Review* 6, no. 23 (November 1839): 426–430.

PRACTICING Historical Thinking

Identify: How does O'Sullivan contrast the past and the future?

Analyze: What does O'Sullivan mean when he states that "entire development of the natural rights of man, in moral, political, and national life" depends on Manifest Destiny?

Evaluate: To what extent does O'Sullivan's view parallel the views of the New England Puritan colonists like John Winthrop (Doc. 2.4)? Consider O'Sullivan's references to monarchy and religion in your response.

APPLYING AP® Historical Thinking Skills

SKILL REVIEW | Synthesis

As you remember from Chapter 7, when historians practice the skill of **synthesis**, they combine different pieces of **evidence** to draw broad and persuasive **conclusions** about a particular era, historical concept, or theme.

Although the documents in this chapter appear to be a collection of often contradictory voices, they all fall broadly under the concept of the Market Revolution. Consider the following prompt, and answer it using at least six of the chapter's nine documents in a cohesive essay that has an introduction with a thesis statement and body paragraphs that support your thesis statement.

> To what extent is the name "Market Revolution" appropriate to describe the changes that happened in the United States between 1800 and 1848? Choose two of these three factors—economics, society, politics—to formulate your response.

PUTTING IT ALL TOGETHER

Revisiting the Main Point

- To what extent did the Market Revolution prove to be a unifying force for the new nation in regional, social, and socioeconomic terms?

- In what ways did the Market Revolution foster migration within the United States? How were these migration patterns different from previous migration within North America? Refer to your textbook and classroom notes to help you answer this question.

- Agree, disagree, or modify this claim: "The Market Revolution fostered a new compassion within the national identity."

BUILDING AP® WRITING SKILLS | **Knowing What and When to Quote**

As you recall from Chapter 7, effective evidence is the key to supporting historical arguments. To develop your understanding of patterns, pay attention to the language that writers use. When patterns become evident in a text, they often highlight a main idea. These patterns may be literal (as in "of the people, by the people, for the people") or conceptual (as in "life, liberty, and the pursuit of happiness").

Historians draw on the language and ideas of others to support their own arguments, and they use such evidence in two ways that both support distinct historical thinking skills. **Explicit evidence** can be a direct quote from another source. It is presented exactly as it appears in the source. Providing direct quotes from primary sources and from other historians can be especially useful when you want to support chronological reasoning and craft historical arguments. **Implicit evidence** can be a reference to the original source that is made in your own words. Implicit evidence is a summary or paraphrase that supports your claim. Whenever you cite the language of another writer—either explicitly or implicitly—you must use appropriate in-text documentation by noting the name of the author and the source or by parenthetically citing a document at the end of a sentence.

As noted above, when we use explicit evidence, we pull direct quotations from other sources. Quoted language requires additional analysis, however. You can't simply present such evidence. You also must provide some analysis of the quoted material. Implicit evidence implies that you have made some level of analysis.

When using quoted material, take care with the language that you use to introduce the quote and to cite the author. As with all historical writing, active language (in which the subject of the sentence does something) is more effective than passive language (in which the subject is acted on). For example, "I wrote this essay" is in the active voice and is more effective than "This essay was written by me," which is in the passive voice. In introducing a quote, use active verbs to reflect your understanding of the author's intent. The following is a partial list of active (and therefore effective) verb choices that you can use to refer to apt quotations:

Active Verbs

advocates	chooses	exhorts	reflects
argues	claims	inspires	signals
believes	decries	laments	urges
celebrates	deplores	questions	

To illustrate, review the following passages from the documents in this chapter, along with the accompanying analysis that exemplifies the historical thinking skill.

Quoting when practicing periodization

Original quote from Eli Whitney's Petition (Doc. 8.1):

> So alluring were the advantages developed by this invention that in a short time the whole attention of the planters of the middle and upper country of the Southern States was turned to planting the green seed cotton. The means furnished by this discovery of cleaning that species of cotton were at once so cheap and expeditious and the prospects of advantage so alluring that it suddenly became the general crop of the country.

Sample analysis:

> Whitney's call for reform features a description of "alluring . . . advantages," which signaled a turning point in the Market Revolution because the cotton gin provided a "cheap and expeditious" (Doc. 8.1) means of turning a profit. Whitney's petition coupled efficiency and cost—markers of an industrial mind-set.

Here the author uses both explicit and implicit evidence. She incorporates several direct quotes from the source within her own summary of Whitney's call for reform. Her clear citation of the original document (Doc. 8.1) shows that she is drawing directly from the original source. Her reference to the Market

Revolution and use of the term "turning point" are evidence that she is practicing periodization, and her use of the active verb "signaled" clarifies that the context and summary of the document are her own.

Quoting when crafting a historical argument

Original quote from John C. Calhoun's "South Carolina Exposition and Protest" (Doc. 8.7):

> The effect on us is to compel us to purchase at a higher price, both what we purchase from them and from others, without receiving a corresponding increase of price for what we sell. The price at which we can afford to cultivate, must depend on the price at which we receive our supplies.

Sample analysis:

> To support his opposition to the federal tariff, Calhoun argues that the result leaves the South in a deficit and that farmers in the South will not receive a "corresponding increase of price" (Doc. 8.7) for their cotton. Calhoun's claim advocates for regional economics over a national economy.

Here a writer offers explicit evidence (in the form of a short direct quotation) as well as implicit evidence. Note how in the second sentence, he uses the active verb "advocates" to attribute the summary argument (presented in his own words) to Calhoun.

Quoting when practicing contextualization

Original quote from John O'Sullivan's editorial on Manifest Destiny (Doc. 8.9):

> It is our unparalleled glory that we have no reminiscences of battle fields, but in defence of humanity, of the oppressed of all nations, of the rights of conscience, the rights of personal enfranchisement.

Sample analysis:

> O'Sullivan's reference to "unparalleled glory" (Doc. 8.9) reflects the era's political version of Manifest Destiny. Unlike the more geographic versions of Manifest Destiny that were discussed during the Jacksonian era, O'Sullivan situates Manifest Destiny in a political context by promising the expansion of voting rights.

Here the writer places her quotation in the context of the era from which it is drawn and then contrasts it with views from another era. She uses quotation marks and citations, not merely referencing the document number but also contrasting Jacksonian era views with what O'Sullivan says "here." This approach keeps the evidence linked to its original source and incorporates the writer's outside knowledge of the subject.

Quotations when practicing synthesis

Quote from Charles Sellers (Applying AP® Historical Thinking Skills, p. 199):

> These early manufacturers succeeded by exploiting efficiently the most vulnerable workers forced into the labor market by agrarian crisis. To utilize the cheapest female and child labor, they hired large families, housing them in company-owned villages or compounds and feeding and clothing them from company stores.

Quote from David Walker Howe (Applying AP® Historical Thinking Skills, p. 200):

> Americans had feared industrialization, lest it create an oppressed, depraved, and turbulent proletariat. But because these women typically worked for only a few years prior to marriage, and did so in a morally protected environment, they did not seem to constitute a permanent separate working class.

Sample analysis:

> The debates focus on the extent to which industrialization marginalized women. Howe believes that women such as the Lowell girls were not a "permanent separate working class," and Sellers argues that these women were "exploit[ed] efficiently." Exploitation to one is emerging independence to another.

Here the writer compares and contrasts two historical analyses by incorporating quotes that are tied to each source ("Howe believes . . ." and "Sellers argues . . ."). He offers some summary of both in his first and last sentences.

Consider the following prompt:

> Agree, disagree, or modify this claim: the Market Revolution proved a unifying force for the new nation in regional, social, and socioeconomic terms.

STEP 1 *Understand the prompt, and identify the key words*

For a review of this step, see Building AP® Writing Skills in Chapter 1 (p. 22).

STEP 2 *Brainstorm*

For a review of this step, see Building AP® Writing Skills in Chapter 4 (p. 111).

STEP 3 *Generate a working thesis*

For a review of this step, see Building AP® Writing Skills in Chapter 1 (p. 22).

STEP 4 *Identify and organize your evidence*

Use your responses for the Applying AP® Historical Thinking Skills exercises in this chapter as a starting point.

Exercise 1: Interpretation of the new working class

Exercise 2: Synthesis of the appropriateness of "Market Revolution" as a name for this era

Complete the following graphic organizer, noting key words, phrases, and patterns that enhance the existing evidence of your body paragraphs:

Document title	Key factor or context	Key words, phrases, and patterns	Supports, refutes, or modifies the claim
	Politics		
	Society		
	Economy		

STEP 5 *Outline your response*

As in previous prompts, your conclusion depends on your ability to understand an abstract concept—in this case, a unifying force. Given that an argument has at least two equally credible positions (as noted in the interpretation exercise above), you can frame this by addressing multiple sides. Because the prompt gives three different categories (regional, social, and socioeconomic), your response will avoid the either/or fallacy because there are at least three different perspectives to consider.

The outline below incorporates an additional feature, which is the language that you quote to support your argument. Understanding the prompt allows you to locate key quotations that align the focus of the claim (for example, a unifying force) to the categories that help you contextualize the claim (such as politics, society, and economy).

A review of the text quoted above reflects how this cited language addresses issues of unity (or disunity) from diverse perspectives:

Alluring advantages

Cheap and expeditious

Corresponding increase of price

Unparalleled glory

Permanent separate working class

Exploit[ed] efficiently

    I. Introduction

   II. First view (claim—for example, how the Market Revolution *failed* to unify)

      A. Key categories (evidence—including political, social, and economic)

        1. Key quotation (for example, text that aligns factors to focus)

        2. Key quotation

      B. Key categories

        1. Key quotation

        2. Key quotation

 III. Second view (claim—for example, how the Market Revolution *did* unify)

      A. Key categories (evidence—including political, social, and economic)

        1. Key quotation (for example, text that aligns factors to focus)

        2. Key quotation

      B. Key categories

        1. Key quotation

        2. Key quotation

  IV. Conclusion

STEP 6 *Draft your essay*

CHAPTER 9

Expansionism: Part 1

T hroughout the first half of the nineteenth century, US policy makers sought to expand American power both internally and abroad. Many American citizens supported this expansion in hopes of expanding their markets and opportunities to exploit land and resources west of the Mississippi River. Many other Americans dissented from these plans and felt that American expansion threatened to provoke internal conflicts and erode the universal human rights that were described in the Declaration of Independence.

As expansion continued westward, the debate over the fate of enslaved Americans became increasingly heated. American policy makers and citizens debated the expansion of slavery into new territories, especially because if slavery was allowed in a new territory, it would become a slave state with corresponding power in Congress. Compromises over the expansion of slavery proved successful in the first half of the nineteenth century but became increasingly difficult toward the middle of the century.

Seeking the Main Point

As you read the documents that follow, keep these broad questions in mind. These questions will help you understand the relationship between the documents in this chapter and the historical changes that they represent. As you reflect on these questions, determine which themes and which documents best address them.

- What were some of the reasons behind American expansion westward? What were some of the debates that it inspired? In what ways did these debates manifest themselves?
- How did economic and environmental factors influence American expansionism?

Expansion, Compromise, and Conflict

DOCUMENT 9.1 | **Map of the Louisiana Purchase**
| 1805

Napoleon Bonaparte surprised Thomas Jefferson's administration with an offer to sell the Louisiana Territory to the United States in 1803. Acquisition of the territory doubled the size of the United States and opened the regions between the Mississippi River and the Rocky Mountains to American settlement.

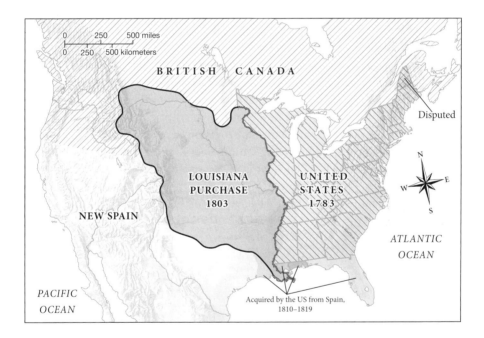

PRACTICING Historical Thinking

Identify: Describe the boundaries and terrain of the Louisiana Purchase.

Analyze: How might doubling the size of the United States shape Americans' perceptions of their nation's Manifest Destiny (see Chapter 8)?

Evaluate: To what extent was the Louisiana Purchase a continuation of European efforts to colonize the New World?

| **Two Opinions on the Missouri Crisis**
1819

The Missouri Territory's application for statehood as a free state in 1819 reopened the debate over the fate of enslaved Americans. Although African Americans and early abolitionists sought an end to slavery, the Missouri Crisis forced American policy makers to face the future of the territories that had been gained in the Louisiana Purchase. In this excerpt from the US Senate debates over the Missouri Compromise, which temporarily settled the issue of slavery in the West, senators from New York and Georgia express the arguments of their respective regions.

Senator Rufus King (New York)

The question respecting slavery in the old thirteen States had been decided and settled before the adoption of the constitution, which grants no power to Congress to interfere with, or to change what had been previously settled—the slave States, therefore, are free to continue or to abolish slavery. Since the year 1808 Congress have possessed power to prohibit and have prohibited the further migration or importation of slaves into any of the old thirteen States, and at all times, under the constitution, have had power to prohibit such migration or importation into any of the new States or territories of the United States. The constitution contains no express provision respecting slavery in a new State that may be admitted into the Union; every regulation upon the subject belongs to the power whose consent is necessary to the formation and admission of new States into the Union. Congress may, therefore, make it a condition of the admission of a new State, that slavery shall be for ever prohibited within the same. . . .

Senator Freeman Walker (Georgia)

I cannot but remark, sir, to what lengths arguments might be carried, predicated upon the supposition of the existence of the power, on the part of congress, to impose conditions and restrictions.

    If you have the authority to impose the one now sought to be imposed, may you not impose any other? If you have the right to inhibit the introduction of slaves into the new state, you have a right to inhibit the introduction of any other species of property. And you may go a step further, and prescribe the manner in which the soil shall be cultivated. In fine, there is no restriction or condition whatever, which may not, with equal propriety, be imposed.

Rufus King, quoted in Frank Moore, *American Eloquence: A Collection of Speeches and Addresses by the Most Eminent Orators of America* (New York: Appleton, 1895), 44; Freeman Walker, quoted in "Missouri Question," *Niles Weekly Register*, February 12, 1820, 411.

DOCUMENT 9.3 | # Missouri Compromise of 1820

The Missouri Compromise of 1820 provided a framework for the division of new territories into slave and free until the Mexican-American War (1846–1848) added nearly one million square miles of new territory to the United States.

Sec. 8. *And be it further enacted*, That in all that Territory ceded by France to the United States under the name of Louisiana which lies north of thirty-six degrees and thirty minutes, north latitude, excepting only such part thereof as is included within the limits of the State contemplated by this act, Slavery and involuntary servitude, otherwise than in the punishment of crime whereof the party shall have been duly convicted, shall be and is hereby forever prohibited. *Provided always*, that any person escaping into the same, from where labor or service is lawfully claimed in any State or Territory of the United States, such fugitive may be lawfully reclaimed and conveyed to the person claiming his or her labor or service as aforesaid.

Horace Greeley, ed., *A History of the Struggle for Slavery Extension or Restriction in the United States from the Declaration of Independence to the Present Day* (New York: Dix, Edwards, 1856), 28.

PRACTICING Historical Thinking

Identify: Explain how the Missouri Compromise limited the growth of slavery.

Analyze: How did the Missouri Compromise reflect regional differences toward slavery?

Evaluate: To what extent did the Missouri Compromise act as a turning point for the political debates about slavery, which culminated with the Emancipation Proclamation?

| **Monroe Doctrine**

| 1823

The Monroe Doctrine, named for President James Monroe (1758–1831), claimed that the entire Western Hemisphere was within the United States' sphere of influence and tried to draw a line between the political systems of the Old World and the New World.

. . . In the discussions to which this interest has given rise, and in the arrangements by which they may terminate, the occasion has been judged proper for asserting as a principle in which the rights and interests of the United States are involved, that the American continents, by the free and independent condition which they have assumed and maintain, are henceforth not to be considered as subjects for future colonization by any European powers. . . .

. . . The citizens of the United States cherish sentiments the most friendly in favor of the liberty and happiness of their fellow-men on that side of the Atlantic. In the wars of the European powers in matters relating to themselves we have never taken any part, nor does it comport with our policy so to do. It is only when our rights are invaded or seriously menaced that we resent injuries or make preparation for our defence. With the movements in this hemisphere we are, of necessity, more immediately connected, and by causes which must be obvious to all enlightened and impartial observers. The political system of the allied powers is essentially different in this respect from that of America. This difference proceeds from that which exists in their respective Governments. And to the defence of our own, which has been achieved by the loss of so much blood and treasure, and matured by the wisdom of their most enlightened citizens, and under which we have enjoyed unexampled felicity, this whole nation is devoted. We owe it, therefore, to candor, and to the amicable relations existing between the United States and those powers, to declare that we should consider any attempt on their part to extend their system to any portion of this hemisphere as dangerous to our peace and safety. . . .

Documents, Legislative and Executive of the Congress of the United States, vol. 5 (Washington, DC: Gales and Seaton, 1858), 246, 250.

PRACTICING Historical Thinking

Identify: How does the Monroe Doctrine establish a difference between American and European powers, as seen in this line: "The political system of the allied powers is essentially different in this respect from that of America"?

Analyze: To what extent was the Monroe Doctrine an extension of the philosophy of Manifest Destiny? Explain.

Evaluate: To what extent did economic considerations shape the creation of the Monroe Doctrine? Consult your textbook for further information.

President Andrew Jackson signed the Indian Removal Act (1830) to compel Native Americans of the so-called Five Civilized Tribes (Cherokee, Chickasaw, Choctaw, Creek, and Seminole) to move from the southeastern United States (Georgia, Mississippi, and Florida) to territories west of the Mississippi River (primarily in modern Oklahoma). The final forced march of these native peoples came to be known as the Trail of Tears.

AN ACT to provide for an exchange of lands with the Indians residing in any of the States or Territories, and for their removal west of the river Mississippi.

Be it enacted, &c., That it shall and may be lawful for the President of the United States to cause so much of any territory belonging to the United States, west of the river Mississippi, not included in any State or organized Territory, and to which the Indian title has been extinguished, as he may judge necessary, to be divided into a suitable number of districts, for the reception of such tribes or nations of Indians as may choose to exchange the lands where they now reside, and remove there; and to cause each of said districts to be so described by natural or artificial marks, as to be easily distinguished from every other.

SEC. 2. *And be it further enacted,* That it shall and may be lawful for the President to exchange any or all of such districts, so to be laid off and described, with any tribe or nation of Indians now residing within the limits of any of the States or Territories, and with which the United States have existing treaties, for the whole or any part or portion of the territory claimed and occupied by such tribe or nation, within the bounds of any one or more of the States or Territories, where the land claimed and occupied by the Indians, is owned by the United States, or the United States are bound to the State within which it lies to extinguish the Indian claim thereto.

SEC. 3. *And be it further enacted,* That in the making of any such exchange or exchanges, it shall and may be lawful for the President solemnly to assure the tribe or nation with which the exchange is made, that the United States will forever secure and guaranty to them, and their heirs or successors, the country so exchanged with them; and if they prefer it, that the United States will cause a patent or grant to be made and executed to them for the same: *Provided always,* That such lands shall revert to the United States, if the Indians become extinct, or abandon the same. . . .

SEC. 8. *And be it further enacted,* That for the purpose of giving effect to the provisions of this act, the sum of five hundred thousand dollars is hereby appropriated, to be paid out of any money in the Treasury, not otherwise appropriated.

Laws of the United States of a Local or Temporary Character, vol. 1 (Washington, DC: Government Printing Office, 1881), 706.

APPLYING AP® Historical Thinking Skills

SKILL REVIEW | Causation and Interpretation

Consider the secondary source below by the historian John Craig Hammond.

Until 1815, the extension of American sovereignty into the Mississippi Valley did little to change either the patterns of slavery's growth and settlement, or the exercise of power between the imperial states that claimed sovereignty over these outposts, and the local settler groups who governed and dominated them. The end of the War of 1812 and the Napoleonic Wars, however, set off an important series of changes in the configurations of slavery and settlement, sovereignty and empire in the greater Mississippi Valley. American sovereignty in the Ohio, Missouri, and Mississippi Valleys, and along the Gulf Coast would be secured as European powers abandoned their claims in the disputed borderlands of the United States. Andrew Jackson's rampages during the war severely weakened Native American resistance to American expansion and resulted in enormous cessions of Indian land in the southern interior between Georgia and the Mississippi River. Potential settler interest in those ceded lands soared as Andrew Jackson's soldiers returned home with tales of abundant and productive land. The onrush of speculators and settlers soon followed. Meanwhile, European demand for cotton, suppressed by the Napoleonic Wars, rose to new heights. Finally, the United States Navy, built up considerably as a result of the War of 1812, turned its attention to interdicting the illegal slave trade along the Gulf Coast, shutting off lower Mississippi Valley planters' main source of slaves. Over the next decade, American slavery from the Atlantic states would expand into the southern interior, the Mississippi Valley, and the Missouri country in an unprecedented, massive push. Only then would the older and isolated slave societies that dotted the American West prior to 1815 be absorbed into a massive and largely uninterrupted American empire for slavery.

John Craig Hammond, "Slavery, Settlement, and Empire: The Expansion and Growth of Slavery in the Interior of the North American Continent, 1770–1820," *Journal of the Early Republic* 32, no. 2 (2012): 175–206, 200.

In a paragraph that includes a claim and evidence that refer to Hammond's paragraph and to Documents 9.1 through 9.5, answer the following prompt:

According to Hammond, what changes took place in the institution of slavery in the Mississippi Valley before and after 1815? What can you infer remained the same about slavery in the Mississippi Valley? Name two documents above that support your understanding of Hammond's arguments about changes in slavery during this period. What in these documents supports your choices?

STEP 1 *Causation*

As you recall from Chapter 1, the term **causation** refers to the ways that things change over time and also to the proximate (short-term) and long-term causes that precede those changes. This prompt asks for two distinct features of slavery before and after 1815 and for the ways that the views of the historian John Craig Hammond agree with two primary documents. Complete the outline below to answer the prompt.

    I. What changes took place regarding the institution of slavery?

        A. Hammond's view

        B. Document from this chapter

        C. Document from this chapter

    II. What stayed the same regarding the institution of slavery?

        A. Hammond's view

        B. Document from this chapter

        C. Document from this chapter

STEP 2 *Interpretation*

The prompt asks you to consider changes in slavery policies before and after 1815. It also asks you to analyze primary source evidence and the points of view expressed in secondary sources. This process of **interpretation** (introduced in Chapter 7) requires you to draw reasonable conclusions that are based on the evidence and your own knowledge of the era and to evaluate the conclusions that have been reached by other historians. How do the documents agree with Hammond's view?

Document	Main points	How it agrees with Hammond	Key words and phrases
Doc. 9.5, Indian Removal Act of 1830		Hammond argues that President Jackson's conquest of native lands led to cessions of land by natives to the United States	Enormous cessions of Indian land
Document 2			
Document 3			

Destinies Manifested

DOCUMENT 9.6 | Texas Declaration of Independence
1836

On March 2, 1836, the Anglo-American settlers who lived in the Mexican state of Texas declared their independence from Mexico.

When a government has ceased to protect the lives, liberty and property of the people, from whom its legitimate powers are derived, and for the advancement of whose happiness it was instituted, and so far from being a guarantee for the enjoyment of those inestimable and inalienable rights, becomes an instrument in the hands of evil rulers for their oppression.

When the Federal Republican Constitution of their country, which they have sworn to support, no longer has a substantial existence, and the whole nature of their government has been forcibly changed, without their consent, from a restricted federative republic, composed of sovereign states, to a consolidated central military despotism, in which every interest is disregarded but that of the army and the priesthood, both the eternal enemies of civil liberty, the everready minions of power, and the usual instruments of tyrants.

When, long after the spirit of the constitution has departed, moderation is at length so far lost by those in power, that even the semblance of freedom is removed, and the forms themselves of the constitution discontinued, and so far from their petitions and remonstrances being regarded, the agents who bear them are thrown into dungeons, and mercenary armies sent forth to force a new government upon them at the point of the bayonet.

When, in consequence of such acts of malfeasance and abdication on the part of the government, anarchy prevails, and civil society is dissolved into its original elements. In such a crisis, the first law of nature, the right of self-preservation, the inherent and inalienable rights of the people to appeal to first principles, and take their political affairs into their own hands in extreme cases, enjoins it as a right towards themselves, and a sacred obligation to their posterity, to abolish such government, and create another in its stead, calculated to rescue them from impending dangers, and to secure their future welfare and happiness.

Nations, as well as individuals, are amenable for their acts to the public opinion of mankind. A statement of a part of our grievances is therefore submitted to an impartial world, in justification of the hazardous but unavoidable step now taken, of severing our political connection with the Mexican people, and assuming an independent attitude among the nations of the earth.

H. P. N. Gammel, ed., *The Laws of Texas, 1822–1897* (Austin, TX: Gammel Book Company, 1898), 4, quoted in Jeffrey D. Schultz, ed., *Encyclopedia of Minorities in American Politics*, vol. 2, *Hispanic Americans and Native Americans* (Santa Barbara, CA: Greenwood, 2000), 539.

PRACTICING Historical Thinking

Identify: Summarize the main points of the declaration.

Analyze: What is the tone of the document? Compare the tone in this document to the tone in the US Declaration of Independence (Doc. 5.6).

Evaluate: This declaration cites the "right of self-preservation" but is silent on the subject of slavery. What role did slavery have in prompting the Anglo rebellion? What other motivations propelled the Texans to sue for independence?

DOCUMENT 9.7 | **"On the Webster-Ashburton Treaty," Brooklyn Daily Eagle**
1842

With the Webster-Ashburton Treaty (1842), the United States settled its northwestern border dispute with Canada, but the question of the Oregon Territory remained unsettled. The *Caroline* affair, mentioned below, refers to an American vessel that was captured by British troops assisting Canadian rebels. The British sent the captured ship with one American still aboard over Niagara Falls in 1837. In the following passage, a Brooklyn newspaper reports on US Senate deliberations over the treaty and the *Caroline* affair.

In the Senate, on Thursday, a resolution of Mr. Rives' [William Cabell Rives, Democrat, Virginia] was adopted, calling for official correspondence between the British Government and Mr. Everett [Edward Everett, Whig, Massachusetts] on the subject of the *Caroline* outrage. A collision between Messrs. Benton [Thomas Hart Benton, Democrat, Missouri] and Rives, which commenced some days ago, in reference to the late treaty, was renewed and continued with much feeling on both sides until its progress was arrested by the chair. The bill to occupy and settle the Oregon Territory was taken up on its final passage, but was laid aside at the suggestion of Mr. Calhoun [John C. Calhoun, Democrat, South Carolina], who wished time to examine it. Mr. Archer [William S. Archer, Whig, Virginia], from the Committee on Foreign Relations, reported a bill to indemnify American citizens for spoliations committed on their commerce prior to 1800. The Senate then went into Executive Session.

"On the Webster-Ashburton Treaty," *Brooklyn Daily Eagle*, January 7, 1843, 2, Brooklyn Public Library, Brooklyn Collection, http://bklyn.newspapers.com/image/50330414/.

DOCUMENT 9.8 | **Democratic Party Platform**
1844

On May 27, 1844, the Democratic Party announced its nominee for the presidency of the United States, James K. Polk (1795–1849). The party's platform paid particular attention to national expansion, states' rights, and slavery. During the campaign that followed, the centerpiece of Polk's campaign was the annexation of Texas from Mexico and the acquisition of the Oregon Territory from Great Britain.

7. *Resolved,* That Congress has no power under the Constitution to interfere with or control the domestic institutions of the several States; and that such States are the sole and proper judges of everything pertaining to their own affairs, not prohibited by the Constitution; that all efforts by Abolitionists or others, made to induce Congress to interfere with questions of slavery, or to take incipient steps in relation thereto, are calculated to lead to the most alarming and dangerous consequences, and that all such efforts have an inevitable tendency to diminish the happiness of the people, and endanger the stability and permanence of the Union, and ought not to be countenanced by any friend to our political institutions. . . .

9. *Resolved,* That the liberal principles embodied by Jefferson in the Declaration of Independence, and sanctioned in the Constitution, which makes ours the land of liberty and the asylum of the oppressed of every nation, have ever been cardinal principles in the Democratic faith; and every attempt to abridge the present privilege of becoming citizens, and the owners of soil among us, ought to be resisted with the same spirit which swept the alien and sedition laws from our statute book. . . .

12. *Resolved,* That our title to the whole of the territory of Oregon is clear and unquestionable; that no portion of the same ought to be ceded to England or any other power, and that the reoccupation of Oregon and the reannexation of Texas

at the earliest practicable period, are great American measures, which this Convention recommends to the cordial support of the Democracy of the Union.

Source: Chandos Fulton, *The History of the Democratic Party from Thomas Jefferson to Grover Cleveland* (New York: Collier, 1892), 158–160.

PRACTICING Historical Thinking

Identify: Summarize the Democratic Party's logic in wanting to annex Texas and the Oregon Territory.

Analyze: To what extent does the party contradict itself by pursuing annexation while at the same advocating states' rights?

Evaluate: Accept, revise, or refute this claim: Territorial expansion allowed the federal government to expand its powers in ways that threaten to violate individual states' rights.

DOCUMENT 9.9 | Parody of the Democratic Party
1848

In this parody of Democratic politics, the artist ridicules the rivalry between conservative proslavery Democrats (riding the pig) and Free Soil Democrats (holding back the pig) who supported restrictions on the spread of slavery. Also portrayed in this cartoon are two former presidents—Millard Fillmore (1800–1874) (left) and Martin Van Buren (1782–1862) (right). Fillmore seeks to stop proslavery Democrats from expanding into the West, and Van Buren chases after the party in support of restrictions on slavery (represented by the "Wilmot Proviso" flag in the background).

Summary of the Cartoon by the Library of Congress

A parody of Democratic politics in the months preceding the party's 1848 national convention.... [T]he artist ridicules the rivalry within the party between Free Soil or antislavery interests, which upheld the Wilmot Proviso, and regular, conservative Democrats or "Hunkers." The "Gilpins" ... are regular Democrats Lewis Cass, Thomas Hart Benton, and Levi Woodbury, who ride a giant sow down "Salt River Lane" away from the "Head Quarters of the Northern Democracy," which displays a Liberty cap and a flag ("Wilmot Proviso").

Cass, a former general and avid expansionist, wears a military uniform and brandishes a sword "Annexation."

Martin Van Buren (right), a Free Soil Democrat, tries to restrain the pig by holding its tail. He remarks, "This is our last hope. If the tail draws out, they are gone for good."

A man at left tries to block the pig's passage shouting, "Stop, stop, Old Hunkers! here's the house!"

Cass orders, "Clear the road. Don't you see that we are fulfilling our manifest destiny!"

Benton asserts, "We are not a whit inclined to tarry there."

On the far right, a stout gentleman chases after them calling, "Hey! hey, there! where upon airth are you going? Come back here to your quarters!"

Meanwhile, former president and Free Soil contender Martin Van Buren is neck-deep in a pool at the lower right. He laments, "Had I served my country with half the zeal with which I served my illustrious predecessor, I should not thus have slumped in the mud." He refers to his service under Andrew Jackson, whom he succeeded as president.

PRACTICING Historical Thinking

Identify: Describe the characterization of the presidents in this image.

Analyze: According to this image, how much power does the president have to restrict the spread of slavery?

Evaluate: Based on this image and your knowledge of the era, determine the power of Congress to legislate for or against slavery during this time period.

APPLYING AP® Historical Thinking Skills

SKILL REVIEW | **Analyzing Evidence: Content and Sourcing, Causation, and Synthesis**

Use the nine documents above, your textbook, and your classroom notes to answer the following prompt:

Analyze the causes and effects of westward expansion between 1800 and 1848. Be sure to examine most of the documents in this chapter in terms of their audience, purpose, point of view, format, argument, and limitations. Place your argument in the context of broad regional, national, and global processes.

STEP 1 Identify documents that present the causes and effects of westward expansion between 1800 and 1848. Analyze the relevant features of each document, including audience, purpose, point of view, and limitations.

STEP 2 Contextualize the documents in terms of broad regional, national, and global processes.

STEP 3 Combine the documents into a clear statement that begins with a main point that is followed by supporting points. Use all nine documents in your response.

Example

The following example illustrates how three sources can be combined in response to the prompt.

Step 1

Document 9.4, Monroe Doctrine, 1823

Document 9.5, Indian Removal Act of 1830

Document 9.6, Texas Declaration of Independence, 1836

Step 2

Source	Audience and purpose	Limitations	Context	Effects and causes
Doc. 9.4, Monroe Doctrine, 1823	To create greater division between America and Europe; audience was isolationists	Endangers the economic interests that thrive on international markets (such as cotton)	Global	Effect: Less reliance on Europe Cause: Development of westward lands
Doc. 9.5, Indian Removal Act of 1830	To garner more land for westward expansion; audience was property holders	Does not address the needs of Native Americans and forgoes inalienable rights	National	Effect: More territory for expansion Cause: Spirit of Manifest Destiny
Doc. 9.6, Texas Declaration of Independence, 1836	To liberate Texas from Mexican control; audience was American landowners	Raises questions about the role of slavery	Regional	Effects: Greater autonomy for states' rights and limitations of federal control Cause: Expansion of slavery

Step 3

Main point: Although westward expansion increased the United States' political and economic power, it also led to the growth of oppressive institutions like slavery and the removal of Native Americans from their lands.

Supporting points: Regionally, nationally, and globally, westward expansion meant more wealth and prosperity for Americans but also limited the capacity of the federal government to ensure equality among all people who lived within its borders. This pattern can be seen in Documents 9.4, 9.5, and 9.6. (Discuss all three documents.)

PUTTING IT ALL TOGETHER

Revisiting the Main Point

- Analyze the connection between westward expansion, economics, and regional interests in the first half of the nineteenth century.
- What political debates were inspired by westward expansion? To what extent were these political debates based on moral considerations?
- How did environmental factors shape American expansionism?

 ## Organizing and Outlining a Reason-Based Historical Argument

In examining ways to support a historical argument, previous chapters have focused on the following areas:

- Patterns in evidence
- Synthesizing written and visual text—knowing what and when to quote

In addition, you should think about different ways of organizing and presenting your points and evidence. A solid organizational structure is an important foundation for making sound historical arguments.

One effective way to organize your evidence is to arrange it in a way that reflects the reasoning behind your position. Typically, you will rely on one of two types of reasoning:

Inductive reasoning is the process of making claims or arguments that are based on generalizations about specific facts, examples, and other evidence. When you use inductive reasoning, you don't necessarily provide absolute proof for your argument, but you do present strong evidence for it.

Deductive reasoning is a process of logically linking specific premises with conclusions.

When you organize your argument around an inductive approach, you work from the "top down," beginning with a specific event, observation, or example and then expanding into a general statement that represents a wider context. For example, consider the Webster-Ashburton Treaty (1842), which determined the northwestern border with Canada but left unresolved the issues that related to the occupation of the Oregon Territory. An inductive approach to examining westward expansion would begin with an analysis of the Webster-Ashburton Treaty and then expand to a discussion of the political or international issues that related to such expansion. Using this inductive model, a logical conclusion would be that the Webster-Ashburton Treaty reflected an American domestic policy that put national interests ahead of international relations. In general, the more significant an event, the more likely that a conclusion (or claim) that is drawn inductively is logical. Visually, such an arrangement appears as a triangle:

Specific event, observation, or example

General statement

When you use a deductive approach, you reason from the "top down," beginning with a pattern of examples, observations, or events from which a main point or claim can be inferred. For example, the Webster-Ashburton Treaty (1842) was followed by the Democratic Party Platform (1844), which advocated the annexation of the Oregon Territory as part of the party's domestic policy. A pattern thus emerges between these two documents, and a logical conclusion (similar to what you arrived at inductively above) would be that the doctrine of Manifest Destiny challenged British or international relations. Such an arrangement appears as an inverted triangle:

Series of examples, observations, or events

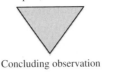

Concluding observation

Both the inductive and the deductive approaches to organization can be applied to debates about westward expansion during an era when the rights of individual states often clashed with the interests of the federal government. A review of state or regional issues deductively leads to a review of the role of the federal government. Similarly, a discussion of a singular state or regional issue inductively presents a discussion about the national or global status.

Consider the following prompt:

> What political debates were inspired by westward expansion? To what extent were these political debates based on moral considerations?

STEP 1 *Understand the prompt, and identify the key words*

For a review of this step, see Building AP® Writing Skills in Chapter 1 (p. 22).

STEP 2 *Generate a working thesis*

For a review of this step, see Building AP® Writing Skills in Chapters 1 through 5 (pp. 22, 51, 79, 111, 142).

STEP 3 *Identify and organize your evidence*

Determine the political debates as presented in this chapter. You may use previous factors to help organize your evidence (for example, economic, geographic, military, and legislative). Use the following chart to identify your evidence, and determine whether a moral consideration figured into the debate. Your determination represents an inductive approach.

Document	Political debate	Moral consideration?
Debates over the Missouri Compromise	Should the expansion of slavery be limited?	Slaves as property; individual states' rights
	What role is played by Native Americans in westward expansion?	
	Does Manifest Destiny mean isolationism from Europe?	
	Was the Anglo-Texans' revolt against Mexico the same as the American colonists' revolution against Great Britain?	
	What economic gains were achieved from the Louisiana Purchase? Who gained the most?	

For example, consider the following analysis of Two Opinions on the Missouri Crisis of 1819 (Doc 9.2):

> Senator Rufus King's speech about extending the role of the federal government to limit slavery addresses the powers that the federal government had to allow a new state into the union and restrict the spread of slavery. This is a legal argument.
>
> Senator Freeman Walker's speech about limiting the role of the federal government to limit states' rights concerns the power of the government to regulate commerce. But there is an implied moral dilemma in terms of individual state autonomy.
>
> Thus, the debate between these two over the expansion of slavery implicity involved morality, but this morality had less to do with human rights and more to do with states' rights.

STEP 4 *Outline your response*

Determine your organizational approach. Use both inductive and deductive methods of organization in your response.

To develop full, coherent outlines, think of an outline in anatomical terms, as both the skeleton of your essay and the muscles that surround that skeleton. The organizational approach (whether an inductive or a deductive model) acts as the skeleton. This is only one part of the outline.

The muscle of your outline supports your claims with at least two substantive pieces of evidence. Having only one example may oversimplify your claim. In your outline, each body paragraph would have the following:

- Claim 1 (which becomes the first sentence of the body paragraph)
  - A. Evidence 1 with explanation
  - B. Evidence 2 with explanation
- Claim 2 (which may represent an inductive or a deductive method)
  - A. Evidence 1 with explanation
  - B. Evidence 2 with explanation

I. Introduction

   The introduction can feature a working **thesis** that introduces the different types of debates and offers reasons that some political debates lent themselves more readily to issues of morality.

II. Political debates with a moral consideration (claim)

   Individual body paragraphs follow an inductive model. The example is cited and is followed by a statement about the nation's perspective on morality. It is helpful to classify the political debates in a reasonable way. This outline suggests debates with and without moral consideration, but you also may organize the debates as a continuum where you look at them as increasingly or decreasingly moral. Either way, the debates you discuss will be your evidence.

III. Political debates without a moral consideration (claim and evidence)

IV. Conclusion

   The final paragraph represents a deductive model. Based on the prior examples, the essay reaches a concluding statement about the level of morality within political debates in this country.

STEP 5 *Draft your essay*

Race and Democracy

America's complex history with race changes during this time period. Westward expansion and the exclusion of Native Americans suggest that President Andrew Jackson pushed for an elitist view of the ruling class. At the same time, the early part of the nineteenth century saw an increase in abolitionists and a strong economy that required contributions from an ever-expanding workforce. The Second Great Awakening saw the beginnings of real reform in the social and economic spheres of America.

You have read various sources that illustrate different approaches toward reform during this period. Now read the two passages below, and consider the extent to which each perspective on the Jacksonian legacy accurately reflects the spirit of this era.

> The Jacksonian South's political discussion of race and slavery revealed a variety of racial attitudes and ideologies ranging from exclusion and marginalization at one end of the spectrum to complete subordination of African Americans at the other end, with a bewildering array of selectively cobbled together variations on either the exclusion or the subordination themes, or both, lying in between. Full-voiced advocates of exclusion sought either to remove African Americans from southern society altogether, or, more realistically, minimize the role of blacks, slave and free, in the civic, social, and economic life of the South. . . .
>
> —Lacy K. Ford, "Making the 'White Man's Country' White: Race, Slavery and State-Building in the Jacksonian South," *Journal of the Early Republic* 19, no. 4 (Winter 1999): 719.

> The old image of the Jacksonians may have exaggerated their liberal egalitarianism; the new image, however, threatens to turn white supremacy into an essential feature of Jacksonian politics, as if racism and proslavery were inevitable ingredients of early nineteenth-century American democratic thought. . . . Such a jaundiced view, however, not only confuses the expediency of some Jacksonian leaders with race hatred. It also slights those Jacksonians who, as early as the 1830s, took principled stands against slavery and against the racism that justified slavery. It ignores the vital contributions these antislavery Jacksonians made toward enlarging the antislavery cause. It suggests that the Jacksonians left behind a single odious legacy on slavery and race, when in fact their legacy was much more complex.
>
> —Sean Wilentz, "Slavery, Antislavery, and Jacksonian Democracy," in *The Market Revolution in America: Social, Political, and Religious Expressions, 1800–1880*, ed. Melvyn Stokes and Stephen Conway (Richmond: University Press of Virginia, 1996), 202–224.

Using the excerpts, respond to the following prompts:

1. Briefly explain one major difference between Ford's and Wilentz's historical interpretations on the perspective of slavery.

2. Briefly explain how one document from the time period that is not explicitly mentioned in the excerpts could be used to support either excerpt.

3. Briefly explain how one document from Chapter 7, 8, or 9 could be used to support the excerpt you did not choose in the second prompt above.

CHAPTER 10

Expansionism: Part 2

The end of the Mexican-American War in 1848 represented only a momentary pause in the United States' territorial and economic expansion in the nineteenth century. Between the 1850s and the 1870s, American policy makers and citizens framed expansion as the country's destiny. During these thirty years (even in the midst of the Civil War), the republic's expansion—through trade, conquest, and settlement and to the eastern reaches of the Pacific Ocean, the Great Plains of the American continent, the western forest of the Oregon Territory in the Northwest, the shores of Caribbean islands, and the coasts of the Gulf of Mexico—appeared boundless.

But this growth fostered conflicts that raised questions about the elasticity of American ideology. Could Irish Catholic immigrants integrate into a republic that claimed universal rights but separated church from state in the First Amendment? Could subjects of the Japanese emperor embrace the concept of free trade and open borders without fear of conquest and loss of cultural integrity? Would a mass resettlement of Americans to new farmland west of the Mississippi fulfill the ideals of the Declaration of Independence? After a war to end racial involuntary servitude of African Americans, would American Indians enjoy the equal rights guaranteed by the new Fourteenth and Fifteenth Amendments?

Seeking the Main Point

As you read the documents that follow, keep these broad questions in mind. These questions will help you understand the relationship between the documents in this chapter and the historical changes that they represent. As you reflect on these questions, determine which themes and which documents best address them.

- In what ways did the concept of Manifest Destiny shape Americans' racial and ethnic identities during this period?
- How did changes in production and transportation shape government policies between 1844 and 1877?
- Analyze the ways in which the environment and the search for resources shaped regional, economic, and political identities and also political developments during this period.
- How did internal and international migration affect US politics and society during this period?
- How did expansionist policies during this period contribute to political and constitutional debates?

Conquest West

DOCUMENT 10.1 | JAMES K. POLK, War Message
1846

James K. Polk (1795–1849) ran for the nomination of the Democratic Party in 1844 on a ticket that promised to annex the independent Republic of Texas (even though it was still claimed by Mexico) and to rival Great Britain for control of the Oregon Territory. After the Mexican army attacked American forces in the Republic of Texas, President Polk made the following war address to the US Senate.

... The Mexican Government ..., after a long-continued series of menaces, have at last invaded our territory, and shed the blood of our fellow-citizens on our own soil. ...

In my message at the commencement of the present session, I informed you that, upon the earnest appeal, both of the congress and convention of Texas, I had ordered an efficient military force to take a position "between the Nueces and the Del Norte [two rivers in southeastern Texas]." This had become necessary, to meet a threatened invasion of Texas by the Mexican forces, for which extensive military preparations had been made. The invasion was threatened solely because Texas had determined, in accordance with a solemn resolution of the Congress of the United States, to annex herself to our Union; and, under these circumstances, it was plainly our duty to extend our protection over her citizens and soil.

This force was concentrated at Corpus Christi, and remained there until after I had received such information from Mexico as rendered it probable, if not certain, that the Mexican government would refuse to receive our envoy. ...

... It became, therefore, of urgent necessity to provide for the defence of that portion of our country. Accordingly, on the 13th of January last, instructions were issued to the general in command of these troops to occupy the left bank of the Del Norte. This river which is the southwestern boundary of the state of Texas, is an exposed frontier. ...

The movement of the troops to the Del Norte was made by the commanding general, under positive instructions to abstain from all aggressive acts toward Mexico or Mexican citizens, and to regard the relations between that republic and the United States as peaceful, unless she should declare war, or commit acts of hostility indicative of a state of war. He was specially directed to protect private property and respect personal rights. ...

The Mexican forces at Matamoras assumed a belligerent attitude, and, on the 12th of April, General Ampudia, then in command, notified General Taylor to break up his camp within twenty-four hours, and to retire beyond the Nueces river; and, in the event of his failure to comply with these demands, announced that arms, and arms alone, must decide the question. But no open act of hostility was committed until the 24th of April. On that day, General Arista, who had succeeded to the command of the Mexican forces, communicated to General Taylor that "he considered hostilities commenced, and should prosecute them." A party of dragoons, of sixty-three men and officers, were on the same day despatched from the American camp up the Rio del Norte, on its left bank, to ascertain whether the Mexican troops had crossed or were preparing to cross the river, "became engaged with a large body of these troops, and after a short affair, in which some sixteen were killed and wounded, appear to have been surrounded and compelled to surrender."

The grievous wrongs perpetrated by Mexico upon our citizens throughout a long period of years remain unredressed; and solemn treaties, pledging her public faith for this redress, have been disregarded. A government either unable or unwilling to enforce the execution of such treaties, fails to perform one of its plainest duties.

Robert Tomes and John Laird Wilson, *Battles of America by Sea and Land* (New York: James S. Virtue, 1878), 585, 587–588.

PRACTICING Historical Thinking

Identify: Identify the chief reasons that Polk provides for engaging in hostilities with Mexico.

Analyze: Infer what Texans' motivations might be for annexing themselves to the United States.

Evaluate: To what extent is Polk's argument based on the Jeffersonian ideals of inalienable rights?

DOCUMENT 10.2 | ABRAHAM LINCOLN, "Spot Resolutions"
1847

Representative Abraham Lincoln (1809–1865), Whig of Illinois, was speaking for the majority of the American Whig Party in Congress when he issued the following "spot resolutions" to protest President Polk's war on Mexico (Doc. 10.1). "Spot resolutions" refers to Lincoln's demand that the president show the exact spot where Mexican forces killed American citizens on American soil (which was one of Polk's justifications for the war).

Resolved by the House of Representatives, That the President of the United States be respectfully requested to inform this House—

1st. Whether the spot on which the blood of our citizens was shed, as in his messages declared, was or was not within the territory of Spain, at least after the treaty of 1819, until the Mexican revolution.

2d. Whether that spot is or is not within the territory which was wrested from Spain by the revolutionary Government of Mexico.

3d. Whether that spot is or is not within a settlement of people, which settlement has existed ever since long before the Texas revolution, and until its inhabitants fled before the approach of the United States army.

4th. Whether that settlement is or is not isolated from any and all other settlements by the Gulf and the Rio Grande on the south and west, and by wide uninhabited regions on the north and east.

5th. Whether the people of that settlement, or a majority of them, or any of them, have ever submitted themselves to the government or laws of Texas or the United States, by consent or compulsion, either by accepting office, or voting at elections, or paying tax, or serving on juries, or having process served upon them, or in any other way.

6th. Whether the people of that settlement did or did not flee from the approach of the United States army, leaving unprotected their homes and their growing crops, *before* the blood was shed, as in the messages stated; and whether the first blood so shed, was or was not shed within the enclosure of one of the people who had thus fled from it.

7th. Whether our *citizens*, whose blood was shed, as in his messages declared, were or were not, at that time, armed officers and soldiers, sent into that settlement by the military order of the President, through the Secretary of War.

8th. Whether the military force of the United States was or was not sent into that settlement after General Taylor had more than once intimated to the War Department that, in his opinion, no such movement was necessary to the defence or protection of Texas.

Henry Raymond, *The Life and Public Services of Abraham Lincoln* (New York: Derby and Miller, 1865), 35–36.

PRACTICING Historical Thinking

Identify: Summarize Lincoln's eight questions in three sentences or less.

Analyze: What is the implied message of these questions?

Evaluate: Compare and contrast the ways in which Lincoln's message and James K. Polk's message (Doc. 10.1) present differing views on Manifest Destiny.

| **"Commodore Perry at the Loo Choo Isles,"** *New York Daily Times*

1853

Commodore Matthew Calbraith Perry (1794–1858) first visited Japan on the orders of President Franklin Pierce to pursue trade opportunities with Japan, which had largely closed itself to trade with the West. On his arrival in Japan in 1853, Perry threatened naval intervention if the kingdom refused American appeals for a trade relationship, and at the Convention of Kanagawa (1854), Japan opened two ports to trade with the United States. The *New York Daily Times* (later the *New York Times*) published this report.

From the *Freeman's Journal*

At last accounts Commodore Perry and Squadron had sailed from the Loo-Choo Islands, the southernmost group of the Japan Empire. Private letters from one of the officers of his Flag-ship give some interesting particulars not published in the Journals. Under date of July 1, this gentleman writes that: "On the 6th of June we marched to Shudi, the capital of the Loo-Choo Islands, with all the officers, marines and sailors, with artillery, &c. It was a march of some three or four miles, over a magnificent paved road, through a rich and highly cultivated country. The clumps of trees and other ornamental embellishments of the way astonished us much less than our heavy cloth uniforms and accoutrements astonished the timid natives, who gathered along our road to gape at us with wonder and poorly concealed disquietude. They cannot tell what to make of this ambiguous demonstration. Poor devils! Their Japanese masters will find out one of these days. The object of this visit was to be received by the Regent of these Islands at his Royal Palace. The honor of the visit may have rebounded to his tawny Excellency, but it is certain the pleasure, such as it was, was all on our side. They are suspicious, and very ill at ease. Commodore Perry was carried in a sedan chair. The rest of us gave the natives a specimen of how Yankees, heavily accoutred, can march under a scorching sun on foot. If the Japanese give us a friendly reception, all will be smooth. If not, we will have a far more effective squadron here, one of these days, and teach them conformity to Christian manners.

"The *Susquehanna* is one of the vessels that disgrace our Navy, and gives boundless annoyances to her officers. The machinery is too light, and is so out of order that the vessel is unfit for service. It is a shame that she is not called home and fitted up under competent inspection.

"Our American Speculators should be on hand. *Commodore Perry has made a purchase at Port Loyd*, on one of the Bonin Islands, north of east of the Loo-Choo group. This must become a dépôt for our steamers. The land is inviting, and is, I think, destined to become a flourishing American colony."

"The Japan Expedition.—Commodore Perry at the Loo-Choo Isles," *New York Daily Times (1851–1857),* October 20, 1853, 1.

PRACTICING Historical Thinking

Identify: Describe the reception that Perry received in Japan, according to the officer who is quoted in the *New York Daily Times.*

Analyze: Why does the officer state that the Japanese are "suspicious, and very ill at ease"?

Evaluate: How did the development of trade relations in the Far East influence the United States' domestic economies? Use your classroom notes and textbook for additional information.

DOCUMENT 10.4 | American (or Know-Nothing) Party Platform
1856

The American (or Know-Nothing) Party sought to reduce immigration to the United States, especially the immigration of Catholics who were arriving from Ireland to urban areas of the Northeast. The Know-Nothing Party took its name from the nativist (or anti-immigrant) secret society from which it grew. The society's members denied the existence of the organization by "knowing nothing" about it. Although the Know-Nothings nominated former president Millard Fillmore in 1856, support for the party declined in popularity after the election.

Resolved, That the American democracy place their trust in the intelligence, the patriotism, and the discriminating justice of the American people. . . .

3. *Americans must rule America;* and to this end *native*-born citizens should be selected for all state, federal, and municipal offices of government employment, in preference to all others. *Nevertheless,*

4. Persons born of American parents residing temporarily abroad, should be entitled to all the rights of native-born citizens.

5. No person should be selected for political station (whether of native or foreign birth), who recognizes any allegiance or obligation of any description to any foreign prince, potentate, or power, or who refuses to recognize the federal and state constitution (each within its sphere) as paramount to all other laws, as rules of political action. . . .

7. The recognition of the right of native-born and naturalized citizens of the United States, permanently residing in any territory thereof, to frame their

constitution and laws, and to regulate their domestic and social affairs in their own mode, subject only to the provisions of the federal constitution, with the privilege of admission into the Union whenever they have the requisite population for one Representative in Congress: *Provided, always,* that none but those who are citizens of the United States under the constitution and laws thereof, and who have a fixed residence in any such territory, ought to participate in the formation of the constitution or in the enactment of laws for said territory or state. . . .

9. A change in the laws of naturalization, making a continued residence of twenty-one years, of all not heretofore provided for, an indispensable requisite for citizenship hereafter, and excluding all paupers and persons convicted of crime from landing upon our shores; but no interference with the vested rights of foreigners.

10. Opposition to any union between church and state; no interference with religious faith or worship; and no test-oaths for office. . . .

13. Opposition to the reckless and unwise policy of the present administration in the general management of our national affairs, and more especially as shown in removing "Americans" (by designation) and conservatives in principle, from office, and placing foreigners and ultraists [abolitionists] in their places; as shown in a truckling subserviency to the stronger, and an insolent and cowardly bravado towards the weaker powers; as shown in reopening sectional agitation, by the repeal of the Missouri Compromise; as shown in granting to unnaturalized foreigners the right of suffrage in Kansas and Nebraska; as shown in its vacillating course on the Kansas and Nebraska question; as shown in the corruptions which pervade some of the departments of the government; as shown in disgracing meritorious naval officers through prejudice or caprice; and as shown in the blundering mismanagement of our foreign relations.

14. Therefore, to remedy existing evils and prevent the disastrous consequences otherwise resulting therefrom, we would build up the "American Party" upon the principles hereinbefore stated.

Walter Raleigh Houghton, *Conspectus of the History of Political Parties and the Federal Government* (Indianapolis, IN: Granger, Davis, 1880), 45.

PRACTICING Historical Thinking

Identify: Identify two features of the American Party's platform that are consistent with the United States Constitution.

Analyze: Who is the intended audience for this platform? Is it the same audience that was intended for the Sedition Act (Doc. 5.18) and the Alien Act? Refer to your textbook and your notes for information on the Alien Act.

Evaluate: To what extent is this party's platform inconsistent with international trade relations, such as those brokered by Commodore Matthew Calbraith Perry (Doc. 10.3)?

SKILL REVIEW | Periodization and Comparison

The first and second halves of the nineteenth century provide an opportunity to compare economic, political, and social trends. Consider the following prompt, which combines several historical thinking skills:

> Was the Civil War a turning point in the development of America's economic, political, and social identities? Or was the formation of this new American identity already in place prior to the Civil War?

STEP 1 Align documents from Chapters 9 and 10 that address similar trends.

Time period	Economic	Social	Political
1800–1848	Doc. 9.7, "On the Webster-Ashburton Treaty"	Doc. 9.8, Democratic Party Platform	Doc. 9.6, Texas Declaration of Independence
1844–1877	Doc. 10.3, "Commodore Perry at the Loo Choo Isles"	Doc. 10.4, American (or Know-Nothing) Party Platform	Doc. 10.2, Abraham Lincoln, "Spot Resolutions"

STEP 2 Write a complete paragraph that begins with a main point that answers the prompt and includes supporting points that synthesize the evidence.

DOCUMENT 10.5 | Homestead Act of 1862

Signed into law by President Abraham Lincoln during the Civil War, the Homestead Act of 1862 encouraged Americans to migrate west of the Mississippi River. Historically, legislative efforts to distribute government lands faced opposition from the South, but this act was passed after secession.

An Act to secure Homesteads to actual Settlers on the Public Domain

Be it enacted by the Senate and House of Representatives of the United States of America in Congress assembled, That any person who is the head of a family, or who has arrived at the age of twenty-one years and is a citizen of the United States, or who shall have filed his declaration of intention to become such, as required by the naturalization laws of the United States, and who has never borne arms against the United States government or given aid and comfort to its enemies, shall, from and after the first January, eighteen hundred and sixty-three, be entitled to enter one quarter section or a less quantity of unappropriated public lands, upon which said person may have filed a pre-emption claim, or which may, at the time the application is made, be subject to pre-emption at one dollar and twenty-five cents or less per acre; or eighty acres or less of such unappropriated lands at two dollars and fifty cents per acre, to be located in a body, in conformity to the legal subdivisions of the public lands, and after the same shall have been surveyed: *Provided*, That any person owning and residing on land may, under the provisions of this act, enter other land lying contiguous to his or her said land, which shall not, with the land so already owned and occupied, exceed in the aggregate one hundred and sixty acres.

Circular from the General Land Office Showing the Manner of Proceeding to Obtain Title to Public Lands (Washington, DC: Government Printing Office, 1870), 16.

PRACTICING Historical Thinking

Identify: Paraphrase the opportunities that were provided by the Homestead Act.

Analyze: In what ways would the North gain an advantage in encouraging migration west of the Mississippi?

Evaluate: As the labor force for both the North and the South was depleted by the war, who stood to gain and lose more by the Homestead Act? Explain.

DOCUMENT 10.6 | **Report from the Spotted Tail Indian Agency**
1877

By the last quarter of the nineteenth century, Native Americans had endured nearly a century of forced removal westward. By the end of the century, American policy makers increasingly sought ways to "civilize" native peoples by undermining traditional settlement and economic patterns and inculcating them with white American values. This excerpt is from the Secretary of the Interior's report to the president regarding Indian education.

The establishment of schools for the instruction of the young is gradually being extended among the Indian tribes under our control. The advantage to be derived from them will greatly depend upon their discipline and the course of instruction. As far as practicable, the attendance of Indian children should be made compulsory. Provision should be made for boarding children at the schools, to bring them more exclusively under the control of educational influences. One of the most important points is that they should be taught to speak and read the English language. Efforts have been made to establish and teach the grammar of Indian dialects and to use books printed in those dialects as a means of instruction. This is certainly a very interesting and meritorious philological work, but as far as the education of Indian children is concerned, the teaching of the English language must be considered infinitely more useful. If Indian children are to be civilized, they must learn the language of civilization.

They will become far more accessible to civilized ideas and ways of thinking when they are enabled to receive those ideas and ways of thinking through the most direct channel of expression. At first, their minds should not be over-burdened with too great a multitude of subjects of instruction, but turned to those practical accomplishments, proficiency in which is necessary to render civilized life possible. In addition to the most elementary schooling boys should be practically instructed in the various branches of husbandry, and girls should receive a good training in household duties and habits of cleanliness. In this way a young generation may be raised up far more open to civilizing influences of a higher kind and more fit for a peaceable and profitable intercourse with the white people.

Friends Intelligencer 34 (University of Michigan, 1877): 699.

PRACTICING Historical Thinking

Identify: What are the greatest obstacles to civilizing the Indians, according to this report?

Analyze: How different is this policy statement from earlier efforts to remove Indians from the native lands? Explain.

Evaluate: Determine the economic, political, and regional factors that influenced the creation of this policy.

APPLYING AP® Historical Thinking Skills

SKILL REVIEW | Synthesis

In the form of a complete essay—with an introduction that includes a thesis and supporting paragraphs that analyze the documents above and relevant information from your textbook and classroom notes—answer the following prompt:

> How did internal and international migration affect the politics and society of the United States from 1844 to 1877? Compare this period with 1800 to 1848 (Chapter 9). To what extent were the causes and effects of internal and international migration to and within North America similar during these two time periods? To what extent were they different?

STEP 1 _Analyzing evidence: content and sourcing_

Determine the effect of internal and international migration on the politics and society of the United States during the years 1844 to 1877. Complete the graphic organizer below.

Internal migration examples	International migration examples	Effect on the politics of the United States	Effect on the society of the United States
Doc. 10.4, American (or Know-Nothing) Party Platform	Doc. 10.1, James K. Polk, War Message		
Doc. 10.5, Homestead Act of 1862	Doc. 10.3, "Commodore Perry at the Loo Choo Isles"		

STEP 2 *Comparison and contrast*

To answer the prompt, you'll need to compare the migration policies and examples from the latter half of the nineteenth century with those from the earlier half (1800 to 1848). Begin with your notes from this chapter's first Applying AP® Historical Thinking Skills exercise (p. 243). Continue with a graphic organizer that is similar to the one above for the first half of the nineteenth century. You may use the first two columns or half of the above table as part of your new table, as is shown here:

1800–1848		1844–1877	
Internal migration examples	International migration examples	Internal migration examples	International migration examples
		Doc. 10.4, American (or Know-Nothing) Party Platform	Doc. 10.1, James K. Polk, War Message
		Doc. 10.5, Homestead Act of 1862	Doc. 10.3, "Commodore Perry at the Loo Choo Isles"

STEP 3 *Synthesis*

After you have completed the second graphic organizer, synthesize the causes and effects of internal and international migration for the entire time period. Determine at least four examples. Below is a table that can help you organize your thoughts.

Causes of migration, 1800–1877	Effects of migration, 1800–1877

PUTTING IT ALL TOGETHER

Revisiting the Main Point

- How did developments in labor and technology influence American expansion westward? To what extent did these developments contribute to domestic political conflicts?
- Describe three ways in which environmental factors contributed to regional identities in the United States between 1844 and 1877.
- In what ways did migration, both internal and from abroad, influence American politics?

BUILDING AP® WRITING SKILLS **Counterarguments in Historical Essays**

Any argument worth making has at least two credible perspectives, and nowhere is this more evident than in an examination of historical debates. A historical argument will have at least two audiences—those who agree and those who disagree. Staking a position and supporting that position become more effective when your argument acknowledges the credibility of those who do not agree with you. When you acknowledge **counterarguments** (positions that oppose your thesis or part of your thesis) in your essay, your own position gains credibility and strength. Failing to acknowledge counterarguments implies that you have not carefully considered alternative ideas on the matter, which harms your credibility.

Counterarguments work in several ways. One way is to acknowledge the other side early in your essay and then refute this other argument with additional evidence. By establishing the counterargument early in the essay, you position yourself to offer your opposing view, called a **refutation**. This tactic has the advantage of drawing in all audiences (those who agree with you and those who disagree) at the beginning of your essay.

Another way to use counterarguments is to present your own arguments first and follow them with the other argument. This method allows you to establish a more original position, rather than frame your argument in reaction to others. If your refutation occurs later in the essay, you are still obliged to conclude your essay by returning to the reasons that your initial claims rule the day.

The way to refute a counterargument is to present a better argument that is backed up with evidence. In Chapters 7 through 9, you learned about the kinds of evidence that offer credible support. Now is your chance to arrange that evidence in ways that will persuade multiple audiences. Consider the following prompt:

> How did developments in labor and technology influence American expansion westward? To what extent did these developments contribute to domestic political conflicts?

STEP 1 *Understand the prompt, and identify the key words*

This prompt, unlike previous prompts, provides *two* questions for you to consider. The key words *how* and *to what extent* ask for you to demonstrate your understanding of two cause-and-effect relationships.

STEP 2 *Generate a working thesis*

Consider and practice the use of subordination in your thesis statement.

STEP 3 *Identify and organize your evidence*

Given the more complex nature of this task, the following suggestions will provide some ideas on how to reflect that complexity in your writing.

- Use a categorical (point-by-point) outline.
- Avoid the either/or fallacy (or provide concessions).

Locating the counterargument means first considering what the opposing sides may be. This prompt features two influences of technological development—westward expansion and domestic political conflicts. There are potential arguments to consider that may run counter to your thesis.

Option 1

Note the construction of the prompt, and determine whether westward expansion opposed domestic political conflicts. The question asks you to reflect on a causal relationship. To what extent did westward expansion influence domestic political conflicts? A review of the documents of this chapter and your class notes suggests that technological influences did have differing effects and that many of the gains that westward expansion provided (by virtue of technological development) were offset by domestic political conflicts, which were highlighted by the Civil War.

Option 2

Consider how each stem of the prompt invites opposing views or counterarguments. Developments in labor and technology may have had both positive and negative influences on domestic policy. Consider, for example, the ongoing subjugation of native peoples or the rise of nativism in response to an international workforce.

Similarly, developments in labor and technology may have both fueled and reduced domestic political conflicts. For example, the depletion of the domestic workforce by legislation such as the Homestead Act created civil strife, but the act also encouraged greater prosperity and eased some of the financial burdens of the struggling Northern and Southern wartime economies.

When looking for counterarguments within a prompt, consider the following oppositions:

Positive/negative influences

Fueled/reduced

Supporters/opponents

Gains/losses

Expansion/restriction

Benefits/losses

Winners/losers

Access/marginalized

STEP 4 *Create an outline*

For this prompt, consider the options above in developing your argument, and create your outline accordingly. The counterargument may appear in any place in your outline. This exercise positions the counterargument early in the essay.

Outline

I. Introduction: This is your original position. It also may be your working thesis.

II. Counterargument(s)

A. Option 1: Developments in labor and technology had a positive influence on domestic policy.

B. Option 2: Developments in labor and technology had a negative influence on domestic policy.

III. Your argument: Provide support for the position that you presented in your introduction. Present your support in opposition to what you identified in the counterargument.

For example, if you selected option 1 above, then your counterargument would respond to this by pointing out why developments in labor and technology negatively influenced domestic policy.

Or if you selected option 2 above, then you would end your essay with a statement about why the lasting influence was more positive than negative.

IV. Conclusion

Note: It is possible to present several counterarguments throughout your essay rather than in the clear-cut division outlined above. For example, the prompt asks you to respond to two distinct claims—one on the causes of westward expansion and another on the influence of domestic policy. Because different causes of westward expansion could have had different influences on domestic policy, your outline may be nuanced as you separate counterarguments by distinct causes and effects. Here is an example of such an outline:

I. Introduction

II. Cause 1 of westward expansion

    A. Discouragement of domestic policy (counterargument)

    B. Encouragement of domestic policy

III. Cause 2 of westward expansion

    A. Discouragement of domestic policy (counterargument)

    B. Encouragement of domestic policy

IV. Conclusion

STEP 5 *Draft your essay*

The Union Undone?

By 1860, debates over territorial expansion, regional economic interests, and demographic changes revolved around the issue of slavery. It was the one abiding issue that consistently divided the nation along sectional lines.

At the time of the election of 1860, many Americans, especially those who lived in slaveholding states, believed that the constitutional system no longer protected their rights and that the constitutionally elected president, Abraham Lincoln, intended to end the republican system that had been instituted by the Framers. By Lincoln's inauguration in March 1861, eleven Southern states had declared their independence from the United States.

Seeking the Main Point

As you read the documents that follow, keep these broad questions in mind. These questions will help you understand the relationship between the documents in this chapter and the historical changes that they represent. As you reflect on these questions, determine which themes and which documents best address them.

* In what ways did the economies and societies of the North and South help shape each region's distinct identity?
* In what ways were the debates over slavery in the 1850s economic arguments? In what ways were they moral arguments? To what extent did these debates divide along political party lines?
* How did internal migration during the 1840s and 1850s fuel sectional antagonism between the North and the South?

The Breakdown of Compromise

DOCUMENT 11.1 | **JOHN C. CALHOUN, "The Clay Compromise Measures"**
| 1850

Senator John C. Calhoun (1782–1850) a South Carolina Democrat, wrote this reaction to the "Clay Compromise Measures" of Henry Clay (1777–1852) (Whig, Kentucky) and Stephen A. Douglas (1813–1861) (Democrat, Illinois). Clay's compromise tried to resolve the debates over the future of slavery in the lands acquired at the end of the Mexican-American War (1846–1848). These measures eventually became the Compromise of 1850.

. . . How can the Union be saved? To this I answer, there is but one way by which it can be, and that is, by adopting such measures as will satisfy the States belonging to the southern section that they can remain in the Union consistently with their honor and their safety. There is, again, only one way by which that can be effected, and that is, by removing the causes by which this belief has been produced. Do *that*, and discontent will cease, harmony and kind feelings between the sections be restored, and every apprehension of danger to the Union removed. The question then is, By what can this be done? . . . There is but one way by which it can with any certainty; and that is, by a full and final settlement, on the principle of justice, of all the questions at issue between the two sections. . . .

But can this be done? Yes, easily; not by the weaker party, for it can of itself do nothing—not even protect itself—but by the stronger. The North has only to will it to accomplish it—to do justice by conceding to the South an equal right in the acquired territory, and to do her duty by causing the stipulations relative to fugitive slaves to be faithfully fulfilled—to cease the agitation of the slave question, and to provide for the insertion of a provision in the Constitution, by an amendment, which will restore to the South in substance the power she possessed of protecting herself, before the equilibrium between the sections was destroyed by the action of this Government. There will be no difficulty in devising such a provision—one that will protect the South, and which at the same time will improve and strengthen the Government, instead of impairing and weakening it.

The Congressional Globe, US Senate, 31st Congress, 1st Session, 1850, Library of Congress, "American Memory: A Century of Lawmaking for a New Nation—U.S. Congressional Documents and Debates, 1874–1875," 453, 455, http://memory.loc.gov.

PRACTICING Historical Thinking

Identify: What is Calhoun's main argument?

Analyze: What does Calhoun mean by his use of the word "equilibrium"?

Evaluate: To what extent was the return of fugitive slaves to the South the main reason for Calhoun's argument?

DOCUMENT 11.2 | HARRIET BEECHER STOWE, *Uncle Tom's Cabin*
1852

Harriet Beecher Stowe's (1811–1896) novel, *Uncle Tom's Cabin: or, Life among the Lowly*, sold over 300,000 copies during its first year of publication. Its strongly antislavery themes, vivid characters, and sentimentalism helped many white readers in the North understand and feel deeply about the plight of slaves. In the following passage, southern slave owner Augustine St. Clare discusses the institution with his Northern abolitionist cousin, Ophelia.

Miss Ophelia stopped her knitting, and looked surprised; and St. Clare, apparently enjoying her astonishment, went on.

"You seem to wonder; but if you will get me fairly at it, I'll make a clean breast of it. This cursed business, accursed of God and man, what is it? Strip it of all its ornament, run it down to the root and nucleus of the whole, and what is it? Why, because my brother Quashy is ignorant and weak, and I am intelligent and strong—because I know how, and *can* do it—therefore, I may steal all he has, keep it, and give him only such and so much as suits my fancy. Whatever is too hard, too dirty, too disagreeable for me, I may set Quashy to doing. Because I don't like work, Quashy shall work. Because the sun burns me, Quashy shall stay in the sun. Quashy shall earn the money, and I will spend it. Quashy shall lie down in every puddle, that I may walk over dryshod. Quashy shall do my will, and not his, all the days of his mortal life, and have such a chance of getting to heaven at last as I find convenient. This I take to be about what slavery *is*. I defy anybody on earth to read our slave-code, as it stands in our law-books, and make anything else of it. Talk of the *abuses* of slavery! Humbug! The *thing itself* is the essence of all abuse! And the only reason why the land don't sink under it, like Sodom and Gomorrah, is because it is *used* in a way infinitely better than it is. For pity's sake, for shame's sake, because we are men born of women, and not savage beasts, many of us do not, and dare not—we would *scorn* to use the full power which our savage laws put into our hands. And he who goes the furthest, and does the worst, only uses within limits the power that the law gives him."

St. Clare had started up, and, as his manner was when excited, was walking, with hurried steps, up and down the floor. His fine face, classic as that of a Greek statue, seemed actually to burn with the fervour of his feelings. His large blue eyes flashed, and he gestured with an unconscious eagerness. Miss Ophelia had never seen him in this mood before, and she sat perfectly silent.

"I declare to you," said he, suddenly stopping before his cousin—"it's no sort of use to talk or to feel on this subject—but I declare to you, there have been times when I have thought, if the whole country would sink, and hide all this injustice and misery from the light, I would willingly sink with it. When I have been traveling up and down on our boats, or about on my collecting tours, and reflected that every brutal, disgusting, mean, low-lived fellow I met, was allowed by our laws to become absolute despot of as many men, women, and children, as he could cheat, steal, or gamble money enough to buy—when I have seen such men in actual ownership of helpless children, of young girls and women—I have been ready to curse my country, to curse the human race!"

"Augustine! Augustine!" said Miss Ophelia, "I'm sure you've said enough. I never, in my life, heard anything like this; even at the North."

"At the North!" said St. Clare, with a sudden change of expression, and resuming something of his habitual careless tone. "Pooh! you northern folks are cold-blooded; you are cool in everything! You can't begin to curse up hill and down, as we can when we get fairly at it."

"Well, but the question is—" said Miss Ophelia.

"O, yes, to be sure, the *question is*—and a deuce of a question it is!—How came *you* in this state of sin and misery? Well, I shall answer in the good old words you used to teach me, Sundays. I came so by ordinary generation. My servants were my father's, and, what is more, my mother's; and now they are mine, they and their increase, which bids fair to be a pretty considerable item. My father, you know, came first from New England; and he was just such another man as your father—a regular old Roman; upright, energetic, noble-minded, with an iron will. Your father settled down in New England, to rule over rocks and stones, and to force an existence out of Nature; and mine settled in Louisiana, to rule over men and women, and force existence out of them. . . .

"Now, an aristocrat, you know, the world over, has no human sympathies, beyond a certain line in society. In England the line is in one place, in Burmah in another, and in America in another; but the aristocrat of all these countries never goes over it. What would be hardship and distress and injustice in his own class, is a cool matter of course in another one. My father's dividing line was that of colour. *Among his equals*, never was a man more just and generous; but he considered the negro, through all possible gradations of colour, as an intermediate link between man and animals, and graded all his ideas of justice or generosity on this hypothesis. I suppose, to be sure, if anybody had asked him, plump and fair, whether they had human immortal souls, he might have hemmed and hawed, and said 'Yes.' But my father was not a man much troubled with spiritualism; religious sentiment he had none, beyond a veneration for God, as decidedly the head of the upper classes." . . .

St. Clare rested his head on his hands, and did not speak for some minutes. After a while, he looked up, and went on:—

"What poor, mean trash this whole business of human virtue is! A mere matter, for the most part, of latitude and longitude, and geographical position, acting with natural temperament. The greater part is nothing but an accident. Your father, for example, settles in Vermont, in a town where all are, in fact, free and equal; becomes a regular church member and deacon, and in due time joins an Abolitionist society, and thinks us all little better than heathens. Yet he is, for all the world, in constitution and habit, a duplicate of my father. I can see it leaking out in fifty different ways—just that same strong, overbearing, dominant spirit. You know very well how impossible it is to persuade some of the folks in your village that Squire Sinclair does not feel above them. The fact is, though he has fallen on democratic times, and embraced a democratic theory, he is to the heart an aristocrat, as much as my father, who ruled over five or six hundred slaves."

Harriet Beecher Stowe, *Uncle Tom's Cabin: or, Life among the Lowly* (London: Ingram, Cooke, 1852), 175–180.

PRACTICING Historical Thinking

Identify: What is the contrast between the two fathers described in this excerpt?

Analyze: Why might St. Clare state that many slave owners "would *scorn* to use the full power which our savage laws put into our hands"?

Evaluate: In what ways does Stowe present the issue of slavery as a moral one?

DOCUMENT 11.3 | MARY HENDERSON EASTMAN, *Aunt Phillis's Cabin*
1852

Mary Henderson Eastman (1818–1887), like many Southerners, was appalled by Harriet Beecher Stowe's powerful use of vivid images and sentimentality in *Uncle Tom's Cabin* (Doc. 11.2). She published *Aunt Phillis's Cabin: or, Southern Life as It Is* as a reaction to Stowe's book. In the following passage, Southerner Arthur Weston discusses slavery with Abel Johnson, a fellow student at Yale University in New Haven, Connecticut.

"Now," said Abel, "having a couple of particularly good cigars, where did we leave off?"

"It's too warm for argument," said Arthur, watching the curling of the gray smoke as it ascended.

"We need not argue," said Abel; "I want to catechize you."

"Begin."

"Do you think that the African slave-trade can be defended?"

"No, assuredly not."

"Well," said Abel, "how can you defend your right to hold slaves as property in the United States?"

"Abel," said Arthur, "when a Yankee begins to question there is no reason to suppose he ever intends to stop. I shall answer your queries from the views of Governor Hammond, of Carolina. They are at least worthy of consideration. What right have you New England people to the farms you are now holding?"

"The right of owning them," said Abel.

"From whom did you get them?" asked Arthur.

"Our fathers."

"And how did they get them?"

"From the Red men, their original owners."

"Well," said Arthur, "we all know how these transactions were conducted all over the country. We wanted the lands of the Red men, and we took them. Sometimes they were purchased, sometimes they were wrested; always, the Red men were treated with injustice. They were driven off, slaughtered, and taken as slaves. Now, God as clearly gave these lands to the Red men as he gave life and freedom to the African. Both have been unjustly taken away."

"But," said Abel, "we hold property in land, you in the bodies and souls of men."

"Granted," said Arthur; "but we have as good a right to our *property* as you to yours—we each inherit it from our fathers. You must know that slaves were recognized as *property* under the constitution. John Q. Adams, speaking of the protection extended to the peculiar interests of the South, makes these remarks: 'Protected by the advantage of representation on this floor, protected by the stipulation in the constitution for the recovery of fugitive slaves, protected by the guarantee in the constitution to the owners of this *species of property*, against domestic violence.' It was considered in England as any other kind of commerce; so that you cannot deny our right to consider them as property now, as well as then."

"But can you advocate the enslaving of your fellow man?" said Abel.

"No," said Arthur, "if you put the question in that manner; but if you come to the point, and ask me if I can conscientiously hold in bondage slaves in the South, I say yes, without the slightest hesitation. I'll tell you why. You must agree with me, if the Bible allow slavery there is no sin it. Now, the Bible does allow it. You must read those letters of Governor Hammond to Clarkson, the English Abolitionist. The tenth commandment, your mother taught you, no doubt: 'thou shalt not covet thy neighbor's house, thou shalt not covet thy neighbor's wife, nor his *man-servant*, nor his *maid-servant*, nor his ox, nor his ass, nor any thing that is thy neighbor's.' These are the words of God, and as such, should be obeyed strictly. In the most solemn manner, the man-servant and the maid-servant are considered the *property* of thy neighbor. Generally the word is rendered slave. This command includes all classes of servants; there is the Hebrew-brother, who shall go out in the seventh year, and the hired-servant, and those 'purchased from the heathen round about,' who were to be bondmen forever. In Leviticus, speaking of the 'bondmen of the heathen which shall be round about,' God says, 'And ye shall take them for an inheritance, for your children after you, to inherit them for a possession; they shall be your bondmen forever.' I consider that God permitted slavery when he made laws for the master and the slave, therefore I am justified in holding slaves. In the times of our Saviour, when slavery existed in its worst form, it was regarded as one of the conditions of human society; it is evident Abolition was not shadowed forth by Christ or his apostles. 'Do unto all men as ye would have them do unto you,' is a general command, inducing charity and kindness among all classes of men; and does not authorize interference with the established customs of society. If, according to this precept of Christ, I am obliged to manumit [free] my slaves, you are equally forced to purchase them. If I were a slave, I would have my master free me; if you were a slave, and your owner would not give you freedom, you would have some rich man to buy you. From the early ages of the world, there existed the poor and the rich, the master and the slave.

"It would be far better for the Southern slaves, if our institution, as regards them, were left to 'gradual mitigation and decay, which time *may* bring about. The course of the Abolitionists, while it does nothing to destroy this institution, greatly adds to its hardships.' Tell me that 'man-stealing' is a sin, and I will agree with you, and will insist that the Abolitionists are guilty of it. In my opinion, those who consider slavery a sin, challenge the truth of the Bible.

"Besides, Abel," continued Arthur, "what right have you to interfere? Your Northern States abolished slavery when it was their interest to do so: let us do the same. In the meantime, consider the condition of these dirty vagabonds, these free blacks, who are begging from me every time I go into the street. I met one the other day, who had a most lamentable state of things to report. He had rheumatism, and a cough, and he spit blood, and he had no tobacco, and he was hungry, and he had the toothache. I gave him twenty-five cents as a sort of panacea, and advised him to travel South and get a good master. He took the money, but not the advice."

Mary Henderson Eastman, *Aunt Phillis's Cabin: or, Southern Life as It Is* (Philadelphia, PA: Lippincott, Grambo, 1852), 132–135.

PRACTICING Historical Thinking

Identify: According to Abel, how does the Bible justify slaveholding?

Analyze: Why does Abel acknowledge the theft of land from the Native Americans at the beginning of this passage?

Evaluate: Find three ways in which Abel's argument counters St. Clare's from *Uncle Tom's Cabin* (Doc. 11.2). How does each argument support the beliefs of each book's author?

| Map of Kansas-Nebraska Act

1854

The Kansas-Nebraska Act (1854) allowed the Kansas and Nebraska Territories to be available for a transcontinental railroad but gained Southern support only because it also allowed popular sovereignty (that is, a vote by residents) to decide whether slavery would be allowed in any states that might be created in the territories. By opening territories to slavery north of Missouri's southern border, the Kansas-Nebraska Act negated the Missouri Compromise (1820) and led to attacks and counterattacks by pro- and antislavery forces in Kansas between 1854 and 1861.

POPULAR SOVEREIGNTY ESTABLISHED
Compromise of 1850/Kansas-Nebraska Act of 1854

Free states

Free territory

Popular sovereignty
(decision on slavery left to the
people of the territory)

Slave states

Slave territory

PRACTICING Historical Thinking

Identify: Examine the borders of the territory that were affected by the Kansas-Nebraska Act. How would voters' decisions in the open territories affect the balance of slave and free states and territories?

Analyze: How could both the North and the South stand to gain economically from the Kansas-Nebraska Act?

Evaluate: To what extent could popular sovereignty have contributed to the Civil War?

In this election song from 1856, Republican presidential candidate John C. Frémont (1813–1890) is portrayed as the protector of American liberty. During the election, the Republican Party's slogan supported restricting the spread of slavery in the West.

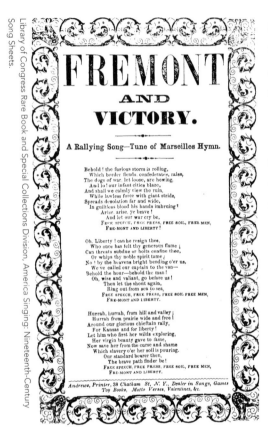

LYRICS (enlarged for readability)

Behold ! the furious storm is rolling,
  Which border fiends, confederates, raise,
The dogs of war, let loose, are howling,
  And lo ! our infant cities blaze,
And shall we calmly view the ruin,
  While lawless force with giant stride,
Spreads desolation far and wide,
  In guiltless blood his hands imbruing?
    Arise, arise, ye brave !
    And let our war cry be,
    FREE SPEECH, FREE PRESS, FREE SOIL, FREE MEN,
    FRE-MONT AND LIBERTY !

Oh, Liberty ! can he resign thee,
  Who once has felt thy generous flame ¿
Can threats subdue or bolts confine thee,
  Or whips thy noble spirit tame ¿
No ! by the heavens bright bending o'er us,
  We've called our captain to the van—
Behold the hour—behold the man !
  Oh, wise and valiant, go before us !
    Then let the shout again,
    Ring out from sea to sea,
    FREE SPEECH, FREE PRESS, FREE SOIL, FREE MEN,
    FRE-MONT AND LIBERTY.

Hurrah, hurrah, from hill and valley;
  Hurrah from prairie wide and free !
Around our glorious chieftain rally,
  For Kansas and for liberty !
Let him who first her wilds exploring,
  Her virgin beauty gave to fame,
Now save her from the curse and shame
  Which slavery o'er her soil is pouring.
    Our standard bearer then,
    The brave path finder be !
    FREE SPEECH, FREE PRESS, FREE SOIL, FREE MEN,
    FRE-MONT AND LIBERTY !

PRACTICING Historical Thinking

Identify: What does "furious storm" refer to in the first stanza?

Analyze: Why does this campaign song make a reference to Kansas? You may need to consult your text and class notes to help you with this question.

Evaluate: In what ways is the campaign song both a moral and a legal call to action?

DOCUMENT 11.6 | ROGER B. TANEY, *Dred Scott v. Sandford*
1857

The opinion by Chief Justice Roger B. Taney (1777–1864) in the US Supreme Court's decision in *Dred Scott v. Sandford* appeared to leave open the possibility that slaves could be transported anywhere in the nation and be protected by federal law. Taney also made explicit that African Americans had no legal recourse in American courts.

The question is simply this: can a negro, whose ancestors were imported into this country and sold as slaves, become a member of the political community formed and brought into existence by the Constitution of the United States, and as such become entitled to all the rights, and privileges, and immunities, guaranteed by that instrument to the citizen. One of those rights is the privilege of suing in a court of the United States in the cases specified in the Constitution. . . .

The words "people of the United States" and "citizens" are synonymous terms, and mean the same thing. They both describe the political body, who, according to our republican institutions, form the sovereignty, and who hold the power and conduct the government through their representatives. They are what we familiarly call the "sovereign people," and every citizen is one of this people, and a constituent member of this sovereignty. The question before us is, whether the class of persons described in the plea in abatement compose a portion of this people, and are constituent members of this sovereignty. We think they are not, and that they are not included, and were not intended to be included, under the word "citizens" in the Constitution, and can, therefore, claim none of the rights and privileges which that instrument provides for and secures to citizens of the United States. On the contrary, they were at that time considered as a subordinate and inferior class of beings, who had been subjugated by the dominant race, and whether emancipated or not, yet remained subject to their authority, and had no rights or privileges but such as those who held the power and the government might choose to grant them. . . .

It is very clear, therefore, that no State can, by any Act or law of its own, passed, since the adoption of the Constitution, introduce a new member into the political community created by the Constitution of the United States. It cannot make him a member of this community by making him a member of its own. And for the same reason it cannot introduce any person, or description of persons, who were not intended to be embraced in this new political family, which the Constitution brought into existence, but were intended to be excluded from it. . . .

In the opinion of the court, the legislation and histories of the times, and the language used in the Declaration of Independence, show, that neither the class of persons who had been imported as slaves, nor their descendants, whether they had become free or not, were then acknowledged as a part of the people, nor intended to be included in the general words used in that memorable instrument.

Scott v. Sandford 60 U.S. 393 (1856).

DOCUMENT 11.7 | ABRAHAM LINCOLN, Speech at Edwardsville, Illinois
1858

In 1858, Abraham Lincoln (1809–1865) gained national attention in his campaign for the United States Senate against Senator Stephen A. Douglas, an Illinois judge and coauthor of the Compromise of 1850 and the Kansas-Nebraska Act. In a series of speeches around Illinois, Lincoln made a moderate case for halting slavery's spread. Lincoln gave the following speech as part of his debates with Douglas.

I have been requested to give a concise statement, as I understand it, of the difference between the Democratic and the Republican parties on the leading issues of this campaign. The question has just been put to me by a gentleman whom I do not know. I do not even know whether he is a friend of mine or a supporter of Judge Douglas in this contest; nor does that make any difference. His question is a pertinent one and, though it has not been asked me anywhere in the State before, I am very glad that my attention has been called to it to-day. Lest I should forget it, I will give you my answer before proceeding with the line of argument I had marked out for this discussion.

The difference between the Republican and the Democratic parties on the leading issue of this contest, as I understand it, is, that the former consider slavery a moral, social and political wrong, while the latter *do not* consider it either a moral, social or political wrong; and the action of each, as respects the growth of the country and the expansion of our population, is squared to meet these views. I will not allege that the Democratic party consider slavery morally, socially and politically *right*; though their tendency to that view has, in may [my] opinion, been constant and unmistakable for the past five years. I prefer to take, as the accepted maxim of the party, the idea put forth by Judge Douglas, that he "don't care whether slavery is voted down or voted up." I am quite willing to believe that many Democrats would prefer that slavery be always voted down, and I am sure that some prefer that it be always "voted up"; but I have a right to insist that their action, especially if it be their *constant and unvarying* action, shall determine their ideas and preferences on the subject. Every measure of the Democratic party of late years, bearing directly or indirectly on the slavery question, has corresponded with this notion of utter indifference whether slavery or freedom shall outrun in the race of empire across the Pacific—every measure, I say, up to the Dred Scott decision, where, it seems to me, the idea is boldly suggested that slavery is *better* than freedom. The Republican party, on the contrary, hold that this government was instituted to secure the blessings of freedom, and that slavery is an unqualified evil to the negro, to the white man, to the soil, and to the State. Regarding it an evil, they will not molest it in the States where it exists; they will not overlook the constitutional guards which our forefathers have placed around it; they will do nothing which can give proper offence to those who hold slaves by legal sanction; but they will use every constitutional method to prevent the evil from becoming larger and involving more negroes, more white men, more soil, and more States in its deplorable consequences. They will, if possible, place it where the public mind shall rest in the belief that it is in course of ultimate peaceable extinction, in God's own good time. And to this end they will, if possible, restore the government to the policy of the fathers—the policy of preserving the new territories from the baneful influence of human bondage, as the Northwestern territories were sought to be preserved by the ordinance of 1787 and the compromise act of 1820. They will oppose, in all its length and breadth, the modern Democratic idea that slavery is as good as freedom, and ought to have room for expansion all over the continent, if people can be found to carry it. All, or very nearly all, of Judge Douglas' arguments about "Popular Sovereignty," as he calls it, are logical if you admit that slavery is as good and as right as freedom; and not one of them is worth a rush if you deny it. This is the difference, as I understand it, between the Republican and the Democratic parties; and I ask the gentleman, and all of you, whether his question is not satisfactorily answered.—[Cries of "Yes, yes."]

The Collected Works of Abraham Lincoln, ed. Roy Prentice Basler, vol. 3 (Norwalk, CT: Easton Press, 1993), 92–94.

PRACTICING Historical Thinking

Identify: Summarize Lincoln's view of the party differences toward slavery.

Analyze: What is Lincoln's tone (or attitude) toward slavery? What words best reflect this tone?

Evaluate: Compare Lincoln's reference to the Framers' intention with Chief Justice Roger B. Taney's reference to their intention (Doc. 11.6). Are these references accomplishing similar goals? Explain.

SKILL REVIEW | **Analyzing Evidence: Content and Sourcing and Contextualization**

Answer the following prompt in a complete essay that includes an introduction and supporting paragraphs. Incorporate both documents above and any outside information from your textbook and class notes that help you support your argument:

> By the end of the 1850s, the debate over slavery appeared unresolvable. Considering the documents above and your knowledge of the time period, what major disagreements about the institution of slavery made these debates seem unresolvable?

STEP 1 *Analyzing evidence: content and sourcing*

Select the documents that address the disagreements about slavery. Summarize their arguments in the table provided below.

Document	For slavery?	Against slavery?
Doc. 11.1, John C. Calhoun, 1850	Return fugitive slaves to rightful owners	
Doc. 11.2, Harriet Beecher Stowe, 1852		
Doc. 11.3, Mary Henderson Eastman, 1852		
Doc. 11.5, Republican Campaign Song, 1856		
Doc. 11.6, Roger B. Taney, 1857		
Doc. 11.7, Abraham Lincoln, 1858		

STEP 2 *Contextualization*

Contextualize the documents to explain the reasons for differing views on slavery.

Document	Context	Explanations
Doc. 11.1, John C. Calhoun, 1850	Legal, geographic, political	
Doc. 11.2, Harriet Beecher Stowe, 1852	Moral	
Doc. 11.3, Mary Henderson Eastman, 1852	Moral	

Document	Context	Explanations
Doc. 11.5, Republican Campaign Song, 1856	Geographic, economic, social	
Doc. 11.6, Roger B. Taney, 1857	Legal	
Doc. 11.7, Abraham Lincoln, 1858	Legal, political	

STEP 3 *Composition*

Write the essay.

Explaining Secession

DOCUMENT 11.8 | JEFFERSON DAVIS, Inaugural Address
1861

Jefferson Davis (1808–1889) served as a senator from Mississippi before he was elected president of the Confederate States of America during the Civil War. He delivered his inaugural address on February 18, 1861.

. . .We have entered upon the career of independence, and it must be inflexibly pursued. Through many years of controversy, with our late associates, the Northern States, we have vainly endeavored to secure tranquillity, and to obtain respect for the rights to which we were entitled. As a necessity, not a choice, we have resorted to the remedy of separation; and henceforth, our energies must be directed to the conduct of our own affairs, and the perpetuity of the Confederacy which we have formed. If a just perception of mutual interest shall permit us, peaceably, to pursue our separate political career, my most earnest desire will have been fulfilled. But, if this be denied to us, and the integrity of our territory and jurisdiction be assailed, it will but remain for us, with firm resolve, to appeal to arms, and invoke the blessing of Providence on a just cause. . . .

Actuated solely by the desire to preserve our own rights and promote our own welfare, the separation of the Confederate States has been marked by no aggression upon others, and followed by no domestic convulsion. Our industrial pursuits have received no check—the cultivation of our fields has progressed as heretofore—and even should we be involved in war, there would be no considerable diminution in the production of the staples which have constituted our exports, and in which the commercial world has an interest scarcely less than our own. This common interest of the producer and consumer, can only be interrupted by exterior force, which should obstruct its transmission [of our staples] to foreign markets—a course of conduct which would be as unjust toward us as it would be detrimental to manufacturing and commercial interests abroad. Should reason guide the action of the Government from which we have separated, a policy so detrimental to the civilized world, the Northern States included, could not be dictated by even the strongest desire to inflict injury upon us; but if otherwise, a terrible responsibility will rest upon it, and the suffering of millions will bear testimony to the folly and wickedness of our aggressors. In the mean time, there will remain to us, besides the ordinary means before suggested, the well-known resources for retaliation upon the commerce of an enemy.

De Bow's Review 5, no. 4 (April 1861): 482–483.

PRACTICING Historical Thinking

Identify: List the main points of Davis's inaugural address.

Analyze: What does Davis's final paragraph suggest about the Confederacy's position toward any action by the North? Explain.

Evaluate: Why does Davis refer to international support for Southern secession?

DOCUMENT 11.9 | ABRAHAM LINCOLN, First Inaugural Address
1861

Abraham Lincoln delivered his first address to the nation as president of the United States on March 4, 1861. In it, he attempted to offer assurances to Southern policy leaders that the institution of slavery was protected where it already existed, but that he was obligated to protect the integrity of the union against succession.

I have no purpose, directly or indirectly, to interfere with the institution of slavery in the States where it exists. I believe I have no lawful right to do so, and I have no inclination to do so. . . .

There is much controversy about the delivering up of fugitives from service or labor. The clause I now read is as plainly written in the Constitution as any other of its provisions:

"No person held to service or labor in one State, under the laws thereof, escaping into another, shall in consequence of any law or regulation therein, be discharged from such service or labor, but shall be delivered up on claim of the party to whom such service or labor may be due."

It is scarcely questioned that this provision was intended by those who made it for the reclaiming of what we call fugitive slaves; and the intention of the lawgiver is the law. All members of Congress swear their support to the whole Constitution—to this provision as much as any other. To the proposition, then, that slaves, whose cases come within the terms of this clause, "shall be delivered up," their oaths are unanimous. Now, if they would make the effort in good temper, could they not, with nearly equal unanimity, frame and pass a law by means of which to keep good that unanimous oath? . . .

I hold that, in contemplation of universal law, and of the Constitution, the Union of these States is perpetual. Perpetuity is implied, if not expressed, in the fundamental law of all National Governments. It is safe to assert that no Government proper ever had a provision in its organic law for its own termination. Continue to execute all the express provisions of our National Constitution, and the Union will endure forever—it being impossible to destroy it, except by some action not provided for in the instrument itself. . . .

I, therefore, consider that, in view of the Constitution and the laws, the Union is unbroken, and, to the extent of my ability, I shall take care, as the Constitution itself expressly enjoins upon me, that the laws of the Union be faithfully executed in all the States. Doing this I deem to be only a simple duty on my part; and I shall perform it, so far as practicable, unless my rightful masters, the American people, shall withhold the requisite means, or, in some authoritative manner, direct the contrary. I trust this will not be regarded as a menace, but only as the declared purpose of the Union that it will constitutionally defend and maintain itself. . . .

Plainly, the central idea of secession is the essence of anarchy. A majority held in restraint by constitutional checks and limitations, and always changing easily with deliberate changes of popular opinions and sentiments, is the only true sovereign of a free people. Whoever rejects it, does, of necessity, fly to anarchy or to despotism. Unanimity is impossible; the rule of a minority, as a permanent arrangement, is wholly inadmissible; so that, rejecting the majority principle, anarchy or despotism in some form is all that is left. . . .

In your hands, my dissatisfied fellow-countrymen, and not in mine, is the momentous issue of civil war. The Government will not assail you. You can have no conflict without being yourselves the aggressors. You have no oath registered in Heaven to destroy the Government, while I shall have the most solemn one to "preserve, protect, and defend it."

I am loth [loath] to close. We are not enemies, but friends. We must not be enemies. Though passion may have strained, it must not break our bonds of affection. The mystic chords of memory, stretching from every battle-field and patriot grave to every living heart and hearth-stone, all over this broad land, will yet swell the chorus of the Union, when again touched, as surely they will be, by the better angels of our nature.

The American Annual Cyclopedia and Register of Important Events of the Year 1861 (New York: D. Appleton, 1864), 600–603.

PRACTICING Historical Thinking

Identify: What does Lincoln say that he will do about slavery?

Analyze: How does Lincoln address both Northern and Southern audiences in this speech?

Evaluate: What could be the "mystic chords of memory" that Lincoln invokes? Why does he end this speech by mentioning them?

JAMES E. TAYLOR, *The Cause of the Rebellion*

Published sometime between 1861 and 1865

James E. Taylor (1839–1901) was an artist who was best known for his depictions of the Civil War. Taylor was from New York and served as a correspondent and an artist for *Frank Leslie's Illustrated Newspaper*.

Library of Congress Prints and Photographs Division, LC-USZ62-49304.

PRACTICING Historical Thinking

Identify: Describe the individual who is pictured here.

Analyze: What images in the setting are most prominent? Why?

Evaluate: How does the choice of an African American man influence the artist's message on the causes or effects of the war?

| EMILY DICKINSON, "Much Madness is Divinest Sense"

1862

New England poet Emily Dickinson (1830–1886) wrote more than seventeen hundred poems in her lifetime, but most of her work was not published until after her death.

> Much madness is divinest sense
> To a discerning eye;
> Much sense the starkest madness.
> 'T is the majority
> In this, as all, prevails.
> Assent, and you are sane;
> Demur, — you're straightway dangerous,
> And handled with a chain.

Emily Dickinson, "Much Madness is Divinest Sense," *Poems by Emily Dickinson*, ed. Mabel Loomis Todd and T. W. Higginson (Boston, MA: Roberts Brothers, 1892), 24.

PRACTICING Historical Thinking

Identify: What does the first line mean?

Analyze: Who might the "you" be? Consider more than one audience here.

Evaluate: While Dickinson was not necessarily talking about political events in this poem, what might the significance of the words "sense," "sadness," and "chain" be in conjunction with the beginning of the Civil War?

APPLYING AP® Historical Thinking Skills

SKILL REVIEW | **Comparison and Synthesis**

Answer the following prompt in a complete essay that includes an introduction and supporting paragraphs that incorporate the documents above and any outside information from your textbook and class notes that helps you support your argument.

> Compare the arguments that Jefferson Davis and Abraham Lincoln make in their inaugural addresses above (Docs. 11.8 and 11.9). Where are their arguments similar, and where are they different? How do their arguments reflect older debates about federal power under the Constitution?

STEP 1 *Compare*

Compare the documents using subject-by-subject organization.

    I. Introduction

    II. Jefferson Davis's Inaugural Address

        A. Point 1

        B. Point 2

    III. Abraham Lincoln's First Inaugural Address

        A. Point 1

        B. Point 2

Determine points of comparison between the two speeches. Use the Identify, Analyze, and Evaluate questions as a starting point.

STEP 2 *Synthesize*

Synthesize older debates about federal power under the Constitution.

    1. What are these debates? Refer to earlier chapters in this textbook and your outside knowledge.

    2. What documents reflect these debates?

Use your response for Step 2 to begin the second half of your response. You may, for example, consider the following format for the second half of your organization:

    IV. Older debates

        A. Similarities to the Jefferson and Lincoln addresses

        B. Differences with the Jefferson and Lincoln addresses

        C. Analysis of context

    V. Conclusion

PUTTING IT ALL TOGETHER

Revisiting the Main Point

- By 1860, Northerners and Southerners claimed to have distinct identities, and Southerners used their identity to justify forming a new nation. What were Southerners' economic, social, and moral arguments for their secession?
- In your opinion, which primarily drove the debate over slavery during the 1850s—moral or economic arguments?
- How did the growth of the United States since 1800 fuel the political crisis of the 1850s? Refer to previous chapters to answer this question.

BUILDING AP® WRITING SKILLS	Addressing Exceptions in Historical Argument: The Role of the Qualifier

Given the amount of evidence that is available to any historical argument, it is nearly impossible to find all of the evidence that supports a single position. Much evidence falls into patterns, as you learned in Chapter 7.

But even if you incorporate a **subordinated thesis statement** (Chapter 4), you will invariably encounter examples that do not support your argument or that even run counter to your argument. These examples often serve as extremes that rarely are repeated and become exceptions to the recognized patterns of evidence. These examples also can serve as **exemplars**—recognized highs and lows and peaks and valleys in the historical record.

Such examples are called **qualifiers**. As a writer, you can choose to leave out the qualifier because it could lessen the credibility of your argument. Sometimes, however, a well-positioned qualifier may strengthen your overall argument. Consider Frederick Douglass (Doc. 7.9) in the discussion of the horrors of slavery. His greatness in history is measured largely by his achievements against impossible circumstances, but comparing others in similar circumstances to Douglass would be an oversimplification.

You cannot ignore Douglass because it undermines your attempt to decry the horrors of slavery. But how do you use the exceptional example to support your argument? There are three ways to use Douglass as an example:

- *As a beacon or aspiration:* Douglass is an exemplar of others' visions, such as Stowe's or Lincoln's.
- *As a recognition that another side exists:* Douglass's example did not serve the goals of the Confederacy.

- *As a portal through which to entertain new ideas:* Douglass's legacy helps redefine slavery in terms of education, not race, which is one reason that his work is still relevant today (even though slavery has been abolished).

Consider the following prompt to illustrate the effective use of qualifying evidence in historical argument:

> In your opinion, which primarily drove the debate over slavery during the 1850s—moral or economic arguments?

STEP 1 *Understand the prompt, and identify the key words*

For a review of this step, see Building AP® Writing Skills in Chapter 1 (p. 22).

STEP 2 *Generate a working thesis*

For a review of Step 2, see Building AP® Writing Skills in Chapters 1 through 5 (pp. 22, 51, 79, 111, 142). Consider and practice the use of subordination in your thesis statement.

STEP 3 *Identify and organize evidence*

By addressing the slavery debate in two key contexts—moral and economic—your argument automatically presents clear divisions about what pieces of evidence will apply. A review of the documents in this chapter suggests that many adhere to either of these two contexts:

Document	Context
Doc. 11.1, John C. Calhoun, 1850	Legal, geographic, political
Doc. 11.2, Harriet Beecher Stowe, 1852	Moral
Doc. 11.3, Mary Henderson Eastman, 1852	Moral
Doc. 11.4, Map of Kansas-Nebraska Act, 1854	Political, economic
Doc. 11.5, Republican Campaign Song, 1856	Geographic, economic, social
Doc. 11.6, Roger B. Taney, 1857	Legal
Doc. 11.7, Abraham Lincoln, 1858	Legal, political
Doc. 11.8, Jefferson Davis, 1861	Political, social
Doc. 11.9, Abraham Lincoln, 1861	Economic, political
Doc. 11.10, James E. Taylor	Moral, economic
Doc. 11.11, Emily Dickinson, 1862	Social, moral

Consider culling all the evidence that addresses the moral aspects of the slavery debate. Your examples may include the following pieces of evidence:

- Harriet Beecher Stowe—favors forgiveness and brotherhood
- Mary Henderson Eastman—favors traditional boundaries of ownership
- James E. Taylor—suggests moral indignation at the cost of war
- Emily Dickinson—implies that slavery is a condition of madness

Given the different messages of these examples, the discussion of morality is influenced by your recognition of the outlier status of any of the examples.

- *A beacon or inspiration:* You could write, for example, that Emily Dickinson (Doc. 11.11) was one of the first to incorporate a transcendental philosophy into the slavery debate, as in these lines:

    Assent, and you are sane;
    Demur, — you're straightway dangerous,
    And handled with a chain.

- *A portal for new ideas:* Alternatively, you could write that James E. Taylor (Doc. 11.10) made the moral debate an economic one, thereby broadening the discussion about morality.

- *A recognition of another side:* Or you could instead write that Mary Henderson Eastman's (Doc. 11.3) moral view was based on a traditional mind-set that gradually lessened with new ways of thinking about slavery and morality.

In your notebook, identify and organize your evidence for the economic aspects of the debate.

STEP 4 *Outline your response*

Use the following outline as a basis for your essay. Note the position of the qualifier as a way to enhance your body paragraphs. The qualifying example may serve as a transition to a new segment of your essay, a counterargument, or an extreme example of all the evidence that you have provided for that portion of the essay.

I. Introduction

II. Moral aspects

    A. Patterns of evidence that agrees

    B. Qualifier example(s)

III. Economic aspects

    A. Patterns of evidence that agrees

    B. Qualifier example(s)

IV. Conclusion

STEP 5 *Write the essay*

Suggestion: As you write, keep in mind the language of counterargument (Chapter 10, p. 247) when introducing qualifying examples.

Both North and South mobilized their economies and societies during the Civil War, and early in the war, the South achieved many victories despite its smaller population and largely agricultural economy. President Abraham Lincoln's issuing of the Emancipation Proclamation in 1862 changed the goal of the conflict from maintaining the Union to assuring freedom for enslaved African Americans in the American South. Ultimately, the North secured victory through its military and economic superiority over the South.

The abolition of slavery with the Thirteenth Amendment proved to be the most far-reaching and immediate result of the war. This sweeping reform was followed by the Fourteenth Amendment, which guaranteed that the federal government would protect civil rights, and the Fifteenth Amendment, which removed racial barriers from voting. Although these three amendments led to temporary political successes for formerly enslaved African Americans throughout the 1870s, Northern support for Reconstruction—the remaking of the South with racial equality and economic justice—faltered as Southern resistance to reforms, often in violent attacks on African Americans and their Northern and Southern supporters, quashed the progress that had been made in the first years after the war.

Seeking the Main Point

As you read the documents that follow, keep these broad questions in mind. These questions will help you understand the relationship between the documents in this chapter and the historical changes that they represent. As you reflect on these questions, determine which themes and which documents best address them.

- Describe the ways in which the arguments over secession and slavery echoed older arguments about state and federal powers.
- Characterize the ways in which Northerners and Southerners identified themselves as distinct peoples in these documents.
- In what ways did white Americans on both sides of the conflict try to define African American identity to their own advantage?
- In what ways might the Civil War have been the inevitable consequence of pre-Revolutionary America?

Emancipation

DOCUMENT 12.1 | **"What to Do with the Slaves When Emancipated,"** *New York Herald*
1862

Not all Northerners agreed with how President Abraham Lincoln conducted the war. In this March 8, 1862, editorial, for example, the *New York Herald* opposed the emancipation of African American slaves as part of the war effort and tended to support the Democratic Party as opposed to Lincoln's Republican Party.

It will be observed that the policy proposed by the President in his Message to Congress is essentially different from any proposition ever made by the abolitionists. They laughed to scorn the idea of the nation purchasing the freedom of the slaves from their owners, inasmuch as it was the right of the negroes to be free, all laws and constitutions to the contrary notwithstanding. Their policy was a sudden and compulsory emancipation. Mr. Lincoln's [idea is] a gradual and voluntary emancipation, which clearly recognizes the sovereignty of the States over their own domestic institutions, and merely offers them assistance to carry out emancipation if they should deem it desirable.

The policy of the abolitionists would be destructive: that of the President is benign. It looks only to the border slave States; for they alone would be willing to accept the proposition. In the cotton States the slave institution is regarded as entirely superior to that of free labor [where workers can freely move from job to job in pursuit of higher wages]. In the border States there is a difference of opinion on the subject; for the climate, unlike the extreme South, is favorable to the labor of the white man; and wherever that is the case slavery necessarily dies out, because it will no longer pay. It was for that reason alone that all the Northern States got rid of it; and were it not for the fanaticism of the abolitionists creating a spirit of antagonism in the slave States, there would not be a slave in Maryland, Missouri, Virginia or Kentucky to-day. In those States free labor pays better than slave labor, and when the war is ended it is extremely probable that those States will deliberately abolish slavery and accept the aid proposed in Mr. Lincoln['s] Message.

Now the question is, What is to be done with the slaves when emancipated? It would not do to let them work or not, as they may think proper. If they were as willing to work as the white man there would be no slavery now in any Southern State. The proposed change would involve the necessity of transferring from the master to the State the superintendence of negro labor, and vagrant laws should be passed compelling negroes to work—laws which exist in many parts of Europe in reference to the white population, but infinitely more necessary for blacks, whose idea of paradise is to have nothing to do. The wages should be regulated by law, and be sufficient not only to procure food and clothing, but to enable the negro to lay up something for sickness and old age. On the whole, the negro would be worse off under this system than in servitude; but if the interests of the white men of the border slave States demand it the interests of the negro must be made subordinate, and the system which now gives him protection by law, and a provision for life, must be abolished. But of their own interests in the matter the citizens of the slave States alone are the proper judges, and the people of the free States have nothing whatever to do with the question.

"What to Do with the Slaves When Emancipated," *New York Herald*, March 8, 1862, Accessible Archives: The Civil War Collection.

PRACTICING Historical Thinking

Identify: What are the writer's main concerns about emancipation?

Analyze: What is the writer's attitude toward enslaved African Americans? Explain your response.

Evaluate: How are the writer's perspectives on slavery different from perspectives of those who lived in Southern states?

DOCUMENT 12.2 | ABRAHAM LINCOLN, Letter to Horace Greeley
1862

Horace Greeley (1811–1872), editor of the *New York Tribune*, challenged President Abraham Lincoln to free enslaved African Americans as part of his war effort. In this open letter published by Greeley in the *Tribune* in August 1862, the president clarifies his position on slavery for Greeley.

Executive Mansion, Washington,
August 22, 1862.
Hon. Horace Greeley—

Dear Sir:

I have just read yours of the 19th, addressed to myself through the New York *Tribune*. If there be in it any statements or assumptions of fact which I may know to be erroneous, I do not now and here controvert them. If there be in it any inferences which I may believe to be falsely drawn, I do not now and here argue against them. If there be perceptible in it an impatient and dictatorial tone, I waive it in deference to an old friend, whose heart I have always supposed to be right.

As to the policy I "seem to be pursuing," as you say, I have not meant to leave any one in doubt.

I would save the Union. I would save it the shortest way under the Constitution. The sooner the National authority can be restored, the nearer the Union will be "the Union as it was." If there be those who would not save the Union unless they could at the same time *save* Slavery, I do not agree with them. If there be those who would not save the Union unless they could at the same time *destroy* Slavery, I do not agree with them. My paramount object in this struggle *is* to save the Union, and is *not* either to save or to destroy Slavery. If I could save the Union without freeing *any* slave, I would do it; and if I could save it by freeing *all* the slaves, I would do it; and if I could save it by freeing some and leaving others alone, I would also do that. What I do about Slavery, and the colored race, I do because I believe it helps to save the Union; and what I forbear, I forbear because I do *not* believe it would help to save the Union. I shall do *less* whenever I shall believe what I am doing hurts the cause, and I shall do *more* whenever I shall believe doing more will help the cause. I shall try to correct errors when shown to be errors; and I shall adopt new views so fast as they shall appear to be true views. I have here stated my purpose according to my view of *official* duty; and I intend no modification of my oft-expressed *personal* wish that all men, every-where, could be free.

Yours,

A. LINCOLN.

Joseph Hartwell Barrett, *Life of Abraham Lincoln* (New York: Moore, Wilstach & Baldwin, 1865), 413–414.

PRACTICING Historical Thinking

Identify: According to Lincoln, what is the relationship between freeing slaves and saving the Union?

Analyze: What does Lincoln mean when he says: "If I could save the Union without freeing *any* slave, I would do it; and if I could save it by freeing *all* the slaves, I would do it"?

Evaluate: Compare Lincoln's argument with the newspaper article about emancipation in Document 12.1. In what ways did the slavery debate change over time from an economic debate to a political one?

ABRAHAM LINCOLN, Emancipation Proclamation

1862

President Lincoln issued the Emancipation Proclamation on September 22, 1862, after Union forces successfully forced the Confederate Army of Northern Virginia out of Maryland.

By the President of the United States of America:

A Proclamation.

Whereas, on the twenty-second day of September, in the year of our Lord one thousand eight hundred and sixty-two, a proclamation was issued by the President of the United States, containing, among other things, the following, to wit:

"That on the first day of January, in the year of our Lord one thousand eight hundred and sixty-three, all persons held as slaves within any State or designated part of a State, the people whereof shall then be in rebellion against the United States, shall be then, thenceforward, and forever free; and the Executive Government of the United States, including the military and naval authority thereof, will recognize and maintain the freedom of such persons, and will do no act or acts to repress such persons, or any of them, in any efforts they may make for their actual freedom.

"That the Executive will, on the first day of January aforesaid, by proclamation, designate the States and parts of States, if any, in which the people thereof, respectively, shall then be in rebellion against the United States; and the fact that any State, or the people thereof, shall on that day be, in good faith, represented in the Congress of the United States by members chosen thereto at elections wherein a majority of the qualified voters of such State shall have participated, shall, in the absence of strong countervailing testimony, be deemed conclusive evidence that such State, and the people thereof, are not then in rebellion against the United States."

Now, therefore I, Abraham Lincoln, President of the United States, by virtue of the power in me vested as Commander-in-Chief, of the Army and Navy of the United States in time of actual armed rebellion against the authority and government of the United States, and as a fit and necessary war measure for suppressing said rebellion, do, on this first day of January, in the year of our Lord one thousand eight hundred and sixty-three, and in accordance with my purpose so to do publicly proclaimed for the full period of one hundred days, from the day first above mentioned, order and designate as the States and parts of States wherein the people thereof respectively, are this day in rebellion against the United States, the following, to wit:

Arkansas, Texas, Louisiana, (except the Parishes of St. Bernard, Plaquemines, Jefferson, St. John, St. Charles, St. James, Ascension, Assumption, Terrebonne,

Lafourche, St. Mary, St. Martin, and Orleans, including the City of New Orleans), Mississippi, Alabama, Florida, Georgia, South Carolina, North Carolina, and Virginia, (except the forty-eight counties designated as West Virginia, and also the counties of Berkley, Accomac, Northampton, Elizabeth City, York, Princess Ann, and Norfolk, including the cities of Norfolk and Portsmouth[)], and which excepted parts, are for the present, left precisely as if this proclamation were not issued.

And by virtue of the power, and for the purpose aforesaid, I do order and declare that all persons held as slaves within said designated States, and parts of States, are, and henceforward shall be free; and that the Executive government of the United States, including the military and naval authorities thereof, will recognize and maintain the freedom of said persons.

And I hereby enjoin upon the people so declared to be free to abstain from all violence, unless in necessary self-defence; and I recommend to them that, in all cases when allowed, they labor faithfully for reasonable wages.

And I further declare and make known, that such persons of suitable condition, will be received into the armed service of the United States to garrison forts, positions, stations, and other places, and to man vessels of all sorts in said service.

And upon this act, sincerely believed to be an act of justice, warranted by the Constitution, upon military necessity, I invoke the considerate judgment of mankind, and the gracious favor of Almighty God.

In witness whereof, I have hereunto set my hand and caused the seal of the United States to be affixed.

Done at the City of Washington, this first day of January, in the year of our Lord one thousand eight hundred and sixty-three, and of the Independence of the United States of America the eighty-seventh.

By the President: ABRAHAM LINCOLN

WILLIAM H. SEWARD, Secretary of State.

"The Emancipation Proclamation: January 1, 1863 A Transcription," Featured Documents, US National Archives and Records Administration.

PRACTICING Historical Thinking

Identify: Summarize the first three paragraphs of the Proclamation.

Analyze: How does Lincoln equate the slaves' freedom with the states' rebellion?

Evaluate: To what extent was the Emancipation Proclamation a document that spurred political action? To what extent was it a document that reflected a new reality? Use your textbook for additional information on these questions.

DOCUMENT 12.4 | "President Lincoln and His Scheme of Emancipation," *Charleston Mercury*
1862

For many Southerners, Lincoln's Emancipation Proclamation was a cynical military ploy to inspire rebellion among Southern slaves, as implied in this excerpt from the *Charleston Mercury* from December 11, 1862.

There is something in Northern Abolitionism which seems, in some way or other, totally to deprave its votaries [followers]. We speak not of its cruel and barbarous exemplifications in practical war, when the passions may be lashed into fury, but of its corrupting tendency in the sober relations of government in civil life. For instance, the Constitution of a country ought to be, in the relations of this world, as sacred as the Bible is in those of the next. Yet Abolitionism teaches a man that there is a higher law than the Constitution of the country, or the Bible itself. Hence, their licentious [unethical] aggressions upon the slave institution of the South, in spite of the Constitution, and even the plain dictates of interest itself. Hence President LINCOLN['s] Proclamation for the abolition of slavery in the Confederate States, without a particle of constitutional authority. And, having committed this impotent and insolent blunder, he follows it up with another still more impotent and absurd. In his late message to the Congress of the United States, he gravely proposes, with a most elaborate dissertation to support it, that all the slaves of loyal masters shall be emancipated, by a law of Congress, in 1900—the close of the century. The slaves of loyal masters will amount to one in twenty or one in one hundred. By his Proclamation, the nineteen out of twenty will be emancipated by the first of next January. Under such circumstances, how is it possible to perpetuate slavery over the twentieth slave? The truth is, his Proclamation is declarative for emancipation to all the slaves of the South. That is what . . . [it] signifies, and that is what he means by it. President LINCOLN is not such a fool as not to know that the emancipation of all the slaves in the South, belonging to the citizens of the Confederate States, is also an emancipation of all the slaves belonging to the few traitors who affect allegiance to the United States. Why, then, propose to Congress, to do that in 1900 which he does next January, so far as the power of the United States can accomplish it? The answer is very simple. The fellow is a rogue. He wishes to disguise the scope and atrocity of his unconstitutional and fiendish policy. His calling upon Congress to do anything in the matter is a flagrant hypocrisy. If he can deprive white men in the United States of their liberties, whenever he pleases, why can he not liberate black men? If his Proclamation is constitutional, what act towards the slaves of the Confederate States can be unconstitutional? He and his bloody associate in criminality, SEWARD, are fully of the opinion of that keen observer of our baser nature, who remarked that "Words are the counters of wise men, but the money of fools." For a man to be an Abolitionist in the United States seems at once to convert him into a knave and a robber.

"President Lincoln and His Scheme of Emancipation," *Charleston Mercury*, December 11, 1862, Accessible Archives: The Civil War Collection.

PRACTICING Historical Thinking

Identify: What is significant about the year 1900 to this newspaper? Is this year mentioned in the Emancipation Proclamation? Use your notes and textbook to help you.

Analyze: What does the writer mean when he states: "Yet Abolitionism teaches a man that there is a higher law than the Constitution of the country, or the Bible itself"? Why would a Southern slave owner reject this notion?

Evaluate: Synthesize the first four documents of this chapter to form a statement on the ways that newspapers in this era tried to shape public opinion.

DOCUMENT 12.5 | **THOMAS NAST, "The Emancipation of the Negroes, January, 1863—The Past and the Future,"** *Harper's Weekly*
1863

The following image appeared in the Northern periodical *Harper's Weekly* on January 24, 1863, to celebrate the Emancipation Proclamation.

Library of Congress Prints and Photographs Division, LC-USZ62-130778.

APPLYING AP® Historical Thinking Skills

SKILL REVIEW | # Comparison, Contextualization, and Argumentation

Regarding the emancipation of enslaved African Americans, compare the five documents above, and answer the following prompt:

Accept, modify, or refute the following: Although Northerners and Southerners debated the status of African Americans, neither side in the Civil War perceived enslaved African Americans and whites as equals. Use the documents above and your knowledge of the 1860s to support your argument.

STEP 1 *Organize your evidence*

Use a simple table to clarify the point of view and context for each piece of evidence. This is the first step toward comparison. Note the point of view and context for each piece.

Document	Point of view on (or perception of) African Americans	Context
Doc. 12.1, "What to Do with the Slaves When Emancipated," *New York Herald*	Antiabolition	Political, economic
Doc. 12.2, Abraham Lincoln, Letter to Horace Greeley		
Doc. 12.3, Abraham Lincoln, Emancipation Proclamation		
Doc. 12.4, "President Lincoln and His Scheme of Emancipation," *Charleston Mercury*	Southern	Political, economic
Doc. 12.5, Thomas Nast, "The Emancipation of the Negroes, January, 1863—The Past and the Future"	Abolitionist	Social, moral

STEP 2 *Evaluate each source*

Determine which of these sources agrees with, disagrees with, or modifies the claim.

Document	Agrees with claim? Why?	Disagrees with claim? Why?	Modifies the claim? Why?
Doc. 12.1, "What to Do with the Slaves When Emancipated," *New York Herald*			
Doc. 12.2, Abraham Lincoln, Letter to Horace Greeley			
Doc. 12.3, Abraham Lincoln, Emancipation Proclamation			
Doc. 12.4, "President Lincoln and His Scheme of Emancipation," *Charleston Mercury*			
Doc. 12.5, Thomas Nast, "The Emancipation of the Negroes, January, 1863— The Past and the Future"			

STEP 3 *Write your response*

Recall Chapter 11's focus on the **outlier** or **qualifying evidence**. How does the *New York Herald*'s criticism of Lincoln's plan for emancipation (Doc. 12.1) fit into your overall argument? (For example, "Because the *Herald* and Lincoln held differing views toward enslaved African Americans . . .") Whether you agree or disagree with the claim, you will find evidence that contradicts or qualifies your position.

TOPIC II

Total War

DOCUMENT 12.6 | **ULYSSES S. GRANT,** *Memoirs*
| 1885

Recollections by Ulysses S. Grant (1822–1885) of his assumption of command of all Union forces in 1863 reflect a change in military strategy from a defensive campaign to an offensive one.

In my first interview with Mr. Lincoln alone he stated to me that he had never professed to be a military man or to know how campaigns should be conducted, and never wanted to interfere in them: but that procrastination on the part of commanders, and the pressure from the people at the North and Congress, *which was always with him*, forced him into issuing his series of "Military Orders"—one, two, three, etc. He did not know but they were all wrong, and did know that some of them were. All he wanted or had ever wanted was some one who would take the responsibility and act, and call on him for all the assistance needed, pledging himself to use all the power of the government in rendering such assistance. Assuring him that I would do the best I could with the means at hand, and avoid as far as possible annoying him or the War Department, our first interview ended. . . .

My general plan now was to concentrate all the force possible against the Confederate armies in the field. There were but two such, as we have seen, east of the Mississippi River and facing north. The Army of Northern Virginia, General Robert E. Lee commanding, was on the south bank of the Rapidan, confronting the Army of the Potomac; the second, under General Joseph E. Johnston, was at Dalton, Georgia, opposed to Sherman, who was still at Chattanooga. Beside these main armies the Confederates had to guard the Shenandoah Valley, a great storehouse to feed their armies from, and their line of communications from Richmond to Tennessee. . . .

. . . Little expeditions could not so well be sent out to destroy a bridge or tear up a few miles of railroad track, burn a storehouse, or inflict other little annoyances. Accordingly I arranged for a simultaneous movement all along the line. Sherman was to move from Chattanooga, Johnston's Army and Atlanta being his objective points.

Ulysses S. Grant, *Personal Memoirs of U. S. Grant* (New York: C. L. Webster, 1894), 407–408, 411–412.

DOCUMENT 12.7	Call for Black Troops
	1863

In this recruitment poster, black troops who enlist and serve in the Union army are assured protection and compensation by the federal government.

DOCUMENT 12.8 | ABRAHAM LINCOLN, Gettysburg Address
1863

After the Battle of Gettysburg, the bloodiest of the war, President Lincoln gave the following address at the dedication of the Gettysburg National Cemetery on November 19, 1863.

Fourscore and seven years ago our fathers brought forth on this continent a new nation, conceived in Liberty, and dedicated to the proposition that all men are created equal.

Now we are engaged in a great civil war, testing whether that nation, or any nation so conceived and so dedicated, can long endure. We are met on a great battle-field of that war. We have come to dedicate a portion of that field, as a final resting-place for those who here gave their lives that that nation might live. It is altogether fitting and proper that we should do this.

But, in a larger sense, we cannot dedicate—we cannot consecrate—we cannot hallow—this ground. The brave men, living and dead, who struggled here, have consecrated it, far above our poor power to add or detract. The world will little note, nor long remember what we say here, but it can never forget what they did here. It is for us the living, rather, to be dedicated here to the unfinished work which they who fought here have thus far so nobly advanced. It is rather for us to be here dedicated to the great task remaining before us—that from these honored dead we take increased devotion to that cause for which they gave the last full measure of devotion—that we here highly resolve that these dead shall not have died in vain—that this nation, under God, shall have a new birth of freedom— and that government of the people, by the people, for the people, shall not perish from the earth.

The Index, vol. VI, "Lincoln's Gettysburg Address," September 23, 1875, 449.

PRACTICING Historical Thinking

Identify: Find three references to the founding of the United States in this document.

Analyze: Examine the last four phrases of the address, beginning with "and that government" and ending with "from the earth." Explain the significance of the order of these phrases.

Evaluate: In Gary Wills's book *Lincoln at Gettysburg*, Wills claims that the Gettysburg Address serves as Lincoln's redefinition—almost a rebirth—of the Declaration of Independence. Find evidence from both documents (the Gettysburg Address above and the Declaration of Independence on p. 122) that could support or refute Wills's claim.

"Emancipation of the Slaves by the Confederate Government," *Charleston Mercury*

1864

As the war became increasingly desperate for the South, the Confederate government offered emancipation to male slaves who were willing to fight for secession. In this excerpt from November 3, 1864, the *Charleston Mercury* comments on this proposal.

Now, if there was any single proposition that we thought was unquestionable in the Confederacy it was this—that the States, and the States alone, have the exclusive jurisdiction and mastery over their slaves. To suppose that any slave-holding country would voluntarily leave it to any other power than its own, to emancipate its slaves, is such an absurdity, that we did not believe a single intelligent man in the Confederacy could entertain it. Still less could we believe that after what had taken place under the United States, with respect to slavery in the Southern States, it was possible that any pretension to emancipate slaves could be set up for the Confederate States. It was because the exclusion of slaves from our Territories by the Government of the United States, looked to their emancipation, that we resisted it. The power to exercise it was never claimed by that Government. The mere agitation in the Northern States to effect the emancipation of our slaves largely contributed to . . . [our] separation from them. And now, before a Confederacy which we established to put at rest forever all such agitation is four years old, we find the proposition gravely submitted that the Confederate Government should emancipate slaves in the States. South Carolina, acting upon the principle that she and she alone had the power to emancipate her slaves, has passed laws prohibiting their emancipation by any of her citizens, unless they are sent out of the State; and no free person of color already free, who leaves the State, shall ever afterwards enter it. She has laws now in force, prohibiting free negroes, belonging either to the Northern States, or to European powers, from entering the States and by the most rigid provisions, they are seized and put into prison should they enter it. These were her rights, under the Union of the United States, recognized and protected by the Government of the United States, and acquiesced in by all foreign nations. And, now, here, it is proposed that the Government of the Confederate States, not only has the right to seize our slaves and to [make] them soldiers, but to emancipate them in South Carolina, and compel us to give them a home amongst us. We confess, that our indignation at such pretensions is so great, that we are at a loss to know how to treat them. To argue against them is self-stultification. They are as monstrous as they are insulting.

The pretext for this policy is, that we want soldiers in our armies. This pretext is set up by the Enquirer [a rival newspaper] in the face of the fact disclosed by the President of the confederate States, that two-thirds of our soldiers, now in the army, are absentees from its ranks. The Enquirer is a devout upholder of President DAVIS and the Administration. It does not arraign the Government for such a state of things. It passes ever the gross mismanagement which has produced them; and cries out, that negroes are wanted to fill the ranks of our armies. The President . . . [reiterates] the assertion. They are not wanted. The freemen of the country are not dependent on slaves for their defence. There are twice as many at home, as are in the field. Why are they not placed in the service? In our opinion, it is the fault of the government, and can be rectified. But if it is the fault of the people, can slaves supply the place of two-thirds of the people, to give the Confederate states independence and liberty? It is vain to attempt to blink the truth. The freemen of the Confederate States, must work out their own redemption, or they must be the slaves of their own slaves. The statesmanship, which looks to any other source for success, is contemptible charlitanry. It is worse—it is treachery to our cause itself. Assert the right in the Confederate Government to emancipate slaves, and it is stone dead.

"Emancipation of Slaves by the Confederate Government," *Charleston Mercury*, November 3, 1864, Accessible Archives: The Civil War Collection.

PRACTICING Historical Thinking

Identify: What is the main argument of the *Charleston Mercury* regarding emancipation?

Analyze: How does this editorial support that argument?

Evaluate: How does this editorial echo older arguments about states' rights versus federal powers?

DOCUMENT 12.10 | **Ruins of Richmond**
| 1865

This photograph, taken shortly after the Union occupation of the Confederate capital of Richmond, Virginia, shows the extent of the damage done to the Confederate infrastructure by the Union army.

Library of Congress Prints and Photographs Division, Civil War Photographs, LC-DIG-cwpb-02879.

PRACTICING Historical Thinking

Identify: What images are the most prominent in this photograph?

Analyze: Compare this photograph with the image painted by James E. Taylor (Doc. 11.10). Do both convey the economic devastation similarly? Explain.

Evaluate: Locate other early examples of photography as a form of documenting the era. How could the emergence of photography help shape a national memory and identity?

APPLYING AP® Historical Thinking Skills

SKILL REVIEW | Causation and Periodization

Consider the following prompt:

> To what extent did the Emancipation Proclamation prove to be a turning point in the Civil War?

STEP 1 *Look for evidence of causation*

Locate and organize the events that are featured in this chapter, both before and after the Emancipation Proclamation. Be sure to include the Emancipation Proclamation as a **turning point**. For each one, note historical trends, patterns, or developments that are reflected in or encompassed by the event. Consider whether and how these patterns shifted around the Emancipation Proclamation.

The following table lists documents and events that followed the Emancipation Proclamation. Complete the chart to reflect general patterns, trends, and developments.

Document	Event	Patterns, trends, developments
Doc. 12.6, Ulysses S. Grant, *Memoirs*		Brutality of war
Doc. 12.7, Call for Black Troops	Call for black troops	Retaliation
Doc. 12.8, Abraham Lincoln, Gettysburg Address		
Doc. 12.9, "Emancipation of the Slaves by the Confederate Government," *Charleston Mercury*		Argument for states' rights
Doc. 12.10, Ruins of Richmond		Economic devastation

STEP 2 *Periodize the evidence*

To periodize this era, consider the evidence in light of the following questions:

1. What did the Emancipation Proclamation represent for freed African Americans in an economic sense? In a social sense? In a political sense?
2. What did the Emancipation Proclamation mean for whites in the North? In the South?
3. To what extent did the Emancipation Proclamation change attitudes toward the war? To what extent did it change the war itself?

Americans were divided about how best to accept this newly freed population. Thus, any characterization of this period must take into account the various points of view toward the Emancipation Proclamation.

STEP 3 *Write your response*

If the Proclamation is a turning point, characterize the periods both before and after the Proclamation. Write your response in your notebook.

Reconstruction

DOCUMENT 12.11 | **Anti-Reconstruction Cartoon,**
Independent Monitor

| 1868

After the war, Northerners—both independently and in organizations like the Freedmen's Bureau—traveled south to assist in the reconstruction of Southern society along lines of racial equality. These transplanted Northerners were derisively termed *carpetbaggers* by Southerners for the type of luggage they carried. Many Southerners who were sympathetic to emancipation also assisted in Reconstruction. They were called *scalawags* by their fellow Southerners. This political cartoon and public threat from the *Independent Monitor* of Tuscaloosa, Alabama, portrays a scalawag, a carpetbagger from Ohio, and a mule branded with the letters KKK (for Ku Klux Klan).

A Prospective Scene in the "City of Oaks," 4th of March, 1869.

Fotosearch/Getty Images.

" Hang, curs, hang! * * * * * *Their* complexion is perfect gallows. Stand fast, good fate, to *their* hanging! * * * * * If they be not born to be hanged, our case is miserable."

The above cut represents the fate in store for those great pests of Southern society—the carpet-bagger and scallawag—if found in Dixie's Land after the break of day on the 4th of March next.

PRACTICING Historical Thinking

Identify: What is the message of this picture?

Analyze: Who is the intended audience for this picture?

Evaluate: Using your knowledge of the time period, evaluate the extent to which Reconstruction efforts were aided or undermined by Northerners.

| # Fourteenth and Fifteenth Amendments
1868 and 1870

The Fourteenth and Fifteenth Amendments to the US Constitution were passed to guarantee full civil and political rights to formerly enslaved African Americans.

Amendment XIV

Section 1. All persons born or naturalized in the United States, and subject to the jurisdiction thereof, are citizens of the United States and of the state wherein they reside. No State shall make or enforce any law which shall abridge the privileges or immunities of citizens of the United States; nor shall any State deprive any person of life, liberty, or property, without due process of law, nor deny to any person within its jurisdiction the equal protection of the laws. . . .

Amendment XV

Section 1. The right of citizens of the United States to vote shall not be denied or abridged by the United States or by any State on account of race, color, or previous condition of servitude.

Section 2. The Congress shall have power to enforce this article by appropriate legislation.

For Amendment 14, *A Century of Lawmaking for a New Nation: U.S. Congressional Documents and Debates, 1774–1875; Statutes at Large, 39th Congress, 1st Session, 358;* for Amendment 15, *A Century of Lawmaking for a New Nation: U.S. Congressional Documents and Debates, 1774–1875; Statutes at Large, 40th Congress, 3rd Session, 346,* Library of Congress.

PRACTICING Historical Thinking

Identify: Summarize the rights guaranteed by the Fourteenth and Fifteenth Amendments.

Analyze: How do these two amendments differ? How are they alike?

Evaluate: Synthesize these amendments with the Emancipation Proclamation (Doc. 12.3) and the Gettysburg Address (Doc. 12.8). To what extent did these federal documents fulfill the promises that were made by the Declaration of Independence?

DOCUMENT 12.13 | # THOMAS NAST, "This Is a White Man's Government"
1874

In the 1870s, as Southerners sought to remove African Americans by force from participating in politics, many white Northerners lost interest in the pursuit of justice for Southern African Americans. In this Thomas Nast cartoon, the caption quotes the Democratic Platform of 1872.

PRACTICING Historical Thinking

Identify: What demographic group does each character in the cartoon represent?

Analyze: Whom do the characters in the image represent, and how does Nast convey his opinion of them?

Evaluate: In what ways were Reconstruction efforts hindered more by political and economic conflicts than by social rejection of freed slaves?

DOCUMENT 12.14 | **Sharecropper Contract**
1882

Sharecropper contracts, such as this from the Grimes family, used debt to tie poor, land-less, formerly enslaved African Americans in the South to an agricultural system that kept them poor and benefited white landowners.

To every one applying to rent land upon shares, the following conditions must be read, and agreed to. To every 30 and 35 acres, I agree to furnish the team, plow, and farming implements, except cotton planters, and I do not agree to furnish a cart to every [share] cropper. The croppers are to have half of the cotton, corn, and fodder (and peas and pumpkins and potatoes if any are planted) if the following conditions are complied with, but—if not—they are to have only two-fifths (2/5). Croppers are to have no part or interest in the cotton seed raised from the crop planted and worked by them. No vine crops of any description, that is, no watermelons, muskmelons, . . . squashes or anything of that kind, except peas and pumpkins, and potatoes, are to be planted in the cotton or corn. All must work under my direction. All plantation work to be done by the croppers. My part of the crop to be housed by them, and the fodder and oats to be hauled and put in the house. All the cotton must be topped about 1st August. If any cropper fails from any cause to save all the fodder from his crop, I am to have enough fodder to make it equal to one-half of the whole if the whole amount of fodder had been saved.

For every mule or horse furnished by me there must be 1000 good sized rails . . . hauled, and the fence repaired as far as they will go, the fence to be torn down and put up from the bottom if I so direct. All croppers to haul rails and work on fence whenever I may order. Rails to be split when I may say. Each cropper to clean out every ditch in his crop, and where a ditch runs between two croppers, the cleaning out of that ditch is to be divided equally between them. Every ditch bank in the crop must be shrubbed down [perhaps to remove underbrush] and cleaned off before the crop is planted and must be cut down every time the land is worked with his hoe and when the crop is "laid by," the ditch banks must be left clean of bushes, weeds, and seeds. The cleaning out of all ditches must be done by the first of October. The rails must be split and the fence repaired before corn is planted. . . .

No cropper is to work off the plantation when there is any work to be done on the land he has rented, or when his work is needed by me or other croppers. Trees to be cut down on Orchard, house field, & Evanson fences, leaving such as I may designate. . . .

Every cropper must feed or have fed, the team he works, Saturday nights, Sundays, and every morning before going to work, beginning to feed his team (morning, noon, and night every day in the week) on the day he rents and feeding it to including the 31st day of December. If any cropper shall from any cause fail to repair his fence as far as 1000 rails will go, or shall fail to clean out any part of his ditches, or shall fail to leave his ditch banks, any part of them, well shrubbed and clean when his crop is laid by, or shall fail to clean out stables, fill them up and haul straw in front of them whenever he is told, he shall have only two-fifths (2/5) of the cotton, corn, fodder, peas, and pumpkins made on the land he cultivates.

If any cropper shall fail to feed his team Saturday nights, all day Sunday and all the rest of the week, morning/noon, and night, for every time he so fails he must pay me five cents. . . .

The sale of every cropper's part of the cotton to be made by me when and where I choose to sell, and after deducting all they owe me and all sums that I may be responsible for on their accounts, to pay them their half of the net proceeds. Work of every description, particularly the work on fences and ditches, to be done to my satisfaction, and must be done over until I am satisfied that it is done as it should be.

No wood to burn, nor light wood, nor poles, nor timber for boards, nor wood for any purpose whatever must be gotten above the house occupied by Henry Beasley—nor must any trees be cut down nor any wood used for any purpose, except for firewood, without my permission.

Grimes Family Papers (#3357), 1882, Southern Historical Collection, University of North Carolina, Chapel Hill, Roy Rosenzweig Center for History and New Media, George Mason University.

PRACTICING Historical Thinking

Identify: Select five details of a sharecropper's job description in this contract and summarize them.

Analyze: What is the writer's attitude toward sharecroppers? How do the details you choose reveal this attitude?

Evaluate: What other kinds of primary sources would help us understand the economic status of African American Southerners after the Civil War?

APPLYING AP® Historical Thinking Skills

SKILL REVIEW | Comparison, Interpretation, and Synthesis

Read the two documents below by historians of Reconstruction. What are the similarities in their arguments? What are the differences? If you were to incorporate a piece of information or a document to support one of these authors, what would you incorporate? In what ways would it support the author?

> Army officers had neither the orders nor the desire to provide military protection for the fledgling Republican state governments created by the Reconstruction Acts. Like any other states in the Union, these were expected to provide for their own security. Anxious to gain political legitimacy in the eyes of a white population who largely regarded them as "regimes," these state governments had strong reasons to downplay the subversive activities within their borders. Instead, . . . [t]hey respected the civil liberties of ex-Confederates and, with only a few exceptions, permitted their bitterest foes full participation [in] the political process. They treated the Ku Klux Klan's extensive campaigns of murder, assault, and intimidation as mere criminal activity. Those accused of such acts therefore enjoyed full access to the courts—and often dominated them.

Mark Grimsley, "Wars for the American South: The First and Second Reconstructions Considered as Insurgencies," *Civil War History* 58, no. 1 (2012): 11–12.

The central role of the military has been underappreciated in the histories of Reconstruction. Studies duly note the use of military force and announce that the South experienced "military rule," but scholars rarely give the army its due as the central agents for social and political change. When they do, the focus most often falls on the Freedmen's Bureau agents and not the troops who operated independently and lasted beyond the demise of this agency, which was largely dismantled in 1869. Nor have they often looked beyond the district level to see the dynamic of relationships in communities between lower-level army officers and citizens. With rare exception, the tendency has been to depict soldiers as pawns in the power struggle between the president and the Radicals in Congress. In fact, with the exception of a few known Radicals such as Phil Sheridan, soldiers have been portrayed as trying to remain apolitical and as unbiased as possible in the administration of their duties, although their prejudices toward a certain brand of free labor have been widely recorded. This approach has left unexamined soldiers' own views on the political situation and what they thought about postwar readjustment. Part of the problem has been the tendency to measure the army's impact through what happened to the freedpeople, when soldiers had a broader mission that started with preserving law and order while attempting to nourish loyalty to the national government, especially among white people who had constituted their former enemies.

William Blair, "The Use of Military Force to Protect the Gains of Reconstruction," *Civil War History* 51, no. 4 (2005): 388–402, 390–391.

STEP 1 *Comparison*

Determine the similarities and differences between the two texts. Answer the following questions about the arguments from Mark Grimsley and William Blair:

- What do both texts say about the state of law and order in the reconstructed South?
- How do both texts characterize the difficulties and damages of Reconstruction?

STEP 2 *Interpretation*

As you learned from previous chapters, qualifying evidence influences your historical argument. Recall that Frederick Douglass (Doc. 7.9) serves as an exceptional, unusual representative of his demographic, not the norm. For example, the second Thomas Nast image in this chapter (Doc. 12.13) aligns more closely with the renegade world depicted by Grimsley and less closely with the description by Blair. Conversely, Document 12.12, which provides excerpts from two new amendments to the US Constitution, lends fuller support to the claims made by Blair.

Examine the final set of documents in this chapter, and align them to either interpretation by completing the chart on the next page.

Document	Aligns with Grimsley. Why?	Aligns with Blair. Why?
Doc. 12.11, Anti-Reconstruction Cartoon		
Doc. 12.12, Fourteenth and Fifteenth Amendments		X
Doc. 12.13, Thomas Nast, "This Is a White Man's Government"	X	
Doc. 12.14, Sharecropper Contract		

STEP 3 *Synthesis*

Write a paragraph that contrasts these historians' views of the military in the reconstructed South. Using all of the documents in the chart, determine which of the two interpretations is more compelling, and explain why.

PUTTING IT ALL TOGETHER

Revisiting the Main Point

- Choose four documents above that reflect differing interpretations of federal power. Connect each of these documents to one or more earlier arguments about federal power from the periods between 1787 and 1848.

- By the end of the Civil War, Northerners and Southerners often identified themselves as distinctly different peoples. What evidence of these different self-definitions can you find in the documents above?

- Using your knowledge of the time period and the documents above, characterize the ways in which white Americans identified African Americans throughout this period. What advantages did white Americans gain by defining African Americans in these various ways?

BUILDING AP® WRITING SKILLS | **Beginning an Argument with Sources: The Preliminary Claim**

Another way of introducing an argument is to begin by discussing a primary source. This approach contrasts with essays that begin paragraphs with main points that are followed by supporting points.

There are four good reasons to begin an essay or a body paragraph with a review of sources. First and foremost, the source acts as a springboard and can provide a preliminary claim. Here you are practicing synthesis by allowing sources to "speak" to each other. By introducing what another author says and then entertaining other positions—sometimes supportive, sometimes competing—you show empathy, patience, and the ability to present an argument that is fully grounded in primary documents.

Second, as you learned in Chapter 9, starting with specific examples provides an inductive approach to your overall essay. These starting points allow you to move into a more thorough illustration of key historical thinking skills—causation and periodization. Sources serve as portals into abstract historical thinking skills, such as contextualization and interpretation.

Third, by beginning with a primary document—when used in the service of historical thinking skills—you increase the credibility of your argument with your readers.

Finally, such a move has distinct effects on your reader: you gain credibility, illustrate a concept from the beginning, and appeal to your audience more fully, depending on your presentation of that document.

Consider the following prompt to illustrate the effective use of qualifying evidence in historical argument:

> Using your knowledge of the time period and the documents above, characterize the ways in which white Americans identified African Americans throughout this period. What advantages did white Americans gain by defining African Americans in these various ways?

STEP 1 *Understand the prompt, and identify the key words*

For a review of this step, see the Building AP® Writing Skills exercise in Chapter 1 (p. 22).

STEP 2 *Generate a working thesis*

For a review of this step, see the Building AP® Writing Skills exercises in Chapters 1 through 5 (pp. 22, 51, 79, 111, 142).

STEP 3 *Identify and organize evidence*

Review the Applying AP® Historical Thinking Skills exercises in this chapter as a way to determine differing points of view toward African Americans.

STEP 4 *Outline your response*

As an exercise, return to Chapter 2, and create a subject-by-subject comparison of different points of views toward African Americans. A sample outline follows:

    I. Introduction
   II. Liberal Northern perspective toward African Americans
       A. Reasons for this perspective
       B. Advantages of this perspective
  III. Conservative Northern perspective toward African Americans
       A. Reasons for this perspective
       B. Advantages of this perspective
   IV. Southern white perspective toward African Americans
       A. Reasons for this perspective
       B. Advantages of this perspective
    V. Conclusion

To continue with this exercise, select one of the body paragraphs and begin the paragraph not with a main point but with a description of one of the primary documents. For example, consider the following as the beginning of a discussion on the Southern white perspective toward African Americans:

Sample paragraph

By claiming that the "pretext for this policy [of freeing and drafting African American slaves] is, that we want soldiers in our armies" (1864), the *Charleston Mercury* (Doc. 12.9) claims that the state unjustly has more control over its citizens than the federal government. South Carolinians, indignant over Lincoln's Emancipation Proclamation, question President Jefferson Davis's emancipation plan as well.

Explanation

Note how the paragraph begins with a summary of the main ideas of the *Charleston Mercury*'s "Emancipation of the Slaves by the Confederate Government" and a statement of causation: the Proclamation led South Carolinians to become indignant. Freeing slaves to fight in Confederate armies is a similar crime against the Constitution, according to the editorial.

In reality, this stance reflected Southerners' belief in the inferiority of African Americans, and they used the United States Constitution as leverage to ignore the moral and social arguments against slavery. By arguing for states' rights in this editorial, the *Mercury* upholds the continuation of the institution of slavery.

STEP 5 *Finalize your thesis, and write your essay*

When you follow an inductive model to organize your body paragraphs, your writing *results* in a claim.

As you finalize your thesis, your essay also will have completed a similar approach toward the other perspectives outlined above—the Northern liberal point of view and the Northern conservative point of view.

The finalized thesis combines these distinct perspectives into a single claim. You have at least two choices for how you might combine these perspectives. A basic form of organization combines three perspectives with subordinate phrases (to evaluate). A template for this basic combination might look like this:

Although perspective 1 reveals that _____, perspectives 2, 3, and 4 more fully demonstrate that _____.

The above template *evaluates* and in so doing creates a broader argument.

A second approach toward combining points of view might engage in a *deductive* process that allows you to synthesize distinct perspectives into a single claim. Such an approach still obliges you to discern patterns or breaks in the patterns of perspectives to create a single statement. A template for such a deduced claim might look like this:

Although all groups share perspective _____ on African Americans, they differ from each other in their view of African Americans' _____.

Such a move requires you to *conceptualize* key ideas that are part of this chapter's debate. These ideas may feature words such as the following:

Autonomous	Patriots
Citizens	Pawns
Equal	Rebels
Freedom	Servitude

Similar to how the body paragraphs follow an inductive model and conclude with a general claim, the essay itself can begin with a working thesis (that tentatively compares the different perspectives) and conclude with a final thesis.

Reconstructions

Historians often mark the Civil War as the turning point in the fortunes of African Americans. Yet events that occurred during Reconstruction suggest that although the US Constitution was modified to prepare for a new era for blacks, most people did not see great improvements in their daily lives. It took many years before African Americans benefited from the civil and economic promises of emancipation and the Fourteenth and Fifteenth Amendments.

The presence of such unfulfilled promises during the era of Reconstruction leads historians to consider two questions: how much was slavery really a cause of the Civil War, and how much did winning the Civil War really serve as the turning point in the fortunes of African Americans? You have already read various sources that illustrate some different perspectives on African Americans during this time period. Now read the two passages below, and consider the extent to which the Civil War marked the genuine turning point in the fortunes of African Americans.

> If blacks failed to achieve the economic independence envisioned in the aftermath of the Civil War, Reconstruction closed off even more oppressive alternatives than the Redeemers' New South. The post-Reconstruction labor system embodied neither a return to the closely supervised gang labor of the antebellum days, nor the complete dispossession and immobilization of the black labor force and coercive apprenticeship systems envisioned by white Southerners in 1865 and 1866. . . . As illustrated by the small but growing number of black landowners, businessmen, and professionals, the doors of economic opportunity that had opened could never be completely closed. Without Reconstruction, moreover, it is difficult to imagine the establishment of a framework of legal rights enshrined in the Constitution that, while flagrantly violated after 1877, created a vehicle for future federal intervention in Southern affairs. As a result of this unprecedented redefinition of the American body politic, the South's racial system remained regional rather than national, an outcome of great importance when economic opportunities at last opened in the North.

> —Eric Foner, *Reconstruction: America's Unfinished Revolution, 1863–1877* (New York: Harper and Row, 1998)

> This Greater Reconstruction [of the whole nation] was even more morally ambiguous than the lesser one [in the South]. It included not one war but three—the Mexican War, Civil War, and War against Indian America—and while it saw the emancipation of one non-white people, it was equally concerned with dominating others. It included the Civil Rights Acts and the 13th, 14th, and 15th Amendments, but it began with U.S. soldiers clashing with a Mexican patrol on disputed terrain along the Rio Grande in 1846. . . . Always the Greater Reconstruction was as much about control as liberation, as much about unity and power as about equality. Indians were given roles they mostly didn't want, and freedmen were

offered roles they mostly did, but both were being told that these were the roles they *would* play, like it or not. . . .

. . . [W]e should . . . not allow the Civil War to continue behaving as it does now in our texts and histories, sitting there like a gravity field, drawing to itself everything around it and bending all meanings to fit its own shape. I am certain that, while we call the mid-nineteenth century the Civil War Era, acquiring the West had at least as much to do with remaking America as the conflict between North and South. I know that race is essential to understanding what happened during those years, and I know that the conquest and integration of the West is essential to understanding race.

—Elliott West, "Reconstructing Race," *Western Historical Quarterly* 34 (Spring 2003): 1–14.

Based on the two interpretations above, complete the following three tasks:

1. Briefly explain the relationship between slavery and economics that is established in the first passage.
2. Briefly explain the relationship between slavery and westward expansion that is established in the second passage.
3. Provide one document from Chapter 10, 11, or 12, and explain how it supports the interpretation of either passage.

CHAPTER 13

A Gilded Age

Mark Twain called the period from the end of the Civil War through the end of the nineteenth century "The Gilded Age" and compared the times to something cheap and ugly disguised by a thin layer of gold. Although Twain's term has stuck to the age, it is a satire that obscures more than it reveals. The generation after the Civil War experienced upheavals and hardships but also opportunities and prosperity.

Two broad changes—a Second Industrial Revolution and millions of immigrants from southern and eastern Europe—defined this age. As a result, many of America's towns and cities grew from ports of trade to centers of industrial production. The conditions in factories and the lives of the Americans who worked in them were often dire, and these production centers led to paradoxical results—increased wealth for most Americans as well as reform movements and worker protests. During this period, the American middle and upper classes continued building the consumer culture that began in the early nineteenth century and became known for their conspicuous consumption, or the purchasing of goods to display wealth and define oneself to others.

For many Americans, however, these years accelerated or simply changed the nature of the oppression that they experienced before the Civil War. Although the institution of slavery had ended, many African Americans were relegated to second-class citizenship by the Jim Crow laws and sharecropping systems, Mexican Americans struggled with growing Anglo settlements in the West, and Hawaiians contended with growing American imperialism.

Seeking the Main Point

As you read the documents that follow, keep these broad questions in mind. These questions will help you understand the relationship between the documents in this chapter and the historical changes that they represent. As you reflect on these questions, determine which themes and which documents best address them.

- How did changes in transportation technologies shape changes in the American economy? In what ways did these changes help transform labor and labor conditions during this period? How did workers and other reformers protest these changes?
- In what ways did American industry situate itself within the world economy? How did the US government assist in this situation?
- What moral arguments were used to question and critique the US economic order in the late nineteenth century?
- How did migration, both within and to the United States, influence economic and social changes during this period? How did migrations from abroad stimulate conflicts over American identity and assimilation?
- Characterize the justification for conservation during this period.

The New Economy

DOCUMENT 13.1	**Completion of the Transcontinental Railroad at Promontory Point**
	1869

The Pacific Railway Act of 1862 offered free land and monetary incentives to railroad developers in return for the completion of a transcontinental line. On May 10, 1869, at Promontory Point, Utah, the transcontinental line was completed. The images below—an engraving from a magazine and a photograph—capture this event.

COMPLETION OF THE PACIFIC RAILROAD—MEETING OF LOCOMOTIVES OF THE UNION AND CENTRAL PACIFIC LINES: THE ENGINEERS SHAKE HANDS.

The Granger Collection, New York.

16-G-99-1-1, Still Picture Records; Photographs and other Graphic Materials; Records of the Office of the Secretary of Agriculture; Record Group 16; National Archives.

DOCUMENT 13.2 | HENRY GRADY, "The New South"
1886

Henry Grady (1850–1889) was a journalist and witness to the Civil War in the South. His plan for the South's reemergence from the war was modeled on the North's industrial economy. He described his plan in a speech in 1886 at a meeting of the New England Society in New York City.

But what is the sum of our work? We have found out that in the general summing up the free negro counts more than he did as a slave. We have planted the school house on the hill top and made it free to white and black. We have sowed towns and cities in the place of theories and put business above politics. We have challenged your spinners in Massachusetts and your iron makers in Pennsylvania. We have learned that the $400,000,000 annually received from our cotton crop will make us rich, when the supplies that make it are home-raised. We have reduced the commercial rate of interest from 24 to 6 per cent. and are floating 4 per cent. bonds. We have learned that one Northern immigrant is worth fifty foreigners and have smoothed the path to the southward, wiped out the place where Mason and Dixon's line used to be, and hung our latch string out to you and yours. We have reached the point that marks perfect harmony in every household, when the husband confesses that the pies which his own wife cooks are as good as those his mother used to bake; and we admit that the sun shines as brightly and the moon as softly as it did "before the war." We have established thrift in city and country. We have fallen in love with work. . . .

Henry Grady, "The New South," *The Critic* (ed. Jeanette Leonard Gilder and Joseph Benson Gilder) 10, no. 157 (1887): 10.

JOSEPH KEPPLER, "Bosses of the Senate,"
Puck

1889

The magazine *Puck* published political satire during the last quarter of the nineteenth century. The cartoon below, like most of the images in *Puck*, reflects contemporary concerns and anxieties.

THE BOSSES OF THE SENATE.

The Granger Collection, New York.

PRACTICING Historical Thinking

Identify: Which figures in this cartoon are most prominent? What do they represent? What details explain what they represent?

Analyze: What is the relationship between the larger and the smaller men in this picture? What does this depiction tell you about the artist's perception of business and government at the time?

Evaluate: **Satire** is the use of humor, irony, ridicule, or exaggeration as a form of criticism. Does this image distort the relationship between big business and the US government? Explain.

DOCUMENT 13.4

New Year's Greetings in *Puck*

1898

This New Year's cartoon in the popular humorous magazine *Puck* features a departing 1897 and an incoming 1898.

Library of Congress Prints and Photographs Division, LC-DIG-ppmsca-28768.

PRACTICING Historical Thinking

Identify: What features of the image are most prominent?

Analyze: How does this image of women reflect a larger development about leisure in America at this time?

Evaluate: In what ways was the pursuit of leisure an important part of America's emerging economy?

DOCUMENT 13.5 | **JOHN FOSTER, Memo to President Grover Cleveland**
1893

American missionaries and sugar planters settled in the kingdom of Hawaii throughout the nineteenth century. In 1893, Americans in Hawaii overthrew Queen Lili'uokalani and requested annexation to the United States. Although President Grover Cleveland rejected annexation overtures, the islands were annexed in 1898 during the term of President William McKinley.

. . . [F]rom an early day the policy of the United States has been consistently and constantly declared against any foreign aggression in the Kingdom of Hawaii inimical [harmful] to the necessarily paramount rights and interests of the American people there, and the uniform contemplation of their annexation as a contingent necessity. But beyond that it is shown that annexation has been on more than one occasion avowed as a policy and attempted as a fact. . . .

In 1871, on the 5th of April, President Grant in a special message significantly solicited some expression of the views of the Senate respecting the advisability of annexation.

In an instruction of March 25, 1873, [Secretary of State] Mr. Fish considered the necessity of annexing the islands in accordance with the wise foresight of those "who see a future that must extend the jurisdiction and the limits of this nation, and that will require the resting spot in midocean between the Pacific Coast and the vast domains of Asia, which are now opening to commerce and Christian civilization." And he directed our minister "not to discourage the feeling which may exist in favor of annexation to the United States," but to seek and even invite information touching the terms and conditions upon which that object might be effected.

Report of the Committee on Foreign Relations, United States Senate, with Accompanying Testimony, and Executive Documents Transmitted to Congress from January 1, 1893 to March 10, 1891, vol. 2 (Washington, DC: Government Printing Office, 1894), 813–814.

PRACTICING Historical Thinking

Identify: What is the main purpose of this message?

Analyze: Describe the changing views toward the annexation of Hawaii as detailed by Foster.

Evaluate: To what extent were these changing views toward annexation driven by political or economic motivations?

DOCUMENT 13.6 | ANDREW CARNEGIE, "The Gospel of Wealth"
| 1889

By the end of the nineteenth century, Andrew Carnegie (1835–1919) had built the Carnegie Steel Company into the largest steel manufacturer in the United States. His essay "The Gospel of Wealth" (originally entitled "Wealth") appeared in the *North American Review* in 1889 at the height of his cultural influence.

There remains, then, only one mode of using great fortunes; but in this way we have the true antidote for the temporary unequal distribution of wealth, the reconciliation of the rich and the poor—a reign of harmony—another ideal, differing, indeed, from that of the Communist in requiring only the further evolution of existing conditions, not the total overthrow of our civilization. It is founded upon the present most intense individualism, and the race is prepared to put it in practice by degrees whenever it pleases. Under its sway we shall have an ideal state, in which the surplus wealth of the few will become, in the best sense, the property of the many, because administered for the common good, and this wealth, passing through the hands of the few, can be made a much more potent force for the elevation of our race than if it had been distributed in small sums to the people themselves. Even the poorest can be made to see this, and to agree that great sums gathered by some of their fellow-citizens and spent for public purposes, from which the masses reap the principal benefit, are more valuable to them than if scattered among them through the course of many years in trifling amounts.

Andrew Carnegie, The "Gospel of Wealth" Essays and Other Writings, ed. David Nasaw (New York: Penguin Books, 2006), 8.

PRACTICING Historical Thinking

Identify: What does Carnegie mean when he says "public purposes" toward the end of this excerpt?

Analyze: How does Carnegie argue that wealth that is held by a few can ultimately benefit the masses?

Evaluate: Evaluate Carnegie's argument by identifying the potential flaws and strengths in his logic. Explain your response.

APPLYING AP® Historical Thinking Skills

SKILL REVIEW | Contextualization

Consider the following prompt:

> Using the documents above and your knowledge of the time period from your text-book and classroom notes, determine to what extent the period between 1865 and 1898 was, in fact, "gilded."

STEP 1 *Organize your evidence*

Using a table, a list, or your own graphic organizer, determine the features of each document that support the notion that this time period was a "gilded age," where deep social and political problems were masked by an outward appearance of wealth and prosperity.

For each document, determine which features reveal one or the other side (or both sides) of the Gilded Age, and note any documents that directly oppose each other.

Clarify the context for each document in terms of the issues that it addresses (for example, social, political, economic, or moral issues).

Which of these documents directly oppose each other?

Provide a brief explanation. Which of these documents oppose each other directly?

Determine the contexts that would or would not define this age as "gilded." Use the following contexts as a starting point:

Economic

Political

Social

Moral

STEP 2 *Develop a working thesis*

STEP 3 *Write your response*

When writing your response, organize your information by context.

Discontents of the New Economy

DOCUMENT 13.7 | "Hopelessly Bound to the Stake," *Puck*
1883

The image below from *Puck* was published on the heels of an economic recession that began in 1882 and ended in 1885. The heads are Jay Gould, Cornelius Vanderbilt, Russell Sage, Roscoe Conkling, Cyrus W. Field, Whitelaw Reid (breathing flames that are labeled "Monopoly Press"), and Chauncey M. Depew (the flames that read "Depew"). Chauncey Depew was a lawyer for Cornelius Vanderbilt.

Library of Congress Prints and Photographs Division, LC-DIG-ppmsca-28415.

DOCUMENT 13.8	**Reaction to African American Agricultural Activism, *St. Louis Globe-Democrat***
	1889

Throughout the late nineteenth century, farmers formed local "alliances" to agitate for economic and political rights. Below is a description of a local reaction to the Colored Farmers' Alliance of Tallahatchie, Mississippi.

Of all the ". . . killings" charged up to Mississippi, the recent campaign in the Tallahatchie country was the worst. The smallest estimate of the number shot is 20. The largest return of casualties is 200 dead. Probably 40 Negroes were murdered before the work ceased. The sole offense which called for such a terrible lesson was the organization of a Colored Farmers' Alliance, and the attempt to put in practice the plan of patronizing an Alliance store. Against the right of the Negro to enjoy the benefits of the Farmers' Alliance organization, the white store-keepers and planters of the Tallahatchie country banded themselves together. They began by exiling Cromwell, the agent of the commercial company. The usual reports now went out that the Negroes were organizing and arming for a race conflict. Then the killing began. . . . There was no battle. There was no resistance by the Negroes. The white store-keepers and planters, armed with Winchesters, rode through the country picking out their victims. . . . The condemned man was made to stand facing a tree, and a volley was fired at his back. Then the white store-keepers and planters rode on to the next place. It is known that at least 20 Negroes were killed in this way. . . . The outline of facts comes from white men and Democrats. . . . When the white store-keepers and planters had concluded their work they met and adopted the following resolutions:

"Whereas, it is the sense of this meeting that the organization known here as the Colored Farmers' Alliance is being diverted from its original or supposed purpose,

"Resolved, that we, the planters and citizens of Tallahatchie River, hereby request the Durant Commercial Company to desist from selling goods or loaning money to said organization . . . and we hereby serve notice that goods or other things shipped to the secretaries or managers of said Alliance shall not be delivered. . . . We do not intend to, and we will not submit to, a combination subversive of our fortunes, our lives, and our property."

Quoted in *The Forum* 9 (1889): 716.

PRACTICING Historical Thinking

Identify: What is the local reaction to the Colored Farmers' Alliance?

Analyze: What does the final phrase suggest about the motivations of the local reaction? Is racism the only reason for the protest?

Evaluate: To what extent did journalism act as a way of addressing social problems during this time period? Consult your textbook and class notes in addition to this document.

DOCUMENT 13.9 | Las Gorras Blancas, *Nuestra Platforma*
1890

Between 1889 and 1891, Mexican night riders known as the Las Gorras Blancas (the White Caps) cut fences and destroyed railroad tracks in an attempt to maintain common use of the Las Vegas Land Grant Commons around Las Vegas, New Mexico, against encroachments by white ranchers and the railroad. Las Gorras Blancas explained their motivations in this manifesto to white ranchers and railroad executives.

Our purpose is to protect the rights and interest of the people in general and especially those of the helpless classes.

We want the Las Vegas Grant settled to the benefit of all concerned, and this we hold is the entire community within the Grant.

We want no "land grabbers" or obstructionists of any sort to interfere. We will watch them.

We are not down on lawyers as a class, but the usual knavery and unfair treatment of the people must be stopped.

Our judiciary hereafter must understand that we will sustain it only when "Justice" is its watchword.

We are down on race issues, and will watch race agitators.

We favor irrigation enterprises, but will fight any scheme that tends to monopolize the supply of water sources to the detriment of residents living on lands watered by the same streams.

The people are suffering from the effects of partisan "bossism" and these bosses had better quietly hold their peace. The people have been persecuted and hauled about in every which way to satisfy their caprices.

We must have a free ballot and fair court and the will of the Majority shall be respected.

We have no grudge against any person in particular, but we are the enemies of bulldozers and tyrants.

If the old system should continue, death would be a relief to our suffering. And for our rights our lives are the least we can pledge.

If the fact that we are law-abiding citizens is questioned, come out to our houses and see the hunger and desolation we are suffering; and "this" is the result of the deceitful and corrupt methods of "bossism" [behind-the-scene control of a political party].

The White Caps, 1,500 Strong and Gaining Daily

Quoted in David J. Weber, ed., *Foreigners in Their Native Land: Historical Roots of the Mexican Americans* (Albuquerque: University of New Mexico Press, 2003), 235–236.

PRACTICING Historical Thinking

Identify: Summarize the main points of the White Caps.

Analyze: To whom are the White Caps referring when they say they are the "enemies of bulldozers and tyrants"?

Evaluate: Compare this document with Document 13.8. To what extent were the situations of African Americans and the White Caps similar in this era?

DOCUMENT 13.10 | JACOB RIIS, *How the Other Half Lives*
1890

Photographer Jacob Riis (1849–1914) published *How the Other Half Lives* in 1890 to introduce middle-class Americans to the living conditions of immigrant people in New York City. These three images portray an immigrant family of cloth cutters in their home, an immigrant family of cigar rollers, and a street in New York's Lower East Side neighborhood.

The Granger Collection, New York.

The Granger Collection, New York.

9696-"How the other half lives" in a crowded Hebrew district, lower East Side, N. Y. City. Copyright 1907 by Underwood & Underwood. U-86189

Library of Congress Prints and Photographs Division, LC-USZ62-63967.

PRACTICING Historical Thinking

Identify: Describe each image.

Analyze: What mood or feeling is created by these images? Explain your response.

Evaluate: Compare these images to that of Document 13.7. Are the figures in Riis's images "hopelessly bound to the stake"? Explain your response.

DOCUMENT 13.11 | BENJAMIN HARRISON, Presidential Proclamation, Wyoming
1891

In this proclamation, President Benjamin Harrison (1833–1901) created the first of what became the national forests, known initially as the Yellowstone Park Timberland Reserve.

Whereas it is provided by section twenty four of an Act approved March the third, eighteen hundred and ninety one, entitled an act to repeal timber-culture laws, and for other purposes: "that the President of the United States may, from time to time, set apart and reserve, in any State or Territory having public land bearing forests, in any part of the public lands wholly or in part covered with timber or undergrowth, whether of commercial value or not, as public reservations, and the President shall, by public proclamation, declare the establishment of such reservations and limits thereof."

Now therefore, I Benjamin Harrison, President of the United States by virtue of the power in me vested, do hereby make known and proclaim that there has been and is hereby reserved from entry or settlement and set apart for a public forest reservation all that tract of land situate in the State of Wyoming contained within the following described boundaries.

Beginning at a point on the parallel of forty four degrees fifty minutes, where said parallel is intersected by the meridian of one hundred and ten degrees west longitude, thence due east along said parallel to the meridian of one hundred and nine degrees and thirty minutes west longitude; thence due south along said meridian to the forty fourth parallel of north latitude; thence due west along said parallel to its point of intersection with the west boundary of the State of Wyoming; thence due north along said boundary line to its intersection with the south boundary of the Yellowstone National Park.

Warning is hereby expressly given to all persons not to enter or make settlement upon the tract of land reserved by this proclamation.

In witness whereof, I have hereunto set my hand and caused the seal of the United States to be affixed.

Done at the City of Washington this 30th day of March in the year of our Lord one thousand eight hundred and ninety one, and of the Independence of the United States the one hundred and fifteenth.

The Statutes at Large of the United States of America from December, 1889, to March, 1891, and Recent Treaties, Conventions, and Executive Proclamations, vol. 26 (Washington, DC: Government Printing Office, 1891), 1565.

DOCUMENT 13.12 | People's Party Platform
1892

The Farmers' Alliance movement of the late nineteenth century culminated in the creation of the People's Party (also known as the Populist Party), which ran James B. Weaver (1833–1912), a former Civil War general, for president in 1892. The Populist Party largely disappeared after the 1896 election. This excerpt is the preamble to its platform.

Assembled upon the 116th anniversary of the Declaration of Independence, the People's party of America, in their first national convention, invoking upon their action the blessing of Almighty God, puts forth, in the name and on behalf of the people of this country, the following preamble and declaration of principles:

The conditions which surround us best justify our co-operation: we meet in the midst of a nation brought to the verge of moral, political, and material ruin. Corruption dominates the ballot-box, the legislatures, the Congress, and touches even the ermine of the bench. The people are demoralized; most of the states have been compelled to isolate the voters at the polling places to prevent universal intimidation or bribery. The newspapers are largely subsidized or muzzled, public opinion silenced, business prostrated, our homes covered with mortgages, labor impoverished, and the land concentrating in the hands of the capitalists. The urban workmen are denied the right of organization for self-protection; imported pauperized labor beats down their wages, a hireling standing army, unrecognized by our laws, is established to shoot them down, and they are rapidly degenerating into European conditions. The fruits of the toil of millions are boldly stolen to build up colossal fortunes for a few, unprecedented in the history of mankind; and the possessors of these, in turn, despise the republic and endanger liberty. From the same prolific womb of governmental injustice we breed the two great classes—tramps and millionaires.

The national power to create money is appropriated to enrich bondhold-ers; a vast public debt payable in legal-tender currency has been funded into gold-bearing bonds, thereby adding millions to the burdens of the people.

Thomas Hudson McKee, ed., *The National Conventions and Platforms of All Political Parties, 1789–1904: Convention, Popular, and Electoral Vote*, 5th ed. (Baltimore, MD: Friedenwald, 1904), 280–285.

PRACTICING Historical Thinking

Identify: List five significant reasons for the formation of the People's Party.

Analyze: What factors encouraged the formation of the People's Party? Were they strictly economic?

Evaluate: To what extent does this platform represent the needs of marginalized groups, such as African Americans and Hispanics?

APPLYING AP® Historical Thinking Skills

SKILL REVIEW | **Causation and Patterns of Continuity and Change over Time**

Consider the following prompt:

Choose three of the documents above that express a desire to revise the status quo of the Gilded Age. In what ways were these documents shaped by historical events that preceded them?

STEP 1 *Organize your evidence*

Select the documents to use, and determine the historical events that preceded these docu-ments. Use your classroom notes and textbook.

STEP 2 *Generate a working thesis*

STEP 3 *Write your response*

Begin with the historical events, and then synthesize these events into a larger statement about the desire for reform. Your response will follow the inductive approach reflected in Chapter 9. In your response, also note patterns of continuity and change over time.

PUTTING IT ALL TOGETHER

Revisiting the Main Point

- To what extent did changes in technology and transportation during the Gilded Age transform labor and also encourage worker protests against the prevailing technological order?
- Compare and contrast the migration patterns of this era with those of the 1840s.
- Compare the ideas in Documents 13.6 and 13.12. In what ways are both products of the Gilded Age? Where do they agree and disagree?
- Although the Civil War was the greatest sectional crisis in US history, regional differences continued to shape the United States during the Gilded Age. Find three documents above that exemplify regional differences, and justify your choices in three paragraphs, one for each of your choices.
- In what ways did debates over the Declaration of Independence and the Constitution continue into the Gilded Age? Choose three documents above that support your opinion.

**BUILDING AP®
WRITING SKILLS** **Contextualizing Historical Argument**

As you learned in Chapter 2 of this textbook, **contextualizing** an argument means determining key factors—such as religion, economics, and politics—that help you understand the broad processes that are associated with a historical event or primary document. The Applying AP® Historical Thinking Skills exercise on contextualization in this chapter furthers this discussion by combining two opportunities to contextualize. You are also looking at the extent to which Mark Twain's assertion about the era as being "gilded" is an accurate one.

The ability to introduce multiple contexts allows you greater versatility in how you create your argument. Consider the following prompt:

> Compare the ideas in Documents 13.6 (Andrew Carnegie's "The Gospel of Wealth") and 13.12 (People's Party Platform). In what ways are both products of the Gilded Age? Where do they agree and disagree?

STEP 1 *Understand the prompt, and identify the key words*

STEP 2 *Generate a working thesis*

For a review of this step, see the Building AP® Writing Skills exercise in Chapter 1 (p. 22).

STEP 3 *Organize your evidence*

This task invites a comparison, even though the documents come from the same era. Review Documents 13.6 and 13.12, and determine where they agree and disagree.

At first glance, these two documents appear to be opposites because they represent the two sides of being "gilded." But note that the prompt also asks you to consider what they have in common. When Andrew Carnegie uses the phrase "the elevation of our race," for example, are his goals very different from those of the People's Party? This phrase suggests an economic or social interest in the welfare of humanity, much as the People's Party platform does. But the second context—the Gilded Age—allows you to approach Carnegie's "Gospel" in a new light.

Historical events influence the creation of new contexts by examining patterns of continuity and change over time. The above Applying AP® Historical Thinking Skills exercise on causation and patterns of continuity and change over time illustrates this concept.

STEP 4 *Outline your response*

One effective outline for such an approach is similar to approaches discussed earlier in this textbook and uses a traditional comparison-and-contrast format:

I. Introduction

II. Context 1: differences (social and economic differences)
   A. Document 1: Andrew Carnegie
   B. Document 2: People's Party

III. Context 2: differences (Gilded Era)
   A. Document 1: Andrew Carnegie
   B. Document 2: People's Party

IV. Conclusion

STEP 5 *Write the essay*

Application of contextualization to a new prompt

With these tips in mind, consider the following prompt:

> In what ways did debates over the Declaration of Independence and the Constitution continue into the Gilded Age? Choose three documents above that support your opinion.

This question examines a broad range of history, and your understanding of larger contexts will enable you to frame the response by examining patterns of continuity and change over time, comparing two very different eras—the Revolutionary period and the Gilded Age.

Formulate an essay using the steps outlined above. You may wish to use the sample outline above as a starting point to begin your response to this question. Use the documents from the Applying AP® Historical Thinking Skills exercises in this chapter as your evidence.

CHAPTER 14

The Throes of Assimilation

PERIOD SIX

1865–1898

By the second half of the nineteenth century, the United States had become an immensely diverse nation. Immigration from northern Europe in the early nineteenth century had been bolstered by immigration from Asia and southern and eastern Europe throughout the mid- to late nineteenth century. These immigrants added to the various white, African American, Native American, and Hispanic peoples who had occupied the North American continent for centuries.

Many Americans assumed that diversity was temporary and that the assimilation of these new Americans would ultimately turn the United States into one vast amalgamation of cultures. This belief was based on the expectation that immigrants and their descendants would embrace the economic, social, and political structures of the predominantly white, northern European American majority. This assimilation process continued throughout this period but not without conflict and resistance.

Seeking the Main Point

As you read the documents that follow, keep these broad questions in mind. These questions will help you understand the relationship between the documents in this chapter and the historical changes that they represent. As you reflect on these questions, determine which themes and which documents best address them.

- Consider the effect of white American migration on native populations in the West. In what ways were the effects of this migration different from the effects of eastern European migration to American cities?
- In what ways did social reformers try to solve the various problems related to migration within and to the United States during this period?
- How did migration to the West raise debates about land use and natural resources?

The Western War against Native Peoples

DOCUMENT 14.1 | **COLUMBUS DELANO, Testimony before the House Committee on Military Affairs**
1874

In his testimony before the House Committee on Military Affairs, Interior Secretary Columbus Delano (1809–1896) revealed the policy of President Ulysses S. Grant's administration toward Native Americans in the West.

The CHAIRMAN. Are the means of independent subsistence by hunting and fishing diminishing very rapidly?

Secretary DELANO. Yes, sir; the buffalo are disappearing rapidly, but not faster than I desire. I regard the destruction of such game as Indians subsist upon as facilitating the policy of the Government, of destroying their hunting habits, coercing them on reservations, and compelling them to begin to adopt the habits of civilization. . . .

Mr. MACDOUGALL. Do you find the Indians pretty generally inclined to live up to treaty stipulations themselves?

Secretary DELANO. Yes, sir. Of course Indians are ignorant. They do not always get correct ideas of their treaties, and we frequently have difficulty in explaining to them and making known to them exactly what they have consented to. But, in my experience, when you have made an Indian understand that he has made an agreement, he will comply with it, especially if you are prepared to show that you will punish him if he does not.

Reports of the Committees of the House of Representatives for the First Session of the Forty-Third Congress, 1873–1874 (Washington, DC: Government Printing Office, 1874), 99, 101.

PRACTICING Historical Thinking

Identify: Explain Delano's position on independent subsistence.

Analyze: What does Delano mean when he hopes that the Indians will "begin to adopt the habits of civilization"?

Evaluate: To what extent did new land opportunities in the West promote a continuation of a belief in America's Manifest Destiny?

| GENERAL PHILIP SHERIDAN, **Description of Custer's Battlefield**

1876

In this dispatch, former Civil War general Philip Sheridan (1831–1888) provides his opinion of the army's decision to attack Lakota, Cheyenne, and Arapaho peoples at the Battle of Little Bighorn in Montana Territory in June 1876.

I have to-day gone carefully over the scene of the Reno defeat and Custer massacre in company with a Sioux warrior who took an active part in both—"War Club" by name. The Indian villages attacked were seven in number, with Crazy Horse and his Sioux on the upper side of the semicircle in which they were placed, and the Cheyennes on the lower side, with the Unepapas next, then coming the Sans-Ares and Minneconjons next in the row—the semicircle of which conformed to the bend in the river at the point, and being close to the trunk of the river. Major Reno charged the village of Crazy Horse from above, while Gen. Custer was to have charged the Cheyennes at the other end; but before the ford was reached, he being on the other side from the village, Crazy Horse had Major Reno whipped and corraled in the high hills opposite, when the entire force attacked Custer with the sad result too well known. To-day a detail of 14 men from each company was made to bury the dead—the dead comrades of Gens. Terry and Gibbon and Major Reno—this being the third attempt to consign all that was left of them to their last sad, homely resting-place. It required the evidence of my own senses to believe this true, and I do not regard it as in any measure my duty to suppress this sad tale. The officers who permitted this should be taught, by the aroused civilized sentiment of the land, that such conduct will not be permitted to go unnoticed and uncondemned, if their own human and soldierly instincts are not sufficient to spur them to a different course.

New York Times, July 21, 1876.

PRACTICING Historical Thinking

Identify: What is Sheridan's opinion of the Battle of Little Bighorn?

Analyze: What is Sheridan's attitude toward the "soldierly instincts" of the army?

Evaluate: In what ways does this conflict between Native Americans and US soldiers resemble similar conflicts from two centuries earlier? In what ways are these conflicts different?

"Educating the Indians," *Frank Leslie's Illustrated Newspaper*

1884

In this image from the cover of *Frank Leslie's Illustrated Newspaper*, a Native American woman is greeted by friends and family members when she returns from a government school that taught her Western subjects and values.

Library of Congress Prints and Photographs Division, LC-USZ62-100543.

PRACTICING Historical Thinking

Identify: Identify the most prominent contrasts in this image.

Analyze: How do these contrasts reflect the overall argument of the image?

Evaluate: To what extent did education become a force for assimilation during the latter half of the nineteenth century? Use your classroom notes and textbook for support here.

| **Dawes Allotment Act**

1887

The Dawes Allotment Act (also called the Dawes Severalty Act) gave the president and his agents authority to divide up reservations and allot parcels of land to individual Indians as private property, with the return promise of US citizenship.

. . . [I]n all cases where any tribe or band of Indians has been, or shall hereafter be, located upon any reservation created for their use, either by treaty stipulation or by virtue of an act of Congress or executive order setting apart the same for their use, the President of the United States be, and he hereby is, authorized, whenever in his opinion any reservation or any part thereof of such Indians is advantageous for agricultural and grazing purposes, to cause said reservation, or any part thereof, to be surveyed, or resurveyed if necessary, and to allot the lands in said reservation in severalty to any Indian located thereon in quantities as follows:

To each head of a family, one-quarter of a section;

To each single person over eighteen years of age, one-eighth of a section;

To each orphan child under eighteen years of age, one-eighth of a section; and

To each other single person under eighteen years now living, or who may be born prior to the date of the order of the President directing an allotment of the lands embraced in any reservation, one-sixteenth of a section. . . .

"Transcript of Dawes Act (1887)," transcription courtesy of the Avalon Project at Yale Law School, National Archives and Records Administration.

PRACTICING Historical Thinking

Identify: Review the era of Andrew Jackson's presidency (1829–1837). How does the Dawes Allotment Act reflect a change in US policy toward Native Americans?

Analyze: What interest would the United States government have in gaining a greater number of Native Americans as US citizens?

Evaluate: How did the US economic policies of this time period—exemplified by the Dawes Allotment Act—contribute to national identity?

DOCUMENT 14.5 | **"Consistency,"** *Puck*

1891

This image from *Puck* magazine portrays the artist's view of the United States' policies toward African and Asian peoples versus its policies toward Native Americans.

PRACTICING Historical Thinking

Identify: Who are the figures in the right, left, and center of the image?

Analyze: Determine the relationship between the central figure and those on either side of him.

Evaluate: Synthesize this lithograph with two other documents from earlier in this chapter. What might explain Uncle Sam's differing relationships in this image?

APPLYING AP® Historical Thinking Skills

SKILL REVIEW | Contextualization and Comparison

Answer the following prompt:

> What social and economic factors shaped Anglo-American contacts with Native Americans between 1865 and 1898? To what extent were these factors similar to those of the period between 1763 and 1800?

STEP 1 *Organize and contextualize your evidence*

Locate the documents that present both social and economic factors that shaped Anglo-American contacts with Native Americans during two different time periods:

Between 1865 and 1898

Document	Social factors	Economic factors
Doc. 14.1, Columbus Delano, Testimony before the House Committee on Military Affairs		X
Doc. 14.2, General Philip Sheridan, Description of Custer's Battlefield	X	

Document	Social factors	Economic factors
Doc. 14.3, "Educating the Indians," *Frank Leslie's Illustrated Newspaper*		
Doc. 14.4, Dawes Allotment Act		
Doc. 14.5, "Consistency," *Puck*		

Between 1763 and 1800

Selected documents may include the following:

Document 2.6, John Martin, Proposal for Subjugating Native Americans, 1622

Document 4.10, Colonel Daniel Brodhead, Letter to General George Washington on an American Expedition into Pro-British Iroquois Territory, 1779

Document 4.2, The Diary of William Trent, 1763

STEP 2 *Compare the two eras*

When you compare these eras, use the social and economic factors as the starting point. Also, use the thematic focus of the documents to help align your comparison. For example, Columbus Delano's statement (Doc. 14.1) represents the federal government's attitude toward Native Americans. Therefore, you would look for a similar document that reflects policy statements toward Native Americans. General Philip Sheridan's account of the Battle at Little Bighorn (Doc. 14.2), for example, may reflect the military's perspective toward Native Americans in the way that Colonel Daniel Brodhead's position (Doc. 4.10) focuses on the military subjugation of Native Americans.

STEP 3 *Outline your response, aligning contexts and documents*

Here is a sample outline:

I. Introduction

II. 1865 to 1898

    A. Social factors

        1. General Sheridan

        2. [Insert evidence here]

    B. Economic factors

        1. [Insert evidence here]

        2. [Insert evidence here]

III. 1763 to 1800

    A. Social factors

        1. Colonel Brodhead

        2. [Insert evidence here]

    B. Economic factors

        1. [Insert evidence here]

        2. [Insert evidence here]

IV. Conclusion

The New Urban Environment

DOCUMENT 14.6 | **JANE ADDAMS, *Twenty Years at Hull House***
1900

Jane Addams (1860–1935) founded Hull House as one of the first settlement houses in the United States. Dedicated to helping Chicago's immigrants on the city's south side, Hull House became the model for the profession of social work. This excerpt is from Addams's popular account of her first twenty years working with Chicago's immigrant communities.

The teacher in a Settlement is constantly put upon his mettle to discover methods of instruction which shall make knowledge quickly available to his pupils, and I should like here to pay my tribute of admiration to the dean of our educational department, Miss Landsberg, and to the many men and women who every winter come regularly to Hull-House, putting untiring energy into the endless task of teaching the newly arrived immigrant the first use of a language of which he has such desperate need. Even a meager knowledge of English may mean an opportunity to work in a factory *versus* nonemployment, or it may mean a question of life or death when a sharp command must be understood in order to avoid the danger of a descending crane.

In response to a demand for an education which should be immediately available, classes have been established and grown apace in cooking, dressmaking, and millinery. A girl who attends them will often say that she "expects to marry a workingman next spring," and because she has worked in a factory so long she knows "little about a house." Sometimes classes are composed of young matrons of like factory experiences. I recall one of them whose husband had become so desperate after two years of her unskilled cooking that he had threatened to desert her and go where he could get "decent food," as she confided to me in a tearful interview, when she followed my advice to take the Hull-House courses in cooking, and at the end of six months reported a united and happy home.

Jane Addams, *Twenty Years at Hull House* (Norwood, MA: Norwood Press, 1911), 437–438.

PRACTICING Historical Thinking

Identify: Describe Addams's goals for Hull House.

Analyze: How did Hull House represent a change in attitudes toward female workers in America? In what ways did it uphold traditional gender roles?

DOCUMENT 14.7 | GEORGE WASHINGTON PLUNKITT, "Honest Graft and Dishonest Graft"

1905

George Washington Plunkitt (1842–1924) was one of New York's best-known "machine politicians." He worked for Tammany Hall, the Democratic Party's political machine that combined voter fraud and corruption (called graft) with social services to maintain power in New York City. Excerpted here is one of the lectures that Plunkitt delivered from the bootblack stand in the New York County Courthouse, which were collected by political reporter William Riordan for publication in 1905.

There's an honest graft, and I'm an example of how it works. I might sum up the whole thing by sayin': "I seen my opportunities and I took 'em."

Just let me explain by examples. My party's in power in the city, and it's goin' to undertake a lot of public improvements. Well, I'm tipped off, say, that they're going to lay out a new park at a certain place.

I see my opportunity and I take it. I go to that place and I buy up all the land I can in the neighborhood. Then the board of this or that makes its plan public, and there is a rush to get my land, which nobody cared particular for before.

Ain't it perfectly honest to charge a good price and make a profit on my investment and foresight? Of course, it is. Well, that's honest graft.

Or supposin' it's a new bridge they're goin' to build. I get tipped off and I buy as much property as I can that has to be taken for approaches. I sell at my own price later on and drop some more money in the bank.

Wouldn't you? It's just like lookin' ahead in Wall Street or in the coffee or cotton market. It's honest graft, and I'm lookin' for it every day in the year. I will tell you frankly that I've got a good lot of it, too.

I'll tell you of one case. They were goin' to fix up a big park, no matter where. I got on to it, and went lookin' about for land in that neighborhood.

I could get nothin' at a bargain but a big piece of swamp, but I took it fast enough and held on to it. What turned out was just what I counted on. They couldn't make the park complete without Plunkitt's swamp, and they had to pay a good price for it. Anything dishonest in that?

Up in the watershed I made some money, too. I bought up several bits of land there some years ago and made a pretty good guess that they would be bought up for water purposes later by the city.

Somehow, I always guessed about right, and shouldn't I enjoy the profit of my foresight? It was rather amusin' when the condemnation commissioners came along and found piece after piece of the land in the name of George Plunkitt of the Fifteenth Assembly District, New York City. They wondered how I knew just what to buy. The answer is—I seen my opportunity and I took it. I haven't confined myself to land; anything that pays is in my line.

William L. Riordan, *Plunkitt of Tammany Hall: A Series of Very Plain Talks on Very Practical Politics, Delivered by Ex-Senator George Washington Plunkitt, the Tammany Philosopher, from His Rostrum—the New York County Court-House Bootblack Stand* (New York: McClure, Phillips, 1905), 3–6.

PRACTICING Historical Thinking

Identify: What does Plunkitt mean by "honest graft"?

Analyze: What is Plunkitt's attitude toward graft? Cite one line to support your response.

Evaluate: Does Plunkitt's statement reflect a paradox within the American identity regarding personal gain and social obligations? Explain.

DOCUMENT 14.8 | **FORRESTER B. WASHINGTON,** *A Study of Negro Employees of Apartment Houses in New York City*
1916

In his book *A Study of Negro Employees of Apartment Houses in New York City*, Forrester B. Washington (1887–1963) applied the methods of the new field of sociology to study the wage status of African Americans who worked in New York apartment buildings.

The average pay of elevator and switch-board men was $27.50 per month. The average pay of door-men was $32.50. There were 90 of the elevator and switch-board men and only 8 door-men.

It was stated by all the men and admitted by most superintendents that tips were not near as high as they had been in the past. The statistics show that the average amount of tips received by the 100 men was $3.00 per month. Adding this to the $28.00 average wage, makes $31.00 per month, the total income of the average colored employee. The income for a week of seven days is $7.00. Thus the typical wage for one of the largest groups of colored working men is two dollars a week less than the minimum wage of $9.00 advocated for women in New York City by the N. Y. State Factory Investigating Committee.

The investigator found that white men in the same neighborhood received more money than the colored men. Twelve out of the 100 colored employees reported that the white men, in the neighborhood received $15.00 more wages per month, 45 reported that the white boys received $10.00 more, 27 reported that the white boys received $5.00 more, 10 reported that the white boys received $2.50 more, and 6 reported that they received the same. Interviews with the superintendents practically confirmed these statements.

Cases were cited to the investigator where the working force had been changed from white to colored and back again. In these cases the wages were raised when the white men were taken on but reduced when colored men were re-employed. When two large department stores failed, for instance, the proprietors used their influence with real estate owners and agents to have colored elevator and switch-board men superseded by the white store employees thrown out of work. There were several houses in the vicinity of West 84th Street where the former dry-goods clerks took the place of colored employees. In each of these houses the wages were raised from the $30.00, which the colored men had been receiving, to $40.00. When, after a short while, the ex-store help was found unsatisfactory and the colored men were called back to their former posts, the wages were reduced to the original wage of $30.00.

Practically every man interviewed complained of the inadequacy of the wages to meet even the mere necessities of life. Of the 100 interviewed, 76 would prefer higher wages without tips; 21 would prefer the present wages with more tips. The objections to tips and the present wages seemed to be that tips were irregular and were gradually diminishing, whereas higher wages were dependable. One point was that adequate wages would insure every man a livelihood whereas tips would not because some men lacked the ability to get tips from tenants. Some men objected to tips because they were "humiliating." Others stated that "people expected too much for tips" and that "tips saddle men down with an enormous number of odd jobs."

Forrester B. Washington, *A Study of Negro Employees of Apartment Houses in New York City* (New York: National Urban League for Social Service among Negroes, 1916), 20–22.

PRACTICING Historical Thinking

Identify: Identify the significant pieces of data in this text, and explain why you chose them.

Analyze: According to Washington, why do some black workers prefer higher wages rather than tips?

Evaluate: To what extent does Washington's account of African Americans parallel the condition of women, Native Americans, and immigrants during this time period? Explain your response.

SKILL REVIEW | Interpretation and Synthesis

STEP 1 *Read the excerpt*

Read the following excerpt by a historian of migration:

> Immigration history, in every respect except for the goal of individual opportunity, the antithesis of pure American and western history, inevitably fell victim to amnesia. Of course, the very subject of immigration has been central, indeed obsessive, to western history and has produced some of its most distinguished imaginative and historical writing. But scholarship and veneration have been limited to the pilgrim years. The Far West's Jamestown has been at Donner Pass [where a party of white migrants spent a winter stranded in the mountains], its Massachusetts Bay in the Salt Lake Valley [where Mormon migrants eventually settled]. In the study of no other region of the United States does the term immigration, except when applied to Asia[ns], almost exclusively denote internal land migration. In no other region . . . did the early settler seek so avidly and so desperately to quick-freeze the pioneer era into a super-American past. Perhaps no other region shifted more abruptly from heroic epic years to statistical drift years, from manifest destiny to the "Great Barbecue." Yet no other region's total history is so contemporary, falling just below the horizon of living memory, and so relevant and instructive for an understanding of the present.
>
> The very rapidity and intensity of change in a region so vast with a population so new and so elusive, so mobile and so diverse, so contemptuous of antecedents and yet so hungry for a past, has made it difficult for the historian to find his bearings. The analytical intelligence, which has been the hallmark of the outstanding historians in stabler and older regions, has been notably deficient here. Eastern and far easterners, southwesterners and midwesterners, immigrants and sons of European immigrants and transmigrants, and those from south of the border as well as north, have swarmed over this intellectually uncharted land.

Moses Rischin, "Beyond the Great Divide: Immigration and the Last Frontier," *Journal of American History* 55, no. 1 (1968): 42–53.

STEP 2 *Answer the following questions*

* What is Rischin's main point in these two paragraphs?
* How does he prove this point?
* In a paragraph, describe three ways that help to resolve the problem in western migration history noted by Rischin. Be sure to support your arguments with references to at least three documents from this chapter.

PUTTING IT ALL TOGETHER

Revisiting the Main Point

- Compare and contrast US policies toward Native Americans. What consistencies are apparent here?
- Compare the social services provided by Jane Addams (Doc. 14.6) and George Washington Plunkitt (Doc. 14.7). In what ways were both beneficial to urban immigrant populations?
- Compare and contrast the struggles of migrant communities in American cities as described in Documents 14.6 and 14.7. To what extent are they similar or different from the struggles of African Americans in the cities, as described in Document 14.8?

BUILDING AP®
WRITING SKILLS | ## Synthesizing Themes in Historical Argument

When you create your historical argument, one way to bridge the vast amount of information that is available to you is to understand **historical themes**. Throughout this textbook, these themes have been identified as part of the prereading Seeking the Main Point questions and thematic learning objectives.

Major historical themes in US history

    Peopling
    Politics and power
    Work, exchange, and technology
    Identity
    Beliefs, cultures, and values
    Environment and geography
    America and the world

Key themes for this chapter

    Peopling
    Politics and power
    Environment and geography

Many of the above themes feature common language, ideas, or features. Typically, historical arguments address multiple themes simultaneously because the complexity of any argument invites an examination of different themes. Much like **contexts**, the more that you can understand history through different lenses, the more balanced, logical, and effective your argument becomes.

For example, consider George Washington Plunkitt's "Honest Graft and Dishonest Graft" (Doc. 14.7). This document addresses issues of politics and power as Plunkitt describes how he used political graft to increase his own profits. This document also addresses issues of peopling because Plunkitt's constituents were mostly recent immigrants.

How do these themes work together? At first, it might appear that they are completely unrelated. **Politics and power** address the government aspects of American history, and **peopling** involves the trends, behaviors, and movements of the common man. Yet people in government sometimes gain when they respond to the needs of the poor by making social services a political issue and wielding money and power in the name of helping the poor.

This relationship recurs in other documents, such as the Dawes Allotment Act (Doc. 14.4), another example of governmental policy (in this case to Native Americans) that is a statement on both American politics and power as well as peopling. Social services were provided to Native Americans in exchange for economic and political gain for white people.

Consider the following prompt:

> Compare the social services that were provided by Jane Addams (Doc. 14.6) and George Washington Plunkitt (Doc. 14.7). In what ways were both beneficial to urban immigrant populations?

STEP 1 *Understand the prompt, and identify the key words*

For a review of this step, see the Building AP® Writing Skills exercise in Chapter 1 (p. 22).

STEP 2 *Generate a working thesis*

For a review of this step, see the Building AP® Writing Skills exercise in Chapter 1 (p. 22).

STEPS 3 AND 4 *Organize and outline your evidence*

Although the prompt includes only two pieces of evidence, you will need outside knowledge to develop your argument, especially to understand the benefits that Addams and Plunkitt provided to urban populations. Consult your history textbook for additional information.

Use the following outline as a starting point. The emphasis in this outline is on incorporating multiple themes into your discussion.

I. Introduction

II. Jane Addams

    A. Analysis of politics and power

    B. Analysis of peopling

III. George Washington Plunkitt

    A. Analysis of politics and power

    B. Analysis of peopling

IV. Evaluation of multiple themes

Note: When you evaluate multiple themes, you may address the following questions:

1. Why were these themes connected in history?

2. Do either of these themes emerge as more prominent than the other? Why?

3. Do additional pieces of evidence also reflect the relationship between these themes?

STEP 5 *Write your essay*

CHAPTER 15

New Ideas and Old Ideas in the New Industrial Age

Although the Gilded Age was an age of economic and technological progress, it also produced new forms of poverty and social dislocation. Throughout the last quarter of the nineteenth century, Americans wrestled with the political and economic legacies of the Industrial Revolution.

Politically, Americans argued over whether the government had an obligation to promote or control corporations for the sake of the common good. Immigrants and African Americans continued to bear the blame for economic woes experienced by urban and rural whites who were adversely affected by constantly shifting economic fortunes.

Throughout this period, reformers and civic leaders debated whether the people who were destabilized by the Industrial Revolution, including small businessmen and the working poor, could be better helped through government intervention or through private philanthropy.

Seeking the Main Point

As you read the documents that follow, keep these broad questions in mind. These questions will help you understand the relationship between the documents in this chapter and the historical changes that they represent. As you reflect on these questions, determine which themes and which documents best address them.

- In what ways did debates about extending civil rights manifest themselves during this time period?
- How did industrialization shape beliefs about progress and the future of the United States as seen in the documents in this chapter?
- Compare the various challenges to the status quo that are presented in this chapter.

Reform Impulses

DOCUMENT 15.1 | **WOMEN OF LORAIN COUNTY, Petition against Woman Suffrage**
1870

The cause of women's suffrage gained popularity throughout the second half of the nineteenth century, but it continued to generate opposition among both men and women. In this petition to the Ohio state legislature, 140 married women from Lorain County, including several female faculty members of Oberlin College, protest against women's suffrage.

We acknowledge no inferiority to men. We claim to have no less ability to perform the duties which God has imposed upon us than they have to perform those imposed upon them. We believe that God has wisely and well adapted each sex to the proper performance of the duties of each. We believe our trusts to be as important and as sacred as any that exist on earth. We feel that our present duties fill up the whole measure of our time and abilities; and that they are such as none but ourselves can perform. Their importance requires us to protest against all efforts to compel us to assume those obligations which cannot be separated from suffrage; but which cannot be performed by us without the sacrifice of the highest interests of our families and of society. It is our fathers, brothers, husbands and sons, who represent us at the ballot-box. Our fathers and brothers love us. Our husbands are our choice, and one with us. Our sons are what *we* make them. We are content that they represent us in the corn-field, the battle-field, at the ballot-box and the jury-box, and we them, in the church, the school-room, at the fireside and at the cradle; believing our representation, even at the ballot-box, to be thus more full and impartial than it could possibly be, were all women allowed to vote. We do, therefore respectively protest against legislation to establish woman suffrage in Ohio.

Elizabeth Cady Stanton et al., *History of Woman Suffrage: 1876–1885*, vol. 3 (Rochester, NY: Susan B. Anthony, 1886), 494.

DOCUMENT 15.2 | SUSAN B. ANTHONY, Speech in Support of Woman Suffrage

1873

Susan B. Anthony (1820–1906), the prominent women's suffrage activist, gave this speech following her arrest for casting an illegal ballot in the 1872 presidential election. She was fined $100 but refused to pay.

FRIENDS AND FELLOW CITIZENS:—I stand before you to-night, under indictment for the alleged crime of having voted illegally at the last Presidential election. I shall endeavor this evening to prove to you that in voting, I not only committed no crime, but simply exercised my "citizen's rights," guaranteed to me and all United States citizens by the National Constitution, beyond the power of any State to deny. . . .

The preamble of the Federal Constitution says:

> We, the people of the United States, in order to form a more perfect union, establish justice, insure domestic tranquillity, provide for the common defense, promote the general welfare, and secure the blessings of liberty to ourselves and our posterity, do ordain and establish this Constitution for the United States of America.

It was we, the people, not we, the white male citizens, nor yet we, the male citizens, but we, the whole people, who formed this Union. And we formed it, not to give the blessings of liberty, but to secure them; not to the half of ourselves and the half of our posterity, but to the whole people—women as well as men. And it is downright mockery to talk to women of their enjoyment of the blessings of liberty while they are denied the use of the only means of securing them provided by this democratic republican government—the ballot. . . .

For any State to make sex a qualification that must ever result in the disfranchisement of one entire half of the people, is to pass a bill of attainder, or an *ex post facto* law, and is therefore a violation of the supreme law of the land. By it, the blessings of liberty are forever withheld from women and their female posterity.

To them, this government has no just powers derived from the consent of the governed. To them this government is not a democracy. It is not a republic. It is an odious aristocracy; a hateful oligarchy; the most hateful ever established on the face of the globe. An oligarchy of wealth, where the rich govern the poor; an oligarchy of learning, where the educated govern the ignorant; or even an oligarchy of race, where the Saxon rules the African, might be endured; but surely this oligarchy of sex, which makes the men of every household sovereigns, masters; the women subjects, slaves; carrying dissension, rebellion into every home of the Nation, can not be endured. . . .

Webster, Worcester and Bouvier all define citizen to be a person, in the United States, entitled to vote and hold office. . . .

The only question left to be settled now, is: Are women persons? And I hardly believe any of our opponents will have the hardihood to say they are not. Being persons, then, women are citizens, and no State has a right to make any new law, or to enforce any old law, that shall abridge their privileges or immunities. Hence, every discrimination against women in the constitutions and laws of the several States, is to-day null and void, precisely as is every one against negroes. . . .

Elizabeth Cady Stanton et al., *History of Woman Suffrage: 1871–1876*, vol. 2 (Rochester, NY: Susan B. Anthony, 1886), 630–631, 635, 638.

PRACTICING Historical Thinking

Identify: What is Anthony's main argument in this speech? Find three different lines that support your response.

Analyze: To whom is Anthony addressing her speech? What allows you to make this inference?

Evaluate: Compare the first two documents of this chapter. How does Anthony's reference to the federal government and education change the context of the argument made in the Petition against Woman Suffrage (Doc. 15.1)?

DOCUMENT 15.3	"A Model Office Seeker," *Puck*
	1881

After failing to acquire a government job, Charles Guiteau (1841–1882) shot President James A. Garfield on July 2, 1881, and the president died on September 19. In this July 13 cartoon on the evils of the political spoils system, which awarded jobs to office seekers in return for political loyalty, Guiteau is depicted as threatening Garfield's life in return for a political appointment.

Library of Congress Prints and Photographs Division, LC-USZC4-6402.

DOCUMENT 15.4 | Chinese Exclusion Act
1882

Bending to political pressure from western legislators, Congress passed the Chinese Exclusion Act in 1882 in an attempt to curtail the number of Chinese laborers, whose presence in the West had angered American nativist politicians and their constituents.

Be it enacted by the Senate and House of Representatives of the United States of America in Congress assembled, That from and after the expiration of ninety days next after the passage of this act, and until the expiration of ten years next after the passage of this act, the coming of Chinese laborers to the United States be, and the same is hereby, suspended; and during such suspension it shall not be lawful for any Chinese laborer to come, or having so come after the expiration of said ninety days to remain within the United States.

SEC. 2. That the master of any vessel who shall knowingly bring within the United States on such vessel, and land or permit to be landed, any Chinese laborer, from any foreign port or place, shall be deemed guilty of a misdemeanor, and on conviction thereof shall be punished by a fine of not more than five hundred dollars for each and every such Chinese laborer so brought, and maybe also imprisoned for a term not exceeding one year. . . .

SEC. 8. That the master of any vessel arriving in the United States from any foreign port or place shall, at the same time he delivers a manifest of the cargo, and if there be no cargo, then at the time of making a report of the entry of the vessel pursuant to law, in addition to the other matter required to be reported, and before landing, or permitting to land, any Chinese passengers, deliver and report to the collector of customs of the district in which such vessels shall have arrived a separate list of all Chinese passengers taken on board his vessel at any foreign port or place, and all such passengers on board the vessel at that time. . . .

SEC. 9. That before any Chinese passengers are landed from any such line vessel, the collector, or his deputy, shall proceed to examine such passenger, comparing the certificate with the list and with the passengers; and no passenger shall be allowed to land in the United States from such vessel in violation of law.

SEC. 10. That every vessel whose master shall knowingly violate any of the provisions of this act shall be deemed forfeited to the United States, and shall be liable to seizure and condemnation in any district of the United States into which such vessel may enter or in which she may be found. . . .

SEC. 12. That no Chinese person shall be permitted to enter the United States by land without producing to the proper officer of customs the certificate in this act required of Chinese persons seeking to land from a vessel. And any Chinese person found unlawfully within the United States shall be caused to be removed therefrom to the country from whence he came, by direction of the President of the United States, and at the cost of the United States, after being brought before some justice, judge, or commissioner of a court of the United States and found to be one not lawfully entitled to be or remain in the United States.

Papers Relating to the Foreign Relations of the United States, Transmitted to Congress, with the Annual Message of the President (Washington, DC: Government Printing Office, 1892), 108.

Identify: Identify the main purposes of this document.

Analyze: Why are the masters of the vessels targeted as much as the Chinese immigrants?

Evaluate: To what extent does this act serve the same purpose as the Sedition Act (Doc. 5.18) from a century earlier? Where else have you seen this type of response from the federal government?

DOCUMENT 15.5 | EDWARD BELLAMY, *Looking Backward, 2000–1887*
1887

Edward Bellamy (1850–1898) wrote *Looking Backward, 2000–1887* from the perspective of someone living over a hundred years in the future as a way to critique the social and economic inequalities of the late nineteenth century.

"Does it then really seem to you," answered my companion, "that human nature is insensible to any motives save fear of want and love of luxury, that you should expect security and equality of livelihood to leave them without possible incentives to effort? Your contemporaries did not really think so, though they might fancy they did. When it was a question of the grandest class of efforts, the most absolute self-devotion, they depended on quite other incentives. Not higher wages, but honor and the hope of men's gratitude, patriotism and the inspiration of duty, were the motives which they set before their soldiers when it was a question of dying for the nation, and never was there an age of the world when those motives did not call out what is best and noblest in men. And not only this, but when you come to analyze the love of money which was the general impulse to effort in your day, you find that the dread of want and desire of luxury was but one of several motives which the pursuit of money represented; the others, and with many the more influential, being desire of power, of social position, and reputation for ability and success. So you see that though we have abolished poverty and the fear of it, and inordinate luxury with the hope of it, we have not touched the greater part of the motives which underlay the love of money in former times, or any of those which prompted the supremer sorts of effort. The coarser motives, which no longer move us, have been replaced by higher motives wholly unknown to the mere wage earners of your age. Now that industry of whatever sort is no longer self-service, but service of the nation, patriotism, passion for humanity, impel the worker as in your day they did the soldier. The army of industry is an army, not alone by virtue of its perfect organization, but by reason also of the ardor of self-devotion which animates its members.

"But as you used to supplement the motives of patriotism with the love of glory, in order to stimulate the valor of your soldiers, so do we. Based as our industrial system is on the principle of requiring the same unit of effort from every man, that is, the best he can do, you will see that the means by which we spur the workers to do their best must be a very essential part of our scheme. With us, diligence in the national service is the sole and certain way to public repute, social distinction, and official power. The value of a man's services to society fixes his rank in it. Compared with the effect of our social arrangements in impelling men to be zealous in business, we deem the object-lessons of biting poverty and wanton luxury on which you depended a device as weak and uncertain as it was barbaric."

Edward Bellamy, *Looking Backward, 2000–1987* (Boston, MA: Ticknor, 1888), 132–135.

PRACTICING Historical Thinking

Identify: What contrast does Bellamy draw between the pursuit of money and the pursuit of honor?

Analyze: Is Bellamy's vision of the future—based on the social conditions of the late nineteenth century—an optimistic one? Explain your response.

Evaluate: What factors of late nineteenth-century society helped to "impel" citizens to pursue a greater national unity rather than individual glory and wealth?

DOCUMENT 15.6 | **ANDREW CARNEGIE,** *Autobiography of Andrew Carnegie*
1920

The following excerpt is from the childhood memories of Andrew Carnegie, owner of Carnegie Steel, the largest manufacturer of steel in the nineteenth century.

One of the chief enjoyments of my childhood was the keeping of pigeons and rabbits. I am grateful every time I think of the trouble my father took to build a suitable house for these pets. Our home became headquarters for my young companions. My mother was always looking to home influences as the best means of keeping her two boys in the right path. She used to say that the first step in this direction was to make home pleasant; and there was nothing she and my father would not do to please us and the neighbors' children who centered about us.

My first business venture was securing my companions' services for a season as an employer, the compensation being that the young rabbits, when such came, should be named after them. The Saturday holiday was generally spent by my flock in gathering food for the rabbits. My conscience reproves me to-day, looking back, when I think of the hard bargain I drove with my young playmates, many of whom were content to gather dandelions and clover for a whole season with me, conditioned upon this unique reward—the poorest return ever made to labor. Alas! what else had I to offer them! Not a penny.

Andrew Carnegie, *Autobiography of Andrew Carnegie*, (New York: Houghton Mifflin Co., 1920), 23.

PRACTICING Historical Thinking

Identify: What business arrangement did young Carnegie make with his friends?

Analyze: Why do you think Carnegie included this story as an example of smart business strategy?

Evaluate: If Carnegie considered this a good business strategy, what can we infer about the business strategies of this period?

DOCUMENT 15.7 | **ROBERT M. LaFOLLETTE, "The Danger Threatening Representative Government"**
| 1897

Robert M. LaFollette (1855–1925), future governor and senator from Wisconsin, gave the following speech on July 4, 1897, in his first bid for the governorship. He eventually was elected governor in 1900.

The existence of the corporation, as we have it with us today, was never dreamed of by the fathers. Until the more recent legislation, of which it is the product, the corporation was regarded as a purely public institution. The corporation of today has invaded every department of business and its powerful but invisible hand is felt in almost all the activities of life. From the control of great manufacturing plants to the running of bargain counters, from the operation of railways to the conduct of cheese factories, and from the management of each of these singly to the consolidation of many into one of gigantic proportions,—the corporation has practically acquired dominion over the business world. The effect of this change upon the American people is radical and rapid. The individual is fast disappearing as a business factor and in his stead is this new device, the modern corporation. I repeat, the influence of this change upon character cannot be overestimated. The business man at one time gave his individuality, stamped his mental and moral characteristics upon the business he conducted. He thought as much of bequeathing his business reputation to his son, as he did of bequeathing the business upon which that reputation had been so deeply impressed. This, made high moral attributes a positive essential in business life, and marked business character everywhere.

Today the business once transacted by individuals in every community is in the control of corporations, and many of the men who once conducted an independent business are gathered into the organization, and all personal identity, and all individuality lost. Each man has become a mere cog in one of the wheels of a complicated mechanism. It is the business of the corporation to get money. It exacts but one thing of its employe[e]s: Obedience to orders. It cares not about their relations to the community, the church, society, or the family. It wants full hours and faithful service, and when they die, wear out or are discharged, it quickly replaces them with new material. The corporation is a machine for making money, but it reduces men to the insignificance of mere numerical figures, as certainly as the private ranks of the regular army. . . .

I do not wish to be misunderstood. The corporation, honestly operated in the function of a public servant and in certain lines as a business instrumentality purely, has an unlimited field of opportunity and usefulness in this country. As a public servant, as a business instrumentality, the corporation is everywhere,— before the courts, in the legislature and at the bar of public opinion, entitled to the same measure of consideration, the same even-handed justice as the individual. . . .

When, whereas, a corporation is used as a subterfuge in crooked dealing, as an incubator of schemes, as a shifty, irresponsible competitor in private business, as a cover for combination in destruction of competition and restraint of trade, and as a pernicious political factor in the state and nation, it is to be deprecated and ought to be destroyed.

Robert M. LaFollette, "The Danger Threatening Representative Government," speech delivered at Mineral Point, 1897, Robert M. LaFollette Papers, State Historical Society of Wisconsin, 8–9, 18.

PRACTICING Historical Thinking

Identify: According to LaFollette, what are the chief responsibilities of the corporation?

Analyze: What is LaFollette's attitude toward the corporation? Does he present a balanced view? Explain.

Evaluate: Does LaFollette's depiction of the corporation establish a relationship with the common working person similar to the one depicted in "A Model Office Seeker" (Doc. 15.3)?

Daniel DeLeon (1852–1914) was a socialist theorist, union organizer, and leader in the American Socialist Party. DeLeon gave this speech during a textile workers' strike in Massachusetts.

The essential principles of sound organization are, accordingly, these:

1st—A trade organization must be clear upon the fact that, not until it has overthrown the capitalist system of private ownership in the machinery of production, and made this the joint property of the people, thereby compelling everyone to work if he wants to live, is it at all possible for the workers to be safe.

2d—A labor organization must be perfectly clear upon the fact that it can not reach safety until it has wrenched the Government from the clutches of the capitalist class; and that it can not do that unless it votes, not for MEN but for PRINCIPLE, unless it votes into power its own class platform and programme: THE ABOLITION OF THE WAGES SYSTEM OF SLAVERY.

3d—A labor organization must be perfectly clear upon the fact that politics are not, like religion, a private concern, any more than the wages and the hours of a workingman are his private concern. For the same reason that his wages and hours are the concern of his class, so is his politics. Politics is not separable from wages. For the same reason that the organization of labor dictates wages, hours, etc., in the interest of the working class, for that same reason must it dictate politics also; and for the same reason that it execrates the scab in the shop, it must execrate the scab at the hustings [during campaigning]. . . .

. . . [M]y best advice to you for immediate action, is to step out boldly upon the streets, as soon as you can; organize a monster parade of the strikers and of all the other working people in the town; and let the parade be headed by a banner bearing the announcement to your employers:

"We will fight you in this strike to the bitter end; your money bag may beat us now; but whether it does or not, that is not the end, it is only the beginning of the song; in November we will meet again at Philippi [site of a battle to avenge Julius Caesar's assassination], and the strike shall not end until, with the falchion [a type of sword] of the Socialist Labor Party ballot we shall have laid you low for all time!"

This is the message that it has been my agreeable privilege to deliver to you in the name of the Socialist Labor party and of the New Trade Unionists or Alliance men of the land.

Daniel DeLeon, What Means This Strike? (New York: New York Labor News Company, 1899), 30–32.

PRACTICING Historical Thinking

Identify: Summarize DeLeon's advice to the strikers.

Analyze: Why does DeLeon draw a contrast between politics and religion? Why does he draw a connection between politics and wages?

Evaluate: To what extent is DeLeon's argument the opposite of Andrew Carnegie's argument (Doc. 13.6)? Explain your response.

SKILL REVIEW | **Periodization and Argumentation**

All of the documents in this chapter are from the same time period, sometimes called the Gilded Age. Name and justify three events that could qualify as the **turning points** that began the Gilded Age. In what ways do at least three of the documents above reflect each of the turning points that you chose? Refer to your textbook and class notes for outside information, as well as chapters 13 and 14, as needed.

PUTTING IT ALL TOGETHER

Revisiting the Main Point

- Choose three of the above documents that are related to the pursuit of civil or economic rights. What do the demands that are made in these documents have in common? How are they different? In what ways do they reflect the interests of the individuals who are making these demands?
- To what extent do the documents above present an optimistic view of the Gilded Age? Use at least four documents to support your answer.
- Compare the various challenges to the status quo that appear in this chapter. Based on these challenges, generalize what the status quo was at this time.

BUILDING AP® WRITING SKILLS	Periodization in Writing Historical Arguments

As a historical thinking skill, **periodization** allows you to frame a series of events through **turning points**, moments that occur at the start or end of an era. Transferring this skill into **historical argument** entails a similar skill, although this time the periodization occurs simultaneous to the development of your thesis.

Consider the following prompt:

> To what extent do the documents above present an optimistic view of the Gilded Age? Use at least four documents to support your answer.

In assessing the Gilded Age—itself a periodized era—you must determine whether the documents present the Gilded Age as an optimistic era. In determining the extent to which an assertion is true, you may rely on contextualizing your argument. For example, you might claim that the Gilded Age was optimistic in a social sense but was pessimistic in an economic sense.

Periodization gives you another option: you can synthesize documents to create a new definition of an era or a new period. For example, many documents in this chapter reflect the discontent, rebellion, and even violence of a frustrated working class. These frustrations were exacerbated by the unprecedented wealth that was visible in many parts of America.

But this era of rebellion also may be construed as a positive sign as the twentieth century neared. Consider Edward Bellamy's vision of the future (Doc. 15.5), in which he presented the late nineteenth century as a time where citizens shed their mercenary qualities in pursuit of a greater whole, not unlike Daniel

DeLeon's call to action (Doc. 15.8) and Jane Addams's efforts on behalf of immigrants and the poor (Doc. 14.6).

Unlike **contextualization**, where traditional ideas about social, political, and economic conditions influence the ways that you use evidence in your argument, periodization provides you with greater opportunities to redefine a time period.

Refer to the Applying AP® Historical Thinking Skills exercises on evidence that appear earlier in this book (Chapters 4, 5, 6, 9, 11) as your starting point with your evidence and observations. In determining how optimistic this time period was, you also can use **qualifiers** to acknowledge disagreement over the degree of optimism that a labor strike, for example, reveals.

STEP 1 *Organize your response*

Organize your response by using one of the two following outlines.

Outline using deductive organization

  I. Introduction
  II. Document 1: Assess the degree of optimism, organizing your evidence chronologically.
  III. Document 2: How does this agree with? disagree with? modify document 1?

  In this approach, be sure to synthesize the sources following the

  IV. Document 3: How does this agree with? disagree with? modify the earlier documents?
  V. Document 4: How does this agree with? disagree with? modify the earlier documents?
  VI. Conclusion—the main claim of the essay

Note: This approach also uses **chronological reasoning**.

Outline using a point-by-point organization

  I. Introduction
  II. Optimistic features of the Gilded Age (the "golden" aspects)
  III. Pessimistic features of the Gilded Age
  IV. Conclusion

STEP 2 *Write your essay*

Economic Consolidation

America's growing wealth had its positive and negative aspects. The country enjoyed an unprecedented rise in economic strength, which resulted in the development of a new middle class that enjoyed greater leisure time. But the distribution of this wealth and the power that this wealth carried remained problematic. Industry fostered a new class of poverty. To what extent was prosperity meant to be shared among all people?

You have already read various sources that illustrate different approaches toward economic growth in this time period. Now read the two passages below, and consider the extent to which America's wealth acquisition sowed the seeds of greater conflict or prosperity—or both.

> The railroads pioneered in developing ways to control prices in the face of excess capacity and heavily fixed costs. During the 1870's, the railroads formed regional associations, of which the Eastern Trunk Line Association was the most powerful. . . .
>
> . . . [T]he manufacturers sought other ways of obtaining firmer legal control over the factories in their industries. They began personally to purchase stock in one another's companies. After 1882 when the Standard Oil Company devised the trust [an arrangement where one company holds property in others] as a way of acquiring legal control of an industry, companies began to adopt that device. . . .
>
> In many cases these new consolidations embarked on a strategy of vertical integration. . . . In the mid-1880's, the trust [Standard Oil] began to build its own distribution network of tank farms and wholesaling offices. Finally, after enlarging its buying organization, it moved in the late-1880's into the taking of crude oil out of the ground.
>
> —Alfred D. Chandler Jr., "The Role of Business in the United States: A Historical Survey," *Daedalus* 98 (Winter 1969): 23–40.

> Despite the clear advantages held by business managers in countering the job actions of workers—access to the policing powers of government, the ability to hire strikebreakers in great numbers, especially with immigrants and African Americans in desperate search of work—the deck obviously was not completely stacked against the strikers. One important weapon they had at their disposal was community support. . . . In the early 1880s, more than 50 percent of all strikes did not involve a formal trade union organization. The proportion of work stoppages orchestrated by unions rose over the next two decades, but by 1900, one-third of all strikes were still waged without union intervention.
>
> —Walter Licht, *Industrializing America* (Baltimore, MD: Johns Hopkins University Press, 1995), 88–89.

Using the excerpts, answer the following:

1. Briefly explain one major difference between Chandler's and Licht's historical interpretations of relations between management and labor.
2. Briefly explain how one document from the time period that is not explicitly mentioned in the excerpts could be used to support one excerpt.
3. Briefly explain how one document from Chapter 13 or 15 could be used to support the excerpt you did not choose in question 2.

CHAPTER 16

Prosperity and Reform

By the 1890s, the Second Industrial Revolution, a second period in US history where industry and transportation transformed US society and economy, had been in effect for nearly twenty-five years and had produced a mature consumer culture and a certain degree of leisure and luxury for the American middle classes. Although laboring Americans continued to do often backbreaking and underpaid work, they also began to desire the consumable goods and leisure activities that were available to middle-class workers. Immigrants and their descendants, especially, began to imagine themselves as taking part in what came to be known as the "American Dream."

The first half of the twentieth century saw astounding flux in the American economy and culture at large. Middle-class Americans reacted with some ambivalence to the rise of big business and urban political machines. While many Americans celebrated success, others saw the rising inequality and corruption as threats to traditional American republicanism and free-market ideology. From these concerns arose an organized and activist reform movement that sought government regulation of elements of the economy and greater democracy in the political arena.

In the midst of this flux, the Great Depression shook the nation to its foundations and inaugurated the creation of a limited welfare state through Franklin Delano Roosevelt's New Deal.

Seeking the Main Point

As you read the documents that follow, keep these broad questions in mind. These questions will help you understand the relationship between the documents in this chapter and the historical changes that they represent. As you reflect on these questions, determine which themes and which documents best address them.

- Trace the ways in which technological and transportation changes in the late nineteenth century shaped the lives of Americans, both for better and for worse, and the ways in which Americans took advantage of these changes and also rebelled against them.
- Consider the ways in which reformers and government programs sought to solve some of the economic and social problems of this era.
- How did reformers and government programs seek to control the social and environmental effects of the Second Industrial Revolution? To what extent were they successful?
- Trace continuities and changes in Americans' sense of themselves as a nation throughout this period.

The Consumer's City

DOCUMENT 16.1 | **UNITED STATES STRIKE COMMISSION, Report on the Chicago Strike**
1894

By the late nineteenth century, George Pullman (1831–1897) had built his sleeping-car company into the major producer of passenger trains in the United States. Pullman required his workers to live in his company town of Pullman, Illinois (near Chicago), reside in Pullman-owned housing, and buy their goods from Pullman-owned businesses. When the Pullman Company lowered wages in an economic recession in 1894, workers struck, led by the future Socialist candidate for president, Eugene Debs (1856–1926). Ultimately, federal troops broke up the strike.

Pullman's Palace Car Company is in the market at all times to obtain all possible contracts to build cars. Its relations with railroads, its large capital and surplus, its complete and well-located plant and efficient management enable it at all times to meet all competitors on at least equal terms. Prior to the business depression of 1893, the company was unusually active in building new cars for itself and for railroads to meet the expanded demands of general business, and for the expected requirements of the Columbian Exposition traffic. Its repair department was also full of work. An average number of 4,497 workmen, during the year ending July 1, 1893, earned $2,760,548.99, or an average of $613.86 each. The wages paid were about the same as paid elsewhere in the business, Mr. Wickes thinks possibly a little higher.

The depression of 1893 naturally affected the business at once, and to a greater extent in some departments than in others. Matters grew worse until, in the fall of 1893, the company closed its Detroit shops, employing about 800, and concentrated its contract and repair business at Pullman. The company and the railroads had a surplus of cars for the decreased traffic obtainable, and hence pending orders were canceled and car building stopped, except as occasional straggling contracts were obtained at prices which averaged less than shop cost, exclusive of interest upon capital or any charge for depreciation of plant or machinery.

WAGES.

From September 18, 1893, until May 1, 1894, the company did contract work at the price of $1,421,205.75, which was $52,069.03, or 3.663 per cent below shop cost for labor and materials. Against this the loss to labor by the reduction of wages paid on this work was over $60,000, making the wages of June, 1893, the basis of comparison. It also had $1,354,276.06 of unaccepted bids, upon which its similar loss would have been $18,303.56, or 1.35 per cent. Assuming that the analysis submitted as to the cost of several lots of cars affords a fair basis for averaging the whole of the contracts, it appears that the average percentage of cost of material in this contract work was about 75 per cent. Hence while the amount of loss was nearly equally divided, it seems that the percentage of loss borne by labor in the reduction of wages was much greater than that sustained by the company upon material. Three-quarters of the loss for the company and the balance for labor would have more fairly equalized the division of loss on these contracts.

Report on the Chicago Strike of June–July, 1894: With Appendices Containing Testimony, Proceedings, and Recommendations (Washington, DC: Government Printing Office, 1895), xxxii.

PRACTICING Historical Thinking

Identify: Describe the successes and challenges of the Pullman Company, as reported by the document above.

Analyze: Does this report depict the company as being fair to its employees? Explain.

Evaluate: What values are expressed by this report's critique of the Pullman Company?

DOCUMENT 16.2 | **LOUIS GILROD AND DAVID MEYROWITZ, "A Boychik Up-to-Date"**
c. 1900

The word *boychick* is a combination of the English word *boy* with the Yiddish word *tshik*, meaning "little" or "cute." The image below is from the cover of a piece of sheet music that someone could play on a home piano or entertainers could perform at a local theater. The writing at the top is in Yiddish, which was the language of European Jews who immigrated to the United States in the late nineteenth century.

א בּוֹיטשִׁיק
אָפּטוּ־דײט.

A BOYCHIK
UP·TO·DATE

WORDS BY
L. GILROD
MUSIC BY
D. MEYROWITZ

SONG 50.   VIOLIN 30.

New York
THEODORE LOHR
286 GRAND STREET

Library of Congress Music Division.

PRACTICING Historical Thinking

Identify: What images are most prominent in this picture? What is its overall purpose?

Analyze: Is this image a flattering one? Explain.

Evaluate: To what extent does this picture depict a new national identity for America that is based on immigration? Or does this image make a statement on the difficulties of assimilation? Explain.

DOCUMENT 16.3 | ## Luna Park, Coney Island
c. 1908

Coney Island in Brooklyn, New York, was a popular seaside destination for pleasure seekers throughout the nineteenth century. By the 1880s, visitors could ride a carousel and one of the first roller coasters. By 1900, Coney Island had become an important destination for New Yorkers of the middle and working classes in search of leisure and fun.

Photo by Geo. P. Hall & Son/The New York Historical Society/ Getty Images.

PRACTICING Historical Thinking

Identify: What are the most significant images in this picture? Explain.

Analyze: How does this form of leisure reflect changes in American identity during this era?

Evaluate: Does this image present a social class that is at odds with American republican ideals? Explain.

DOCUMENT 16.4 | **Two Women Reading Employment Advertisements**

1909

By the first decades of the twentieth century, it was more and more common for young, single women to work in the service industry. This photograph shows two young women sitting on a park bench as they scan a newspaper looking for job openings.

Lewis W. Hine.

PRACTICING Historical Thinking

Identify: Describe the women's apparel.

Analyze: To what extent does this image represent a new social identity for women?

Evaluate: Based on your knowledge of US history, compare this image with earlier ones that describe women's working conditions (such as Harriet Robinson's description of the Lowell mill girls in Doc. 8.6 or Jane Addams's description of Hull House in Doc. 14.6), and determine the reasons for the changes in women's economic and social status. Your textbook and class notes will help you here.

SKILL REVIEW | Contextualization

Using the documents above, describe how each of the following individuals might react toward the Pullman Strike of 1894 (Doc. 16.1). Justify your responses with reference to the context in which these individuals form these opinions.

- A young woman who is looking for work in an office
- A young man who is enjoying the day at Coney Island
- A young man living in Chicago whose parents were Jewish immigrants from Eastern Europe

STEP 1 *What does the text say?*

Review your answers to the "Identify" questions to determine each text's main message or purpose.

Text	Overall purpose or message
Doc. 16.2, Louis Gilrod and David Meyrowitz, "A Boychik Up-to-Date"	For the son of Jewish immigrants:
Doc. 16.3, Luna Park, Coney Island	For the young man enjoying the day at Coney Island:
Doc. 16.4, Two Women Reading Employment Advertisements	For the young woman looking for office work:

STEP 2 *What is the context of each?*

Text	Context
Doc. 16.2, Louis Gilrod and David Meyrowitz, "A Boychik Up-to-Date"	For the son of Jewish immigrants:
Doc. 16.3, Luna Park, Coney Island	For the young man enjoying the day at Coney Island:
Doc. 16.4, Two Women Reading Employment Advertisements	For the young woman looking for office work:

STEP 3 *Create a historical argument using context.*

Consider the following prompt:

> In what ways would the context of the three individuals described above shape their reaction to the Pullman Strike? Refer to the documents above and your textbook or class notes to structure your response.

The Progressive Critique and New Deal Response

DOCUMENT 16.5 | **LINCOLN STEFFENS,** *The Shame of the Cities*
| 1904

Lincoln Steffens (1866–1936) first published his exposé of political corruption in American cities as a series in *McClure's Magazine*. The popularity of this series encouraged Steffens to republish his articles as a book entitled *The Shame of the Cities*. This excerpt is from the introduction of Steffens's book.

There is hardly an office from United States Senator down to Alderman in any part of the country to which the business man has not been elected; yet politics remains corrupt, government pretty bad, and the selfish citizen has to hold himself in readiness like the old volunteer firemen to rush forth at any hour, in any weather, to prevent the fire; and he goes out sometimes and he puts out the fire (after the damage is done) and he goes back to the shop sighing for the business man in politics. The business man has failed in politics as he has in citizenship. Why?

Because politics is business. That's what's the matter with it. That's what's the matter with everything—art, literature, religion, journalism, law, medicine,— they're all business, and all—as you see them. Make politics a sport, as they do in England, or a profession, as they do in Germany, and we'll have—well, something else than we have now,—if we want it, which is another question. But don't try to reform politics with the banker, the lawyer, and the dry-goods merchant, for these are business men and there are two great hindrances to their achievement of reform: one is that they are different from, but no better than, the politicians; the other is that politics is not "their line." There are exceptions both ways. Many politicians have gone out into business and done well (Tammany ex-mayors, and nearly all the old bosses of Philadelphia are prominent financiers in their cities), and business men have gone into politics and done well (Mark Hanna, for example). They haven't reformed their adopted trades, however, though they have sometimes sharpened them most pointedly. The politician is a business man with a specialty. When a business man of some other line learns the business of politics, he is a politician, and there is not much reform left in him. Consider the United States Senate, and believe me.

The commercial spirit is the spirit of profit, not patriotism; of credit, not honor; of individual gain, not national prosperity; of trade and dickering, not principle. "My business is sacred," says the business man in his heart. "Whatever prospers my business, is good; it must be. Whatever hinders it, is wrong; it must be. A bribe is bad, that is, it is a bad thing to take; but it is not so bad to give one, not if it is necessary to my business." "Business is business" is not a political sentiment, but our politician has caught it. He takes essentially the same view of the bribe, only he saves his self-respect by piling all his contempt upon the bribe-giver, and he has the great advantage of candor. "It is wrong, maybe," he says, "but if a rich merchant can afford to do business with me for the sake of a convenience or to increase his already great wealth, I can afford, for the sake of a living, to meet him half way. I make no pretensions to virtue, not even on Sunday." And as for giving bad government or good, how about the merchant who gives bad goods or good goods, according to the demand?

But there is hope, not alone despair, in the commercialism of our politics. If our political leaders are to be always a lot of political merchants, they will supply any demand we may create. All we have to do is to establish a steady demand for good government. The boss has us split up into parties. To him parties are nothing but means to his corrupt ends. He "bolts" his party, but we must not; the bribe-giver changes his party, from one election to another, from one county to another, from one city to another, but the honest voter must not. Why? Because if the honest voter cared no more for his party than the politician and the grafter, then the honest vote would govern, and that would be bad—for graft. It is idiotic, this devotion to a machine that is used to take our sovereignty from us. If we would leave parties to the politicians, and would vote not for the party, not even for men, but for the city, and the State, and the nation, we should rule parties, and cities, and States, and nation. If we would vote in mass on the more promising ticket, or, if the two are equally bad, would throw out the party that is in, and wait till the next election and then throw out the other party that is in—then, I say, the commercial politician would feel a demand for good government and he would supply it. That process would take a generation or more to complete, for the politicians now really do not know what good government is. But it has taken as long to develop bad government, and the politicians know what that is. If it would not "go," they would offer something else, and, if the demand were steady, they, being so commercial, would "deliver the goods."

Lincoln Steffens, *The Shame of the Cities* (New York: Courier Dover, 2012), 6–9.

PRACTICING Historical Thinking

Identify: Summarize Steffens's claim about the relationship between the business-man and the politician.

Analyze: Why does Steffens mean when he says, "All we have to do is to establish a steady demand for good government"?

Evaluate: Does Steffens's statement rely more on reforming politicians or reforming citizens to respond differently to their political leaders? Explain.

DOCUMENT 16.6 | UPTON SINCLAIR, *The Jungle*
1906

Upton Sinclair (1878–1968) published his novel *The Jungle* as an exposé of the unfairness of the American industrial economy to the working class in the United States. However, his description of the meatpacking process gained the greatest public attention and contributed to the passage of the Pure Food and Drug Act and the creation of the Food and Drug Administration.

They sat and stared out of the window. They were on a street which seemed to run on forever, mile after mile—thirty-four of them, if they had known it—and each side of it one uninterrupted row of wretched little two-story frame buildings. Down every side street they could see, it was the same,—never a hill and never a hollow, but always the same endless vista of ugly and dirty little wooden buildings. Here and there would be a bridge crossing a filthy creek, with hard-baked mud shores and dingy sheds and docks along it; here and there would be a railroad crossing, with a tangle of switches, and locomotives puffing, and rattling freight cars filing by; here and there would be a great factory, a dingy building with innumerable windows in it, and immense volumes of smoke pouring from the chimneys, darkening the air above and making filthy the earth beneath. But after each of these interruptions, the desolate procession would begin again—the procession of dreary little buildings.

A full hour before the party reached the city they had begun to note the perplexing changes in the atmosphere. It grew darker all the time, and upon the earth the grass seemed to grow less green. Every minute, as the train sped on, the colors of things became dingier; the fields were grown parched and yellow, the landscape hideous and bare. And along with the thickening smoke they began to notice another circumstance, a strange, pungent odor. They were not sure that it was unpleasant, this odor; some might have called it sickening, but their taste in odors was not developed, and they were only sure that it was curious. Now, sitting in the trolley car, they realized that they were on their way to the home of it—that they had traveled all the way from Lithuania to it. It was now no longer something far-off and faint, that you caught in whiffs; you could literally taste it, as well as smell it—you could take hold of it, almost, and examine it at your leisure. They were divided in their opinions about it. It was an elemental odor, raw and crude; it was rich, almost rancid, sensual, and strong. There were some who drank it in as if it were an intoxicant; there were others who put their handkerchiefs to their faces. The new emigrants were still tasting it, lost in wonder, when suddenly the car came to a halt, and the door was flung open, and a voice shouted—"Stockyards!"

They were left standing upon the corner, staring; down a side street there were two rows of brick houses, and between them a vista: half a dozen chimneys, tall as the tallest of buildings, touching the very sky—and leaping from them half a dozen columns of smoke, thick, oily, and black as night. It might have come from the centre of the world, this smoke, where the fires of the ages still smoulder. It came as if self-impelled, driving all before it, a perpetual explosion. It was inexhaustible; one stared, waiting to see it stop, but still the great streams rolled out. They spread in vast clouds overhead, writhing, curling; then, uniting in one giant river, they streamed away down the sky, stretching a black pall as far as the eye could reach.

Then the party became aware of another strange thing. This, too, like the odor, was a thing elemental; it was a sound, a sound made up of ten thousand little sounds. You scarcely noticed it at first—it sunk into your consciousness, a vague disturbance, a trouble. It was like the murmuring of the bees in the spring, the whisperings of the forest; it suggested endless activity, the rumblings of a world in motion. It was only by an effort that one could realize that it was made by animals, that it was the distant lowing of ten thousand cattle, the distant grunting of ten thousand swine.

Upton Sinclair, *The Jungle* (New York: New American Library), 27–29.

PRACTICING Historical Thinking

Identify: What is the smoke that Sinclair describes? What are the sounds that Sinclair describes?

Analyze: How does Sinclair's use of the word "elemental" make a larger statement about the values of this society?

Evaluate: Does Sinclair's *The Jungle* represent an illustration of what Lincoln Steffens warns against in Document 16.5? To what extent is it an extension of the relationship that businesses have with their laborers, as seen in the Pullman Strike (Doc. 16.1)? Explain.

DOCUMENT 16.7 | **IDA M. TARBELL, *The Business of Being a Woman***
1921

Ida Tarbell (1857–1944) is best known for *The History of the Standard Oil Company*, her exposé of Standard Oil's monopolistic tactics. Tarbell was a prominent reformer and published a number of articles on contemporary topics, including this one on the social status of women in the early twentieth century.

The most conspicuous occupation of the American woman of to-day, dressing herself aside, is self-discussion. It is a disquieting phenomenon. Chronic self-discussion argues chronic ferment of mind, and ferment of mind is a serious handicap to both happiness and efficiency. Nor is self-discussion the only exhibit of restlessness the American woman gives. To an unaccustomed observer she seems always to be running about on the face of things with no other purpose than to put in her time. He points to the triviality of the things in which she can immerse herself—her fantastic and ever-changing raiment, the welter of lectures and other culture schemes which she supports, the eagerness with which she transports herself to the ends of the earth—as marks of a spirit not at home with itself, and certainly not convinced that it is going in any particular direction or that it is committed to any particular worth-while task.

Perhaps the most disturbing side of the phenomenon is that it is coincident with the emancipation of woman. At a time when she is freer than at any other period of the world's history—save perhaps at one period in ancient Egypt—she is apparently more uneasy.

Ida M. Tarbell, "The Uneasy Woman," *American Magazine* 73, no. 4 (January 1912): 259.

PRACTICING Historical Thinking

Identify: Is Tarbell for or against the emancipation of women? Explain.

Analyze: Why does Tarbell call the women of her day "uneasy"?

Evaluate: To what extent is Tarbell's statement about women's "fantastic and ever-changing raiment" an indictment of the job-seeking women shown in Document 16.4? Explain.

DOCUMENT 16.8 | CLIFFORD K. BERRYMAN, "Dr. New Deal"
1934

President Franklin Delano Roosevelt (1882–1945) was elected in a landslide victory in 1932 in the midst of the Great Depression, the greatest economic crisis the United States had ever faced. Roosevelt's "New Deal" was largely an attempt to use governmental power to improve the economic crisis through programs such as the Civilian Conservation Corps (CCC) and the National Recovery Act (NRA).

The Granger Collection, New York.

DOCUMENT 16.9 | **FRANKLIN D. ROOSEVELT, Message to Congress on Making the Civilian Conservation Corps a Permanent Agency**
1937

In this message to Congress, President Franklin Delano Roosevelt expresses his desire to expand the powers of the federal executive branch by making permanent one of the more popular New Deal programs, the Civilian Conservation Corps.

On March 21, 1933, I addressed a message to the Congress in which I stated:

"I propose to create a civilian conservation corps to be used in simple work, not interfering with normal employment, and confining itself to forestry, the prevention of soil erosion, flood control and similar projects. I call your attention to the fact that this type of work is of definite, practical value, not only through the prevention of great present financial loss, but also as a means of creating future national wealth." . . .

It is not necessary to go into detail regarding the accomplishments of the Corps. You are acquainted with the physical improvements that have taken place in our forests and parks as a result of the activities of the Corps and with the wealth that is being added to our natural resources for the benefit of future generations. More important than the material gain, however, is the improvement we find in the moral and physical well-being of our citizens who have been enrolled in the Corps and of their families who have been assisted by monthly allotments of pay. The functions of the Corps expire under authority of present law on June 30, 1937.

In my Budget Message to Congress on January 5 of this year I indicated that the Corps should be continued and recommended that legislation be enacted during the present session to establish the Corps as a permanent agency of the Government. Such continuance or establishment is desirable notwithstanding the great strides that have been made toward national recovery, as there is still need for providing useful and healthful employment for a large number of our youthful citizens.

I am convinced that there is ample useful work in the protection, restoration and development of our national resources, upon which the services of the Corps may be employed advantageously for an extended future period. It should be noted that this program will not in any respect reduce normal employment opportunities for our adult workers; in fact, the purchase of simple materials, of food and clothing and of other supplies required for the operations of the Corps tends to increase employment in industry.

I recommend, therefore, that provision be made for a permanent Corps of 300,000 youths (and war veterans), together with 10,000 Indians and 5,000 enrollees in our territories and insular possessions. It would appear, after a careful study of available information, that, with improved business conditions, these numbers represent the maximum expected enrollment. To go beyond this number at this time would open new and difficult classifications of enrollment, and the additional cost would seriously affect the financial position of the Treasury.

Franklin D. Roosevelt, Message to Congress on Making the Civilian Conservation Corps a Permanent Agency, April 5, 1937, *The American Presidency Project*, ed. Gerhard Peters and John T. Woolley, www.presidency.ucsb.edu/ws/?pid=15384.

PRACTICING Historical Thinking

Identify: What are Roosevelt's reasons for making the Civilian Conservation Corps a permanent program?

Analyze: When else has the government used natural resources in times of economic hardship?

Evaluate: When he states that the CCC will enhance the "moral and physical well-being" of its employees, to what extent might Roosevelt be responding to the concerns expressed by Lincoln Steffens (Doc. 16.5) and Upton Sinclair (Doc. 16.6)?

| CLIFFORD K. BERRYMAN, "Old Reliable"

c. 1938

Many Americans were uneasy with the new powers that were granted to the federal government during the New Deal. Likewise, many Americans perceived the deficit spending necessitated by New Deal programs to be dangerous to the future of the country.

The Granger Collection, New York.

PRACTICING Historical Thinking

Identify: Describe the images here. What is happening?

Analyze: Explain the role Roosevelt plays here. What is the meaning behind this role?

Evaluate: Synthesize this document with two others from this chapter, and formulate a statement on the roles that government sometimes plays during economically turbulent times. How does this cartoon highlight potential circumstances of this role?

DOCUMENT 16.11 | CHARLES FUSCO, Interview on the New Deal
1938

In this interview, Charles Fusco, an Italian-born munitions worker, gives his impression of the best and worst of Franklin Delano Roosevelt's New Deal programs.

. . . In the nine years of this depression even though I didn't feel it much because I always gave myself a push but think of the others who are weak—what about them? You know there shouldn't be a depression in this country. You know we have everything—even the most money but all you hear today is the same old baloney—the Democrats are in power and the Republicans won't let loose with the money. Well I say that the money men started this thing and I believe the government should make laws to force these capitalist to bring back prosperity. They can do it if they wanted to. But all you hear nowadays is lets balance the budget. I don't believe this budget has been balanced since the indians were here so why the hell do it now. I don't mean that we should go overboard on everything and start spending money left and right because I am against chislers and flukey jobs but lets get down to business and start manufacturing things and sell them to everybody who got the cash—and to those who haven't the cash give them enough credit and a job so that they can pay.

You know sometimes I wonder what way we are drifting—some of the laws that was passed in the last few years were very good for the people and I guess you know what happened. You take the N.R.A. I think that was very good—it gave everybody a chance except those who are misers and are never satisfied if they make 100 dollars a week. This other law the Social Security I believe is the best. The only fault I find is that a man has to reach the age of 65 before he can collect. Well how many do? They tell you nowadays that a person lives longer—well they used to before this depression but [expletive] today you worry your [expletive] head off on how to meet both ends and that makes your life much shorter. You see what I mean that this government wants to do something good for the people and does but [expletive] they put strings to it. Tell me how many reach the age of 65? Very few. Why [expletive] don't they give a person a break and say at 56 years old you should retire from work and enjoy life instead of waiting until he is almost dead they give him a few dollars a month. I think the whole shooting match is wrong. And unless we get the crooks and chislers out of Washington we'll remain the same.

Charles Fusco, interview, in "Roosevelt Is a Damned Good Man," *American Life Histories: Manuscripts from the Federal Writers' Project, 1936–1940*, Library of Congress.

APPLYING AP® Historical Thinking Skills

SKILL REVIEW | Patterns of Continuity and Change over Time

Answer the following prompt in a complete essay:

> Trace the problems described by reformers in the early part of the twentieth century and the extent to which the New Deal solved them. Consult the documents above, your textbook, and your class notes to answer this question.

STEP 1 *Determine patterns*

What problems do reformers describe in the early twentieth century?

Reformer	Problem addressed
Doc. 16.5, Lincoln Steffens	Business too closely aligned with politics
Doc. 16.6, Upton Sinclair	Industry operators exploit workers
Doc. 16.7, Ida M. Tarbell	Anxieties for modern women

What patterns do you see? What changes do you see?

STEP 2 *Connect these patterns*

When you connect these patterns to New Deal legislation, consider the following questions:

How well did the New Deal address the relationship between business and politics?

How well did the New Deal address unlawful or abusive industry operators?

How well did the New Deal respond to anxieties of modern women?

STEP 3 *Consult your textbook and class notes*

STEP 4 *Write your essay*

PUTTING IT ALL TOGETHER

Revisiting the Main Point

- What were some of the positive and negative economic and social effects of the Second Industrial Revolution that were experienced during the late nineteenth and early twentieth century?
- Analyze the ways in which reformers and government programs sought to control the negative effects. To what extent were these reformers and programs successful? What accounted for their lack of success?
- Trace the continuities and changes in Americans' sense of themselves as a nation throughout this period. How did immigrant assimilation and the rise of a consumer economy shape Americans' self-identity?

BUILDING AP® WRITING SKILLS Evaluating Evidence: Discovering Turning Points

In writing historical argument, selecting evidence is a discrete process. You find the examples that best support the prompt, and you organize this evidence in a way that will help support your position.

Finding evidence is more than just an automatic, fill-in-the-blank procedure, and reviewing carefully selected evidence may influence the direction of your essay. Past chapters, for example, have looked at the notion of a **working thesis**, which is an initial claim that the evidence might help confirm as the essay continues. You also have studied the role that is played by the **outlier**, or marginal example, which can provide a qualification or exception to the norm and therefore increase an argument's credibility.

There is an additional move you can make to create a fuller argument, and that is to incorporate actual turning points and **periodization** in prompts that do not explicitly ask for periodization. Consider the following prompt:

> Trace the continuities and changes in Americans' sense of themselves as a nation throughout this period. How did immigrant assimilation and the rise of a consumer economy shape American identity?

At first glance, the period is defined for you in this prompt—"immigrant assimilation" and "the rise of a consumer economy." But the actual turning points are up to you to decide. Additionally, you may choose to create a new period to address this prompt more fully.

For example, this textbook provides an extensive overview of **historical themes**, or bridges between different concepts. Both assimilation and consumerism shape American **self-identity**, so the following questions may enable you to create a new period:

- How does assimilation influence a national identity?
- How does consumerism influence a national identity?
- What ideas, words, or concepts best characterize the new national identity that emerged during this period?

If, for example, you selected a term such as "inflated confidence" to describe the national identity, this term would predict the Great Depression that quickly followed this era. Determining that this era marked a period of "unprecedented expectations for social services" would invite a discussion of the two Applying AP® Historical Thinking Skills exercises in this chapter—where you examined the relationship between a rising leisure time and a government that was responsible for an increasing number of social issues.

Thus, a potential outline for this response is the following:

    I. Introduction

   II. Determination of a new period (for example, "inflated confidence")

      A. Determination of the turning point

      B. Explanation of what period the turning point introduces

 III. Examination of subperiod* 1: assimilation

 IV. Examination of subperiod* 2: consumerism

   V. Conclusion

*By *subperiod* we mean a related lens or factor through which to examine the overall period.

STEPS 1–4

Steps 1 through 4 of the writing sequence have been outlined in earlier chapters, which may be consulted for review.

STEP 5 *Write the essay*

CHAPTER 17

Challenges to the Status Quo

B y the end of the nineteenth century, consumption was rising, a middle class of consumers was growing, and the national transportation infrastructure was expanding. At the same time, exploding urban populations raised their vibrant and varied voices against rising consumerism, persistent racism, and rising class divisions. These conflicts were temporarily eased by strict government controls on dissent and the United States' involvement in the First World War between 1917 and 1918.

By the 1920s and into the 1930s, challenges to the status quo came from diverse quarters—young middle-class Americans who inaugurated a Jazz Age, African Americans who migrated to northern cities and initiated a cultural renaissance based primarily in Harlem in New York City, and young Latinos who struggled for social and cultural space in California.

Seeking the Main Point

As you read the documents that follow, keep these broad questions in mind. These questions will help you understand the relationship between the documents in this chapter and the historical changes that they represent. As you reflect on these questions, determine which themes and which documents best address them.

- Trace the ways in which technological and transportation changes in the late nineteenth century shaped the lives of Americans, both for better and for worse, and the ways in which Americans took advantage of those changes and also rebelled against them.
- Trace the ways in which African Americans challenged the social, political, and economic status quo during this era.
- During this era, how did changes in transportation reflect changes and consistencies in American values?

- Which of the documents or arguments below could be considered "modern" during this time period?
- To what extent did challenges to civil liberties during the First World War reflect earlier examples of similar challenges?
- In what ways did migration into American cities continue to shape urban culture during this time period?

Modernity

DOCUMENT 17.1 | Chicago Streetcar
1900

By the early twentieth century, electric streetcars had replaced most horse-drawn street-cars and become increasingly popular forms of public transportation in American cities. This photograph was taken in the late nineteenth century at the intersection of State Street and Madison Street in Chicago.

Photo by American Stock Archive/Archive Photos/Getty Images.

PRACTICING Historical Thinking

Identify: What is happening in the photograph?

Analyze: Does technology appear to divide or unite people in this image? Explain.

Evaluate: How did greater mobility influence the development of a new urban identity? Compare this image with the description of the view from a Chicago streetcar in Upton Sinclair's *The Jungle* (Doc 16.6).

| **"Our Superb 1914 Model Peerless Bicycle"**
1914

Bicycles became popular both as modes of transportation and as means of leisure for Americans in the late nineteenth century with the invention of the chain-driven "safety" bicycle with two wheels of equal size. This advertisement appeared in one of Sears, Roebuck & Co's mail-order catalogs.

Emergence of Advertising in America Digital Collection—A0055-05 Advertising Ephemera Collection. John W. Hartman Center for Sales, Advertising, and Marketing History. David M. Rubenstein Rare Book and Manuscript Library, Duke University.

PRACTICING Historical Thinking

Identify: What images are most prominent in this advertisement?

Analyze: Who might be the intended audience for this product?

Evaluate: Does this document provide the same message as the photograph of the Chicago streetcar in Document 17.1? Explain.

DOCUMENT 17.3 | **Model T Fords Coming Off the Assembly Line**
1900

Henry Ford (1863–1947) perfected the mass production of low-cost, easy-to-repair automobiles in the early twentieth century and put them within the economic reach of many Americans. This photograph shows finished Model T cars being driven off the assembly line at the Ford Motor Company's plant in Highland Park, Michigan.

Library of Congress Prints and Photographs Division, LC-USZ62-20077.

PRACTICING Historical Thinking

Identify: What features of this car do you think would be easiest to mass-produce?

Analyze: To what extent does the Model T represent a turning point in mass consumption of transportation? Consult your textbook and class notes to help you explain.

Evaluate: Defend or challenge the following statement: The Model T fostered the development of a new national identity more than it hindered it.

DOCUMENT 17.4 | **Clarence Darrow versus William Jennings Bryan**
1925

Biology teacher John Scopes (1900–1970) was prosecuted by the state of Tennessee in the case *State of Tennessee v. John Thomas Scopes* for teaching evolution to his high school classes. In the following excerpt from the July 1925 trial, Clarence Darrow (1857–1938), the famous Chicago attorney who defended Scopes, questions a witness—William Jennings Bryan (1860–1925), who was a three-time Democratic Party candidate for president, US secretary of state under Woodrow Wilson, and the lead prosecutor in the trial, representing the state of Tennessee.

Q [Mr. Darrow]. You have given considerable study to the Bible, haven't you, Mr. Bryan?

A [Mr. Bryan]. Yes, sir, I have tried to.

Q. Then you have made a general study of it.

A. Yes, I have; I have studied the Bible for about fifty years, or sometime more than that, but, of course, I have studied it more as I have become older than when I was but a boy.

Q. You claim that everything in the Bible should be literally interpreted?

A. I believe everything in the Bible should be accepted as it is given there; some of the Bible is given illustratively. For instance: "Ye are the salt of the earth." I would not insist that man was actually salt, or that he had flesh of salt, but it is used in the sense of salt as saving God's people. . . .

Q. But when you read that Jonah swallowed the whale—or that the whale swallowed Jonah—excuse me please—how do you literally interpret that?

A. When I read that a big fish swallowed Jonah—it does not say whale.

Q. Doesn't it? Are you sure?

A. That is my recollection of it. A big fish, and I believe it, and I believe in a God who can make a whale and can make a man and can make both do what He pleases. . . .

Q. Now, you say, the big fish swallowed Jonah, and he there remained how long—three days—and then he spewed him upon the land. You believe that the big fish was made to swallow Jonah?

A. I am not prepared to say that; the Bible merely says it was done.

Q. You don't know whether it was the ordinary run of fish, or made for that purpose?

A. You may guess; you evolutionists guess.

Q. But when we do guess, we have a sense to guess right.

A. But do not do it often.

Q. You are not prepared to say whether that fish was made especially to swallow a man or not?

A. The Bible doesn't say, so I am not prepared to say. . . .

Q. But do you believe He made them—that He made such a fish and that it was big enough to swallow Jonah?

A. Yes sir. Let me add: One miracle is just as easy to believe as another. . . .

Q. Just as hard?

A. It is hard to believe for you, but easy for me. A miracle is a thing performed beyond what man can perform. When you get beyond what man can do, you get within the realm of miracles; and it is just as easy to believe the miracle of Jonah as any other miracle in the Bible.

Q. Perfectly easy to believe that Jonah swallowed the whale?

A. If the Bible said so; the Bible doesn't make as extreme statements as evolutionists do.

Q. That may be a question, Mr. Bryan, about some of those you have known?

A. The only thing is, you have a definition of fact that includes imagination.

Q. And you have a definition that excludes everything but imagination?

Gen. Stewart [attorney general]. I object to that as argumentative. . . .

Mr. Darrow. The Witness must not argue with me, either.

The World's Most Famous Court Trial: Tennessee Evolution Case: A Complete Stenographic Report of the Famous Court Test of the Tennessee Anti-Evolution Act, at Dayton, July 10 to 21, 1925, Including Speeches and Arguments of Attorneys (Clark, NJ: Lawbook Exchange, 1925), 285.

PRACTICING Historical Thinking

Identify: Summarize the arguments presented by both sides.

Analyze: Explain the meaning of this line: "The only thing is, you have a definition of fact that includes imagination."

Evaluate: To what extent did the Scopes trial symbolize a rival national identity that was driven by technology, reason, and science?

DOCUMENT 17.5 | F. SCOTT FITZGERALD, *The Great Gatsby*
1925

With the publication of *The Great Gatsby*, its twenty-eight-year-old author F. Scott Fitzgerald (1896–1940) became the recognized voice of the Jazz Age of the 1920s. In this excerpt, the novel's narrator, Nick Carraway, reflects on the story's Long Island setting.

Most of the big shore places were closed now and there were hardly any lights except the shadowy, moving glow of a ferryboat across the Sound. And as the moon rose higher the inessential houses began to melt away until gradually I became aware of the old island here that flowered once for Dutch sailors' eyes—a fresh, green breast of the new world. Its vanished trees, the trees that had made way for Gatsby's house, had once pandered in whispers to the last and greatest of all human dreams; for a transitory enchanted moment man must have held his breath in the presence of this continent, compelled into an æsthetic contemplation he neither understood nor desired, face to face for the last time in history with something commensurate to his capacity for wonder.

And as I sat there brooding on the old, unknown world, I thought of Gatsby's wonder when he first picked out the green light at the end of Daisy's dock. He had come a long way to this blue lawn, and his dream must have seemed so close that he could hardly fail to grasp it. He did not know that it was already behind him, somewhere back in that vast obscurity beyond the city, where the dark fields of the republic rolled on under the night.

Gatsby believed in the green light, the orgastic future that year by year recedes before us. It eluded us then, but that's no matter—to-morrow we will run faster, stretch out our arms farther. . . . And one fine morning—

So we beat on, boats against the current, borne back ceaselessly into the past.

F. Scott Fitzgerald, *The Great Gatsby* (Oxford: Oxford University Press, 1998), 143–144.

PRACTICING Historical Thinking

Identify: What role is played by the Dutch sailors at the beginning of this passage?

Analyze: Does the speaker see his own goals as consistent with the goals of the Dutch sailors? Are Gatsby's goals consistent with those of the Dutch sailors? Explain.

Evaluate: Does the final line indict the modern America of its times? Explain.

DOCUMENT 17.6	ZORA NEALE HURSTON, "How It Feels to Be Colored Me"
	1928

One of the most emblematic writers of the Harlem Renaissance, Zora Neale Hurston (1891–1960) brought African American culture to a wider audience. Rediscovered in the latter half of the twentieth century, Hurston today is widely recognized as a writer whose anthropological interests enabled her to express the values and complexities of her own culture.

Someone is always at my elbow reminding me that I am the granddaughter of slaves. It fails to register depression with me. Slavery is sixty years in the past. The operation was successful and the patient is doing well, thank you. The terrible struggle that made me an American out of a potential slave said "On the line!" The Reconstruction said "Get set!"; and the generation before said "Go!" I am off to a flying start and I must not halt in the stretch to look behind and weep. Slavery is the price I paid for civilization, and the choice was not with me. It is a bully adventure and worth all that I have paid through my ancestors for it. No one on earth ever had a greater chance for glory. The world to be won and nothing to be lost. It is thrilling to think—to know that for any act of mine, I shall get twice as much praise or twice as much blame. It is quite exciting to hold the center of the national stage, with the spectators not knowing whether to laugh or to weep.

The position of my white neighbor is much more difficult. No brown specter pulls up a chair beside me when I sit down to eat. No dark ghost thrusts its leg against mine in bed. The game of keeping what one has is never so exciting as the game of getting.

I do not always feel colored. Even now I often achieve the unconscious Zora of Eatonville before the Hegira [exodus or migration, named for Muhammad's departure from Mecca to escape persecution]. I feel most colored when I am thrown against a sharp white background.

For instance at Barnard [College in New York City]. "Beside the waters of the Hudson" I feel my race. Among the thousand white persons, I am a dark rock surged upon, and overswept, but through it all, I remain myself. When covered by the waters, I am; and the ebb but reveals me again.

Sometimes it is the other way around. A white person is set down in our midst, but the contrast is just as sharp for me. For instance, when I sit in the drafty basement that is The New World Cabaret with a white person, my color comes. We enter chatting about any little nothing that we have in common and are seated by the jazz waiters. In the abrupt way that jazz orchestras have, this one plunges into a number. It loses no time in circumlocutions, but gets right down to business. It constricts the thorax and splits the heart with its tempo and narcotic harmonies. This orchestra grows rambunctious, rears on its hind legs and attacks the tonal veil with primitive fury, rending it, clawing it until it breaks through to the jungle beyond. I follow those heathen—follow them exultingly. I dance wildly inside myself; I yell within, I whoop; I shake my assegai [spear] above my head, I hurl it true to the mark yeeeeooww! I am in the jungle and living in the jungle way. My face is painted red and yellow and my body is painted blue. My pulse is throbbing like a war drum. I want to slaughter something—give pain, give death to what, I do not know. But the piece ends. The men of the orchestra wipe their lips and rest their fingers. I creep back slowly to the veneer we call civilization with the last tone and find the white friend sitting motionless in his seat, smoking calmly.

Zora Neale Hurston, *I Love Myself When I Am Laughing . . . and Then Again When I Am Looking Mean and Impressive* (New York: CUNY Press, 1979), 153–154.

PRACTICING Historical Thinking

Identify: When does the speaker feel "colored"? When does it matter to her?

Analyze: In the title of this piece, what does the author mean by "colored me"?

Evaluate: To what extent does this essay advocate or oppose assimilation into mainstream culture? Explain.

APPLYING AP® Historical Thinking Skills

SKILL REVIEW | **Patterns of Continuity and Change over Time, Contextualization, and Argumentation**

Answer the following prompt in the form of a complete essay, using the documents above, your textbook, and your class notes for historical context:

> Accept, modify, or refute this statement: The first thirty years of the twentieth century represented a new era in American history.

STEP 1 *Determine continuity or change over time*

Establish a graphic organizer that determines whether the documents above represented more of continuity or more of change, and why.

Document	Continuity and why?	Change and why?
Doc. 17.1, Chicago Streetcar, 1900		
Doc. 17.2, "Our Superb 1914 Model Peerless Bicycle," 1914		
Doc. 17.3, Model T Fords Coming Off the Assembly Line, 1900		
Doc. 17.4, Clarence Darrow versus William Jennings Bryan, 1925		
Doc. 17.5, F. Scott Fitzgerald, *The Great Gatsby*, 1925		
Doc. 17.6, Zora Neale Hurston, "How It Feels to Be Colored Me," 1928		

STEP 2 *Contextualize*

For each *why* statement that you provided above, contextualize the era. You may choose local forms of context (such as political, economic, and social contexts) or broad contexts (such as the themes of peopling, identity, and work, exchange, and technology).

Document (example of either continuity or change over time)	Local contexts: politics and power, environment and technology	Broad contexts: peopling, identity, and work, exchange, and technology
Doc. 17.1, Chicago Streetcar, 1900		
Doc. 17.2, "Our Superb 1914 Model Peerless Bicycle," 1914		
Doc. 17.3, Model T Fords Coming Off the Assembly Line, 1900		
Doc. 17.4, Clarence Darrow versus William Jennings Bryan, 1925		
Doc. 17.5, F. Scott Fitzgerald, *The Great Gatsby*, 1925		
Doc. 17.6, Zora Neale Hurston, "How It Feels to Be Colored Me," 1928		

STEP 3 *Formulate your position*

After you have completed the second table, you may formulate your position (**argumentation**) on the statement "The first thirty years of the twentieth century represented a new era in American history." If all your responses indicate a change, then you would accept the statement. If all your responses indicate continuity, then you would refute the statement. And if some of your responses indicate a change and others indicate continuity, then you would modify the statement.

Beyond the initial response (to accept, refute, or modify the statement), your argument also must contextualize. For example, you may choose to see the Model T Ford as a continuation of the assembly-plant approach that Eli Whitney used with the cotton gin nearly fifty years earlier. From an economic perspective, this represents continuity.

The development of a new national identity, however, was enhanced by transportation and technology. This changed the meaning of technology. It became more than a means of mass production as it ushered in an era of mass migration and distribution of wealth. You may reasonably argue that in terms of work, exchange, and technology, there was a new national identity that made the Model T a symbol of a new era.

Challenges to Civil Liberties

DOCUMENT 17.7 | **Espionage Act**
| 1917

The Espionage Act of 1917 was passed by Congress soon after the United States entered World War I, and it reflected popular anxieties about the loyalties of recent immigrants from countries that were now at war with the nation.

Sec. 2. (a) Whoever, with intent or reason to believe that it is to be used to the injury of the United States or to the advantage of a foreign nation, communicates, delivers, or transmits, or attempts to, or aids or induces another to, communicate, deliver, or transmit, to any foreign government, or to any faction or party or military or naval force within a foreign country, whether recognized or unrecognized by the United States, or to any representative, officer, agent, employe[e], subject, or citizen thereof, either directly or indirectly, any document, writing, code book, signal book, sketch, photograph, photographic negative, blue print, plan, map, model, note, instrument, appliance, or information relating to the national defence, shall be punished by imprisonment for not more than 20 years. . . .

Sec. 3. Whoever, when the United States is at war, shall willfully make or convey false reports or false statements with intent to interfere with the operation or success of the military or naval forces of the United States or to promote the success of its enemies and whoever, when the United States is at war, shall willfully cause or attempt to cause insubordination, disloyalty, or refusal of duty, in the military or naval forces of the United States, or shall willfully obstruct the recruiting or enlistment service of the United States, to the injury of the service or of the United States, shall be punished by a fine of not more than $10,000 or imprisonment for not more than 20 years, or both. . . .

Sec. 5. Whoever harbors or conceals any person who he knows, or has reasonable grounds to believe or suspect, has committed, or is about to commit, an offence under this title shall be punished by a fine of not more than $10,000 or by imprisonment for not more than two years, or both. . . .

Sec. 8. The provisions of this title shall extend to all territories, possessions, and places subject to the jurisdiction of the United States whether or not contiguous thereto, and offences under this title when committed upon the high seas or elsewhere within the admiralty and maritime jurisdiction of the United States and outside the territorial limits thereof shall be punishable hereunder.

United States Naval Institute Proceedings, vol. 43, pt. 2 (Annapolis, MD: US Naval Institute), 1582–1583.

DOCUMENT 17.8	**Sedition Act**
	1918

One year after Congress passed the Espionage Act, it passed the Sedition Act of 1918, which amended the earlier law to include the fining and imprisonment of United States citizens who were found guilty of committing sedition against the government.

SECTION 3. Whoever, when the United States is at war, shall willfully make or convey false reports or false statements with intent to interfere with the operation or success of the military or naval forces of the United States, or to promote the success of its enemies, or shall willfully make or convey false reports, or false statements, . . . or . . . incite . . . insubordination, disloyalty, mutiny, or refusal of duty, in the military or naval forces of the United States, or shall willfully obstruct . . . the recruiting or enlistment service of the United States, . . . [or] shall willfully utter, print, write, or publish any disloyal, profane, scurrilous, or abusive language about the form of government of the United States, or the Constitution of the United States, or the military or naval forces of the United States, . . . or shall willfully display the flag of any foreign enemy, or shall willfully . . . urge, incite, or advocate any curtailment of production . . . [or] advocate, teach, defend, or suggest the doing of any of the acts or things in this section enumerated, and whoever shall by word or act support or favor the cause of any country with which the United States is at war or by word or act oppose the cause of the United States therein, shall be punished by a fine of not more than $10,000 or imprisonment for not more than twenty years, or both. . . .

1919 Supplement to United States Compiled Statutes, vol. 2 (St. Paul, MN: West, 1920), 2355–2356.

DOCUMENT 17.9 | **EUGENE DEBS, Speech in Canton, Ohio**
1918

Eugene Debs (1855–1926) was the country's most famous socialist in his day. He condemned both the Espionage Act and the Sedition Act and extolled the virtues of socialism. A few weeks after delivering the June 16, 1918, speech excerpted below, Debs was arrested for violating the Espionage Act.

I realize that, in speaking to you this afternoon, there are certain limitations placed upon the right of free speech. I must be exceedingly careful, prudent, as to what I say, and even more careful and prudent as to how I say it. I may not be able to say all I think; but I am not going to say anything that I do not think. I would rather a thousand times be a free soul in jail than to be a sycophant and coward in the streets. They may put those boys in jail—and some of the rest of us in jail—but they can not put the Socialist movement in jail. Those prison bars separate their bodies from ours, but their souls are here this afternoon. They are simply paying the penalty that all men have paid in all the ages of history for standing erect, and for seeking to pave the way to better conditions for mankind. . . .

Are we opposed to Prussian militarism? Why, we have been fighting it since the day the Socialist movement was born; and we are going to continue to fight it, day and night, until it is wiped from the face of the earth. Between us there is no truce—no compromise. . . .

Socialism is a growing idea; an expanding philosophy. It is spreading over the entire face of the earth: It is as vain to resist it as it would be to arrest the sunrise on the morrow. It is coming, coming, coming all along the line. Can you not see it? If not, I advise you to consult an oculist. There is certainly something the matter with your vision. It is the mightiest movement in the history of mankind. What a privilege to serve it! I have regretted a thousand times that I can do so little for the movement that has done so much for me. The little that I am, the little that I am hoping to be, I owe to the Socialist movement. It has given me my ideas and ideals; my principles and convictions, and I would not exchange one of them for all of Rockefeller's bloodstained dollars. It has taught me how to serve—a lesson to me of priceless value. It has taught me the ecstasy in the handclasp of a comrade. It has enabled me to hold high communion with you, and made it possible for me to take my place side by side with you in the great struggle for the better day; . . . to realize . . . that to serve them [my fellow socialists] and their cause is the highest duty of my life. . . .

Organize industrially and make your organization complete. Then unite in the Socialist Party. Vote as you strike and strike as you vote. . . .

When we unite and act together on the industrial field and when we vote together on election day we shall develop the supreme power of the one class that can and will bring permanent peace to the world. We shall then have the intelligence, the courage and the power for our great task. In due time industry will be organized on a cooperative basis. We shall conquer the public power. . . . We shall then have industrial democracy. We shall be a free nation whose government is of and by and for the people. . . .

Yes, in good time we are going to sweep into power in this nation and throughout the world. We are going to destroy all enslaving and degrading capitalist institutions and re-create them as free and humanizing institutions. The world is daily changing before our eyes. The sun of capitalism is setting; the sun of socialism is rising. It is our duty to build the new nation and the free republic. . . .

In due time the hour will strike and this great cause triumphant—the greatest in history—will proclaim the emancipation of the working class and the brotherhood of all mankind.

Loren Baritz, ed., *The American Left: Radical Political Thought in the Twentieth Century* (New York: Basic Books, 1971), 98.

PRACTICING Historical Thinking

Identify: Paraphrase this sentence: "When we unite and act together on the industrial field and when we vote together on election day we shall develop the supreme power of the one class that can and will bring permanent peace to the world."

Analyze: How does Debs's speech demonstrate his awareness of context? What are his views toward the Espionage Act and the Sedition Act?

Evaluate: How does Debs's use of the word "emancipation" further his argument?

DOCUMENT 17.10 | **Meeting of the Communist Labor Party,**
New York Times
| 1919

The "Red Scare" of 1919 was ostensibly in reaction to the Russian Bolshevik Revolution of 1917, which created the communist Union of Soviet Socialist Republics (USSR). However, as seen in this *New York Times* article, the Red Scare also revealed underlying social and ethnic tensions among Americans that predated the First World War. The Lusk Committee mentioned in this document refers to a New York State commission to investigate individuals and organizations suspected of sedition.

"Jim" Larkin and ex-Assemblyman Benjamin Gitlow, both of whom are at liberty in $15,000 bail under an indictment for criminal anarchy, addressed a mass meeting last night at which more than 500 men and women rose to their feet and took the Communist oath to fight for and remain true to the party's tenets repeated by Larkin. The meeting, which was held in the Manhattan Lyceum, 66 East Fourth Street, under the auspices of the Communist Labor Party of America, was presided over by Dr. Morris Zucker, a Brownsville dentist, who was sentenced to fifteen years in the Federal prison for violation of the Espionage act and is now out on $15,000 bail pending appeal. It was called to raise funds to defend Larkin and Gitlow. About $300 was raised.

Every reference to Soviet Russia, "the coming revolution in America," Trotzky, Lenin, and Eugene Debs was vigorously cheered and applauded by the audience. And with equal vigor did the radicals show their hostility by hissing to Senator Lusk, Archibald Stevenson, Assistant District Attorney Alexander I. Rorke, Samuel Gompers, the King of Belgium, the Prince of Wales, and the King of Italy. . . .

Dr. Zucker, who assumed the duties of a chairman after he made a speech, struck a responsive note when he declared that perhaps the time would come when the workers would have to take up guns and pistols to protect themselves against the masters of capitalism. He said he had been subpoenaed to appear before the Extraordinary Grand Jury, and asserted that when he did go before that body they would not get a word out of him. The Communists wanted to act in a lawful manner in attaining their aims, he maintained, but were prevented by those who tried to disrupt their organization.

"This meeting is a conclusive answer to the Lusk Committee and Mr. Rorke [interrupted by plenty of hisses] that Communism can't be destroyed by putting Communists in jail," he said. "Every time you put one of us in prison a thousand others spring up to take our places. Some day we will overthrow this damnable capitalistic system and establish a Soviet republic in America."

Gitlow related his recent experiences with the Lusk Committee and the authorities. The acts of the Lusk Committee in the past three weeks had clarified the evolutionary movement in the United States, and "no scissor bill like Archibald Stevenson can stop its progress," he declared. . . .

Gitlow served notice on the Lusk Committee that the next ruling class in this country would be the working class and the Government would be patterned after the Soviet form, which, he added, was best suited for the workers.

"And for the benefit of the Lusk Committee let me say that I am a Bolshevist," Gitlow said. . . .

Larkin told of his recent "honor" of being arrested in his home by a detective, "a being of a low mental type," who, he asserted, was masquerading as a newspaperman in order to reach him. The officer told him, he said, that the Lusk Committee wanted to see him.

"We had in Russia the Black Hundred, the Lusk Committee of Russia," Larkin went on to say. "The people of Russia rose in their might and took them and they went out of history."

Larkin discredited the discovery of TNT chemicals used in bomb manufacture in a secret room of the Union of Russian Workers at 133 East Fifteenth Street last Tuesday. He wondered if the police thought the American people were so stupid as to believe the combustibles were really there as claimed.

"We don't use such weapons," Larkin declared. "We use mental bombs to blow a new idea, a new ideal, into life."

Just as he was closing, Larkin, in urging the workers to spread the tidings of communism and of the oath which they were about to take, walked to the edge of the platform and said:

"We've got to organize a Soviet army here"—he paused for a moment while his audience was breathless for his next words. Then he added, ironically: "Of course, I mean that we have got to meet together in a drilled manner, come early, stay throughout the meeting and then be dismissed by the Chairman. Such a proceeding will cause fear in the minds of capitalists."

Before and during the meeting copies of such radical publications as *The Communist World*, *The Communist*, *The Revolutionary Age*, *The Rebel Worker*, and *The Hobo News* were sold among the audience.

"Larkin Pledges Five Hundred to Communism," *New York Times*, November 29, 1919.

PRACTICING Historical Thinking

Identify: Summarize Larkin's defense of communism.

Analyze: In what ways does Larkin skirt the dictates of the Sedition Act in this speech?

Evaluate: What motivations could have shaped the *New York Times*'s portrayal of Larkin's speech? How did the context of world affairs in 1919 shape this portrayal?

DOCUMENT 17.11 | **JOHN VACHON, Picket Line, Chicago**
| 1941

During the First World War, African American citizens in the southern United States began to move to northern cities in search of economic opportunities and redress from the racist Jim Crow laws of southern states. However, racism in the North proved to be nearly as prevalent as in the South, and people experienced low pay, low-prestige work, physical isolation, and overcrowding. This photograph shows protesters as they picket a realty company in Chicago in 1941.

Library of Congress Prints and Photographs Division, FSA-OWI Collection, LC-USZ62-130701.

PRACTICING Historical Thinking

Identify: What are these demonstrators' concerns, as evidenced by the signs they are holding?

Analyze: In what ways is this protest a product of the legacy of Reconstruction after the Civil War?

Evaluate: Compare this image with the photograph of a Chicago streetcar in Document 17.1. How are they similar and different to other portrayals of public life in Northern cities (for example in Doc. 17.1)?

DOCUMENT 17.12 | **LAWRENCE E. DAVIES, "Zoot Suits Become Issue on Coast,"** *New York Times*
| 1943

During the Second World War, young men who dressed in "zoot suits" (bright-colored suits with long jackets, wide lapels, and loose, pegged-legged pants) rioted and shocked the sensibilities of middle-class Americans, who had assumed a unified front in the face of total war, as reported in this *New York Times* article.

LOS ANGELES, June 12—The zoot suit with the reat pleat [or reet pleat], the drape shape and the stuff cuff has been the object of much amusement and considerable derision from Harlem to the Pacific during the last two or three years. Psychiatrists may have their own ideas about it, but, according to the reasoning of many newcomers to the armed services, especially hundreds of young sailors in this area, the zoot suit has become the symbol these last ten days of a fester on the body politic which should be removed by Navy vigilantes, if police will not or cannot do the job.

    Adventurers of the Navy boys in trying to accomplish their purpose have been watched with such interest in all quarters—bringing cheers from some and causing concern to others—that newspapers were snatched up eagerly on downtown street corners the other day when newsboys handling late afternoon and morning "bulldog" editions shouted:

"No more zoot suits!"

"Navy bans Los Angeles!"

"Out of Bounds"

These headlines referred to the action of Rear Admiral David W. Bagley, commandant of the Eleventh Naval District, in placing this city under "temporarily restricted liberty for naval personnel." This means that only in special cases could sailors be at large in the city.

This greatly reduced, if it failed to stop altogether, clashes between small bands of zoot-suit wearers, chiefly of Mexican descent, and groups of Navy seamen out to retaliate for attacks on lone sailors or their girls by the pork-pie-hatted hoodlums.

Library of Congress Prints and Photographs Division, FSA/OWI Collection, LC-USF34-011543-D.

PRACTICING Historical Thinking

Identify: Above is an image of two young men in zoot suits. Describe how they are dressed. According to this article, why were the men who wore zoot suits considered a threat?

Analyze: How does this conflict illustrate ethnic tensions in the United States during the Second World War?

Evaluate: Where else in this chapter—or others—does appearance take on a political aspect? How does this costume criticize American values of its era?

SKILL REVIEW | # Comparison, Analyzing Evidence: Content and Sourcing, and Contextualization

Consider the following prompt:

> Compare the speech by Eugene Debs in Canton, Ohio (Doc. 17.9), and the newspaper article about a meeting of the Communist Labor Party (Doc. 17.10). How does each document characterize socialist activism in the United States? What contextual factors created the similarities and differences between them?

STEP 1 *Compare and use evidence appropriately*

Use your response to the "Evaluate" question for Document 17.10 as a starting point for comparison and analysis of the content and sources of evidence. Organize your information in a subject-by-subject outline:

   I. Introduction

  II. Eugene Debs speech

      A. Language of the speech

      B. Key examples of the speech

  III. Communist Labor Party meeting

      A. Language of the speech

      B. Key examples of the speech

STEP 2 *Contextualize and use evidence appropriately*

Determine what contexts were most influential in the years 1918 and 1919 for contextualization and analysis of the contents and sources of evidence.

- Economic?
- Social?
- Political?

Consider the broad context of America in the world (one of the key themes of this course). How did the end of World War I and the broad, international context influence the perception of communism in the United States?

PUTTING IT ALL TOGETHER

Revisiting the Main Point

- Choose two examples of transportation technology that are described in documents in this chapter. In what ways did each example shape American society and economics?
- To what extent did African Americans find justice in American cities?
- What values expressed above might be seen as threatening by a social conservative from this time period?
- Compare the Sedition Act of 1918 (Doc. 17.8) to the Sedition Act of 1798 (Doc. 5.18). What are some similarities and differences between the two acts? What accounts for the similarities and differences between them?
- Compare the above excerpts from Zora Neale Hurston (Doc. 17.6) and F. Scott Fitzgerald (Doc. 17.5). In what ways do both express notions that are at odds with the American status quo of this period?

**BUILDING AP®
WRITING SKILLS** **Evaluating Context and Multiple Perspectives**

In the last chapter, you learned about ways to broaden your historical argument by incorporating a wide range of **contexts**. Much like you saw in the Applying AP® Historical Thinking Skills exercise on comparison, analysis of content and sources of evidence, and contextualization above, you may broaden these contexts by incorporating large themes that allow your argument to cover more historical content.

When you evaluate context or **multiple perspectives**, you make a judgment about the following:

- Which context is more important?
- How are the contexts similar to each other?
- How do the contexts differ from each other?

More sophisticated arguments will **evaluate**, or judge, these broad contexts. When you evaluate, you must support your reasoning with carefully selected evidence, clear comparisons, and logical organization. To say, for example, that the economic context outweighs the social context is an arbitrary statement. Only by providing support can you strengthen your argument.

This support comes from your ability to negotiate various contexts at the same time. For example, in the above Applying AP® Historical Thinking Skills exercise on comparison, analysis of the content and sources of evidence, and contextualization, the international context clearly influences the American perception of the Communist Party. Although working people joined social and economic movements in the early 1900s, the end of World War I signaled the end of isolationism for the United States and opened the doors to ideologies that threatened the economic fabric.

Socialism and communism shared some similar economic concerns, but they differed because of historical events that reshaped America's role in the world. Consider the following prompt:

> Compare the above excerpts from Zora Neale Hurston (Doc. 17.6) and
> F. Scott Fitzgerald (Doc. 17.5). In what ways do both express notions that
> are at odds with the American status quo of this period?

Using literature as a primary document automatically contextualizes a historical discussion because authors are influenced by the context in which they write and their work archives the era.

In the documents referred to in the above prompt, for example, Fitzgerald's vision of the endless pursuit of wealth seems as romanticized as Hurston's tribute to her race. Both voices seek to paint a picture of America that is distant from its reality, and both paint a picture that is prettier than reality. Why?

Preparing an answer to such a question allows you to evaluate key contexts or perspectives. Which ones most prominently influenced these writers? First, consider the contexts that apply:

- Social
- Economic
- Demographic

Next, evaluate the most (or least) important contexts, or determine if they carry equal weight in their influence. When you make these evaluative statements, use transitional words that show judgment, such as the following:

Even more important

Less significant

To an equal extent

Most important

Far less noteworthy

Finally, your outline requires you to compare two documents that accomplish the same goal, so you have the freedom to evaluate the contexts differently. For example, matters of race (a social context) and class (an economic context) may figure differently in each author's vision. A sample outline is provided below:

I. Introduction: what goals do these writers share?

II. Subject 1: Hurston

    A. Context 1 (evaluated relative to the other choices)

    B. Context 2

    C. Context 3

III. Subject 2: Fitzgerald

    A. Context 1 (evaluated relative to the other choices)

    B. Context 2

    C. Context 3

IV. Did both writers accomplish their goal? Use your notes from your textbook and classroom discussion to conclude your essay.

STEPS 1–4

Steps 1 through 4 of the writing sequence have been outlined in earlier chapters, which may be consulted for review.

STEP 5 *Write the essay*

CHAPTER 18

Isolated No More

T he role played by the United States in world affairs shifted substantially in the first half of the twentieth century. The era began with the so-called closing of the American frontier west of the Mississippi and ended as the United States stood as one of two superpowers able to exert global power. Between these two events, Americans debated the place of their overseas military ventures within the context of traditional American ideals.

For President William McKinley's administration, Spain's attempt to suppress an independence movement in Cuba represented a threat to republican liberties throughout the Western Hemisphere. Ironically, by the end of the Spanish-American War (1898), the United States itself controlled the colonies of Guam, Puerto Rico, and the Philippines and battled Filipino rebels who demanded independence. Throughout this era, many Americans questioned the compatibility of republicanism and imperialism, culminating in the Anti-Imperialist League and the popular neutrality of Americans during the First World War and again in the 1930s. Conversely, presidents like Woodrow Wilson and Franklin Delano Roosevelt used the rhetoric of republicanism to offer compelling justification for American involvement in foreign wars in the name of democracy.

The tensions between Americans who held isolationist and those who held internationalist sentiments continued throughout the twentieth century, and both sides used the rights-based rhetoric of the American Revolution to justify their positions. This created a dynamic and high-stakes argument around American conceptions of liberty and equality.

Seeking the Main Point

As you read the documents that follow, keep these broad questions in mind. These questions will help you understand the relationship between the documents in this chapter and the historical changes that they represent. As you reflect on these questions, determine which themes and which documents best address them.

- How did America's legacy of individualism manifest itself at home and abroad during the first half of the twentieth century?
- To what extent did war both assist and hinder American progress on social, economic, and political levels?
- To what extent did isolationism shape American identity from 1915 to 1945? Analyze the political, social, and economic factors that helped shape the American identity in this period.

From Frontier to Empire

DOCUMENT 18.1 | **FREDERICK JACKSON TURNER, The Closing of the Frontier**
| 1893

At the Columbian Exposition in Chicago in 1893, Frederick Jackson Turner (1861–1932), a young historian from the University of Wisconsin, publicly presented his now famous "frontier thesis" regarding the significance of the frontier on American history and its closing in 1890.

Up to our own day American history has been in a large degree the history of the colonization of the Great West. The existence of an area of free land, its continuous recession, and the advance of American settlement westward explain American development. Behind institutions, behind constitutional forms and modifications lie the vital forces that call these organs into life and shape them to meet changing conditions. Now the peculiarity of American institutions is the fact that they have been compelled to adapt themselves to the changes of an expanding people—to the changes involved in crossing a continent, in winning a wilderness, and in developing at each area of this progress out of the primitive economic and political conditions of the frontier into the complexity of city life.

Said Calhoun in 1817, "We are great, and rapidly—I was about to say fearfully—growing!" So saying, he touched the distinguishing feature of American life. All peoples show development: the germ theory of politics has been sufficiently emphasized. In the case of most nations, however, the development has occurred in a limited area; and if the nation has expanded, it has met other growing peoples whom it has conquered. But in the case of the United States we have a different phenomenon.

Limiting our attention to the Atlantic Coast, we have the familiar phenomenon of the evolution of institutions in a limited area, such as the rise of representative government; the differentiation of simple colonial governments into complex organs; the progress from primitive industrial society, without division of labor, up to manufacturing civilization. But we have in addition to this *a recurrence of the process of evolution in each western area reached in the process of expansion.* Thus American development has exhibited not merely advance along a single line but a return to primitive conditions on a continually advancing frontier line, and a new development for that area.

American social development has been continually beginning over again on the frontier. This perennial rebirth, this fluidity of American life, this expansion westward with its new opportunities, its continuous touch with the simplicity of primitive society, furnish the forces dominating American character. The true point of view in the history of this nation is not the Atlantic Coast, it is the Great West. Even the slavery struggle, which is made so exclusive an object of attention by writers like Professor von Holst, occupies its important place in American history because of its relation to westward expansion.

Frederick Jackson Turner, "The Significance of the Frontier in American History" (1893), *Primary Sources: Workshops in American History*, www.learner.org, reprinted from *Annals of America* © 1968, 1976 Encyclopaedia Britannica, Inc.

PRACTICING Historical Thinking

Identify: Summarize Turner's argument.

Analyze: What does Turner mean when he says that the "true point of view . . . is the Great West"?

Evaluate: Do you think the closing of the American frontier lead to (or will lead to) policies that were more isolationist or more expansionist? Explain.

DOCUMENT 18.2 | **US Diplomatic Cable to the Spanish Ambassador**
1898

Beginning in the mid-1890s, American newspapers reported on the conflicts between the Spanish government and Cuban rebels. By 1898, President William McKinley's administration began to take an active interest in removing Cuba from Spanish control and giving the island independence within an American sphere of influence. This March 26, 1898, statement to the governor general of Cuba, Ramón Blanco, explains the official US position on the uprising in Cuba.

. . . The President's desire is for peace. He cannot look upon the suffering and starvation in Cuba save with horror. The concentration of men, women, and children in the fortified towns, and permitting them to starve, is unbearable to a Christian nation geographically so close as ours to Cuba. All this has shocked and inflamed the American mind, as it has the civilized world, where its extent and character are known.

It was represented to him in November that the Blanco government would at once release the suffering and so modify the Weyler order as to permit those who were able to return to their homes and till the fields from which they had been driven. There has been no relief to the starving except such as the American people have supplied. The reconcentration order has not been practically superseded.

There is no hope of peace through the Spanish arms. The Spanish government seems unable to conquer the insurgents. More than half of the island is under control of the insurgents. For more than three years our people have been patient and forbearing; we have patrolled our coast with zeal and at great expense, and have successfully prevented the landing of any armed force on the island. The war has disturbed the peace and tranquility of our people.

We do not want the island. The President has evidenced in every way his desire to preserve and continue friendly relations with Spain. He has kept every international obligation with fidelity. He wants an honorable peace. He has repeatedly urged the government of Spain to secure a peace. She still has the opportunity to do it, and the President appeals to her from every consideration of justice and humanity to do it. Will she? Peace is the desired end.

For your own guidance, the President suggests that if Spain will revoke the reconcentration order and maintain the people until they can support themselves, and offer the Cubans full self-government with reasonable indemnity, the President will gladly assist in its consummation. If Spain should invite the United States to mediate for peace and the insurgents would make like request, the President might undertake such office of friendship.

French Ensor Chadwick, *The Relations of the United States and Spain: Diplomacy* (New York: Charles Scribner's Sons, 1909), 557–558.

PRACTICING Historical Thinking

Identify: According to the cable, what conditions must Spain meet prior to US involvement in Cuban affairs?

Analyze: Why, according to this official US communication, does McKinley avoid acting unilaterally without Spanish involvement?

Evaluate: Determine the political and economic advantages to the United States of influence over Cuban affairs.

DOCUMENT 18.3 | ## Platform of the American Anti-Imperialist League
1899

Anti-Imperialist League members like Jane Addams and Mark Twain protested the United States' control of "protectorates" like the Philippines, Puerto Rico, and Guam after the Spanish-American War (1898).

We hold that the policy known as imperialism is hostile to liberty and tends towards militarism, an evil from which it has been our glory to be free. We regret that it has become necessary in the land of Washington and Lincoln to reaffirm that all men, of whatever race or color, are entitled to life, liberty and the pursuit of happiness. We maintain that governments derive their just powers from the consent of the governed. We insist that the subjugation of any people is "criminal aggression" and open disloyalty to the distinctive principles of our government.

We earnestly condemn the policy of the present national administration in the Philippines. It seeks to extinguish the spirit of 1776 in those islands. We deplore the sacrifice of our soldiers and sailors, whose bravery deserves admiration even in an unjust war. We denounce the slaughter of the Filipinos as a needless horror. We protest against the extension of American sovereignty by Spanish methods.

We demand the immediate cessation of the war against liberty, begun by Spain and continued by us. We urge that congress be promptly convened to announce to the Filipinos our purpose to concede to them the independence for which they have so long fought and which of right is theirs.

The United States have always protested against the doctrine of international law which permits the subjugation of the weak by the strong. A self-governing state cannot accept sovereignty over an unwilling people. The United States cannot act upon the ancient heresy that Might makes Right.

"Platform of the American Anti-Imperialist League," *The Commons* 39 (October 31, 1899): 2.

PRACTICING Historical Thinking

Identify: What rationale does the Anti-Imperialist League provide for the United States to leave these smaller islands?

Analyze: To what extent is US control over these protectorates similar to British control over the American colonies? Explain.

Evaluate: Compare this document to 18.2—the communique to the Spanish ambassador. Would the Anti-Imperialist League support this diplomatic cable and the war thereafter?

SKILL REVIEW | ## Periodization, Patterns of Continuity and Change over Time, Causation, and Argumentation

Reread John L. O'Sullivan's "The Great Nation of Futurity," a statement about the United States' Manifest Destiny (Doc. 8.9). Accept, modify, or refute the following statement. Use your textbook and your class notes for additional support.

Frederick Jackson Turner's claim that the American frontier was "closed" (Doc. 18.1) fundamentally altered US expansionist policies.

STEP 1 *Patterns of continuity and change over time and causation*

In addition to reviewing the claims of John L. O'Sullivan and Frederick Jackson Turner, examine the patterns of United States expansionist policies between 1845 and 1890. Review events, and consider the motivations behind such US policies.

What was happening in the second half of the nineteenth century that influenced America's worldview? What were the economic, political, and social expectations about expansionist thinking?

Also, consider whether the United States regarded the international world as an extension of the frontier. Did the United States continue to conquer new "wildernesses" in the form of other countries?

Consider how some of the themes presented in this textbook may help frame your thinking about US expansionist policies. For example, were these policies related to the development of work, exchange, and technology? Values, beliefs, and culture? Peopling?

STEP 2 *Periodization*

Using 1890 as a starting point, review some of Turner's key claims. For example, he states the following:

> Thus American development has exhibited not merely advance along a single line but a return to primitive conditions on a continually advancing frontier line, and a new development for that area. . . . This perennial rebirth, this fluidity of American life, this expansion westward with its new opportunities, its continuous touch with the simplicity of primitive society, furnish the forces dominating American character.

Paraphrase Turner's claims here to help frame your thinking. Consider the meanings of "new opportunities," the "simplicity of primitive society," and Turner's claims about the American character. This will help guide your understanding of policies formed in 1890 and beyond.

Review the competing messages from Documents 18.2 and 18.3. The cable to the Spanish ambassador and the platform of the American Anti-Imperialist League provide conflicting messages about international expansion. The Spanish-American War (1898) represents a break in the pattern and a potential **turning point** that marks a new period of US expansionist policies. Your textbook and class notes may suggest additional ideas for turning points.

STEP 3 *Argumentation*

The breaks in the pattern qualify as a potential turning point and the beginning of a new period—in this case, the alteration of US expansionist policies. If there are no breaks in the pattern, then you would refute Turner's thesis. Finding some breaks in the pattern suggests a modification. For example, the United States' economic motivations may have remained the same, but its worldview changed dramatically. An acceptance of Turner's claim would show a shift in US expansionist policies.

War in the Name of Democracy?

DOCUMENT 18.4 | **WOODROW WILSON, Remarks to the Senate**
1917

President Woodrow Wilson (1856–1924) finished his first term in 1917 with a rhetorical and diplomatic push for the United States' entrance into the First World War, including these remarks to the Senate on January 22, 1917. But many Americans felt ambivalent about entering the war, and Wilson himself had campaigned for reelection in 1916 on the slogan "He kept us out of war."

Gentlemen of the Senate:

On the eighteenth of December last I addressed an identic[al] note to the governments of the nations now at war requesting them to state, more definitely than they had yet been stated by either group of belligerents, the terms upon which they would deem it possible to make peace. I spoke on behalf of humanity and of the rights of all neutral nations like our own, many of whose most vital interests the war puts in constant jeopardy. The Central Powers united in a reply which stated merely that they were ready to meet their antagonists in conference to discuss terms of peace. The Entente Powers have replied much more definitely and have stated, in general terms, indeed, but with sufficient definiteness to imply details, the arrangements, guarantees, and acts of reparation which they deem to be the indispensable conditions of a satisfactory settlement. We are that much nearer a definite discussion of the peace which shall end the present war. We are that much nearer the discussion of the international concert which must thereafter hold the world at peace. In every discussion of the peace that must end this war it is taken for granted that that peace must be followed by some definite concert of power which will make it virtually impossible that any such catastrophe should ever overwhelm us again. Every lover of mankind, every sane and thoughtful man, must take that for granted. . . .

It is inconceivable that the people of the United States should play no part in that great enterprise. To take part in such a peace will be the opportunity for which they have sought to prepare themselves by the very principles and purposes of their polity and the approved practices of their Government ever since the days when they set up a new nation in the high and honourable hope that it might in all that it was and did show mankind the way to liberty. They cannot in honour withhold the service to which they are now about to be challenged. They do not wish to withhold it. . . .

No covenant of cooperative peace that does not include the peoples of the New World can suffice to keep the future safe against war; and yet there is only one sort of peace that the peoples of America could join in guaranteeing. The elements of that peace must be elements that engage the confidence and satisfy the principles of the American governments, elements consistent with their political faith and with the practical convictions which the peoples of America have once for all embraced and undertaken to defend.

Committee on Public Information, *How the War Came to America* (Washington, DC: Committee of Public Information, 1917), 17–18.

PRACTICING Historical Thinking

Identify: What does Wilson say is "inconceivable" regarding the war?

Analyze: How does Wilson's reference to a "covenant of cooperative peace" shape possible American involvement in the war?

Evaluate: To what extent does Wilson's speech mark an end to American isolationism? How might this end relate back to Frederick Jackson Turner's thesis on the closing of the American frontier (Doc. 18.1)?

DOCUMENT 18.5 | WOODROW WILSON, On the League of Nations
1919

President Wilson imagined the end of the First World War as an opportunity to make the world safe for democracy and free of warfare. An international legislature, known as the League of Nations, was an important part of his vision, but it was rejected by Republicans, who controlled the US Senate. The following speech was delivered on September 25, 1919, and was one of Wilson's final addresses in support of the League of Nations.

. . . Reflect, my fellow citizens, that the membership of this great league is going to include all the great fighting nations of the world, as well as the weak ones. It is not for the present going to include Germany, but for the time being Germany is not a great fighting country. All the nations that have power that can be mobilized are going to be members of this league, including the United States. And what do they unite for? They enter into a solemn promise to one another that they will never use their power against one another for aggression; that they never will impair the territorial integrity of a neighbor; that they never will interfere with the political independence of a neighbor; that they will abide by the principle that great populations are entitled to determine their own destiny and that they will not interfere with that destiny; and that no matter what differences arise amongst them they will never resort to war without first having done one or other of two things—either submitted the matter of controversy to arbitration, in which case they agree to abide by the result without question, or submitted it to the consideration of the council of the league of nations, laying before that council all the documents, all the facts, agreeing that the council can publish the documents and the facts to the whole world, agreeing that there shall be six months allowed for the mature consideration of those facts by the council, and agreeing that at the expiration of the six months, even if they are not then ready to accept the advice of the council with regard to the settlement of the dispute, they will still not go to war for another three months. In other words, they consent, no matter what happens, to submit every matter of difference between them to the judgment of mankind, and just so certainly as they do that, my fellow citizens, war will be in the far background, war will be pushed out of that foreground of terror in which it has kept the world for generation after generation, and men will know that there will be a calm time of deliberate counsel. The most dangerous thing for a bad cause is to expose it to the opinion of the world. The most certain way that you can prove that a man is mistaken is by letting all his neighbors know what he thinks, by letting all his neighbors discuss what he thinks, and if he is in the wrong you will notice that he will stay at home, he will not walk on the street. He will be afraid of the eyes of his neighbors. He will be afraid of their judgment of his character. He will know that his cause is lost unless he can sustain it by the arguments of right and of justice. The same law that applies to individuals applies to nations.

Woodrow Wilson, Address at Pueblo, Colorado, *Senate Documents*, vol. 11, 66th Congress, 1st Session (Washington, DC: Government Printing Office, 1919), 361–362.

PRACTICING Historical Thinking

Identify: Reread Wilson's speech, noting all references to words related to violence (such as "war" and "terror"). What effect does this language have on the overall speech?

Analyze: What does Wilson mean when he states, "The most dangerous thing for a bad cause is to expose it to the opinion of the world"? What assumption does he make about the global society?

Evaluate: According to Wilson, what will give the league its authority? How will this authority, in theory, keep aggressive nations from attacking others?

DOCUMENT 18.6 | **Kellogg-Briand Pact**
1928

The Kellogg-Briand Pact, officially known as the General Treaty for Renunciation of War as an Instrument of National Policy, began as a pact against war between the United States and France but soon was transformed into a multinational agreement to forgo war.

Article I

The High Contracting Parties solemnly declare in the names of their respective peoples that they condemn recourse to war for the solution of international controversies, and renounce it, as an instrument of national policy in their relations with one another.

Article II

The High Contracting Parties agree that the settlement or solution of all disputes or conflicts of whatever nature or of whatever origin they may be, which may arise among them, shall never be sought except by pacific [peaceful] means.

Article III

The present Treaty shall be ratified by the High Contracting Parties named in the Preamble in accordance with their respective constitutional requirements, and shall take effect as between them as soon as all their several instruments of ratification shall have been deposited at Washington.

This Treaty shall, when it has come into effect as prescribed in the preceding paragraph, remain open as long as may be necessary for adherence by all the other Powers of the world. Every instrument evidencing the adherence of a Power shall be deposited at Washington and the Treaty shall immediately upon such deposit become effective as; between the Power thus adhering and the other Powers parties hereto.

It shall be the duty of the Government of the United States to furnish each Government named in the Preamble and every Government subsequently adhering to this Treaty with a certified copy of the Treaty and of every instrument of ratification or adherence. It shall also be the duty of the Government of the United States telegraphically to notify such Governments immediately upon the deposit with it of each instrument of ratification or adherence.

IN FAITH WHEREOF the respective Plenipotentiaries have signed this Treaty in the French and English languages both texts having equal force, and hereunto affix their seals.

DONE at Paris, the twenty seventh day of August in the year one thousand nine hundred and twenty-eight.

Charles Irving Bevans, *Treaties and Other International Agreements of the United States of America, 1776–1949: Multilateral, 1918–1930* (Washington, DC: Department of State Publication, 1969), 734.

PRACTICING Historical Thinking

Identify: List three to five significant points made in the Kellogg-Briand Pact.

Analyze: What contextual factors shaped this pact?

Evaluate: Although the Kellogg-Briand Pact casts the United States as an international force, in what ways does the pact also help to preserve American power?

RUSSELL LEE, Japanese American Child on the Way to Internment

1942

Under Executive Order 9066 (1942), more than 110,000 Japanese Americans were relocated and interred throughout the United States for the duration of the Second World War. This photo by Russell Lee (1903–1986) shows a young child being evacuated to the internment camp in Owens Valley, California.

Library of Congress Prints and Photographs Division, FSA/OWI Collection LC-USF33-013290-M1.

PRACTICING Historical Thinking

Identify: Note five details from the image.

Analyze: How does the framing of this photograph create sympathy for the child?

Evaluate: Synthesize this image with the image of "Rosie the Riveter" (Doc. 18.8) and Woodrow Wilson's call for a League of Nations (Doc. 18.5). How do all three of these documents describe America's vision of itself in a global society?

"Rosie the Riveter," Office of War Information

1943

During World War II, "Rosie the Riveter" encouraged women to commit to the industrial workforce to replace male workers who had been recruited or drafted into the armed services.

"I've found the job where I fit best!"

FIND YOUR WAR JOB
In Industry – Agriculture – Business

Library of Congress Prints and Photographs Division, LC-USZ62-99103.

PRACTICING Historical Thinking

Identify: What features of the advertisement—both the imagery and the text—appeal to audiences?

Analyze: In what ways does this image uphold traditional images of American women? In what ways does it challenge those images?

Evaluate: To what extent does this advertisement portray new opportunities for American women?

DOCUMENT 18.9 | ## CARL MURPHY, An Open Letter Home during World War II

1943

Carl Murphy (1889–1967) was president of the *Baltimore Afro-American* newspaper and a civil rights leader who, in publishing this open letter, questioned the justice of racial segregation in the US armed forces. The United States Army was desegregated by President Harry Truman in 1948.

. . . I, a commissioned officer of the United States Army, am denied the rights and privileges of an officer. I am excluded by members of my own rank and station in the Army. I am denied the privilege to use the Officer's Club. Although members of my race are used as waiters and general help around the club, I am denied the privilege of using it. It has been a source of embarrassment for a Negro soldier working there to ask me if I am denied the privilege of the club. I ask you, gentlemen, what would you say or do if a soldier, who respected you as an officer of the Army, knew that you, an officer sworn to up-hold and defend the principles of this democracy, were being denied the very thing you are and asking them to lay down their life for. How can we demand the respect of men under our command when we are not respected by members of our own rank.

Gentlemen, I have seen men come from States of the South where my race is persecuted beyond belief. I have seen them come cowed. I have seen them come with no self respect. I have seen them come eager in the belief of what their state did to them, their government would not uphold. I have heard them upon entering the Army say, that an Army post is under Federal regulations and that they would not be subjected to injustices of State rule. Yet these men have been let down by the very government they swore to uphold. They see their government inflict upon them and a large number of the white race a segregation neither one desires.

They see a great Federal government built on the principle of "Liberty and justice for all" being swayed by sectional customs and traditions that were defeated in a war seventy-five years ago.

Gentlemen, at the first touch of these injustices, the men of my race naturally turn to me, a commissioned officer, to explain the reasons and policies of the government. Am I to tell them that the great and powerful government of the United States of America is being swayed by a small state government? I ask you, gentlemen, what am I to say? Am I to admit that we are fighting for ideals for another country or people when America has not yet established these ideals at home? These are the problems of the Negro officer. He is being constantly appealed to by the men under his command to correct the injustices that exist on the post and yet, the post, knowing that these injustices do exist, take[s] no step to correct them. What would you do?

These type of conditions seriously injure the morale of the Negro soldier and tend to give him an air of indifference that he is sure to carry with him to civilian life. I have heard it expressed openly, hundreds of times by Negro soldiers that they would just as soon give their life fighting the injustices inflicted upon him right here in the United States than to fight to correct the injustices of other people they know nothing about on foreign soil. This state of mind has been brought about by the reluctance of the federal government to uphold firmly the rights of all men.

Gentlemen, it would be foolish of me to expect that these injustices could be wiped out immediately. For that reason I am making several suggestions that would not solve the problem but would alleviate the tenseness of the situation and increase the morale of the Negro troops. . . .

Philip McGuire, ed., *Taps for a Jim Crow Army: Letters from Black Soldiers in World War II* (Lexington: University Press of Kentucky, 1993), 42–43.

DOCUMENT 18.10 | FRANKLIN DELANO ROOSEVELT, **State of the Union Address**
| 1944

President Franklin Delano Roosevelt gave his January 11, 1944, State of the Union address on the topic of further organizing the American economy and society for the war effort.

Let us remember the lessons of 1918. In the summer of that year the tide turned in favor of the Allies. But this government did not relax, nor did the American people. In fact, our national effort was stepped up. In August 1918, the draft age limits were broadened from twenty-one to thirty-one, all the way to eighteen to forty-five. The president called for "force to the utmost," and his call was heeded. And in November, only three months later, Germany surrendered.

That is the way to fight and win a war—all out—and not with half an eye on the battlefronts abroad and the other eye and a half on personal, selfish, or political interests here at home.

Therefore, in order to concentrate all of our energies, all of our resources on winning this war, and to maintain a fair and stable economy at home, I recommend that the Congress adopt:

First, a realistic and simplified tax law—which will tax all unreasonable profits, both individual and corporate, and reduce the ultimate cost of the war to our sons and our daughters. The tax bill now under consideration by the Congress does not begin to meet this test.

Secondly, a continuation of the law for the renegotiation of war contracts— which will prevent exorbitant profits and assure fair prices to the government. For two long years I have pleaded with the Congress to take undue profits out of war.

Third, a cost of food law—which will enable the government to place a reasonable floor under the prices the farmer may expect for his production; and to place a ceiling on the prices a consumer will have to pay for the necessary food he buys. This should apply, as I have intimated, to necessities only and this will require public funds to carry it out. It will cost in appropriations about 1 percent of the present annual cost of the war.

Fourth, an early reenactment of the stabilization statute of October 1942. This expires this year, June 30, 1944, and if it is not extended well in advance, the country might just as well expect price chaos by summertime.

We cannot have stabilization by wishful thinking. We must take positive action to maintain the integrity of the American dollar.

And fifth, a national service law—which, for the duration of the war, will prevent strikes, and, with certain appropriate exceptions, will make available for war production or for any other essential services every able-bodied adult in this whole nation.

Franklin Delano Roosevelt, *Public Papers of the Presidents of the United States: F. D. Roosevelt, 1944–1945, Volume 13* (Washington, DC: Government Printing Office, 1950), 36–37.

PRACTICING Historical Thinking

Identify: What are Roosevelt's reasons for taking steps to ensure a stable economy?

Analyze: How did a wartime economy allow Roosevelt to impose greater restrictions on capitalism?

Evaluate: Compare Roosevelt's State of the Union address with Woodrow Wilson's remarks to the Senate (Doc. 18.4). Explain how the two documents differ in the ways that they present the United States' reasons for engaging in international conflicts.

APPLYING AP® Historical Thinking Skills

SKILL REVIEW | **Patterns of Continuity and Change over Time, Comparison, and Synthesis**

Address the following prompt in a complete essay using the documents above and appropriate information from your textbook and classroom notes as support:

Analyze the extent to which the First and Second World Wars contributed to increasing the civil rights of women and minorities in the first half of the twentieth century. Compare the progress of civil rights reforms during wartime to one other period in US history.

STEP 1 *Patterns of continuity and change over time and comparison*

Review the documents in this chapter and your classroom notes to determine the ways in which the civil rights of women and minorities developed during wartime. Two documents present competing views—the advertisement of "Rosie the Riveter" (Doc. 18.8) and the letter home from Carl Murphy (Doc. 18.9). Both women and minorities served the war effort, but they were treated vastly differently.

This task asks for two comparisons. The first comparison that you make is between two different groups—women and minorities. The examples above suggest that women made strides toward equality during the war but that segregation in the armed forces thwarted equality for African American men, at least until 1948 when the armed forces were desegregated by executive order.

STEP 2 *Comparison and synthesis*

The second comparison—of your own choosing—looks at the ways in which both of these groups (women and minorities) were treated during another wartime period in US history. Whether you choose the Revolutionary War, the Civil War, or a different war, your comparisons double because you also are looking at the ways in which women and minorities were treated between two different eras.

Synthesis allows you to broaden your comparisons more fully, especially when you consider the thematic ideas of US history. For example, the theme of a national identity focuses on a long history of oppression of both women and minorities. Thus, how does the economic advances of one group (women) compare with the military advances of African Americans? Looked at another way, how do the expectations of women who conformed to male work standards compare with the expectations of African Americans who performed military duties but still experienced segregation from the American mainstream?

At issue with identity are competing terms—*progress* and *acceptance*. Synthesizing your comparisons into a larger theme such as identity provides you with the ideas and language to develop your response.

STEP 3 *Write your response*

PUTTING IT ALL TOGETHER

Revisiting the Main Point

- Compare the ways in which Presidents Woodrow Wilson (Doc. 18.5) and Franklin Delano Roosevelt (Doc. 18.10) characterize the conclusions of the First and Second World Wars, respectively. How does each characterization view American identity?
- In what ways did the period between 1890 and 1945 represent an era of fulfillment of the ideals of the Declaration of Independence (Doc. 5.6) and the Gettysburg Address (Doc. 12.8)?
- In what ways did technological advances during this era influence three to five of the documents above? You may need to refer to Chapters 16 and 17 and your textbook to help you answer this question.

BUILDING AP® WRITING SKILLS **Implications in Historical Argument**

As your study of history covers a wider arc, your ability to discern **implications** means that you can draw conclusions based on patterns that can be traced over longer periods of time. Like ripples in a pond, implications suggest a far-reaching causation and allow for creative and original historical argument.

Consider the following prompt:

> In what ways did the period between 1890 and 1945 represent an era of fulfillment of the ideals of the Declaration of Independence (Doc. 5.6) and the Gettysburg Address (Doc. 12.8)?

This task—unlike any other that you have seen in this textbook—spans nearly two hundred years. Further, the implications of a key document—such as the Declaration of Independence or Gettysburg Address—represent a body of thought and action that is representative of an era. Coincidentally, both of these documents were products of war.

One helpful metaphor to bear in mind when thinking about implications is "windows and mirrors." A document serves not just as a mirror of its time, reflecting events as they were, but also acts as a window—as a gateway through which, in retrospect, hints of the future might be discerned. For example, the Declaration of Independence is a reflection or mirror of its times, and it also serves as a window through which we can trace countless events that have shaped our history. In general, visionary documents begin as mirrors; only time can tell if they also serve as windows.

STEPS 1–3

Steps 1 through 3 of the writing sequence have been outlined in earlier chapters, which may be consulted for review.

STEP 4 *Outline your essay*

Organizing this task requires an understanding of key documents and events and a synthesis of the ideals that different eras represented. The following outline is a possible beginning point for organization:

    I. Introduction

   II. Declaration of Independence

 III. Gettysburg Address

 IV. Period of 1890 to 1945

This chronology invites an understanding of the actual ideals of each era. Use your historical thinking exercises in this chapter as a starting point. To review, these include the closure of the American frontier (the Turner thesis) and the ambiguous progress made by women and minorities during the nineteenth and twentieth centuries.

Integrating historical themes also allows you to contextualize your arguments even further. When you consider the fulfillment of the ideals of the Declaration of Independence and Gettysburg Address, you also consider which of the historical themes best apply. Two that may apply are "identity" and "work, exchange, and technology."

Thus, a revised outline for this prompt could incorporate these themes, moving away from the documents as the sole organizing agent. The outline below allows you to create a framework for your essay that is organized around a few themes and then to examine those themes through both mirror and window lenses for each document. We have started the outline for you by filling in the first main point (identity) for the first document.

    I. Introduction

   II. Declaration of Independence

      A. THEME: IDENTITY. At issue in the struggle for equal rights from the time of the founding through the twentieth century is the notion of American IDENTITY—who we are as a nation and who is entitled to the "natural rights" that are outlined in our founding documents.

         1. MIRROR: The Declaration reflects ideas of its time and sidesteps issues of rights for women and people of color. This relates to the theme IDENTITY, with women and people of color being less identifiable as Americans or citizens.

2. WINDOW: The language of the Declaration focuses on natural rights and leaves room for interpretation. Women and former slaves eventually pointed to it and used it as evidence in their own struggles for equality. Although not a requirement, using the word *implications* works well with a discussion of the window metaphor.

   B. THEME: WORK, EXCHANGE, AND TECHNOLOGY

   1. MIRROR: (As shown above, examine the ways in which the Declaration of Independence—with its emphasis on inalienable rights—reflects the economic status of this society.)

   2. WINDOW: (And as before, in what ways does the language of the Declaration anticipate future ambiguities for opportunities, especially as these opportunities relate to issues of identity?)

III. Gettysburg Address (While you are repeating the same moves for the Gettysburg Address, you are also drawing comparisons with the Declaration. Thus, there is an additional component to this outline.)

   A. THEME:

   1. MIRROR:

   2. WINDOW:

   3. Comparison and contrast with observations on the Declaration of Independence

   B. THEME:

   1. MIRROR:

   2. WINDOW:

   3. Comparison and contrast with observations on the Declaration of Independence

IV. Period of 1890 to 1945

   A. THEME:

   1. MIRROR: (Here you will examine how the era reflects the promises of the Declaration and Gettysburg Address relative to one theme.)

   2. WINDOW: (Here you may examine how the era *has yet* to fulfill these same promises. This portion of your essay may also prevent you from presenting an either/or fallacy about the question of fulfillment.)

   B. THEME:

   1. MIRROR:

   2. WINDOW:

   V. Conclusion

STEP 5 *Write the essay*

International and Grassroots Progressivism

To what extent did the Progressive era owe its origins to an increasingly global society? Although the United States began its economic growth in a developing global market, it also began to see itself through the lens of other developed nations and their approaches toward social politics.

The origins of reform in the first half of the twentieth century remain ambiguous. The Progressive era represented a grassroots approach to the fulfillment of the inalienable rights of the Declaration of Independence. But what other factors encouraged the legislative leaders to formalize such movements, with attention to the Seventeenth and Nineteenth Amendments (election of senators and women's right to vote, respectively)?

You have already read various sources that illustrate different interpretations about the origins of reforms during this time period. Now read the two passages below, and consider the factors that promulgated reform during this time period.

> The years between 1900 and 1920 marked the maturation of the political culture of middle-class women. Able to vote in only a few states before 1910, excluded by law from public office in most states, and perceived as outsiders by lawmakers in Congress, and in state and municipal governments, women had to find ways to overcome these gender-specific "disabilities" if they were to affect public policy. They did so by drawing on the most fundamental and enduring features of women's political culture—the strength of its grass-roots organizations, and the power of its moral vision.
>
> Structured representationally, women's organizations, even those with strong national leaders like the National Consumers' League, gave great weight to the views of state and local affiliates. This sparked grass-roots initiative. It also fostered belief in democratic processes and the capacity of large social organizations—like state and federal governments—to respond positively to social needs. Whereas the predominant moral vision of men's political culture tended to regard the state as a potential enemy of human liberty, the moral vision of women's political culture viewed the state as a potential guarantor of social rights. . . .

—From "The Historical Foundations of Women's Power in the Creation of the American Welfare State, 1880–1920," in Seth Koven and Sonya Michel, eds., *Mothers of a New World: Maternalist Politics and the Origins of Welfare States* (New York: Routledge, 1993), 68.

> By the first decade of the twentieth century there was no party system within the North Atlantic economy that had not been profoundly shaken by the new social politics. In Britain, the Liberal government of 1906–1914 embarked on a flurry of legislation that, a quarter century later, still stuck in Franklin Roosevelt's mind for its daring. For the aged poor, it inaugurated an old-age pension system borrowed from New Zealand; for the crippling economic effects of sickness, a program of compulsory wage-earners' health insurance borrowed from Germany; for the most exploited of workers, a set of Australian-style wage boards empowered to establish legal minimum wages; for the sake of fiscal justice, progressive land and

income taxes; for the unemployed, a German-style network of state-run employment offices; and, for workers in trades of particularly uneven labor demand, an untried experiment in pooling the risks of unemployment through state-administered insurance. The Radical coalitions that governed France between 1899 and 1914, though their failures were greater, proposed no less: progressive income taxation, public medical assistance to the elderly poor, a legally fixed maximum working day, tax subsidies for trade union unemployment benefits, public mediation of labor disputes, and—in a policy reversal that hinted at the international volatility of the new social politics—German-modeled, compulsory, old-age insurance. In timing and content, the prewar progressive movement in American politics fit, as fragment to whole, into this broader North Atlantic pattern.

—From Daniel T. Rogers, *Atlantic Crossings: Social Politics in a Progressive Age* (Cambridge, MA: Belknap Press of Harvard University Press, 1998), 56.

Using the two excerpts, answer the following questions:

1. Briefly explain one major difference between Koven and Michel's and Roger's historical interpretations of the reform movement.
2. Briefly explain how one document from the time period not explicitly mentioned in the excerpts could be used to support either excerpt.
3. Briefly explain how one document from Chapter 16, 17, or 18 could be used to support the excerpt you did not choose in question 2.

CHAPTER 19

Containment and Conflict

he postwar period promised to be expansive for American interests and ideals. After the United States, Soviet Union, and other allied powers defeated the aggressive fascist nations of Europe and Asia, they set in motion an international order that was grounded in the new United Nations and in statutes that protected universal human rights. However, in the waning days of the Second World War, the United States and the USSR established the parameters of a global conflict that lasted for nearly fifty years, approximately a quarter of US history.

The Cold War was waged between people living in two fundamentally different political and economic systems and reflected a precarious balance between the two world powers left standing in the aftermath of 1945. The destructive capabilities of modern warfare, especially after the invention of nuclear weaponry, made direct conflict between these two "superpowers" unthinkable for most leaders. Instead, in Europe, Asia, and the Caribbean, a series of "proxy wars" on the fringes of each nation's sphere of influence broke out regularly throughout this period. These proxy wars inspired an ongoing culture of preparedness and anxiety domestically, including debates over the power of the federal government over individuals in an age of constant fear of war, and they shaped American consciousness until the eve of the twenty-first century.

Seeking the Main Point

As you read the documents that follow, keep these broad questions in mind. These questions will help you understand the relationship between the documents in this chapter and the historical changes that they represent. As you reflect on these questions, determine which themes and which documents best address them.

- Analyze the effects of the Second World War and the Cold War on Americans' sense of themselves as an isolated nation.
- To what extent did the Second World War and the Cold War shape American debates about civil liberties?
- Compare and contrast the influence of the Second World War and the influence of the Cold War on the relationship between American voters and the government.

The Origins of the Cold War

DOCUMENT 19.1 | **HARRY S. TRUMAN, On Atomic Technology**
1945

When Harry S. Truman (1884–1972) became president after Franklin Delano Roosevelt's death in 1945, it fell to him to bring to fruition the United States' nuclear weapons program. In this speech, which Truman gave after meeting with Joseph Stalin, leader of the Soviet Union, and Clement Attlee, prime minister of Great Britain, at an Allied conference in Potsdam, Germany, the president revealed the existence of the atomic bomb to the American people.

... We now have two great plants and many lesser works devoted to the production of atomic power. Employment during peak construction numbered 125,000 and over 65,000 individuals are even now engaged in operating the plants. Many have worked there for two and a half years. Few know what they have been producing. They see great quantities of material going in and they see nothing coming out of these plants, for the physical size of the explosive charge is exceedingly small. We have spent two billion dollars on the greatest scientific gamble in history—and won.

But the greatest marvel is not the size of the enterprise, its secrecy, nor its cost, but the achievement of scientific brains in putting together infinitely complex pieces of knowledge held by many men in different fields of science into a workable plan. And hardly less marvelous has been the capacity of industry to design and of labor to operate, the machines and methods to do things never done before so that the brainchild of many minds came forth in physical shape and performed as it was supposed to do. Both science and industry worked under the direction of the United States Army, which achieved a unique success in managing so diverse a problem in the advancement of knowledge in an amazingly short time. It is doubtful if such another combination could be got together in the world. What has been done is the greatest achievement of organized science in history. It was done under high pressure and without failure.

We are now prepared to obliterate more rapidly and completely every productive enterprise the Japanese have above ground in any city. We shall destroy their docks, their factories, and their communications. Let there be no mistake; we shall completely destroy Japan's power to make war.

It was to spare the Japanese people from utter destruction that the ultimatum of July 26 was issued at Potsdam. Their leaders promptly rejected that ultimatum. If they do not now accept our terms they may expect a rain of ruin from the air, the like of which has never been seen on this earth. Behind this air attack will follow sea and land forces in such number and power as they have not yet seen and with the fighting skill of which they are already well aware. . . .

The fact that we can release atomic energy ushers in a new era in man's understanding of nature's forces. Atomic energy may in the future supplement the power that now comes from coal, oil, and falling water, but at present it cannot be produced on a basis to compete with them commercially. Before that comes there must be a long period of intensive research. It has never been the habit of the scientists of this country or the policy of this government to withhold from the world scientific knowledge. Normally, therefore, everything about the work with atomic energy would be made public.

But under present circumstances it is not intended to divulge the technical processes of production or all the military applications, pending further examination of possible methods of protecting us and the rest of the world from the danger of sudden destruction.

Harry S. Truman Library and Museum, www.trumanlibrary.org/publicpapers/index.php?pid=100&st=atomic&st1=bomb.

PRACTICING Historical Thinking

Identify: Identify three or four significant reasons that Truman provides for praising atomic weaponry.

Analyze: Do these reasons primarily pursue progress in the name of peace and technology, or something else? Explain.

Evaluate: To what extent does the "unique success" that Truman describes represent a continuation of the ways that American technology paved the way for economic and political power?

DOCUMENT 19.2 | **GEORGE F. KENNAN, The Long Telegram**
1946

George Kennan (1904–2005) was an American diplomat who was based in Moscow when he wrote his famous long telegram to the US State Department to persuade Washington policy makers to take a more cautious policy toward the Soviet Union (USSR).

(1) Our first step must be to apprehend, and recognize for what it is, the nature of the movement with which we are dealing. We must study it with same courage, detachment, objectivity, and same determination not to be emotionally provoked or unseated by it, with which doctor studies unruly and unreasonable individual.

(2) We must see that our public is educated to realities of Russian situation. I cannot over-emphasize importance of this. Press cannot do this alone. It must be done mainly by Government, which is necessarily more experienced and better informed

on practical problems involved. In this we need not be deterred by [ugliness?] of picture. I am convinced that there would be far less hysterical anti-Sovietism in our country today if realities of this situation were better understood by our people. There is nothing as dangerous or as terrifying as the unknown. It may also be argued that to reveal more information on our difficulties with Russia would reflect unfavorably on Russian-American relations. I feel that if there is any real risk here involved, it is one which we should have courage to face, and sooner the better. But I cannot see what we would be risking. Our stake in this country, even coming on heels of tremendous demonstrations of our friendship for Russian people, is remarkably small. We have here no investments to guard, no actual trade to lose, virtually no citizens to protect, few cultural contacts to preserve. Our only stake lies in what we hope rather than what we have; and I am convinced we have better chance of realizing those hopes if our public is enlightened and if our dealings with Russians are placed entirely on realistic and matter-of-fact basis.

(3) Much depends on health and vigor of our own society. World communism is like malignant parasite which feeds only on diseased tissue. This is point at which domestic and foreign policies meets. Every courageous and incisive measure to solve internal problems of our own society, to improve self-confidence, discipline, morale and community spirit of our own people, is a diplomatic victory over Moscow worth a thousand diplomatic notes and joint communiqués. If we cannot abandon fatalism and indifference in face of deficiencies of our own society, Moscow will profit—Moscow cannot help profiting by them in its foreign policies.

(4) We must formulate and put forward for other nations a much more positive and constructive picture of sort of world we would like to see than we have put forward in past. It is not enough to urge people to develop political processes similar to our own. Many foreign peoples, in Europe at least, are tired and frightened by experiences of past, and are less interested in abstract freedom than in security. They are seeking guidance rather than responsibilities. We should be better able than Russians to give them this. And unless we do, Russians certainly will.

(5) Finally we must have courage and self-confidence to cling to our own methods and conceptions of human society. After A1, the greatest danger that can befall us in coping with the problem of Soviet communism, is that we shall allow ourselves to become like those with whom we are coping.

Akis Kalaitzidis and Gregory W. Streich, eds., *U.S. Foreign Policy: A Documentary and Reference Guide* (Santa Barbara, CA: ABC-CLIO, 2011), 144–145.

PRACTICING Historical Thinking

Identify: Paraphrase Kennan's concerns about the rise of Communism, as well as his beliefs about how Americans should cultivate their values.

Analyze: Kennan states: "I feel that if there is any real risk here involved, it is one which we should have courage to face, and sooner the better. But I cannot see what we would be risking. Our stake in this country, even coming on heels of tremendous demonstrations of our friendship for Russian people, is remarkably small." Given this statement, why does Kennan feel that it is important for the United States to pay attention to the Soviet Union?

Evaluate: How does Kennan's long telegram revise American isolationist policy? And is this revision primarily a political one? An economic one? Explain.

DOCUMENT 19.3 | **HARRY S. TRUMAN, On Greece and Turkey**
1947

In the face of communist rebellions in Greece and Turkey and an appeal from Great Britain for assistance in preventing the rise of communist governments in these nations, in 1947, President Harry S. Truman asked Congress to authorize the funding of counter-insurgency efforts in Greece and Turkey. This established the "Truman Doctrine" as the broad anti-Soviet policy of the United States throughout the Cold War.

It would be an unspeakable tragedy if these countries, which have struggled so long against overwhelming odds, should lose that victory for which they sacrificed so much. Collapse of free institutions and loss of independence would be disastrous not only for them but for the world. Discouragement and possibly failure would quickly be the lot of neighboring peoples striving to maintain their freedom and independence.

Should we fail to aid Greece and Turkey in this fateful hour, the effect will be far reaching to the West as well as to the East.

We must take immediate and resolute action.

I, therefore, ask the Congress to provide authority for assistance to Greece and Turkey in the amount of $400,000,000 for the period ending June 30, 1948. In requesting these funds, I have taken into consideration the maximum amount of relief assistance which would be furnished to Greece out of the $350,000,000 which I recently requested that the Congress authorize for the prevention of starvation and suffering in countries devastated by the war.

In addition to funds, I ask the Congress to authorize the detail of American civilian and military personnel to Greece, and Turkey, at the request of those countries, to assist in the tasks of reconstruction, and for the purpose of supervising the use of such financial and material assistance as may be furnished. I recommend that authority also be provided for the instruction and training of selected Greek and Turkish personnel.

Finally, I ask that the Congress provide authority which will permit the speediest and most effective use, in terms of needed commodities, supplies, and equipment, of such funds as may be authorized.

Harry Truman, *Public Papers of the Presidents of the United States: Harry S. Truman, 1947, Volume 3* (Washington, DC: Government Printing Office, 1963), 56.

DOCUMENT 19.4	JOHN N. WHEELER, Letter Home from Korean War
	1950

The Korean Conflict (1950–1953) grew from the division of Korea in the aftermath of the Second World War. When communist North Korea invaded US-supported South Korea, the United States found itself compelled to apply the Truman Doctrine to Asia. Although the United States fought under a United Nations mandate, US and South Korean soldiers did most of the fighting throughout the conflict.

Can't say as I blame you, Dad, for your opinions of Mr. Truman and his administration. However, you must remember that his opinions as well as his actions represent the vast majority of the "Soft-bellied Americans" who, for the life of them, couldn't see giving up a few of the needless luxuries of life to support a military machine big enough to protect the peace and liberty that they take for granted. Only those who have visited foreign countries can realize what they mean. It would be a good lesson to the Americans if they had to fight a war on their own soil, and had to lie for a short time under the sadistic rule of this band of perverted sadists who call themselves communists. They claim that they want to help the "worker"—all they want to do is to help themselves. Mass murder, rape torture, and starvation is the rule and not the exception with them. They have proved it here as well as everywhere else. I could see nothing more fitting for a young man to do then to devote his entire life to killing everyone of them.

Andrew Carroll, ed, *War Letters: Extraordinary Correspondence from American Wars* (New York: Simon & Schuster), 2001.

| **CENTRAL INTELLIGENCE AGENCY, A Study of Assassination**

1953

The following excerpt on assassination is from a manual published by the Central Intelligence Agency (CIA) in 1953 as part of the United States' attempt to prevent the rise of socialist and communist governments in Latin America.

Definition

Assassination is a term thought to be derived from "Hashish," a drug similar to marijuana, said to have been used by Hasan-Dan-Sabah to induce motivation in his followers, who were assigned to carry out political and other murders, usually at the cost of their lives.

It is here used to describe the planned killing of a person who is not under the legal jurisdiction of the killer, who is not physically in the hands of the killer, who has been selected by a resistance organization for death, and whose death provides positive advantages to that organization.

Employment

Assassination is an extreme measure not normally used in clandestine operations. It should be assumed that it will never be ordered or authorized by any U.S. Headquarters, though the latter may in rare instances agree to its execution by members of an associated foreign service. This reticence is partly due to the necessity for committing communications to paper. No assassination instructions should ever be written or recorded. Consequently, the decision to employ this technique must nearly always be reached in the field, at the area where the act will take place. Decision and instructions should be confined to an absolute minimum of persons. Ideally, only one person will be involved. No report may be made, but usually the act will be properly covered by normal news services, whose output is available to all concerned.

Justification

Murder is not morally justifiable. Self-defense may be argued if the victim has knowledge which may destroy the resistance organization if divulged. Assassination of persons responsible for atrocities or reprisals may be regarded as just punishment. Killing a political leader whose burgeoning career is a clear and present danger to the cause of freedom may be held necessary.

But assassination can seldom be employed with a clear conscience. Persons who are morally squeamish should not attempt it.

Nick Cullather, *Secret History: The CIA's Classified Account of Its Operations in Guatemala, 1952–1954* (Palo Alto, CA: Stanford University Press, 1999), 137–138.

PRACTICING Historical Thinking

Identify: Summarize the message of this passage.

Analyze: How does the manual distinguish assassination from murder?

Evaluate: Does the CIA's involvement in Central America during the 1950s differ from America's first steps into international alliances, as seen during the Woodrow Wilson administration (Docs. 18.4 and 18.5)? Explain.

DOCUMENT 19.6 | ## PETE SEEGER, Testimony before the House Un-American Activities Committee
1955

Throughout the late 1940s and early 1950s, the House Un-American Activities Committee (HUAC) sought to root out communists in the American government and entertainment community. HUAC's greatest power lay in its ability, as a congressional committee, to subpoena individuals to appear before the committee in public hearings, as it did on August 18, 1955, with the folksinger Pete Seeger.

MR. TAVENNER: The Committee has information obtained in part from the *Daily Worker* indicating that, over a period of time, especially since December of 1945, you took part in numerous entertainment features. I have before me a photostatic copy of the June 20, 1947, issue of the *Daily Worker*. In a column entitled "What's On" appears this advertisement: "Tonight—Bronx, hear Peter Seeger and his guitar, at Allerton Section housewarming." May I ask you whether or not the Allerton Section was a section of the Communist Party?

MR. SEEGER: Sir, I refuse to answer that question whether it was a quote from the *New York Times* or the *Vegetarian Journal*.

MR. TAVENNER: I don't believe there is any more authoritative document in regard to the Communist Party than its official organ, the *Daily Worker*.

MR. SCHERER: He hasn't answered the question, and he merely said he wouldn't answer whether the article appeared in the *New York Times* or some other magazine. I ask you to direct the witness to answer the question.

CHAIRMAN WALTER: I direct you to answer.

MR. SEEGER: Sir, the whole line of questioning—

CHAIRMAN WALTER: You have only been asked one question, so far.

MR. SEEGER: I am not going to answer any questions as to my association, my philosophical or religious beliefs or my political beliefs, or how I voted in any election, or any of these private affairs. I think these are very improper questions for any American to be asked, especially under such compulsion as this. I would be very glad to tell you my life if you want to hear of it.

MR. TAVENNER: Has the witness declined to answer this specific question?

CHAIRMAN WALTER: He said that he is not going to answer any questions, any names or things.

MR. SCHERER: He was directed to answer the question.

MR. TAVENNER: I have before me a photostatic copy of the April 30, 1948, issue of the *Daily Worker* which carries under the same title of "What's On," an advertisement of a "May Day Rally: For Peace, Security and Democracy." The advertisement states: "Are you in a fighting mood? Then attend the May Day rally." Expert speakers are stated to be slated for the program, and then follows a statement, "Entertainment by Pete Seeger." At the bottom appears this: "Auspices Essex County Communist Party," and at the top, "Tonight, Newark, N.J." Did you lend your talent to the Essex County Communist Party on the occasion indicated by this article from the *Daily Worker*?

MR. SEEGER: Mr. Walter, I believe I have already answered this question, and the same answer.

CHAIRMAN WALTER: The same answer. In other words, you mean that you decline to answer because of the reasons stated before?

MR. SEEGER: I gave my answer, sir.

CHAIRMAN WALTER: What is your answer?

MR. SEEGER: You see, sir, I feel—

CHAIRMAN WALTER: What is your answer?

MR. SEEGER: I will tell you what my answer is. I feel that in my whole life I have never done anything of any conspiratorial nature and I resent very much and very deeply the implication of being called before this Committee that in some way because my opinions may be different from yours, or yours, Mr. Willis, or yours, Mr. Scherer, that I am any less of an American than anybody else. I love my country very deeply, sir.

U.S. House Committee on Un-American Activities, Investigation of Communist Activities Hearings: New York Area (Entertainment), 84th Congress, August 18, 1955, in "'I Have Sung in Hobo Jungles, and I Have Sung for the Rockefellers': Pete Seeger Refuses to 'Sing' for HUAC," *History Matters: The U.S. Survey Course on the Web*, George Mason University, http://historymatters.gmu.edu/d/6457.

PRACTICING Historical Thinking

Identify: What does the committee want from Seeger? And what is Seeger's reply?

Analyze: What "implication" concerns Seeger in the final paragraph above?

Evaluate: Compare this HUAC interrogation with the excerpt from the CIA manual (Doc. 19.5). How do both documents signal a shift in America's worldview?

DOCUMENT 19.7 | DWIGHT D. EISENHOWER, Farewell Address
1961

Dwight D. Eisenhower (1890–1969) served as commander of US forces in Europe during the D-Day invasion before he was elected president of the United States in 1952. Like Harry S. Truman, Eisenhower advocated the "containment" of communism worldwide, but in his farewell address to the nation, he questioned the expansion of a permanent armament industry as a result of the Cold War.

A vital element in keeping the peace is our military establishment.

Our arms must be mighty, ready for instant action, so that no potential aggressor may be tempted to risk his own destruction.

Our military organization today bears little relation to that known by any of my predecessors in peacetime, or indeed by the fighting men of World War II or Korea.

Until the latest of our world conflicts, the United States had no armaments industry.

American makers of plowshares could, with time and as required, make swords as well.

But now we can no longer risk emergency improvisation of national defense; we have been compelled to create a permanent armaments industry of vast proportions.

Added to this, three and a half million men and women are directly engaged in the defense establishment.

We annually spend on military security more than the net income of all United States Corporations.

This conjunction of an immense military establishment and a large arms industry is new in the American experience.

The total influence—economic, political, even spiritual—is felt in every city, every State house, every office of the Federal government.

We recognize the imperative need for this development.

Yet we must not fail to comprehend its grave implications.

Our toil, resources and livelihood are all involved; so is the very structure of our society.

In the councils of government, we must guard against the acquisition of unwarranted influence, whether sought or unsought, by the military-industrial complex.

The potential for the disastrous rise of misplaced power exists and will persist.

We must never let the weight of this combination endanger our liberties or democratic processes.

We should take nothing for granted.

Only an alert and knowledgeable citizenry can compel the proper meshing of the huge industrial and military machinery of defense with our peaceful methods and goals, so that security and liberty may prosper together.

Farewell address by President Dwight D. Eisenhower, January 17, 1961, final TV talk 1/17/61 (1), box 38, Speech Series, Papers of Dwight D. Eisenhower as President, 1953–1961, Eisenhower Library, National Archives and Records Administration, 12–16.

PRACTICING Historical Thinking

Identify: Summarize Eisenhower's warning.

Analyze: What contrasts does Eisenhower draw between wartime and peacetime? Do you see any irony in the development of the American military establishment?

Evaluate: Develop a position on the extent to which American political reactions to global conflict justified the development of the American military establishment.

DOCUMENT 19.8 | NIKITA KHRUSHCHEV, **Diplomatic Cable to Fidel Castro**
| 1962

When Fidel Castro (b. 1926) overthrew Fulgencio Batista's government in Havana, Cuba, in 1959 and started to receive support from the Soviet Union in 1960, the United States began to seek to overthrow this communist government ninety miles off its shore. In 1962, the Soviet Union placed short-range nuclear missiles in Cuba, and President John F. Kennedy (1917–1963) responded with a military blockade that threatened to escalate into a full-scale conflict with the USSR. In the letter below, Soviet Premier Nikita Khrushchev (1894–1971) informed Castro that the Soviet Union had negotiated the removal of its short-range missiles from Cuba.

Dear Comrade Fidel Castro:

Our October 27 message to President Kennedy allows for the question to be settled in your favor, to defend Cuba from an invasion and prevent war from breaking out. Kennedy's reply, which you apparently also know, offers assurances that the United States will not invade Cuba with its own forces, nor will it permit its allies to carry out an invasion. In this way the president of the United States has positively answered my messages of October 26 and 27, 1962.

We have now finished drafting our reply to the president's message. I am not going to convey it here, for you surely know the text, which is now being broadcast, over the radio.

With this motive I would like to recommend to you now, at this moment of change in the crisis, not to be carried away by sentiment and to show firmness. I must say that I understand your feelings of indignation toward the aggressive actions and violations of elementary norms of international law on the part of the United States.

But now, rather than law, what prevails is the senselessness of the militarists at the Pentagon. Now that an agreement is within sight, the Pentagon is searching for a pretext to frustrate this agreement. This is why it is organizing the provocative flights. Yesterday you shot down one of these, while earlier you didn't shoot them down when they overflew your territory. The aggressors will take advantage of such a step for their own purposes.

Therefore, I would like to advise you in a friendly manner to show patience, firmness and even more firmness. Naturally, if there's an invasion it will be necessary to repulse it by every means. But we mustn't allow ourselves to be carried away by provocations, because the Pentagon's unbridled militarists, now that the solution to the conflict is in sight and apparently in your favor, creating a guarantee against the invasion of Cuba, are trying to frustrate the agreement and provoke you into actions that could be used against you. I ask you not to give them the pretext for doing that.

On our part, we will do everything possible to stabilize the situation in Cuba, defend Cuba against invasion, and assure you the possibilities for peacefully building a socialist society.

I send you greetings, extensive to all your leadership group.

October 28, 1962

N. KHRUSHCHEV

James G. Blight, Bruce J. Allyn, and David A. Welch, *Cuba on the Brink: Castro, the Missile Crisis, and the Soviet Collapse* (Lanham, MD: Rowman and Littlefield, 2002), 510–511.

PRACTICING Historical Thinking

Identify: What does Khrushchev mean when he states: "But now, rather than law, what prevails is the senselessness of the militarists at the Pentagon"?

Analyze: What is Khrushchev's tone? Defensive? Conciliatory? Bitter? Explain your response.

Evaluate: To what extent can this document be regarded as a blow for Communism? Or to what extent can this document be regarded as a warning against American international aggression?

DOCUMENT 19.9 | **"The Commune Comes to America,"** *Life*
1969

While throughout US history Americans have experimented with utopian and communal living, in the late 1960s mainstream media outlets, like *Life* magazine, provided Americans with images of contemporary countercultures that challenged popular beliefs.

THE YOUTH COMMUNES
New Way of Living Confronts the U.S.

JULY 18 · 1969 · 40¢

Photo by John Olson/The LIFE Premium Collection/Getty Images.

PRACTICING Historical Thinking

Identify: "Counterculture" designates a culture often in conscious opposition to the mainstream. Identify three elements of this image that designate it a picture of a "counterculture" to mainstream society in the 1960s.

Analyze: Explain in what ways the three elements you chose are countercultural.

Evaluate: How does the text in the upper right-hand corner shape the reader's interpretation of this image? Is the text sympathetic, critical, or a combination of both? Explain.

DOCUMENT 19.10 | JIMMY CARTER, Inaugural Address
1977

Jimmy Carter (b. 1924) was elected president in 1976 after President Richard M. Nixon resigned because of his involvement in the Watergate scandal. Nixon had impeded an investigation into the role played by his administration in a 1972 break-in at the

Democratic National Committee headquarters at the Watergate office complex in Washington, DC. In the 1976 campaign, Carter promised honest government and a humbler American foreign policy. He delivered his inaugural address on January 20, 1977.

The American dream endures. We must once again have full faith in our country—and in one another. I believe America can be better. We can be even stronger than before.

Let our recent mistakes bring a resurgent commitment to the basic principles of our Nation, for we know that if we despise our own government we have no future. We recall in special times when we have stood briefly, but magnificently, united. In those times no prize was beyond our grasp.

But we cannot dwell upon remembered glory. We cannot afford to drift. We reject the prospect of failure or mediocrity or an inferior quality of life for any person. Our Government must at the same time be both competent and compassionate.

We have already found a high degree of personal liberty, and we are now struggling to enhance equality of opportunity. Our commitment to human rights must be absolute, our laws fair, our natural beauty preserved; the powerful must not persecute the weak, and human dignity must be enhanced.

We have learned that "more" is not necessarily "better," that even our great Nation has its recognized limits, and that we can neither answer all questions nor solve all problems. We cannot afford to do everything, nor can we afford to lack boldness as we meet the future. So, together, in a spirit of individual sacrifice for the common good, we must simply do our best.

Our Nation can be strong abroad only if it is strong at home. And we know that the best way to enhance freedom in other lands is to demonstrate here that our democratic system is worthy of emulation.

To be true to ourselves, we must be true to others. We will not behave in foreign places so as to violate our rules and standards here at home, for we know that the trust which our Nation earns is essential to our strength.

Jimmy Carter, *A Government as Good as Its People* (Plains, GA: Carter Foundation for Governmental Affairs, 1977), 222.

PRACTICING Historical Thinking

Identify: Paraphrase Carter's statement: "We have already found a high degree of personal liberty, and we are now struggling to enhance equality of opportunity. Our commitment to human rights must be absolute, our laws fair, our natural beauty preserved; the powerful must not persecute the weak, and human dignity must be enhanced."

Analyze: According to Carter, what is the relationship between American liberties and international responsibility?

Evaluate: To what extent does Carter's vision return American foreign policy to its roots in the early part of the twentieth century? Explain.

SKILL REVIEW | Contextualization and Interpretation

Read the following excerpt from Martin Halpern's "'I'm Fighting for Freedom': Coleman Young, HUAC, and the Detroit African American Community." Determine the following with assistance from your textbook and classroom notes as necessary:

1. What is Halpern's thesis? Hint: Examine the ways in which Halpern develops both sides of the argument, and determine the extent to which policy makers succumbed to an either/or approach to a solution.

2. To what extent does Halpern's thesis contradict American policy makers' justifications for Cold War domestic policy?

3. If you were going to incorporate a piece of evidence from this chapter to support Halpern's thesis, what document or documents might you choose? Justify your choice.

4. To what extent does this **synthesis** of evidence show that HUAC's stance was over-simplified? Hint: As you determine Halpern's thesis, consider how HUAC **synthesizes** various aspects of "left-wing" phenomena:

- African American advocacy
- Organized labor
- Unions in support of global peace

Although the FBI records released under the Freedom of Information Act do not disclose the identities of its informants, it is likely that the informant referred to by Hoover was Bereneice Baldwin, an African American woman whose story identifying twenty-eight Detroiters as Communists before the Subversive Activities Control Board in Washington produced banner headlines in the motor city just ten days prior to Hoover's wire. A plan to open the Detroit hearings with Baldwin's testimony was dropped, however, because she was being cross-examined in Washington.[1] The idea of leading off with an African American informer was probably no accident since committee investigators knew that its list of witnesses likely to be "unfriendly" included a disproportionate number of prominent African American Detroiters. Moreover, the committee's most visible public opposition came from the Civil Rights Congress, within which African Americans played a conspicuous role. Indeed, African Americans were often at center stage during the Detroit hearings.

Although the committee's general goal was to expose Communists in defense industries, its main Detroit target was Local 600 of the United Auto Workers, which represented sixty thousand workers at the Ford Motor Company's River Rouge complex and was the largest local union in the world. The vast Rouge complex included sixteen buildings each of which had its own full time union officials. The committee's second target was a group of African American leaders, Communist and non-Communist, who rejected the cold war consensus but retained a good deal of influence within Detroit's African American community. HUAC's purpose in holding local hearings was not to gather information relevant to national security legislation but rather to arouse public animosity to Communists and their allies and thereby undermine the ability of leftist individuals and organizations to function politically. Committee member Charles E. Potter (R-Michigan) told the *Detroit News* that the FBI knew the facts "but this will be the public's first knowledge of what is going on."[2]

In targeting UAW Local 600, HUAC was selecting one of the bulwarks of left-wing influence in the United States. To be sure, HUAC's assumption that communists dominated the local was inaccurate.[3] However, the left had played a decisive part in the early underground phase of the unionization effort at Ford and in winning unity between African American and white workers. Communists continued to function in the local's progressive caucus, which retained a sizeable following in the local. In the March 1951 local union election, candidates affiliated with the progressive caucus had won three of the four highest offices in the local, the presidencies of several units (buildings), and about half the seats on the local's executive board and general council. The sizeable left and progressive presence in the membership and leadership of Local 600 often led the organization to take controversial stands on both trade union and political matters. Local 600 was one of the few large organizations advocating a cease fire in Korea in 1951. It spoke out "for international peace and cooperation of all nations" and against "an impending World War III" during the Korean War when such ideas were branded as Communist in the mass media.[4]

Contributing to the orthodox concern with Local 600 was the fact that it served as an important base of support for radicalism within the African American community. This situation occurred because of the employment of a large number of African Americans, the inclusion of African Americans in leadership at the unit and local levels, and the significant role the local played in community affairs. The Ford Rouge complex became the Detroit area's largest employer of African American workers in the 1920s and about twelve thousand African American workers were employed at the complex in 1952. The highest ranking African American official, William Hood, the local's recording secretary, served as the president of the National Negro Labor Council (NNLC), a left-led national organization of African American trade unionists.[5]

Although influential in Local 600, the left was also vulnerable there. The anti-communist Walter Reuther had won control of the UAW's national leadership in November 1947. An opponent of the left, Carl Stellato, was elected president of Local 600 in 1950 and initiated an anti-communist campaign that included a requirement that all 550 elected and appointed local representatives sign a loyalty oath. Stellato attempted to remove five unit officers from their positions on the grounds that they were Communists and, thus, not eligible for office under the union's constitution. Substantial opposition to the anti-communist campaign, however, led to the defeat of the purge effort and Stellato's abandonment of his anti-communist effort. He retained the presidency of the local in a close 1951 election. Although dropped by Local 600's president, HUAC recalled Stellato's charges during its 1952 hearings as did the UAW international leadership when it took action against Local 600 in the wake of the HUAC public relations onslaught.[6]

Among other important organizations that HUAC interrogated in Detroit were the Civil Rights Congress (CRC) and the National Negro Labor Council (NNLC). The Civil Rights Congress was formed in 1946 as a merger of the International Labor Defense and the National Federation for Constitutional Liberties. As an organization whose focus was the defense of democratic rights, the Civil Rights Congress was involved in campaigns for justice for the Martinsville Seven, Willie McGee, and other victims of racist repression. In 1951 Paul Robeson and William Patterson presented to the United Nations the CRC petition, *We Charge Genocide* which chronicled the violence and denial of African American people's rights taking place in the United States. Although modest in numbers, with five hundred to one thousand members, the Detroit chapter of the CRC had an active staff and broad community support. Anne Shore, the Detroit CRC's Director of Organization, recalled that the organization "depended on a coalition of labor, white, black, middle class, and intellectual and it had been a very effective organization over the years." African Americans were prominent in the leadership of the Civil Rights Congress, including Detroit's Rev. Charles A. Hill, a national board member, and Arthur C. McPhaul, the full-time executive secretary of the Detroit chapter.[7]

Martin Halpern, "'I'm Fighting for Freedom': Coleman Young, HUAC, and the Detroit African American Community," *Journal of American Ethnic History* 17, (1) (1997): 19.

Notes

1. *Detroit Times*, 13 February 1952; *Detroit News*, 13, 24 February 1952.

2. *Detroit News*, 24 February 1952.

3. Andrew provides a critique of the charge that Local 600 was "Communist-dominated." William D. Andrew, "Factionalism and Anti-Communism: Ford Local 600," *Labor History*, 20 (Spring 1979): 227–55.

4. *Ford Facts*, 2 June 1951; Letter, Carl Stellato et al., to Walter Reuther, 13 March 1952, Nat Ganley Collection, Box 6, Archives of Labor History and Urban Affairs, Wayne State University, Detroit (hereafter WSU). *Fortune* commented that in backing Sen. Edwin C. Johnson's (D-Colorado) cease-fire proposal Local 600 was endorsing "a program of ending the Korean war that had received virtually no labor support outside of the party-line unions." "Mutiny at Ford," *Fortune*, 44 (August 1951): 44.

5. Martin Halpern, *UAW Politics in the Cold War Era* (Albany: State University of New York Press, 1988), pp. 257–62. According to a UAW survey in February and March 1947, blacks were 21.5 percent of 74,500 workers in four Detroit area Ford plants. The percentage of blacks at the Rouge complex was certainly higher since plants outside the Rouge had relatively few black employees. In 1952 employment of union members at the Rouge complex was about 60,000. Memorandum, J. H. Wishart to Walter Reuther, 11 April 1947 and attached UAW Research Department, Employment Survey—February–March 1947, Walter Reuther Collection, Box 33, WSU; *Proceedings of the Thirteenth Convention of the UAW-CIO, April 1–6 1951*, Cleveland, Ohio, p. 470.

6. Andrew, "Factionalism and Anti-Communism: Ford Local 600," pp. 239–55; Halpern, *UAW Politics*, pp. 259–60.

7. Gerald Horne, *Communist Front? The Civil Rights Congress, 1946–1956* (Rutherford, NJ: Fairleigh Dickinson University Press, 1988), p. 71; Art McPhaul Statement, Detroit Civil Rights Congress Collection, Box 41, WSU; Interview with Art McPhaul, 6 October 1984; William L. Patterson, ed., *We Charge Genocide: The Historic Petition to the United Nations for Relief from a Crime of the United States Government against the Negro People* (New York: International Publishers, 1951); William L. Patterson, *The Man Who Cried Genocide: An Autobiography* (New York: International Publishers, 1971), pp. 146–208; Oral History Interview with Anne Shore, 1982, Oral History of the American Left, Tamiment Library, New York University.

PUTTING IT ALL TOGETHER

Revisiting the Main Point

* Analyze the effects of the Second World War and the Cold War on Americans' sense of themselves as an "isolated" nation.
* To what extent did the Second World War and the Cold War shape American debates about civil liberties?

**BUILDING AP®
WRITING SKILLS** **Organizing Themes in Historical Arguments**

Sophisticated historical arguments apply historical thinking skills to your argument, through a discussion of broader themes.

Consider the following prompt:

> To what extent did the Second World War and the Cold War shape American debates about civil liberties?

STEP 1 *Understand the prompt, and identify the key words*

Answering this question requires you to look at American ideas, beliefs, and cultures as a product of distinct moments in American history. Unlike Chapter 18, which assessed a relationship between distinct entities (seminal documents in history), this prompt examines the relationship between distinct events and "American debates."

Assessing a debate may take the following approaches:

* Examining the pros and cons of civil liberties
* Evaluating directions as healthy or harmful (understanding implications, from Chapter 18)
* Determining new definitions about civil liberties

Several historical thinking skills are available to you as you develop this response, including the following:

* Causation and historical evidence
* Contextualization (noting how the Second World War and Cold War reflected the mind-set of America)
* Comparison (examining how distinct events produce complex results)

- Synthesis (understanding how a particular theme—in this case, ideas, beliefs, and culture—reflects a combination of disparate events, perspectives, and documents)

This prompt also allows for a creative interplay of distinct historical themes. The theme of ideas, beliefs, and culture also permits a discussion of other themes, including peopling, identity, and even work, exchange, and technology. Earlier chapters featured the primary documents in the service of historical thinking skills, but now you may paint broader strokes by using historical thinking skills in the service of broader themes.

STEP 2 *Generate a working thesis*

STEP 3 *Identify and organize your evidence*

STEP 4 *Outline your response*

Thus, one outline for this prompt suggests this organization:

Introduction
I. Historical theme 1 (such as ideas, beliefs, and culture)
   A. Second World War and Cold War
   B. Influence on theme
      1. Primary documents and historical evidence in support
      2.
II. Historical theme 2 (such as identity)
   A. Second World War and Cold War
   B. Influence on theme
      1. Primary documents and historical evidence in support
      2.
Conclusion

As the essay continues, you should evaluate the relationship between themes. One theme may be subordinate to another, or a theme may contribute to the development of another. For example, the theme of Americans ideas, beliefs, and culture (which includes a discussion of civil liberties) may at its core be directly related to the theme of America's identity.

STEP 5 *Write the essay*

Remember that the use of primary documents and historical evidence occupies a distinct place in your essay.

CHAPTER 20

The Breakdown of Consensus

B y the early 1960s, the Vietnam War and the civil rights movement dominated newspaper headlines in the United States and inspired movements for gender and sexual equality and for African American, Latin American, and Native American rights. These movements for civil rights especially influenced millions of young Americans who were coming of age in high schools and colleges. By the end of the decade, the assassinations of Martin Luther King Jr., Malcolm X, and Robert F. Kennedy and riots in the poor and predominately African American ghettos of American cities ignited widespread calls for reform.

These revolutionary sentiments also produced a countermovement of self-proclaimed conservatives like Ronald Reagan and Phyllis Schlafly who took inspiration from the (unsuccessful) presidential candidacy of Barry Goldwater in 1964 and looked back to an unspecified time when American society was at peace and the American economy in a state of prosperity. These sentiments provided the seeds of a revitalized conservatism in the 1970s and 1980s, breaking through on the federal level with the election of Ronald Reagan as president in 1980.

Seeking the Main Point

As you read the documents that follow, keep these broad questions in mind. These questions will help you understand the relationship between the documents in this chapter and the historical changes that they represent. As you reflect on these questions, determine which themes and which documents best address them.

- To what extent was the post–World War II American identity an acceptance of diversity? Or was this era a time when a sweeping effort was made to homogenize previously marginalized voices?
- Compare and contrast the office of the presidency with grassroots advocacy groups in terms of how they each wielded power.
- In what ways did the civil rights movements of the 1960s and 1970s reshape and realign American politics?

The Beginnings of the Modern Civil Rights Movement

DOCUMENT 20.1 | **DWIGHT D. EISENHOWER, On Earl Warren and the *Brown* Decision**
| 1954

President Dwight D. Eisenhower (1890–1969) appointed former governor of California Earl Warren (1891–1974) to the United States Supreme Court in 1953. In May of the following year, Warren delivered the landmark *Brown v. Board of Education* decision, in which the justices unanimously overturned the Court's decision in *Plessy v. Ferguson* (1896) and declared that separate educational facilities were "inherently unequal." In the following excerpt from a letter written in October 1954, Eisenhower defends his appointment of Warren.

. . . The Chief Justice has a great many administrative tasks, as well as obvious responsibilities involving personal leadership. Along with this, he must be a statesman and, in my opinion (since I have my share of egotism), I could not do my duty unless I appointed a man whose philosophy of government was somewhat along the lines of my own. All this finally brought me down to Warren, especially as I refused to appoint anyone to the Supreme Court who was over 62 years of age. It seems to me completely futile to try to use a Supreme Court vacancy as a mere reward for long and brilliant service. If I should be succeeded by a New Deal President, a judge who is now 69 or 70 would probably create a vacancy very soon to be filled by the left-wingers. So—it seems to me that prudence demands that I secure relatively young men for any vacancies that may occur. I *wish* that I could find a number of outstanding jurists in the low 50's.

The segregation issue will, I think, become acute or tend to die out according to the character of the procedure orders that the Court will probably issue this winter. My own guess is that they will be very moderate and accord a maximum of initiative to local courts.

"Letter from President Dwight D. Eisenhower to E. E. 'Swede' Hazlett, October 23, 1954," Dwight D. Eisenhower Library, www.archives.gov/education/lessons/brown-v-board.

Identify: According to Eisenhower, why did he nominate Earl Warren to the US Supreme Court?

Analyze: Why does Eisenhower refer to his own "egotism"?

Evaluate: To what extent does Eisenhower's statement present a close relationship between the judicial and executive branches of government?

DOCUMENT 20.2 | **STUDENTS FOR A DEMOCRATIC SOCIETY, Port Huron Statement**
1962

Students for a Democratic Society (SDS) was formed at the University of Michigan in 1962 as a student organization concerned with American domestic politics and foreign policy. By the late 1960s, SDS had chapters on American universities across the nation and functioned as the epicenter of the student antiwar movement.

We are people of this generation, bred in at least modest comfort, housed now in universities, looking uncomfortably to the world we inherit.

When we were kids the United States was the wealthiest and strongest country in the world: the only one with the atom bomb, the least scarred by modern war, an initiator of the United Nations that we thought would distribute Western influence throughout the world. Freedom and equality for each individual, government of, by, and for the people—these American values we found good, principles by which we could live as men. Many of us began maturing in complacency.

As we grew, however, our comfort was penetrated by events too troubling to dismiss. First, the permeating and victimizing fact of human degradation, symbolized by the Southern struggle against racial bigotry, compelled most of us from silence to activism. Second, the enclosing fact of the Cold War, symbolized by the presence of the Bomb, brought awareness that we ourselves, and our friends, and millions of abstract "others" we knew more directly because of our common peril, might die at any time. We might deliberately ignore, or avoid, or fail to feel all other human problems, but not these two, for these were too immediate and crushing in their impact, too challenging in the demand that we as individuals take the responsibility for encounter and resolution.

While these and other problems either directly oppressed us or rankled our consciences and became our own subjective concerns, we began to see complicated and disturbing paradoxes in our surrounding America. The declaration "all men are created equal . . ." rang hollow before the facts of Negro life in the South and the big cities of the North. The proclaimed peaceful intentions of the United States contradicted its economic and military investments in the Cold War status quo. . . .

"Port Huron Statement of the Students for a Democratic Society, 1962," courtesy of the Office of Senator Tom Hayden, www.h-net.org/~hst306/documents/huron.html.

PRACTICING Historical Thinking

Identify: List the major forms of "degradation" that are listed in the Port Huron Statement.

Analyze: How does the statement's use of the word "complacency" represent a changing position toward domestic and foreign policies?

Evaluate: Was the Port Huron Statement a function of Cold War politics? Consult your textbook and class notes for additional information.

DOCUMENT 20.3 | **BETTY FRIEDAN,** *The Feminine Mystique*
1963

Betty Friedan (1921–2006) was a journalist before publishing *The Feminine Mystique* in 1963. Today historians consider the book to be one of the catalysts of the modern feminist movement in the United States.

The problem lay buried, unspoken, for many years in the minds of American women. It was a strange stirring, a sense of dissatisfaction, a yearning that women suffered in the middle of the twentieth century in the United States. Each suburban wife struggled with it alone. As she made the beds, shopped for groceries, matched slipcover material, ate peanut butter sandwiches with her children, chauffeured Cub Scouts and Brownies, lay beside her husband at night—she was afraid to ask even of herself the silent question—"Is this all?"

For over fifteen years there was no word of this yearning in the millions of words written about women, for women, in all the columns, books and articles by experts telling women their role was to seek fulfillment as wives and mothers. Over and over women heard in voices of tradition and of Freudian sophistication that they could desire no greater destiny than to glory in their own femininity. Experts told them how to catch a man and keep him, how to breastfeed children and handle their toilet training, how to cope with sibling rivalry and adolescent rebellion; how to buy a dishwasher, bake bread, cook gourmet snails, and build a swimming pool with their own hands; how to dress, look, and act more feminine and make marriage more exciting; how to keep their husbands from dying young and their sons from growing into delinquents. They were taught to pity the neurotic, unfeminine, unhappy women who wanted to be poets or physicists or presidents. They learned that truly feminine women do not want careers, higher education, political rights—the independence and the opportunities that the old-fashioned feminists fought for. Some women, in their forties and fifties, still remembered painfully giving up those dreams, but most of the younger women no longer even thought about them. A thousand expert voices applauded their femininity, their adjustment, their new maturity. All they had to do was devote their lives from earliest girlhood to finding a husband and bearing children. . . .

By the end of the fifties, the United States birthrate was overtaking India's. The birth-control movement, renamed Planned Parenthood, was asked to find a method whereby women who had been advised that a third or fourth baby would be born dead or defective might have it anyhow. Statisticians were especially astounded at the fantastic increase in the number of babies among college women. Where once they had two children, now they had four, five, six. Women who had once wanted careers were now making careers out of having babies. So rejoiced *Life* magazine in a 1956 paean to the movement of American women back to the home.

In a New York hospital, a woman had a nervous breakdown when she found she could not breastfeed her baby. In other hospitals, women dying of cancer refused a drug which research had proved might save their lives: its side effects were said to be unfeminine. "If I have only one life, let me live it as a blonde," a larger-than-life-sized picture of a pretty, vacuous woman proclaimed from newspaper, magazine, and drugstore ads. And across America, three out of every ten women dyed their hair blonde. They ate a chalk called Metrecal, instead of food, to shrink to the size of the thin young models. Department-store buyers reported that American women, since 1939, had become three and four sizes smaller. "Women are out to fit the clothes, instead of vice-versa," one buyer said.

Interior decorators were designing kitchens with mosaic murals and original paintings, for kitchens were once again the center of women's lives. Home sewing became a million-dollar industry. Many women no longer left their homes, except to shop, chauffeur their children, or attend a social engagement with their husbands. Girls were growing up in America without ever having jobs outside the home. In the late fifties, a sociological phenomenon was suddenly remarked: a third of American women now worked, but most were no longer young and very few were pursuing careers. They were married women who held part-time jobs, selling or secretarial, to put their husbands through school, their sons through college, or to help pay the mortgage. Or they were widows supporting families. Fewer and fewer women were entering professional work. The shortages in the nursing, social work, and teaching professions caused crises in almost every American city. Concerned over the Soviet Union's lead in the space race, scientists noted that America's greatest source of unused brainpower was women. But girls would not study physics: it was "unfeminine." A girl refused a science fellowship at Johns Hopkins to take a job in a real-estate office. All she wanted, she said, was what every other American girl wanted—to get married, have four children and live in a nice house in a nice suburb.

PRACTICING Historical Thinking

Identify: List the significant roles for mid-twentieth-century American women that Friedan describes. What patterns do you observe?

Analyze: Who is the intended audience for Friedan's statement? Explain your response.

Evaluate: To what extent does a solution to the problems that Friedan identifies depend on persuading men to change their views toward cultural norms?

DOCUMENT 20.4 | MARTIN LUTHER KING JR., "I Have a Dream"
| 1963

Martin Luther King Jr. (1929–1969) became the de facto leader of the postwar civil rights movement during the Montgomery bus boycott of 1955. Using tactics of nonviolent resistance to racial segregation in the South, King helped bring the inequalities experienced by African Americans to the forefront of American consciousness in the 1950s and 1960s. On August 28, 1963, in his seminal speech during the March on Washington, King eloquently expressed his vision of a racially just America.

. . . I have a dream that my four little children will one day live in a nation where they will not be judged by the color of their skin but by the content of their character. I have a dream . . . I have a dream that one day in Alabama, with its vicious racists, with its governor having his lips dripping with the words of interposition and nullification, one day right there in Alabama little black boys and black girls will be able to join hands with little white boys and white girls as sisters and brothers.

I have a dream today . . . I have a dream that one day every valley shall be exalted, every hill and mountain shall be made low. The rough places will be made plain, and the crooked places will be made straight. And the glory of the Lord shall be revealed, and all flesh shall see it together. This is our hope. This is the faith that I go back to the South with. With this faith we will be able to hew out of the mountain of despair a stone of hope. With this faith we will be able to transform the jangling discords of our nation into the beautiful symphony of brotherhood. With this faith we will be able to work together, to pray together, to struggle together, to go to jail together, to stand up for freedom together, knowing that we will be free one day. . . .

"I Have a Dream . . . ," speech by the Reverend Martin Luther King Jr. at the March on Washington, August 28, 1963, www.archives.gov/press/exhibits/dream-speech.pdf.

PRACTICING Historical Thinking

Identify: What is King's dream?

Analyze: Why does King say that this is "the faith that I go back to the South with"?

Evaluate: Are the "jangling discords" to which King refers the same conflicts that inspired Betty Friedan's vision (Doc. 20.3)? Explain.

DOCUMENT 20.5 | Civil Rights Act of 1964

When President John F. Kennedy called on Congress to enact civil rights legislation, the bill was stalled by segregationist legislators. Only after Kennedy's assassination was President Lyndon B. Johnson able to secure its passage. Johnson signed the Civil Rights Act into law on July 2, 1964.

To enforce the constitutional right to vote, to confer jurisdiction upon the district courts of the United States to provide injunctive relief against discrimination in public accommodations, to authorize the Attorney General to institute suits to protect constitutional rights in public facilities and public education, to extend the Commission on Civil Rights, to prevent discrimination in federally assisted programs, to establish a Commission on Equal Employment Opportunity, and for other purposes. . . .

(2) No person acting under color of law shall—

(A) in determining whether any individual is qualified under State law or laws to vote in any Federal election, apply any standard, practice, or procedure different from the standards, practices, or procedures applied under such law or laws to other individuals within the same county, parish, or similar political subdivision who have been found by State officials to be qualified to vote;

(B) deny the right of any individual to vote in any Federal election because of an error or omission on any record or paper relating to any application, registration, or other act requisite to voting, if such error or omission is not material in determining whether such individual is qualified under State law to vote in such election; or

(C) employ any literacy test as a qualification for voting in any Federal election unless (i) such test is administered to each individual and is conducted wholly in writing, and (ii) a certified copy of the test and of the answers given by the individual is furnished to him within twenty-five days of the submission of his request made within the period of time during which records and papers are required to be retained and preserved pursuant to title III of the Civil Rights Act of 1960 (42 U.S.C. 1974—74e; 74 Stat. 88): Provided, however, That the Attorney General may enter into agreements with appropriate State or local authorities that preparation, conduct, and maintenance of such tests in accordance with the provisions of applicable State or local law, including such special provisions as are necessary in the preparation, conduct, and maintenance of such tests for persons who are blind or otherwise physically handicapped, meet the purposes of this subparagraph and constitute compliance therewith. . . .

Civil Rights Act of 1964, Public Law 88-352, *Revised Statutes*, Volume 78, page 241. July 2, 1964.

PRACTICING Historical Thinking

Identify: Identify the rights conferred on people from minority groups by this legislation.

Analyze: Compare these rights to the ones that are articulated in the Declaration of Independence and Gettysburg Address. How similar are they?

Evaluate: In what ways do these rights respond to an early movement toward equity—the Progressive movement during the early 1900s?

DOCUMENT 20.6 | **CESAR CHAVEZ, "We Shall Overcome"**
1965

Cesar Chavez (1927–1993) cofounded the United Farm Workers (UFW) union and was instrumental in bringing the issues of Latino American economic rights to public attention. The following item appeared in the farm workers' underground newspaper, *El Malcriado*, on January 16, 1965, at the beginning of the Delano, California, grape strike. Its title, "We Shall Overcome," became a rallying cry for the movement. The strike continued for more than five years.

In a 400-square-mile area halfway between Selma and Weedpatch, California, a general strike of farm workers has been going on for six weeks. The Filipinos, under AWOC AFL-CIO, began the strike for a $1.40 per hour guarantee and a union contract. They were joined by the independent Farm Workers Association, which has a membership of several thousand Mexican Americans.

Filipino, Mexican American and Puerto Rican workers have been manning picket lines daily for 41 days in a totally non-violent manner. Ranchers in the area, which include DiGiorgio Fruit, Schenley, and many independent growers, did not take the strike seriously at first. By the second or third week, however, they began taking another look and striking back. Mechanized agriculture began picketing the pickets, spraying them with sulfur, running tractors by them to create dust storms, building barricades of farm machinery so that scabs could not see the pickets. These actions not only increased the determination of the strikers, but convinced some of the scabs that the ranchers were, in fact, less than human. Scabs quit work and the strike grew.

The growers hired security guards for $43 a day. They began driving their Thunderbirds, equipped with police dogs and rifles, up and down the roads. The people made more picket signs, drew in their belts, and kept marching.

Production was down 30 percent and the growers began looking for more and more scabs. They went to Fresno and Bakersfield and Los Angeles to find them. They didn't tell the workers that they would be scab crews. The pickets followed them into every town and formed ad hoc strike committees to prevent scabbing. They succeeded in these towns. Within two weeks, only one bus, with half a dozen winos escorted by a pearl gray Cadillac, drove into the strike zone. A new plan was formed. The ranchers would advertise in South Texas and old Mexico. They bring these workers in buses and the workers are held in debt to the rancher before they even arrive in town. We have a new and more difficult task ahead of us with these scabs.

As our strike has grown, workers have matured and now know why and how to fight for their rights. As the strike has grown into a movement for justice by the lowest paid workers in America, friends of farm workers have begun to rally in support of *La Causa*. Civil rights, church, student and union groups help with food and money.

We believe that this is the beginning of a significant drive to achieve equal rights for agricultural workers. In order to enlist your full support and to explain our work to you, I would like to bring some of our pickets and meet with you.

Cesar Chavez, "We Shall Overcome," *El Malcriado*, September 16, 1965, in Cesar Chavez, *An Organizer's Tale: Speeches*, ed. and introduction by Ilan Stavans (New York: Penguin Group, 2008).

PRACTICING Historical Thinking

Identify: Identify the significant numbers in Chavez's statements. Why did you select these?

Analyze: Who is Chavez's intended audience? Use your class notes and textbook to assist you.

Evaluate: Synthesize Chavez's statement with Martin Luther King Jr.'s (Doc. 20.4) and Betty Friedan's (Doc. 20.3). To what extent do all three documents present a shift in power away from the federal government to a more populist approach toward reform?

SKILL REVIEW | Causation and Argumentation

Accept, modify, or refute the following statement:

> The *Brown v. Board of Education* decision was a turning point in the twentieth-century civil rights movement.

STEP 1 *Causation*

The claim that *Brown v. Board of Education* began a series of events—or **period**—requires you to visualize the relationship between the legislative decision and key features of the civil rights movement. Consider the chronology of the documents in this chapter:

Document 20.1, Dwight D. Eisenhower, On Earl Warren and the *Brown* Decision, 1954

Document 20.2, Students for a Democratic Society, Port Huron Statement, 1962

Document 20.3, Betty Friedan, *The Feminine Mystique,* 1963

Document 20.4, Martin Luther King Jr., "I Have a Dream," 1963

Document 20.5, Civil Rights Act of 1964

Document 20.6, Cesar Chavez, "We Shall Overcome," 1965

Thematically, these documents share similar features. Consider the following questions as you determine other features of causation:

1. What events in the years leading up to *Brown* may have contributed to the civil rights movement?

2. Following *Brown*, what other events contributed to the civil rights movement?

3. To what extent was *Brown* an actual turning point? What other events might have acted as a clearer turning point for the modern civil rights movement?

4. What is the relationship between education and civil rights? Did other landmark Supreme Court cases address inalienable rights?

STEP 2 *Argumentation*

As you have learned from previous chapters, effective argumentation presents at least two sides, so whether you agree or disagree with a claim, your ability to recognize the counter-argument enhances your overall position. Your answers to the questions above will help you address these different points of view as you create your argument.

The Shattering Consensus

DOCUMENT 20.7 | **Lyndon B. Johnson Campaign Poster**
| 1964

President Lyndon Baines Johnson (1908–1973) inherited the Vietnam War from the John F. Kennedy administration but escalated the conflict and raised the number of American troops in South Vietnam to over 500,000. Domestic protests, both against the war and against racial injustice, undermined his series of social reforms, which collectively are known as the Great Society.

Virginia Historical Society.

PRACTICING Historical Thinking

Identify: Describe the imagery in this poster.

Analyze: What broader message do the images communicate?

Evaluate: All four of the presidents who are depicted in this poster were involved in international conflicts. What accounted for the domestic reaction to Johnson's role in the Vietnam conflict? To what extent was Johnson's success domestically compromised by his failed foreign policy?

| ## H. RAP BROWN, Speech at Free Huey Rally

1968

H. Rap Brown (b. 1943) the fourth became chairman of the Student Non-Violent Coordinating Committee (SNCC) in 1967 after Stokely Carmichael (1941–1998) declared that the organization would be dedicated to "Black Power." Brown gave this speech on February 17, 1968, at a rally in support of the jailed Black Panther leader, Huey Newton (1942–1989).

First of all, I'd like to start out by thanking brother Cleaver and the Black Panther Party for Self Defense. See, unlike America would have us believe, the greatest problem confronting this country today is not pollution and bad breath. [laughter] It's black people. It's black people. See, that's just one of the big lies that America tells you and that you go for 'cause you chumps. You go for it. One of the lies that we tell ourselves is that we're making progress; but Huey's chair's empty. We're not making progress. We tend to equate progress with concessions. We can no longer make that mistake. . . . They gave you Thurgood Marshall, and you said we were making progress. Thurgood Marshall is a tom of the highest order. . . . You put Adam Clayton Powell in office and you couldn't keep him; what you think they gonna do with Thurgood Marshall when they get tired of him? . . . See, it's no in between: you're either free or you're a slave. There's no such thing as second-class citizenship. That's like telling me you can be a little bit pregnant. [laughter, applause]

The only politics in this country that's relevant to black people today is the politics of revolution . . . none other. [applause] There is no difference between the Democratic and Republican party. The similarities are greater than the difference of those parties. What's the difference between Lyndon Johnson and Goldwater? None! But a lot of you running around talking about you Democrats, and the Democrats got you in the biggest trick going. They tell you, "It ain't our fault, it's the Dixiecrats." No such thing as a Dixiecrat. The only difference between George Wallace and Lyndon Johnson is one of them's wife's got cancer. [uproar . . . applause?] That's the only difference. But you go for it! You go for it because you chumps! You go for it! The only thing that's going to free Huey is gun powder. . . . Huey Newton is the only living revolutionary in this country today. He has paid his dues! He paid his dues!

How many white folks you kill today? [uproar] . . . But you revolutionaries! You are revolutionaries! Che Guevara says they only two ways to leave the battlefield: victorious or dead. Huey's in jail! That's no victory, that's a concession. When black people become serious about the revolutionary struggle that they are caught up in, whether they recognize it or not . . . when they begin to go down and knock off people who are oppressing them, and begin to render these people impotent, that's when the revolutionary struggle unfolds . . . not until. [applause]

DOCUMENT 20.9 | **MARTIN LUTHER KING JR., Address at Mason Temple, Memphis**
1968

Martin Luther King Jr. gave the speech excerpted below on April 3, 1968, at a strike by Memphis sanitation workers. He was assassinated in Memphis the next day.

. . . I can remember (Applause.) I can remember when Negroes were just going around as [Rev.] Ralph [Abernathy] has said, so often, scratching where they didn't itch, and laughing when they were not tickled. (Laughter, applause.) But that day is all over. (Yeah.) (Applause.) We mean business now, and we are determined to gain our rightful place in God's world. (Yeah.) (Applause.) And that's all this whole thing is about. We aren't engaged in any negative protest and in any negative arguments with anybody. We are saying that we are determined to be men. We are determined to be people. (Yeah.) We are saying that we are God's children. (Yeah.) (Applause.) And that if we are God's children, we don't have to live like we are forced to live.

Now, what does all of this mean in this great period of history? It means that we've got to stay together. (Yeah.) We've got to stay together and maintain unity. You know, whenever Pharaoh wanted to prolong the period of slavery in Egypt, he had a favorite, favorite formula for doing it. What was that? He kept the slaves fighting among themselves. (Applause.) But whenever the slaves get together, something happens in Pharaoh's court, and he cannot hold the slaves in slavery. When the slaves get together, that's the beginning of getting out of slavery. (Applause.) Now let us maintain unity.

Secondly, let us keep the issues where they are. (Right.) The issue is injustice. The issue is the refusal of Memphis to be fair and honest in its dealings with its public servants, who happen to be sanitation workers. Now, we've got to keep attention on that. (That's right.) That's always the problem with a little violence. You know what happened the other day, and the press dealt only with the window-breaking. (That's right.) I read the articles. They very seldom got around to mentioning the fact that one thousand, three hundred sanitation workers were on strike, and that Memphis is not being fair to them, and that Mayor Loeb is in dire need of a doctor. They didn't get around to that. (Yeah.) (Applause.)

Now we're going to march again, and we've got to march again, in order to put the issue where it is supposed to be—and force everybody to see that there are thirteen hundred of God's children here suffering, sometimes going hungry, going through dark and dreary nights wondering how this thing is going to come out. That's the issue. And we've got to say to the nation: We know how it's coming out. For when people get caught up with that which is right and they are willing to sacrifice for it, there is no stopping point short of victory. . . .

Martin Luther King Jr., "I've Been to the Mountaintop," in Martha Simmons and Frank A. Thomas, eds., *Preaching with Sacred Fire: An Anthology of African American Sermons, 1750 to the Present* (New York: Norton, 2010), 518–519.

PRACTICING Historical Thinking

Identify: What is King's purpose in this speech?

Analyze: What does King mean by his use of the word "sacrifice" in the context of this speech?

Evaluate: King's speech refers to the past as a prelude to his vision. What other documents in this chapter follow the same pattern? Why are prophetic visions often grounded in a deep knowledge of the past?

DOCUMENT 20.10 | **EDMUND WHITE, Letter to Ann and Alfred Corn**
1969

Edmund White (b. 1940) followed his partner from the Midwest to New York and witnessed the birth of the gay rights movement in the riots that started at the Stonewall Inn in Greenwich Village on June 28, 1969. In this July 8, 1969, letter to friends, he describes the initial riot.

Dear Ann and Alfred,

Well, the big news here is Gay Power. It's the most extraordinary thing. It all began two weeks ago on a Friday night. The cops raided the . . . [Stonewall Inn], that mighty Bastille which you know has remained impregnable for three years, so brazen and so conspicuous that one could only surmise that the Mafia was paying off the pigs handsomely. Apparently, however, a new public official, Sergeant Smith, has taken over the Village, and he's a peculiarly diligent lawman. In any event, a mammoth paddy wagon, as big as a school bus, pulled up to the Wall and about ten cops raided the joint. The kids were all shooed into the street; soon other gay kids and straight spectators swelled the ranks to, I'd say, about a thousand people. Christopher Street was completely blocked off and the crowds swarmed from the [*Village*] *Voice* office down to the Civil War hospital.

As the Mafia owners were dragged out one by one and shoved into the wagon, the crowd would let out Bronx cheers and jeers and clapping. Someone shouted "Gay Power," others took up the cry—and then it dissolved into giggles. A few more gay prisoners—bartenders, hatcheck boys—a few more cheers, someone starts singing "We Shall Overcome"—and then they started camping on it. A drag queen is shoved into the wagon; she hits the cop over the head with her purse. The cop clubs her. Angry stirring in the crowd. The cops, used to the cringing and disorganization of the gay crowds, snort off. But the crowd doesn't disperse. Everyone is restless, angry and high-spirited. No one has a slogan, no one even has an attitude, but something's brewing.

Some adorable butch hustler boy pulls up a *parking meter*, mind you, out of the pavement, and uses it as a battering ram (a few cops are still inside the Wall, locked in). The boys begin to pound at the heavy wooden double doors and windows; glass shatters all over the street. Cries of "Liberate the Bar." Bottles (from hostile straights?) rain down from the apartment windows. Cries of "We're the Pink Panthers." A mad Negro queen whirls like a dervish with a twisted piece of metal in her hand and breaks the remaining windows. The door begins to give. The cop turns a hose on the crowd (they're still within the Wall). But they can't aim it properly, and the crowd sticks. Finally the door is broken down and the kids, as though working to a prior plan, systematically dump refuse from the waste cans into the Wall, squirting it with lighter fluid, and ignite it. Huge flashes of flame and billows of smoke.

Now the cops in the paddy wagon return, and two fire engines pull up. Clubs fly. The crowd retreats. . . .

Edmund White, Letter to Ann and Alfred Corn, "We're Part of a Vast Rebellion of All the Repressed," Out History, http://outhistory.org/exhibits/show/stonewall-riot-police-reports /related-items/edmund-white-letter.

PRACTICING Historical Thinking

Identify: What similarities do you see between this letter and earlier documents in this chapter?

Analyze: Compare the tone of White's letter to that of H. Rap Brown's speech (Doc. 20.8). Explain the similarities and differences in purpose and tone.

Evaluate: How does this letter broaden the perspective of an increasingly diverse, complex, and disjointed national identity?

| **WEATHERMAN UNDERGROUND, Communiqué No. 1**

1970

The radical leftist wings of Students for a Democratic Society (SDS)—especially the Ann Arbor, Michigan–based Weatherman (later known as Weather Underground or simply the Weathermen)—were instrumental in SDS's dissolution in the late 1960s. After a series of high-profile acts of militant protest, Weatherman went "underground" and continued its activism as a terrorist revolutionary organization.

Hello. This is Bernardine Dohrn.

I'm going to read A DECLARATION OF A STATE OF WAR.

This is the first communication from the Weatherman underground.

All over the world, people fighting Amerikan imperialism look to Amerika's youth to use our strategic position behind enemy lines to join forces in the destruction of the empire.

Black people have been fighting almost alone for years. We've known that our job is to lead white kids into armed revolution. We never intended to spend the next five or twenty-five years of our lives in jail. Ever since SDS became revolutionary, we've been trying to show how it is possible to overcome the frustration and impotence that comes from trying to reform this system. Kids know the lines are drawn[,] revolution is touching all of our lives. Tens of thousands have learned that protest and marches don't do it. Revolutionary violence is the only way.

Now we are adapting the classic guerrilla strategy of the Viet Cong and the urban guerrilla strategy of the Tupamaros to our own situation here in the most technically advanced country in the world. . . .

The hundreds and thousands of young people who demonstrated in the Sixties against the war and for civil rights grew to hundreds of thousands in the past few weeks actively fighting Nixon's invasion of Cambodia and the attempted genocide against black people. The insanity of Amerikan "justice" has added to its list of atrocities six blacks killed in Augusta, two in Jackson and four white Kent State students, making thousands more into revolutionaries. . . .

Within the next fourteen days we will attack a symbol or institution of Amerikan injustice. This is the way we celebrate the example of Eldridge Cleaver and H. Rap Brown and all black revolutionaries who first inspired us by their fight behind enemy lines for the liberation of their people.

The Berkeley Tribe/The Red Mountain Tribe, July 31, 1970. As it appears in Timothy Patrick McCarthy and John Campbell McMillian, eds., *The Radical Reader: A Documentary History of the American Radical Tradition* (New York: New Press, 2003).

DOCUMENT 20.12 | **AMERICAN INDIAN MOVEMENT GOVERNING COUNCIL, Trail of Broken Treaties: 20-Point Proposal**
1972

Starting in the late 1960s, Native American activists sought to raise American awareness of Native American rights at protests like the occupations of Alcatraz (1970) and Wounded Knee (1973). The following excerpt from the American Indian Movement's 20 Point Proposal calls for the renewal of contracts and reconstruction of Indian communities in America.

Commission to Review Treaty Commitments & Violations

The President should immediately create a multi-lateral, Indian and non-Indian Commission to review domestic treaty commitments and complaints of chronic violations and to recommend or act for corrective actions including the imposition of mandatory sanctions or interim restraints upon violative activities, and including formulation of legislation designed to protect the jeopardized Indian rights and eliminate the unending patterns of prohibitively complex lawsuits and legal defenses—which habitually have produced indecisive and interment results, only too frequently forming guidelines for more court battles, or additional challenges and attacks against Indian rights. (Indians have paid attorneys and lawyers more than $40,000,000 since 1962. Yet many Indian people are virtually imprisoned in the nation's courtrooms in being forced constantly to defend their rights, while many tribes are forced to maintain a multitude of suits in numerous jurisdictions relating to the same or a single issue, or a few similar issues. There is less need for more attorney assurances than there is for institution of protections that reduce violations and minimize the possibilities for attacks upon Indian rights).

Resubmission of Unratified Treaties to the Senate

The President should resubmit to the U.S. Senate of the next Congress those treaties negotiated with Indian nations or their representatives, but never heretofore ratified nor rendered moot by subsequent treaty contract with such Indians not having ratified treaties with the United States. The primary purpose to be served shall be that of restoring the rule of law to the relationships between such Indians and the United States, and resuming a recognition of rights controlled by treaty relations where the failure to ratify prior treaties operated to affirm the cessions and loss of title to Indian lands and territory, but failed to secure and protect the reservations of lands, rights, and resources reserved against cession, relinquishment, or loss, the Senate should adopt resolutions certifying that a prior de facto ratification has been affected by the Government of the United States, and direct that appropriate actions be undertaken to restore to such Indians an equitable measure of their reserved rights and ownership in lands, resources, and rights of self-government. Additionally, the President and the Congress should direct that reports be concluded upon the disposition of land rights and land title which were lawfully vested or held, for people of Native Indian blood under the 1840 Treaty of Guadalupe Hidalgo with Mexico.

Timothy Patrick McCarthy and John McMillian, eds., *Protest Nation: Words That Inspired a Century of American Radicalism* (New York: New Press, 2010), 187–188.

PRACTICING Historical Thinking

Identify: Summarize the demands of the American Indian Movement.

Analyze: Why does the AIM ask for the "rights of self-government"? Does this extend beyond the scope of restoration?

Evaluate: Compare the plight of Native Americans with that of other marginalized groups (such as African Americans, women, and members of the working class) during this period. Are all of these groups demanding something similar? Explain.

DOCUMENT 20.13 | RONALD REAGAN, Address to the First Conservative Political Action Conference
1974

Ronald Reagan (1911–2004), a former actor and president of the Screen Actors Guild, served as governor of California from 1967 to 1976. He called the National Guard to occupy the town of Berkeley during student protests at the University of California there and quickly became the voice of conservative reactions to 1960s civil rights and anti-war activism. In this speech, Reagan addresses the first conservative political action conference.

I thought that tonight, rather than talking on the subjects you are discussing, or trying to find something new to say, it might be appropriate to reflect a bit on our heritage.

You can call it mysticism if you want to, but I have always believed that there was some divine plan that placed this great continent between two oceans to be sought out by those who were possessed of an abiding love of freedom and a special kind of courage.

This was true of those who pioneered the great wilderness in the beginning of this country, as it is also true of those later immigrants who were willing to leave the land of their birth and come to a land where even the language was unknown to them. Call it chauvinistic, but our heritage does set us apart. Some years ago a writer, who happened to be an avid student of history, told me a story about that day in the little hall in Philadelphia where honorable men, hard-pressed by a King who was flouting the very law they were willing to obey, debated whether they should take the fateful step of declaring their independence from that king. I was told by this man that the story could be found in the writings of Jefferson. I confess, I never researched or made an effort to verify it. Perhaps it is only legend. But story, or legend, he described the atmosphere, the strain, the debate, and that as men for the first time faced the consequences of such an irretrievable act, the walls resounded with the dread word of treason and its price—the gallows and the headman's axe. As the day wore on the issue hung in the balance, and then, according to the story, a man rose in the small gallery. He was not a young man and was obviously calling on all the energy he could muster. Citing the grievances that had brought them to this moment, he said, "Sign that parchment. They may turn every tree into a gallows, every home into a grave and yet the words of that parchment can never die. For the mechanic in his workshop, they will be words of hope, to the slave in the mines—freedom." And he added, "If my hands were freezing in death, I would sign that parchment with my last ounce of strength. Sign, sign if the next moment the noose is around your neck, sign even if the hall is ringing with the sound of headman's axe, for that parchment will be the textbook of freedom, the bible of the rights of man forever." And then it is said he fell back exhausted. But 56 delegates, swept by his eloquence, signed the Declaration of Independence, a document destined to be as immortal as any work of man can be. And according to the story, when they turned to thank him for his timely oratory, he could not be found nor were there any who knew who he was or how he had come in or gone out through the locked and guarded doors. . . .

Scott J. Hammond, Kevin R. Hardwick, and Howard Leslie Luber, eds., *Classics of American Political and Constitutional Thought: Reconstruction to the Present* (Indianapolis, IN: Hackett, 2007), 818.

APPLYING AP® Historical Thinking Skills

SKILL REVIEW | Causation, Periodization, and Interpretation

Read the following two interpretations of the origins of the civil rights movement in the 1960s. In addition to the documents in this chapter, consult your textbook and class notes for additional details on this topic.

> The impact of the civil rights movement on race relations and the nation's social fabric has been monumental. . . . One of the key outcomes is the creation of self-perpetuating momentum that allowed for other movements to occur. By showing that human oppression is not inevitable and that collective action can generate change, the civil rights movement aided in the conceptualization of the women's movement as well as the Latino civil rights movement. . . . The sentiments of these collective movements drive public opinion, both in terms of change and in terms of the people involved in change. To clarify, movements create and perpetuate attitudes toward progress as well as attitudes toward specific groups responsible for a particular movement. . . .

Antwan Jones, "Race and the 'I Have a Dream' Legacy: Exploring Predictors of Positive Civil Rights Attitudes," *Journal of Black Studies* 37, no. 2 (2006): 194–195.

> Although they never attained the scope of the black civil rights movement, the Hispanic movements had natural histories that paralleled the black movement in many respects: the growth of large barrios [Latin American neighborhoods], creating the human resources necessary to start and sustain protest movements; the emergence of charismatic leaders who used existing ethnic networks (e.g., the church, neighborhood gangs, social clubs, schools, and universities) to generate "nonviolent" and sometimes successful demonstrations; the rise of militant leaders and groups; the growth of urban riots, when demands for change outran more orderly and organized means.

Gregg Lee Carter, "Hispanic Rioting during the Civil Rights Era," *Sociological Forum* 7, no. 2 (1992): 302.

1. Identify Jones's main point in the first interpretation. Which documents in this chapter best support Jones's argument in his passage above? Explain your answer.

2. Identify Carter's main point in the second interpretation. Which documents in this chapter best support his argument in their passage above? Explain your answer.

3. Finally, which of these interpretations analyzes the civil rights movements as a series of causes and effects? Which of these interpretations analyzes the civil rights movements as a product of a broader context? How do these respective "lenses" shape the arguments in each interpretation?

PUTTING IT ALL TOGETHER

Revisiting the Main Point

- In the era after World War II, in what ways did Americans struggle with the ideas of national unity and diversity?
- Compare the civil rights statements in this chapter. What are some of the similar grievances? What are some examples of differences between the movements?
- How did US policy makers and local law enforcement agencies engage the civil rights movements in different ways? What, in your opinion, caused these differences?

BUILDING AP® WRITING SKILLS **Analyzing and Evaluating Persona in Documents**

Until this point, the writing instruction has examined primary documents in the service of historical thinking skills. Combining these skills creatively allows you to use sophisticated approaches to historical arguments, including complex arrangements of evidence and sophisticated constructions of the overall shape of the argument.

This chapter provides a new dimension in historical argument—analyzing and evaluating persona in documents. A **persona** is the "voice" that emerges in a primary document and that reflects the writer's or speaker's experiences, emotions, vision, and rhetorical style. For example, Martin Luther King Jr.'s "I Have a Dream" speech, in both its written and spoken forms, conveys not only King's message but also his vision, commitment, and charisma.

In many ways, persona relates to point of view, so recognizing key features of the persona influences your understanding of the text. Consider the following questions when determining persona:

1. What is the tone of the writer or speaker?
2. What features of language does the writer or speaker use to communicate a message?
3. How does the audience influence the message itself?

For example, note this excerpt from Ronald Reagan's address to the first conservative political action conference (Doc. 20.13):

I was told by this man that the story could be found in the writings of Jefferson. I confess, I never researched or made an effort to verify it.

Reagan presents himself in a grandfatherly, humble, folksy manner. He acknowledges the writings of the founding fathers but presents his concern as preserving that heritage rather than authenticating it.

Given the varied voices that are found in our increasingly pluralistic world, a speaker's ability to communicate a message matters as much as the message itself. There can also be a persona to a group document. For example, the American Indian Movement's 20 Point Proposal (Doc. 20.12) carries a slightly less urgent persona than the Weatherman Underground's Communiqué No. 1 (Doc. 20.11). Consider the following prompt:

> In the era after World War II, in what ways did Americans struggle with the ideas of national unity and diversity?

STEP 1 *Understand the prompt, and identify the key words*

STEP 2 *Generate a working thesis*

STEP 3 *Identify and organize your evidence*

As you have done with previous chapters, organize your evidence around various voices. The following graphic organizer provides some suggestions about how to monitor the relationship between persona and historical significance:

Document	Key words	Persona	Intended effect upon audience
Reagan address (Doc. 20.13)	"abiding love of freedom"	folksy/nostalgic	Presentation of American independent ideas
MLK "I Have a Dream" (Doc. 20.4)	"beautiful symphony of brotherhood"	moral/uplifting	Beautiful symphony of brotherhood
AIM proposal (Doc. 20.12)	"There is less need for more attorney assurances than there is for institution of protections that reduce violations and minimize the possibilities for attacks upon Indian rights"	rational/determined	Dual demand: sovereignty over a cultural heritage and governmental protection of these rights and liberties

STEP 4 *Outline your response*

This prompt invites a study of persona, given that its use of the words "unity" and "diversity" encourage you to analyze the different personas that are presented in the civil rights documents. This prompt also invites a comparison between unity and diversity, so a prospective outline may feature the following:

   I. Introduction

  II. Voices of unity: More than just listing documents here—such as Reagan's speech—consider the broad contexts or themes that contribute to the national sense of unity.

 III. Voices of diversity: How you define *unity* and *diversity* requires you to examine historical context.

  IV. Evaluation: Beyond analyzing the persona, the **evaluation** allows you to make an informed judgment. In ending a comparison, one conclusion to draw would be hierarchical: which voices prevailed during this era? Another conclusion to draw would be comparative: what similarities and differences can be found in the overall effect of these voices?

STEP 5 *Write your essay*

Discontinuities

For many Americans, the forty years after the Second World War represent a time when all that had gone smoothly before seemed suddenly to have become jagged and out of alignment. Already anxious from the Cold War and the ongoing threat of global nuclear destruction, they felt further threatened by new value systems that challenged old conventions, by the emergence of new interest groups that demanded recognition and respect, and by the arrival of new immigrants from locations outside of Europe.

The instability of American society and culture initiated a political backlash that claimed to represent traditional American values and interests. This conservative backlash grew in intensity throughout the 1970s and came to fruition with the election of Ronald Reagan as president in 1980.

Seeking the Main Point

* Describe two social and cultural changes during the 1960s and 1970s, and choose appropriate documents below to support your description.
* In what ways did government fuel the desire for change in the 1960s and 1970s?
* In what ways did technological changes in the first half of the twentieth century shape environmental and social anxieties in the second half of the twentieth century?
* In what ways are both conformity and rebellion elements of the documents below? In other words, to what do the subjects below conform? What do they rebel against?

Conflicting Postwar Visions

DOCUMENT 21.1 | **Levittown**
| 1948

Levittown, New York, was the first mass-produced suburban community. It began after the Second World War with two thousand homes in 1947 and, aided by Federal Housing Administration loans, grew to over four thousand homes by the early 1950s.

Associated Press.

> ### PRACTICING Historical Thinking
>
> *Identify:* Describe the patterns visible in the photo.
>
> *Analyze:* What do these patterns reveal about perceptions of suburban life in the 1950s?
>
> *Evaluate:* In what ways did the government's support of housing help redefine the role that government played in the social welfare of its citizens?

DOCUMENT 21.2 | **WILLIAM FAULKNER, Nobel Prize Acceptance Speech**
| 1950

William Faulkner (1897–1962) used his acceptance speech for the Nobel Prize in Literature to comment on modern anxieties caused by the threat of nuclear war.

I feel that this award was not made to me as a man, but to my work—life's work in the agony and sweat of the human spirit, not for glory and least of all for profit, but to create out of the materials of the human spirit something which did not exist before. So this award is only mine in trust. It will not be difficult to find a dedication for the money part of it commensurate with the purpose and significance of its origin. But I would like to do the same with the acclaim too, by using this moment as a pinnacle from which I might be listened to by the young men and women already dedicated to the same anguish and travail, among whom is already that one who will some day stand where I am standing.

Our tragedy today is a general and universal physical fear so long sustained by now that we can even bear it. There are no longer problems of the spirit. There is only the question: When will I be blown up? Because of this, the young man or woman writing today has forgotten the problems of the human heart in conflict with itself which alone can make good writing because only that is worth writing about, worth the agony and the sweat.

He must learn them again. He must teach himself that the basest of all things is to be afraid; and, teaching himself that, forget it forever, leaving no room in his workshop for anything but the old verities and truths of the heart, the universal truths lacking which any story is ephemeral and doomed—love and honor and pity and pride and compassion and sacrifice. Until he does so, he labors under a curse. He writes not of love but of lust, of defeats in which nobody loses anything of value, of victories without hope and, worst of all, without pity or compassion. His griefs grieve on no universal bones, leaving no scars. He writes not of the heart but of the glands.

Robert G. Torricelli and Andrew Carroll, eds., *In Our Own Words: Extraordinary Speeches of the American Century* (New York: Kodansha, 1999), 179–180.

PRACTICING Historical Thinking

Identify: What is Faulkner calling for in his speech?

Analyze: Explain Faulkner's view on fear and its effects.

Evaluate: How is Faulkner using this acceptance speech to make an argument? How does he prove this argument?

DOCUMENT 21.3 | Trans World Airlines Advertisement
1953

In the years after the Second World War, rising affluence at home, an interest in American tourism abroad, and the maturation of jet travel allowed citizens of the United States greater access to overseas travel. Like other advertisers in the early twentieth century, airline carriers such as Trans World Airlines (TWA) appealed to customers in ways that reflected the cultural values of the period. This advertisement appeared in the *New Yorker*, whose readership tended to be relatively affluent and educated.

Advertising Archive/Courtesy Everett Collection.

TEXT (enlarged for readability):

Who Says, "IT'S A MAN'S WORLD"?

Not the woman who flies TWA. For since she's discovered the swiftness of TWA Constellation flight, her whole outlook has changed. Her horizons are broader...she's found new freedom and greater opportunity to see and enjoy. Not only that, she can travel alone without a worry in the world, enjoying service that befits a queen. Meals are served right at her seat; friendly TWA hostesses are always on hand to help smooth her way. Yes, women of all ages are going more places in the world today because of world-proved TWA.

PRACTICING Historical Thinking

Identify: Describe three ways in which the images in this advertisement correspond to the written text.

Analyze: Who is the intended audience for this advertisement? What does the intended audience tell us about social trends in the years after World War II?

Evaluate: To what extent does this image represent an intersection of technological, economic, and social forces?

DOCUMENT 21.4 | SENATE SUBCOMMITTEE TO INVESTIGATE JUVENILE DELINQUENCY, Interim Report on Comic Books and Juvenile Delinquency
1955

By the early 1950s, many Americans were concerned over a perceived rise in juvenile delinquency in the United States. Although historians still debate the extent to which there was an increase in juvenile delinquency in the 1950s, anxiety over the issue was linked with the rise of youth culture and suburban living. This US Senate report was part of an investigation into juvenile delinquency and focuses on the effects of horror and crime-related comic books.

. . . Over a period of several months the subcommittee has received a vast amount of mail from parents expressing concern regarding the possible deleterious effect upon their children of certain of the media of mass communication. This led to an inquiry into the possible relationship to juvenile delinquency of these media.

Members of the subcommittee have emphatically stated at public hearings that freedom of speech and freedom of the press are not at issue. They are fully aware of the long, hard, bitter fight that has been waged through the ages to achieve and maintain those freedoms. They agree that these freedoms, as well as other freedoms in the Bill of Rights, must not be abrogated.

The subcommittee has no proposal for censorship. It moved into the mass media phase of its investigations with no preconceived opinions in regard to the possible need for new legislation.

Consistent with this position, it is firmly believed that the public is entitled to be fully informed on all aspects of this matter and to know all the facts. It was the consensus that the need existed for a thorough, objective investigation to determine whether, as has been alleged, certain types of mass communication media are to be reckoned with as contributing to the country's alarming rise in juvenile delinquency. These include: "crime and horror" comic books and other types of printed matter; the radio, television, and motion pictures.

In its investigations of mass media, as in its investigation of other phases of the total problem, the subcommittee has not been searching for "one cause." Delinquency is the product of many related causal factors. But it can scarcely be questioned that the impact of these media does constitute a significant factor in the total problem.

Juvenile delinquency in America today must be viewed in the framework of the total community-climate in which children live. Certainly, none of the children who get into trouble live in a social vacuum. One of the most significant changes of the past quarter century has been the wide diffusion of the printed word, particularly in certain periodicals, plus the phenomenal growth of radio and television audiences.

The child today in the process of growing up is constantly exposed to sights and sounds of a kind and quality undreamed of in previous generations. As these sights and sounds can be a powerful force for good, so too can they be a powerful counterpoise working evil. Their very quantity makes them a factor to be reckoned with in determining the total climate encountered by today's children during their formative years. . . .

United States Congress, Senate Committee on the Judiciary, *Juvenile Delinquency: Comic Books, Motion Pictures, Obscene and Pornographic Materials, Television Programs* (Westport, CT: Greenwood, 1955), 1–2.

Identify: Summarize the committee's chief concerns.

Analyze: In what ways does this committee reflect the era's focus on conformity?

Evaluate: In what ways could the concern expressed by this committee be a result of the living arrangements portrayed in Doc. 21.1?

DOCUMENT 21.5	RACHEL CARSON, *Silent Spring*
	1962

Marine biologist and conservationist Rachel Carson (1907–1964) inspired the modern environmentalist movement in the United States with her 1962 book *Silent Spring*. In her work, Carson called into question the morality and benefits of scientific and technological progress and offered a vision of an economy and society that would not undermine health and resources.

The history of life on earth has been a history of interaction between living things and their surroundings. To a large extent, the physical form and the habits of the earth's vegetation and its animal life have been molded by the environment. Considering the whole span of earthly time, the opposite effect, in which life actually modifies its surroundings, has been relatively slight. Only within the moment of time represented by the present century has one species—man—acquired significant power to alter the nature of his world.

During the past quarter century this power has not only increased to one of disturbing magnitude but it has changed in character. The most alarming of all man's assaults upon the environment is the contamination of air, earth, rivers, and sea with dangerous and even lethal materials. This pollution is for the most part irrecoverable; the chain of evil it initiates not only in the world that must support life but in living tissues is for the most part irreversible. In this now universal contamination of the environment, chemicals are the sinister and little-recognized partners of radiation in changing the very nature of the world—the very nature of its life. Strontium 90, released through nuclear explosions into the air, comes to the earth in rain or drifts down as fallout, lodges in soil, enters into the grass or corn or wheat grown there, and in time takes up its abode in the bones of a human being, there to remain until his death. Similarly, chemicals sprayed on croplands or forests or gardens lie long in soil, entering into living organisms, passing from one to another in a chain of poisoning and death. Or they pass mysteriously by underground streams until they emerge and, through the alchemy of air and sunlight, combine into new forms that kill vegetation, sicken cattle, and work unknown harm on those who drink from once pure wells. As Albert Schweitzer has said, "Man can hardly even recognize the devils of his own creation."

Rachel Carson, *Silent Spring* (Boston, MA: Houghton Mifflin, 2002), 5–6.

DOCUMENT 21.6 | **ABBIE HOFFMAN,** *Steal This Book*
1970

Abbie Hoffman (1936–1989) became an icon of the youth counterculture movement when he formed the Youth International Party in 1967. Yippies, as the party's members were called, took part in the antiwar demonstrations at the 1968 Democratic National Convention in Chicago, and Hoffman and six other antiwar leaders of the protests were tried for inciting riots. Hoffman's book *Steal This Book* was a popular summation of countercultural and antiwar sentiments that were held by many members of the New Left in the late 1960s.

It's perhaps fitting that I write this introduction in jail—the graduate school of survival. Here you learn how to use toothpaste as glue, fashion a shiv out of a spoon and build intricate communication networks. Here too, you learn the only rehabilitation possible—hatred of oppression.

Steal This Book is, in a way, a manual of survival in the prison that is Amerika. It preaches jailbreak. It shows you where and exactly how to place the dynamite that will destroy the walls. The first section—SURVIVE!—lays out a potential action program for our new Nation. The chapter headings spell out the demands for a free society. A community where the technology produces goods and services for whoever needs them, come who may. It calls on the Robin Hoods of Santa Barbara Forest to steal from the robber barons who own the castles of capitalism. It implies that the reader already is "ideologically set," in that he understands corporate feudalism as the only robbery worthy of being called "crime," for it is committed against the people as a whole. Whether the ways it describes to rip-off . . . [things] are legal or illegal is irrelevant. The dictionary of law is written by the bosses of order. Our moral dictionary says no heisting from each other. To steal from a brother or sister is evil. To *not* steal from the institutions that are the pillars of the Pig Empire is equally immoral.

Community within our Nation, chaos in theirs; that is the message of SURVIVE!

Abbie Hoffman, *Steal This Book* (New York: Four Walls Eight Windows, 2002), xxi–xxii.

DOCUMENT 21.7	GOVERNOR'S INVESTIGATING COMMITTEE ON PROBLEMS OF WISCONSIN'S SPANISH-SPEAKING COMMUNITIES, Report to the Governor
	1971

After the passage of the Immigration and Nationality Act of 1965, immigration from Latin America and Asia grew rapidly. These new immigrants faced a nation that had largely closed itself to mass immigration since the 1920s. The excerpt below portrays the extent to which immigration had become an issue even for states that had not faced issues of immigration since the early twentieth century.

TASK FORCE RECOMMENDATIONS
Education

1. The Area Technical Colleges should employ teacher aides to assist teachers conducting English and Adult Basic Education classes for Latins. The colleges should recruit Latins to serve on the faculty and to become advisers to Latin students enrolled in other curricula. These actions should be taken in areas with Latin populations such as Milwaukee, Waukesha, Racine, Kenosha, etc.

2. The Area Technical Colleges should provide realistic scholarships for low income Latins interested in vocational education and should intensify efforts to recruit Latins for promising occupations identified by the Wisconsin State Employment Service.

3. The Milwaukee School District and school districts near Latin population centers should hire more professional, technical and paraprofessional personnel of Latin ancestry in elementary and secondary schools to help serve the Latin children.

4. Transition centers should be developed by the Milwaukee School District and school districts near Latin population centers to help children of newly settled migrant families to make an orderly transition into the school districts. The transition centers should employ bilingual personnel to help the children learn English and to evaluate the educational ability of the children. Tests should be reevaluated to determine if they are relevant.

5. The University of Wisconsin, the Wisconsin State University system and the University Extension system should intensify recruiting efforts and increase scholarships for Latins interested in enrolling at the various campuses.

6. The State Motor Vehicle Division should have its driver's manual translated into Spanish for Latins with limited English background and should modify its driver's license examination so Latins are required to know only essential English words needed to drive safely, such as words on highway signs.

Wisconsin Historical Society, *Report to the Governor: Governor's Investigating Committee on Problems of Wisconsin's Spanish-Speaking Communities*, 1971, 9, http://content.wisconsinhistory.org/cdm4/document.php?CISOROOT=/tp&CISOPTR=48410&CISOSHOW=48371.

PRACTICING Historical Thinking

Identify: List the recommendations that the investigating committee made to improve the conditions of immigrants who were living in Wisconsin.

Analyze: How do the committee's recommendations reflect the values that the state placed on education as an assimilating agent for immigrants?

Evaluate: To what extent do this committee's recommendations represent a departure from attitudes toward immigrants before World War II?

DOCUMENT 21.8 | PHYLLIS SCHLAFLY, **Interview with the** *Washington Star*
| 1976

Phyllis Schlafly (b. 1924), lawyer and conservative activist, led the movement against adding the Equal Rights Amendment (ERA) to the US Constitution. The ERA would have guaranteed civil rights to all citizens regardless of gender. In the interview below with a reporter for the *Washington Star*, Schlafly presents her critique of the ERA.

Q: Do you think that women would be as well off today were it not for the women's movement?

Schlafly: I certainly do. There were more women in Congress prior to the women's movement than there are today.

Q: Well, haven't there been a lot of other gains, though? There are many more women working today and a lot of them are getting better salaries too.

Schlafly: And a lot of them who are working would prefer to be in the home. They are working for economic reasons.

Q: But if they have to work then it's important that they make as much money as they can, at least as much as men, for what they are doing.

Schlafly: I believe in equal pay for equal work. I do not believe in hiring unqualified women over qualified men to remedy some alleged oppression of 25 years ago.

Q: Do you think that people are being forced to hire this way?

Schlafly: Yes, we had a good example of that recently in a federal court, a ruling that has ordered the Chicago Police Department to hire 16 percent women, on a quota. Now in order to do this they have got to throw out the physical qualifications that are required to be a policeman on the Chicago police force. And I feel this is absolutely wrong.

It's hurtful to men, it's hurtful to women and it's hurtful to the community. And it will do nothing but demoralize and destroy the police force.

Q: You think the women will not be able to perform the job as well as men?

Schlafly: That's correct. The same thing's true in the military. There is an honorable place for women in the military. They have the best of both worlds in the military today. They are protected from combat service and from some of the dangerous and unpleasant jobs in the military.

PRACTICING Historical Thinking

Identify: What is Schlafly's argument against the Equal Rights Amendment?

Analyze: How is her argument a product of the women's rights movement of the early twentieth century?

Evaluate: To what extent does Schlafly's argument reflect a conservative response to the liberal reforms of the 1960s?

APPLYING AP® Historical Thinking Skills

SKILL REVIEW | **Causation, Analyzing Evidence: Content and Sourcing, Interpretation, and Synthesis**

Read the passage below, and consider the following prompt:

Choose three documents above that express sentiments that helped give rise to the New Right as Lisa McGirr describes them below. Justify each of your choices with specific references to the history of the 1960s and 1970s. You may use your textbook and class notes to help you answer this question.

By 1960, Orange County's [California] economy and social structure had become remarkably complex. Rapid growth had deepened and magnified elements of social strain. Moreover, the community's very newness meant that its values and mores were, to some extent, up for grabs—to be determined in the cultural battles that would be fought in the decade to come. Yet these factors do not, in themselves, explain how the Right found a home, since many communities shared the region's experience of rapid growth, yet few witnessed a conservative mobilization of the strength and magnitude of that in Orange County during the 1960s. Rather, it was the convergence of a particular set of social, economic, and political forces within the region that contributed to the germination of a conservative culture.

The county's cultural traditions, its conservative regional elite, its mode of development, and the kinds of migrants who made their home there provided the ingredients from which the Right would create a movement. First, there were the "old-timers," the large ranchers and small farmers, merchants, shop owners, and middle-class townspeople who had embraced a strong individualism and strict moralism for many years. Added to this older conservatism were the southland's "cowboy capitalists," the new boom-time entrepreneurs who made their fortunes in the post–World War II era of affluence and spent their capital and their energy spreading the gospel of laissez-faire capitalism and an anti-Washington ethos. Together with ranchers-turned-property-developers, county boosters, and real estate speculators, they created a built world that affirmed the values of privacy, individualism, and property rights and weakened a sense of cohesive community, providing an opening for organizations, churches, and missionary zealots that could provide one. Into this setting came the homogeneous group of migrants who populated Orange County. Although they had not necessarily embraced right-wing politics before they came West, the environment of Orange County reinforced strands of social conservatism they had brought in their cultural baggage. Finally, the specific economic dynamics of the Cold War–related industries reinforced the connection between anticommunism and prosperity in the minds of both newcomers and old-time residents.

Taken together, these forces magnified conservative strands of political culture within the region, creating a fertile ground for right-wing growth. Once catalyzed, this fermentation developed a dynamic of its own. The conservative ethos of the county, for example, drew like-minded folk to settle there, making it more likely that large numbers of Orange Countians would hear the Right's message and heed its call.

Lisa McGirr, *Suburban Warriors: The Origins of the New American Right* (Princeton, NJ: Princeton University Press, 2001), 29–30.

To answer the prompt, you will need to employ several of the historical thinking skills that are addressed in previous chapters:

* Causation: Determine the relationship between the primary documents and the claims made in McGirr's essay.
* Analyzing Evidence: Content and Sourcing: Determine the ways in which different documents both support and refute the claims in McGirr's essay.
* Interpretation and Synthesis: Determine the ways in which the combination of the primary documents agree with, disagree with, or modify the claims in McGirr's essay.

PUTTING IT ALL TOGETHER

Revisiting the Main Point

- To what extent were cultural and economic changes in this era a product of widespread demographic changes?
- Analyze whether government policies were a driving force in cultural and social changes between 1945 and 1965. Were other factors more influential?
- How did technological and demographic changes shape society, the economy, and the environment?
- To what extent were the years 1945 to 1989 a period of relative conformity? To what extent was it an era for rebellion? How did both conformity and rebellion shape each other during these years?

**BUILDING AP®
WRITING SKILLS** | **Incorporating Secondary Sources into Historical Argument**

Up to this point, creating your historical arguments has depended on your interpretations of primary documents. Although some secondary sources have been featured in these chapters, the majority of the prompts have invited a study of historical thinking skills with historical themes.

Bringing in secondary sources can enhance your overall argument as long as your argument remains central to the task. The secondary source—which is someone else's interpretation—may serve as the linchpin to your overall argument.

Your argument becomes a larger **conversation** where your own interpretation joins with another's interpretation. When you use secondary sources for your own historical argument, keep in mind these four guiding principles:

1. How does your own argument *validate* another interpretation?
2. How does another interpretation *challenge* your own argument?
3. How might different interpretations arise through a different combination of primary sources?
4. How might secondary sources compare with each other for a new insight?

Consider the following prompt:

> To what extent were the years 1945 to 1989 a period of relative conformity? To what extent was it an era for rebellion? How did both conformity and rebellion shape each other during these years?

STEP 1 *Understand the prompt, and identify the key words*

STEP 2 *Generate a working thesis*

STEP 3 *Identify and organize your evidence*

This chapter, along with the previous ones, brings in compelling arguments that may further your own answer. Lisa McGirr's essay, for example, provides a discussion on the development of the New Right. Martin Halpern's essay (Chapter 19) addresses the House Un-American Activities Committee's intimidation of left-leaning activists in the Detroit area. Antwan Jones and Gregg Lee Carter (Chapter 20) provide rationales for how marginalized groups—such as Latinos—gained political power after World War II.

All of these examples illustrate the ways in which a secondary source can address issues of conformity and rebellion in a given era. In fact, Jones and Carter provide differing views on how Latinos gained access, so one possibility is to determine which of the two views carries more weight in response to a given prompt.

STEP 4 *Outline your response*

In their book *They Say / I Say: The Moves That Matter in Academic Discourse*, authors Gerald Graff and Cathy Birkenstein observe the importance of entering into existing conversations. To this end, your outline may begin with a synthesis of secondary voices, especially when they offer competing views. For example, your outline may begin as follows:

   I. Introduction

  II. Conformity during the period 1945 to 1989

     A. Martin Halpern: oppression and greater conformity over marginalized groups

     B. Antwan Jones and Gregg Lee Carter: greater access and empowerment for marginalized groups

     C. Your own central claim about conformity during this period

Such an approach represents a deductive method of organizing information. For a review of deductive reasoning, see Chapter 9.

STEP 5 *Write your essay*

PERIOD EIGHT
1945–1980

Civil Rights Leadership

Dr. Martin Luther King Jr. launched a new phase in the reform era. He almost singlehand-edly changed the landscape of race relations in the United States. Such a powerful figure ran the risk of outdistancing the needs of other marginalized groups in the United States during this time, including women, Native Americans, and Latinos. Does reform depend on extraordinary talent and appeal (as with King), and if so, do such movements expect King's counterpart to emerge as a spokesperson for their group?

King's influence also asks historians to reflect on the ways in which reform is spread equally among all groups or is spread narrowly so that only individual groups take signifi-cant steps in social and economic contexts.

You already have read various sources that illustrate different perspectives on civil rights during this era. Now read the two passages below, and consider the extent to which the civil rights era fulfilled the promise of the Declaration of Independence.

Appreciating King's own understanding of his role and responsibilities is really *more* crucial than anything else, I would contend, to comprehending the kind of leadership that Martin Luther King, Jr., gave to the American black freedom strug-gle of the 1950s and 1960s. By 1963–1964, as that role and those responsibilities grew, King thought increasingly about his own destiny and what he termed "this challenge to be loyal to something that transcends our immediate lives." . . .

King's understanding of his life underwent a significant deepening when he was awarded the 1964 Nobel Peace Prize. The prize signaled the beginning of a fundamental growth in King's own sense of mission and in his willingness to accept a prophetic role. . . .

More and more in those years King thought of his own life in terms of the cross. . . .

More than anything else, the Vietnam War issue brought King face to face with what was becoming a consciously self-sacrificial understanding of his role and fate. . . . [I]n early 1967, King resolved to take on Lyndon B. Johnson's war publicly as never before.

—David J. Garrow, "Martin Luther King, Jr., and the Spirit of Leadership," *Journal of American History* 74 (September 1987): 444–445.

The one glaring flaw that should have concerned all women activists, whatever their ideological persuasion, was feminism's failure to escape its narrow class and race boundaries. Despite the ambitious aspirations of socialist feminists for a cross-class, cross-race coalition, most feminist activists were white, middle class, and college-educated. There were occasional black feminist groups, such as the National Black Feminist Organization, and each feminist organization boasted some participation by African-American or Latina women. Yet on balance, the numbers were infinitesimally small. Both the language and the programs of fem-inist groups seemed to reflect a white middle-class approach. Until women of all classes and backgrounds felt attracted to and welcomed by feminist groups, there was little likelihood that the promise of a universal sisterhood could become a reality.

—William H. Chafe, "The Road to Equality, 1962–Today," in Nancy Cott, ed., *No Small Courage: A History of Women in the United States* (New York: Oxford University Press, 2000).

Based on the two interpretations above, complete the following three tasks:

1. Briefly explain the perspective on reform agents that is presented by the first passage.
2. Briefly explain the perspective on reform agents that is presented by the second passage.
3. Select one document from Chapter 21, and explain how it supports the interpretation of either passage.

A Conservative Tenor

T he United States entered the twenty-first century in the midst of economic prosperity and peace. Drawing lessons from the collapse of the Soviet Union, the United States celebrated the Cold War policies that supported containment and encouraged capitalism around the world to bring an end to what Ronald Reagan called an "evil empire."

In hindsight, some Americans called the election of Ronald Reagan to the presidency in 1980 the beginning of the "Reagan revolution." Although there is debate over the meaning of this phrase, most historians agree that Reagan's election represented a shift in American political rhetoric and policy. It seemed that the liberal project that began with Franklin Delano Roosevelt and reached its high tide with the Great Society programs of Lyndon B. Johnson had come to an end.

Reagan's election represented the political maturity of two divergent social movements that began in the early 1960s—the New Right and the New Left. In these two ideologies, free-market economics and "traditional" moral certitudes collided with civil rights activism, identity politics, and environmentalism. This shift in sensibilities, especially regarding a government and society overseen by experts, bound both the New Right and the New Left to each other and raised the tensions between the two throughout this period.

In the aftermath of the terrorist attacks of September 11, 2001, the nation seemed to overcome, at least temporarily, these debates in an attempt to reinvigorate the ideals that united the nation. But that unified front proved short-lived. The Bush administration's response to the attacks, the administration's attempts to overhaul key New Deal legislation, and lingering anger over the contested presidential election of 2000 deepened the ideological divide and signaled the dawn of a new era of bitter political partisanship and cultural conflict.

Seeking the Main Point

As you read the documents that follow, keep these broad questions in mind. These questions will help you understand the relationship between the documents in this chapter and the historical changes that they represent. As you reflect on these questions, determine which themes and which documents best address them.

- To what extent did the United States' role in the world change during these years?
- How did international concerns shift during this period, both on the part of the United States and on the part of other world regions like Europe, Latin America, and Asia? What were the primary economic and political causes of this shift? In what ways did science play a role?
- Between 1980 and 2001, the United States shifted from fighting a Cold War with a global superpower to fighting a war on terror with stateless terrorist networks. How did this change shape American citizens' and policy makers' sense of America in the world and of the role that should be played by the American government?
- By 2001, the United States had moved from being primarily an industrial economy to a service or information economy. What are some examples of this change that you can extrapolate from these documents?
- How did migration patterns change during this period? How did they remain the same?

TOPIC I

An End to the Twentieth Century

DOCUMENT 22.1 | **JIMMY CARTER**, "Crisis of Confidence" Speech
| 1979

In a televised speech on July 15, 1979, President Jimmy Carter (b. 1924) spoke to the nation on the subjects that he believed had caused a crisis of confidence among the American people. This speech became later known as Carter's "malaise" speech (though he never used the word).

The erosion of our confidence in the future is threatening to destroy the social and the political fabric of America.

The confidence that we have always had as a people is not simply some romantic dream or a proverb in a dusty book that we read just on the Fourth of July.

It is the idea which founded our nation and has guided our development as a people. Confidence in the future has supported everything else—public institutions and private enterprise, our own families, and the very Constitution of the United States. Confidence has defined our course and has served as a link between generations. We've always believed in something called progress. We've always had a faith that the days of our children would be better than our own.

Our people are losing that faith, not only in government itself but in the ability as citizens to serve as the ultimate rulers and shapers of our democracy. As a people we know our past and we are proud of it. Our progress has been part of the living history of America, even the world. We always believed that we were part of a great movement of humanity itself called democracy, involved in the search for freedom, and that belief has always strengthened us in our purpose. But just as we are losing our confidence in the future, we are also beginning to close the door on our past. . . .

As you know, there is a growing disrespect for government and for churches and for schools, the news media, and other institutions. This is not a message of happiness or reassurance, but it is the truth and it is a warning.

These changes did not happen overnight. They've come upon us gradually over the last generation, years that were filled with shocks and tragedy.

We were sure that ours was a nation of the ballot, not the bullet, until the murders of John Kennedy and Robert Kennedy and Martin Luther King Jr. We were taught that our armies were always invincible and our causes were always just, only to suffer the agony of Vietnam. We respected the presidency as a place of honor until the shock of Watergate.

We remember when the phrase "sound as a dollar" was an expression of absolute dependability, until ten years of inflation began to shrink our dollar and our savings. We believed that our nation's resources were limitless until 1973, when we had to face a growing dependence on foreign oil.

Jimmy Carter, *Public Papers of the Presidents of the United States, Jimmy Carter: 1979,* Book 2, *June 23 to December 31, 1979* (Washington, DC: Government Printing Office, 1980), 1237.

PRACTICING Historical Thinking

Identify: Summarize Carter's attitude toward America's past.

Analyze: Is Carter's speech more optimistic or more pessimistic about the future? Cite evidence to explain your response.

Evaluate: How does Carter's concern about loss of respect for the presidency represent a shift in thinking about the role that the president plays in the lives of American citizens?

| DOCUMENT 22.2 | **REGINALD STUART, "Michigan Requests Federal Loan to Bolster Unemployment Fund,"** *New York Times*
1980 |

Beginning in the 1970s, American businesses began to shift industrial production to overseas manufacturers and to lose customers to new foreign competitors. According to this *New York Times* article from January 17, 1980, Detroit, Michigan, the heart of the American automobile industry, was especially hurt by competition from Japan.

The state of Michigan, its economy shaken by the prolonged slump in the nation's automobile industry, has asked the Federal Government for a $260 million loan so it can continue paying unemployment benefits over the next three months, the Michigan Employment Security Commission disclosed today.

Gov. William G. Milliken requested the funds from the Department of Labor, stating that a rising load of unemployment claims and the repayment of earlier Federal loans would "exhaust" Michigan's unemployment compensation trust fund, although no specific time was given. By law, according to the employment commission, such requests must cover a three-month period, and Michigan's request will carry the fund from Feb. 1 through April 30, it said. . . .

Michigan's unemployment rate rose to 8.5 percent in December from 7.9 percent in November, and the state employment commission estimated that 369,000 of its residents were out of work last month. Some 250,000 residents were drawing unemployment benefits last month, the commission reported, including 88,000 people who signed up in the week end[ing] Dec. 27. . . .

PRACTICING Historical Thinking

Identify: What is Governor Milliken's reason for requesting funds from the US Department of Labor?

Analyze: Why does Milliken believe that the federal government has a role to play in this crisis? How does this request signal a change in the relationship between federal control and states rights?

Evaluate: In what ways does this document agree with or disagree with President Jimmy Carter's speech (Doc. 22.1)?

DOCUMENT 22.3 | **"Morning in America" Campaign Television Commercial**
1984

In the aftermath of the Jimmy Carter presidency, President Ronald Reagan (1911–2004) promised to restore Americans' confidence by deregulating the economy and freeing government constraints on American companies. Although prosperity returned for some Americans between 1981 and 1984, this campaign commercial for Reagan's second term claims that the president reawakened broad economic prosperity and therefore should be reelected for a second term.

It's morning again in America. Today more men and women will go to work than ever before in our country's history. With interest rates at about half the record highs of 1980, nearly 2,000 families today will buy new homes, more than at any time in the past four years. This afternoon 6,500 young men and women will be married, and with inflation at less than half of what it was just four years ago, they can look forward with confidence to the future. It's morning again in America, and under the leadership of President Reagan, our country is prouder and stronger and better. Why would we ever want to return to where we were less than four short years ago?

DOCUMENT 22.4 | **RONALD REAGAN, Speech at the Berlin Wall**
1987

Starting in 1985, the Soviet Union began rapidly opening its economy and civic life. In this June 12, 1987, speech at the Berlin Wall, Ronald Reagan sought to hasten this process by demanding that the Soviets remove their troops from East Berlin and East Germany and return sovereignty to the German people.

. . . We hear much from Moscow about a new policy of reform and openness. Some political prisoners have been released. Certain foreign news broadcasts are no longer being jammed. Some economic enterprises have been permitted to operate with greater freedom from state control. Are these the beginnings of profound changes in the Soviet state? Or are they token gestures, intended to raise false hopes in the West, or to strengthen the Soviet system without changing it? We welcome change and openness; for we believe that freedom and security go together, that the advance of human liberty can only strengthen the cause of world peace.

There is one sign the Soviets can make that would be unmistakable, that would advance dramatically the cause of freedom and peace. General Secretary Gorbachev, if you seek peace, if you seek prosperity for the Soviet Union and Eastern Europe, if you seek liberalization: Come here to this gate! Mr. Gorbachev, open this gate! Mr. Gorbachev, tear down this wall!

Ronald Reagan, *Public Papers of the Presidents of the United States, Book 1, January 1 to July 3, 1987* (Washington, DC: Government Printing Office, 1987), 633.

PRACTICING Historical Thinking

Identify: What reasons does Reagan provide to "tear down" the Berlin Wall?

Analyze: Who is Reagan's intended audience? In what ways does this audience represent America's new role in foreign policy?

Evaluate: Is Reagan's statement more of an invitation or a threat? Explain your response.

| **RONALD REAGAN, Speech at the University of Virginia**

1988

Ronald Reagan made the following speech when his presidency was in its final year and the Cold War was quickly coming to an end. During the previous year, Reagan's administration had been embroiled in the Iran-Contra affair, where members of the Reagan administration were accused of illegally selling weapons to Iran and using the money to fund anti-Communist rebels in Nicaragua and to negotiate for hostages held by the Iranian terrorist organization Hezbollah.

But now the question: How do we keep the world moving toward the idea of popular government? Well, today I offer three thoughts—reflections and warnings at the same time—on how the Soviet-American relationship can continue to improve and how the cause of peace and freedom can be served.

First, the Soviet-American relationship: Once marked by sterility and confrontation, this relationship is now characterized by dialog—realistic, candid dialog—serious diplomatic progress, and the sights and sounds of summitry. All of this is heady, inspiring. And yet my first reflection for you today is: All of it is still in doubt. And the only way to make it last and grow and become permanent is to remember we're not there yet.

Serious problems, fundamental differences remain. Our system is one of checks and balances. Theirs, for all its reforms, remains a one-party authoritarian system that institutionalizes the concentration of power. Our foreign relations embrace this expanding world of democracy that I've described. Theirs can be known by the company they keep: Cuba, Nicaragua, Ethiopia, Libya, Vietnam, North Korea. Yes, we welcome Mr. Gorbachev's recent announcement of a troop reduction, but let us remember that the Soviet preponderance in military power in Europe remains, an asymmetry that offends our Jeffersonian senses and endangers our future.

So, we must keep our heads, and that means keeping our skepticism. We must realize that what has brought us here has not been easy, not for ourselves nor for all of those who have sacrificed and contributed to the cause of freedom in the postwar era.

So, this means in our treaty negotiations, as I've said: Trust, but verify. I'm not a linguist, but I learned to say that much in Russian and have used it in frequent meetings with Mr. Gorbachev: "Dovorey no provorey." It means keeping our military strong. It means remembering no treaty is better than a bad treaty. It means remembering the accords of Moscow and Washington summits followed many years of standing firm on our principles and our interests, and those of our allies.

And finally, we need to recall that in the years of detente we tended to forget the greatest weapon the democracies have in their struggle is public candor: the truth. We must never do that again. It's not an act of belligerence to speak to the fundamental differences between totalitarianism and democracy; it's a moral imperative. It doesn't slow down the pace of negotiations; it moves them forward. Throughout history, we see evidence that adversaries negotiate seriously with democratic nations only when they know the democracies harbor no illusions about those adversaries.

Miller Center, University of Virginia, millercenter.org/academic/gage/colloquia/detail/5470.

PRACTICING Historical Thinking

Identify: Name the three major principles that according to Reagan shape America's new relationship with the Soviet Union.

Analyze: Explain what Reagan means by "a moral imperative" to speak the truth. Whose point of view does he represent?

Evaluate: In noting the "company" that the Soviet Union keeps, Reagan cites some of America's enemies. Why? To what extent does Reagan's speech redefine the president's role in international affairs since the early 1900s?

DOCUMENT 22.6 | FRANCIS FUKUYAMA, "The End of History?"
1989

After the end of the Cold War, political scientist Francis Fukuyama (b. 1952) reflected the optimism of many Americans that the future was assured for democracy and free-market capitalism.

In watching the flow of events over the past decade or so, it is hard to avoid the feeling that something very fundamental has happened in world history. The past year has seen a flood of articles commemorating the end of the Cold War, and the fact that "peace" seems to be breaking out in many regions of the world. Most of these analyses lack any larger conceptual framework for distinguishing between what is essential and what is contingent or accidental in world history, and are predictably superficial. If Mr. Gorbachev were ousted from the Kremlin or a new Ayatollah proclaimed the millennium for a desolate Middle Eastern capital, these same commentators would scramble to announce the rebirth of a new era of conflict. . . .

What we may be witnessing . . . [is] not just the end of the Cold War, or the passing of a particular period of post-war history, but the end of history as such: that is, the end point of mankind's ideological evolution and the universalization of Western liberal democracy as the final form of human government. This is not to say that there will no longer be events to fill the pages of *Foreign Affairs*'s yearly summaries of international relations, for the victory of liberalism has occurred primarily in the realm of ideas or consciousness and is as yet incomplete in the real or material world. But there are powerful reasons for believing that it is the ideal that will govern the material world *in the long run*. To understand how this is so, we must first consider some theoretical issues concerning the nature of historical change. . . .

Francis Fukuyama, "The End of History," *National Interest* 16 (Summer 1989): 3–18.

PRACTICING Historical Thinking

Identify: According to Fukuyama, what has ended?

Analyze: What does Fukuyama mean when he states that "it is the ideal that will govern the material world *in the long run*"?

Evaluate: To what extent has Fukuyama's prediction come true? Consult your textbooks for additional information.

DOCUMENT 22.7 | **BILL CLINTON, Address on Health Care Reform**
| 1993

In an attempt to revive liberal policies after twelve years of conservative executives, President Bill Clinton (b. 1946) unveiled his comprehensive health care legislation on September 22, 1993, during his first year in office. The bill failed to pass Congress.

Every one of us knows someone who's worked hard and played by the rules and still been hurt by this system that just doesn't work for too many people. But I'd like to tell you about just one. Kerry Kennedy owns a small furniture store that employs seven people in Titusville, Florida. Like most small business owners, he's poured his heart and soul, his sweat and blood into that business for years. But over the last several years, again like most small business owners, he's seen his health care premiums skyrocket, even in years when no claims were made. And last year, he painfully discovered he could no longer afford to provide coverage for all his workers because his insurance company told him that two of his workers had become high risks because of their advanced age. The problem was that those two people were his mother and father, the people who founded the business and still work in the store.

This story speaks for millions of others. And from them we have learned a powerful truth. We have to preserve and strengthen what is right with the health care system, but we have got to fix what is wrong with it.

Now, we all know what's right. We're blessed with the best health care professionals on Earth, the finest health care institutions, the best medical research, the most sophisticated technology. My mother is a nurse. I grew up around hospitals. Doctors and nurses were the first professional people I ever knew or learned to look up to. They are what is right with this health care system. But we also know that we can no longer afford to continue to ignore what is wrong.

Millions of Americans are just a pink slip away from losing their health insurance and one serious illness away from losing all their savings. Millions more are locked into the jobs they have now just because they or someone in their family has once been sick and they have what is called the preexisting condition. And on any given day, over 37 million Americans, most of them working people and their little children, have no health insurance at all. . . .

William J. Clinton, *Public Papers of the Presidents of the United States, William J. Clinton: 1993, Book 2, August 1 to December 31, 1993* (Washington, DC: Government Printing Office, 1994), 1557.

PRACTICING Historical Thinking

Identify: What are Clinton's reasons for wanting to improve health care?

Analyze: Compare Clinton's tone with Jimmy Carter's (Doc. 22.1) and with Ronald Reagan's (Docs. 22.4 and 22.5). How does each frame his tone to enforce an argument?

Evaluate: To what extent does Clinton's story represent the ideology espoused by Francis Fukuyama in Document 22.6?

DOCUMENT 22.8 | REPUBLICAN PARTY, Contract with America
1994

In the 1994 midterm election, the Republican Party acquired a majority in the United States House of Representatives for the first time since 1952. The House Republican victory was partially orchestrated by Representative Newt Gingrich of Georgia, who offered a "Contract with America" as a unified congressional conservative platform for economic and social reforms. The contract included a vow to bring a collection of related bills to the House floor for debate within the first hundred days of the 104th Congress with a hope to "restore the bonds of trust between the people and their elected representatives."

1. THE FISCAL RESPONSIBILITY ACT: A balanced budget/tax limitation amendment and a legislative line-item veto to restore fiscal responsibility to an out-of-control Congress, requiring them to live under the same budget constraints as families and businesses.

2. THE TAKING BACK OUR STREETS ACT: An anti-crime package including stronger truth-in-sentencing, "good faith" exclusionary rule exemptions, effective death penalty provisions, and cuts in social spending from this summer's "crime" bill to fund prison construction and additional law enforcement to keep people secure in their neighborhoods and kids safe in their schools.

3. THE PERSONAL RESPONSIBILITY ACT: Discourage illegitimacy and teen pregnancy by prohibiting welfare to minor mothers and denying increased AFDC for additional children while on welfare, cut spending for welfare programs, and enact a tough two-years-and-out provision with work requirements to promote individual responsibility.

4. THE FAMILY REINFORCEMENT ACT: Child support enforcement, tax incentives for adoption, strengthening rights of parents in their children's education, stronger child pornography laws, and an elderly dependent care tax credit to reinforce the central role of families in American society.

5. THE AMERICAN DREAM RESTORATION ACT: A $500 per child tax credit, begin repeal of the marriage tax penalty, and creation of American Dream Savings Accounts to provide middle class tax relief.

6. THE NATIONAL SECURITY RESTORATION ACT: No U.S. troops under U.N. command and restoration of the essential parts of our national security funding to strengthen our national defense and maintain our credibility around the world.

7. THE SENIOR CITIZENS FAIRNESS ACT: Raise the Social Security earnings limit which currently forces seniors out of the work force, repeal the 1993 tax hikes on Social Security benefits and provide tax incentives for private long-term care insurance to let Older Americans keep more of what they have earned over the years.

8. THE JOB CREATION AND WAGE ENHANCEMENT ACT: Small business incentives, capital gains cut and indexation, neutral cost recovery, risk assessment/cost-benefit analysis, strengthening the Regulatory Flexibility Act and unfunded mandate reform to create jobs and raise worker wages.

9. THE COMMON SENSE LEGAL REFORM ACT: "Loser pays" laws, reasonable limits on punitive damages and reform of product liability laws to stem the endless tide of litigation.

10. THE CITIZEN LEGISLATURE ACT: A first-ever vote on term limits to replace career politicians with citizen legislators. . . .

www.nationalcenter.org/ContractwithAmerica.html.

PRACTICING Historical Thinking

Identify: Select three elements of the above Contract with America, and summarize their intent.

Analyze: Do the elements that you have chosen represent (or does the contract itself represent) a change in thinking about the relationship between the federal government and its citizens? Explain.

Evaluate: To what extent does Gingrich's contract directly oppose Bill Clinton's call for health care reform (Doc. 22.7)? Cite specific evidence in your response.

| ## SOUTHERN BAPTIST CONVENTION EXECUTIVE COMMITTEE, "Resolution on Homosexual Marriage"

1996

The culmination of a generation of so-called culture wars among the baby-boomer generation, the issue of homosexual marriage served as a lightning rod for American conservatives and liberals in the closing years of the twentieth century. At issue was whether individual states could legalize homosexual marriage. As the largest Protestant denomination in the United States, the Southern Baptist Convention used its broad influence to lobby against this possibility.

BE IT RESOLVED, That we, the messengers of the one hundred thirty-ninth meeting of the Southern Baptist Convention, assembled in New Orleans, Louisiana, June 11–13, 1996, do clearly and steadfastly oppose the legalization of homosexual marriage by the state of Hawaii, or by any other state, or by the United States of America; and

BE IT FURTHER RESOLVED, That we affirm the Bible's teaching that promotion of homosexual conduct and relationships by any society, including action by the governments to sanction and legitimize homosexual relationships by the legalization of homosexual marriages, is an abominable sin calling for God's swift judgment upon any such society (Lev. 18:22, 28; Isa. 3:9); and

BE IT FURTHER RESOLVED, That we commit ourselves to pray faithfully against the legalization of homosexual marriages in American law, and to preach and teach the truth concerning what the Bible says about homosexuality, homosexual conduct and the institution of marriage, and against the foolishness, danger and moral wickedness of any government action to accept, sanction, approve, protect, or promote homosexual marriage; and

BE IT FURTHER RESOLVED, That we commit ourselves to pray for, affirm, and support legislative and legal efforts and all persons involved in efforts to oppose the legalization of homosexual marriages through judicial actions, through public policy decisions and through legislation introduced at both the state and federal levels of government; and we call upon all judges, all persons in public office, and all candidates for public office, to do all they can to resist and oppose the legalization of homosexual marriages; and

BE IT FINALLY RESOLVED, That because any law, or any policy or regulation supporting a law, that legalizes homosexual marriage is and must be completely and thoroughly wicked according to God's standards revealed in the Bible, we do most solemnly pledge our decision never to recognize the moral legitimacy of any such law, policy or regulation, and we affirm that, whatever the stakes (Dan. 3:17–18), we will never conform to or obey (Acts 4:19) anything required by any governing body to implement, impose or act upon any such law. So help us God.

Southern Baptist Convention, "Resolution on Homosexual Marriage," New Orleans, Louisiana, 1996, www.sbc.net/resolutions/amResolution.asp?ID=614.

PRACTICING Historical Thinking

Identify: Summarize the position that is stated by the Southern Baptist Convention in this resolution.

Analyze: What rationale does the Southern Baptist Convention provide for its stance?

Evaluate: To what extent does the battle over legalizing gay marriage represent a clash between people on the far right and far left?

APPLYING AP® Historical Thinking Skills

SKILL REVIEW | Contextualization and Synthesis

Answer the following question in the form of a complete essay. Use the documents above and information from your textbook and classwork to support your arguments.

Characterize the major economic, social, and political debates during the last quarter of the twentieth century (1975–2001). To what extent do these debates reflect controversies and concerns from the third quarter of the twentieth century (1950–1975)?

STEP 1 *Contextualization*

Using the graphic organizer below, determine how key contexts shaped key debates.

1950–1975	1975–2001
Historical context (events and trends that shaped these years)	**Historical context (events and trends that shaped these years)**
Economic debates	Economic debates
Social debates	Social debates
Political debates	Political debates

STEP 2 *Synthesis*

Next, compare the two periods, using a subject-by-subject method of comparison. Your outline may also present contrasts, as shown here:

I. Introduction

II. 1975 to 2001

III. 1950 to 1975

    A. Similarities to later era

    B. Differences from later era

IV. Conclusion

An End to History's End

DOCUMENT 22.10 | GEORGE W. BUSH, Presidential Nomination Acceptance Speech
2000

After a bitter primary battle with Senator John McCain (b. 1936), former Texas governor George W. Bush (b. 1946), son of President George H. W. Bush (b. 1924), laid out his plan for "compassionate conservatism" in his 2000 acceptance address at the Republican National Convention in Philadelphia, Pennsylvania.

Tonight, in this hall, we resolve to be . . . not the party of repose, but the party of reform. We will write, not footnotes, but chapters in the American story. We will add the work of our hands to the inheritance of our fathers and mothers, and leave this nation greater than we found it. We know the tests of leadership. The issues are joined.

We will strengthen Social Security and Medicare for the greatest generation, and for generations to come. Medicare does more than meet the needs of our elderly, it reflects the values of our society. We will set it on firm financial ground, and make prescription drugs available and affordable for every senior who needs them.

Social Security has been called the "third rail of American politics," the one you're not supposed to touch because it might shock you. But, if you don't touch it, you can't fix it. And I intend to fix it. To the seniors in this country, you earned your benefits, you made your plans, and President George W. Bush will keep the promise of Social Security. No changes, no reductions, no way.

Our opponents will say otherwise. This is their last, parting ploy, and don't believe a word of it.

Now is the time for Republicans and Democrats to end the politics of fear and save Social Security, together.

For younger workers, we will give you the option—your choice—to put a part of your payroll taxes into sound, responsible investments. This will mean a higher return on your money, and, over 30 or 40 years, a nest egg to help your retirement, or pass on to your children. When this money is in your name, in your account, it's not just a program, it's your property.

Now is the time to give American workers security and independence that no politician can ever take away.

On education, too many American children are segregated into schools without standards, shuffled from grade-to-grade because of their age, regardless of their knowledge. This is discrimination, pure and simple—the soft bigotry of low expectations. And our nation should treat it like other forms of discrimination. . . . We should end it.

One size does not fit all when it comes to educating our children, so local people should control local schools.

And those who spend your tax dollars must be held accountable. When a school district receives federal funds to teach poor children, we expect them to learn. And if they don't, parents should get the money to make a different choice. . . .

I will use this moment of opportunity to bring common sense and fairness to the tax code. And I will act on principle.

On principle, every family, every farmer and small businessperson, should be free to pass on their life's work to those they love. So we will abolish the death tax.

On principle, no one in America should have to pay more than a third of their income to the federal government. So we will reduce tax rates for everyone, in every bracket.

On principle, those in the greatest need should receive the greatest help. So we will lower the bottom rate from 15% to 10% and double the child [tax] credit.

Now is the time to reform the tax code and share some of the surplus with the people who pay the bills. . . .

Big government is not the answer.

But the alternative to bureaucracy is not indifference. It is to put conservative values and conservative ideas into the thick of the fight for justice and opportunity.

This is what I mean by compassionate conservatism. And on this ground we will lead our nation.

Los Angeles Times, August 4, 2000, http://articles.latimes.com/2000/aug/04/news/mn-64431/2.

PRACTICING Historical Thinking

Identify: List five initiatives that Bush outlines in his acceptance speech.

Analyze: Are these initiatives more within the scope of liberal or conservative thinking? Explain.

Evaluate: Compare Bush's goals with those of earlier presidents from this era, especially Jimmy Carter (Doc. 22.1) and Bill Clinton (Doc. 22.7). Are their purposes dramatically different? How does Bush's speech signal a shift in thinking about the relationship that the president has with the citizens of the country?

OFFICE OF THE PRESIDENT, Proposal to Create the Department of Homeland Security

2002

The proposal for a Department of Homeland Security was authorized by President George W. Bush in 2002 in response to the attacks of September 11, 2001. The following is from the opening pages of the document describing this new department.

The President proposes to create a new Department of Homeland Security, the most significant transformation of the U.S. government in over a half-century by largely transforming and realigning the current confusing patchwork of government activities into a single department whose primary mission is to protect our homeland. The creation of a Department of Homeland Security is one more key step in the President's national strategy for homeland security.

Immediately after last fall's attack, the President took decisive steps to protect America—from hardening cockpits and stockpiling vaccines to tightening our borders. The President used his maximum legal authority to establish the White House Office of Homeland Security and the Homeland Security Council to ensure that our federal response and protection efforts were coordinated and effective. The President also directed Homeland Security Advisor Tom Ridge to study the federal government as a whole to determine if the current structure allows us to meet the threats of today while anticipating the unknown threats of tomorrow. After careful study of the current structure—coupled with the experience gained since September 11 and new information we have learned about our enemies while fighting a war—the President concluded that our nation needs a more unified homeland security structure. In designing the new Department, the Administration considered a number of homeland security organizational proposals that have emerged from outside studies, commissions, and Members of Congress.

President George W. Bush, "The Department of Homeland Security, 2002," Department of Homeland Security website, www.dhs.gov/xlibrary/assets/book.pdf.

PRACTICING Historical Thinking

Identify: According to the president's proposal, what are the reasons for creating the Department of Homeland Security?

Analyze: To what extent does the creation of this new department represent a shift in US foreign policy?

Evaluate: Compare this department to previous attempts to protect American citizens. Does the creation of this department signal a turning point in domestic policy? Support your response with documents from this chapter, your textbook, and your class notes.

| ## GEORGE W. BUSH, On Iraq
2003

During 2002 and 2003, the Bush administration argued that an invasion of Iraq would serve as an essential front in the "War on Terror." The excerpt that follows comes from President George W. Bush's March 6, 2003, opening remarks for a national press conference in which he announced the capture of a key 9/11 conspirator and laid out accusations against Saddam Hussein's regime in Iraq.

This has been an important week on two fronts on our war against terror. First, thanks to the hard work of American and Pakistani officials, we captured the mastermind of the September the 11th attacks against our nation. Khalid Sheikh Mohammed conceived and planned the hijackings and directed the actions of the hijackers. We believe his capture will further disrupt the terror network and their planning for additional attacks.

Second, we have arrived at an important moment in confronting the threat posed to our nation and to peace by Saddam Hussein and his weapons of terror. In New York tomorrow, the United Nations Security Council will receive an update from the chief weapons inspector. The world needs him to answer a single question: Has the Iraqi regime fully and unconditionally disarmed, as required by Resolution 1441, or has it not?

Iraq's dictator has made a public show of producing and destroying a few missiles—missiles that violate the restrictions set out more than 10 years ago. Yet, our intelligence shows that even as he is destroying these few missiles, he has ordered the continued production of the very same type of missiles.

Iraqi operatives continue to hide biological and chemical agents to avoid detection by inspectors. In some cases, these materials have been moved to different locations every 12 to 24 hours, or placed in vehicles that are in residential neighborhoods.

We know from multiple intelligence sources that Iraqi weapons scientists continue to be threatened with harm should they cooperate with U.N. inspectors. Scientists are required by Iraqi intelligence to wear concealed recording devices during interviews, and hotels where interviews take place are bugged by the regime.

These are not the actions of a regime that is disarming. These are the actions of a regime engaged in a willful charade. These are the actions of a regime that systematically and deliberately is defying the world. If the Iraqi regime were disarming, we would know it, because we would see it. Iraq's weapons would be presented to inspectors, and the world would witness their destruction. Instead, with the world demanding disarmament, and more than 200,000 troops positioned near his country, Saddam Hussein's response is to produce a few weapons for show, while he hides the rest and builds even more.

White House Archives, press release, "President George Bush Discusses Iraq in National Press Conference," March 6, 2003.

DOCUMENT 22.13	**GEORGE W. BUSH,** On Social Security Reform
	2005

After his reelection in 2004, George W. Bush initiated a campaign to reform social security. He sought to transform it from a government program that used a payroll tax to collect payments from workers to a system where individuals could open personal accounts to invest in five diversified index funds and a "lifecycle" fund. The legislation was never officially brought to a vote before Congress because it was expected to have little support on Capitol Hill.

First of all, let me explain why I think we—I know we have a problem. When Social Security was designed, there were 16 workers for every beneficiary in 1950—actually, designed in the thirties. In 1950, there were 16 workers for every beneficiary. That meant it was a lot easier to afford that which the Government promised. When you've got 16 people paying in for one person, it—you can see why the system was solvent.

What's happened since the design of the system, however, is that people are living longer—thankfully. [*Laughter*] That's good news. [*Laughter*] What else is happening since the system was designed is we had what's called the baby boomers—that would be me, Baucus, others, you know—[*laughter*]—people whose hair is getting grayer on a regular basis. And we're fixing to retire in big numbers. So you're living longer and you've got bigger—you've got big numbers retiring, and fewer workers paying into the system, 3.3 workers per beneficiary. Plus, Congress over the years has promised an increase of benefits. So think about the math. Fewer people paying into the system, more people living longer, more people retiring, for greater benefits.

Now, that is—and because Social Security is a pay-as-you-go system, there's not a great big trust of money. The money that goes in from your paycheck goes out to the beneficiaries. That's how it works. And so, obviously, as the demand for money increases as a result of more people retiring and people living longer and benefits going up, more has to come in.

Now, if you look at this chart up there, in 2018 the Social Security system goes negative. That means more money is going out than is coming into the system. And every year after that, as you can see, the cash deficit—that is, the money going out is greater than the money coming in—increases. In 2027, it's about

$200 billion a year. That's above and beyond the payroll taxes we're collecting. Ten years later, it's about $300 billion. Every year, the situation gets worse.

So you can imagine what will be happening if we don't do anything. You know, Congress is going to show up, and somebody says, "We're $200 billion short. Where are you going to get the money?" Well, you can tax somebody to get the money; you can get rid of the benefits that you promised; you can cut other programs; or you can keep borrowing debt. That's why I think we've got a problem.

George Bush, *Public Papers of the President of the United States: George W. Bush, Book 1, January 1 to June 30, 2005* (Washington, DC: Government Printing Office, 2009), 135–136.

PRACTICING Historical Thinking

Identify: Summarize Bush's concerns about social security.

Analyze: Are Bush's concerns about social security similar to the concerns for citizens that he expresses in his presidential nomination acceptance speech on "compassionate conservatism" (Doc. 22.10)? Explain.

Evaluate: Compare Bush's justifications for this reform with Lyndon B. Johnson's Great Society (Doc. 20.7). To what extent do Johnson's justifications parallel Bush's?

DOCUMENT 22.14 | **UNITED NATIONS, Kyoto Protocol on Emissions**
| 2008

In 1997, the United Nations Framework Convention on Climate Change, under the auspices of the United Nations, generated the Kyoto Protocol to achieve a leveling of greenhouse gases and decrease global warming. Over 190 nations agreed to the protocols, but the United States Senate never ratified the treaty.

Climate change is increasingly recognized as one of the most critical challenges ever to face humankind. With the release of the Fourth Assessment Report of the Intergovernmental Panel on Climate Change (IPCC), the international scientific community has significantly advanced public understanding of climate change and its impacts. In this report, the IPCC concluded that "warming of the climate system is unequivocal, as is now evident from observations of increases in average global air and ocean temperatures, widespread melting of snow and ice and rising average global sea level." The conclusions of the IPCC report made the case for action against climate change stronger than ever before.

Climate change is a global problem that requires a global response embracing the needs and interests of all countries. The United Nations Framework Convention on Climate Change, which came into effect in 1994, and its Kyoto Protocol that came into effect in 2005—sharing the objective of the Convention to stabilize atmospheric concentrations of greenhouse gases—enable such a global response to climate change.

United Nations Framework Convention on Climate Change, *Kyoto Protocol Reference Manual* (Bonn, Germany: UNFCCC Secretariat, 2008), 4.

PRACTICING Historical Thinking

Identify: What was the purpose of the Kyoto Protocol?

Analyze: Analyze the relationship between science and environmentalism as presented in the protocol.

Evaluate: To what extent does the Kyoto Protocol present environmental concerns as a key issue for political reforms at the beginning of the twenty-first century?

DOCUMENT 22.15 | Border Fence with Mexico
2009

The following image depicts part of the barrier constructed along the border between the United States and Mexico from Yuma, Arizona, to Calexico, California. The fifteen-foot-tall fence was constructed as part of the Secure Fence Act of 2006 and was intended to stem the flow of drugs and illegal immigrants from Mexico into border states.

David McNew/Getty Images.

DOCUMENT 22.16 | **BARACK OBAMA, Address to Congress on Health Care**
| 2011

Although the health care legislation that President Barack Obama (b. 1961) proposed successfully passed Congress, it passed by a partisan vote and remained a contentious issue throughout the Obama administration.

I am not the first President to take up this cause, but I am determined to be the last. (Applause.) It has now been nearly a century since Theodore Roosevelt first called for health care reform. And ever since, nearly every President and Congress, whether Democrat or Republican, has attempted to meet this challenge in some way. A bill for comprehensive health reform was first introduced by John Dingell Sr. in 1943. Sixty-five years later, his son continues to introduce that same bill at the beginning of each session. (Applause.)

Our collective failure to meet this challenge—year after year, decade after decade—has led us to the breaking point. Everyone understands the extraordinary hardships that are placed on the uninsured, who live every day just one accident or illness away from bankruptcy. These are not primarily people on welfare. These are middle-class Americans. Some can't get insurance on the job. Others are self-employed. and can't afford it, since buying insurance on your own costs you three times as much as the coverage you get from your employer. Many other Americans who are willing and able to pay are still denied insurance due to previous illnesses or conditions that insurance companies decide are too risky or too expensive to cover.

We are the only democracy—the only advanced democracy on Earth—the only wealthy nation—that allows such hardship for millions of its people. There are now more than 30 million American citizens who cannot get coverage. In just a two-year period, one in every three Americans goes without health care coverage at some point. And every day, 14,000 Americans lose their coverage. In other words, it can happen to anyone.

But the problem that plagues the health care system is not just a problem for the uninsured. Those who do have insurance have never had less security and stability than they do today. More and more Americans worry that if you move, lose your job, or change your job, you'll lose your health insurance too. More and more Americans pay their premiums, only to discover that their insurance company has dropped their coverage when they get sick, or won't pay the full cost of care. It happens every day. . . .

Then there's the problem of rising cost. We spend one and a half times more per person on health care than any other country, but we aren't any healthier for it. This is one of the reasons that insurance premiums have gone up three times faster than wages. It's why so many employers—especially small businesses—are forcing their employees to pay more for insurance, or are dropping their coverage entirely. It's why so many aspiring entrepreneurs cannot afford to open a business in the first place, and why American businesses that compete internationally—like our automakers—are at a huge disadvantage. And it's why those of us with health insurance are also paying a hidden and growing tax for those without it—about $1,000 per year that pays for somebody else's emergency room and charitable care.

Finally, our health care system is placing an unsustainable burden on taxpayers. When health care costs grow at the rate they have, it puts greater pressure on programs like Medicare and Medicaid. If we do nothing to slow these skyrocketing costs, we will eventually be spending more on Medicare and Medicaid than every other government program combined. Put simply, our health care problem is our deficit problem. Nothing else even comes close. Nothing else.

Office of the Press Secretary, The White House, press release, "Remarks by the President to a Joint Session of Congress on Health Care," September 9, 2009.

PRACTICING Historical Thinking

Identify: List five reasons that Obama provides for reforming health care.

Analyze: Explain the significance of the reasons that you chose.

Evaluate: To what extent does Obama's call for health care reform echo Bill Clinton's (Doc. 22.7)? How does Obama's call for reform make the case differently? Speculate as to the reasons for the difference.

DOCUMENT 22.17 | **BARACK OBAMA, Speech on the Middle East**
2011

In the following speech from May 19, 2011, President Barack Obama details support for a wave of democratic protest movements across the Middle East.

. . . For six months, we have witnessed an extraordinary change taking place in the Middle East and North Africa. Square by square, town by town, country by country, the people have risen up to demand their basic human rights. Two leaders have stepped aside. More may follow. And though these countries may be a great distance from our shores, we know that our own future is bound to this region by the forces of economics and security, by history and by faith.

Today, I want to talk about this change—the forces that are driving it and how we can respond in a way that advances our values and strengthens our security.

. . . [A]lready, we've done much to shift our foreign policy following a decade defined by two costly conflicts. After years of war in Iraq, we've removed 100,000 American troops and ended our combat mission there. In Afghanistan, we've broken the Taliban's momentum, and this July we will begin to bring our troops home and continue a transition to Afghan lead. And after years of war against al Qaeda and its affiliates, we have dealt al Qaeda a huge blow by killing its leader, Osama bin Laden. . . .

The story of this revolution, and the ones that followed, should not have come as a surprise. The nations of the Middle East and North Africa won their independence long ago, but in too many places their people did not. In too many countries, power has been concentrated in the hands of a few. In too many countries, a citizen like that young vendor had nowhere to turn—no honest judiciary to hear his case; no independent media to give him voice; no credible political party to represent his views; no free and fair election where he could choose his leader.

. . . [T]his lack of self-determination—the chance to make of your life what you will—has applied to the region's economy as well. Yes, some nations are blessed with wealth in oil and gas, and that has led to pockets of prosperity. But in a global economy based on knowledge, based on innovation, no development strategy can be based solely upon what comes out of the ground. Nor can people reach their potential when you cannot start a business without paying a bribe.

In the face of these challenges, too many leaders in the region tried to direct their people's grievances elsewhere. The West was blamed as the source of all ills, a half century after the end of colonialism. Antagonism toward Israel became the only acceptable outlet for political expression. Divisions of tribe, ethnicity and religious sect were manipulated as a means of holding on to power, or taking it away from somebody else.

But the events of the past six months show us that strategies of repression and strategies of diversion will not work anymore. Satellite television and the Internet provide a window into the wider world—a world of astonishing progress in places like India and Indonesia and Brazil. Cell phones and social networks allow young people to connect and organize like never before. And so a new generation has emerged. And their voices tell us that change cannot be denied.

Office of the Press Secretary, The White House, press release, "Remarks by the President on the Middle East and North Africa," State Department, Washington, DC, May 19, 2011.

DOCUMENT 22.18	SAM SCHLINKERT, "Facebook Is Invading Your Phone," *Daily Beast*
	2013

The social network site Facebook grew quickly during the first decade of its existence, counting over a billion members by 2012. In this April 4, 2013, article for an online magazine, a journalist reacts to Facebook's announcement of a new mobile platform.

It's a phone! It's an app! It's . . . just an app.

The long-awaited Facebook phone has finally arrived, making its debut Thursday afternoon to a crowd of tech journalists sitting at the social network's headquarters at 1 Hacker Way in Menlo Park, California.

"Today we're finally gonna talk about that Facebook phone," Facebook founder Mark Zuckerberg said as he strode on the stage to muted laughter, clutching an oversized microphone, citing the moniker that for years has followed Facebook's gradual prioritization of mobile.

Would it be hardware designed by Zuck? Would it just be a Facebook button?

We know now the "Facebook Phone" moniker is a misnomer. It's just a collection of apps called "Home"—and it can live on any Android device.

"Today our phones are designed around apps, not people," the hoodie-wearing Zuckerberg proclaimed. Rather than an app-centric phone, he asked, what would it feel like if our phones were designed around people?

Facebook Home will be deeply integrated, with your friends' photos, faces, and messages displayed front and center, on what Zuckerberg calls "a great social phone."

There is Cover Feed, which brings your lock screen to life. There are Chat Heads, a new way of messaging with friends and family. And there's App Launcher, which keeps you close lest your mind were to wander to an app outside of Facebook's environment.

Cover Feed transforms your phone's lock screen by making it a rotating gallery of ever-present Facebook photos on which you can "like" and leave comments.

With Chat Heads, SMS and Facebook messages display on top of any app you're already using, with your friends coming up as circular profile pictures (thus the name Chat Heads).

And then there's the App Launcher, which contains all of the apps on your phone—in the demo this pointedly included Google Maps, Tumblr, DropBox, and other potential competitors. In a sense it's a replacement for your home screen, so you never leave Home.

The software will be available for download beginning April 12 on a variety of Android phones. In a few months, you can get it for tablets as well.

Underscoring the company's commitment to being mobile first, with Wall Street investors anxiously looking on, Zuckerberg proclaimed, "We think this is the best version of Facebook there is."

He later added, "At one level, this is just the next mobile version of Facebook. At a deeper level this will start to be a change to the relationship with how we use these computing devices."

In other words, Zuck wants to make his relationship with your phone "Facebook official." The question is, will you hit accept?

PRACTICING Historical Thinking

Identify: According to Mark Zuckerberg, what are the attractive features of the new application for Facebook on smartphones?

Analyze: How does this new application influence the social lives of Americans?

Evaluate: To what extent does the smartphone—as seen by Zuckerberg—present the same democratizing value in America as it did in the Middle East—as seen by Barack Obama (Doc. 22.17)?

DOCUMENT 22.19 | **JENNIFER MEDINA, "New Suburban Dream Born of Asia and Southern California,"** ***New York Times***
| 2013

The Immigration and Nationality Act of 1965 eliminated quotas favoring immigration from northern Europe and transformed the populations of the southwest and western United States. This April 28, 2013, article from the *New York Times* examines the changing demographics of one California city.

SAN MARINO, Calif.—Beneath the palm trees that line Huntington Drive, named for the railroad magnate who founded this Southern California city, hang signs to honor families who have helped sponsor the centennial celebration here this year. There are names like Dryden, Crowley and Telleen, families that have lived here for generations. But there are newer names as well: Sun, Koo and Shi.

A generation ago, whites made up roughly two-thirds of the population in this rarefied Los Angeles suburb, where most of the homes are worth well over $1 million. But Asians now make up over half of the population in San Marino, which has long attracted some of the region's wealthiest families and was once home to the John Birch Society's Western headquarters.

The transformation illustrates a drastic shift in California immigration trends over the last decade, one that can easily be seen all over the area: more than twice as many immigrants to the nation's most populous state now come from Asia than from Latin America.

And the change here is just one example of the ways immigration is remaking America, with the political, economic and cultural ramifications playing out in a variety of ways. The number of Latinos has more than doubled in many Southern states, including Alabama, Georgia and North Carolina, creating new tensions. Asian populations are booming in New Jersey, and Latino immigrants are reviving small towns in the Midwest.

Much of the current immigration debate in Congress has focused on Hispanics, and California has for decades been viewed as the focal point of that migration. But in cities in the San Gabriel Valley—as well as in Orange County and in Silicon Valley in Northern California—Asian immigrants have become a dominant cultural force in places that were once largely white or Hispanic.

"We are really looking at a different era here," said Hans Johnson, a demographer at the Public Policy Institute of California who has studied census data. "There are astounding changes in working-class towns and old, established, wealthy cities. It is not confined to one place."

Asians have become a majority in more than half a dozen cities in the San Gabriel Valley in the last decade, creating a region of Asian-dominated suburbs that stretches for nearly 30 miles east of Los Angeles. In the shopping centers, Chinese-language characters are on nearly every storefront, visible from the freeways that cut through the area. . . .

PRACTICING Historical Thinking

Identify: Summarize the changing statistics on Asian immigration, according to the article.

Analyze: Why have these changes occurred?

Evaluate: To what extent might immigration in the twenty-first century redefine the American identity?

SKILL REVIEW | **Periodization and Comparison**

Answer the following question in the form of a complete essay. Use the documents above and information from your textbook and classwork to support your arguments.

> To what extent were the September 11, 2001, attacks on the World Trade Center and the Pentagon a turning point in American domestic and foreign policy when compared with the twenty-five years before 9/11?

PUTTING IT ALL TOGETHER

Revisiting the Main Point

- Choose three documents from this chapter that characterize the United States' changing role in the world between 1975 and 2013. In what ways do these documents represent broader shifts in the country and the rest of the world?
- During this period, how did international concerns shift on the part of the United States? What were the primary economic and political causes of this shift? In what ways did science play a role?
- Compare US foreign policy before and after the 9/11 attacks by using four documents from above.
- Choose three documents that characterize changes in the American economy during the last quarter of the twentieth century—and into the twenty-first century. What broader economic changes do these documents represent?
- Characterize changing migration patterns in the United States during this period by analyzing at least three documents and explaining the ways in which they characterize these changing migration patterns.

**BUILDING AP®
WRITING SKILLS** | ## Rethinking Audience and Voice in Primary Documents

Incorporating primary documents into historical argument gives your argument credibility. You can bolster that credibility by showing some understanding of the voice behind the document and its intended audience. By noting the **point of view**, you can contextualize the document and are better situated to understand how this document responds to other documents.

For example, consider the following two documents from this chapter:

Document 22.12, George W. Bush, On Iraq, 2003

Document 22.17, Barack Obama, Speech on the Middle East, 2011

Both the voice and the audience for either speech reflects differing political ideologies. Bush's press conference on Iraq features this language:

> These are not the actions of a regime that is disarming. These are the actions of a regime engaged in a willful charade. These are the actions of a regime that systematically and deliberately is defying the world. **If** the Iraqi regime were disarming, we would know it, because we **would** see it. Iraq's weapons **would** be presented to inspectors, and the world **would** witness their destruction.

In proposing American intervention abroad, Bush's language reflects a clear position and an understanding of implications, as noted by the emphasized words. An aggressive foreign policy reflects a certainty that mirrors the speaker's confidence and comforts an audience that is fearful of outsiders.

Responding to the Arab Spring's protests against dictatorships in the Middle East, President Barack Obama made these remarks (Doc. 22.17):

> In the face of these challenges, too many leaders in the region tried to direct their people's grievances elsewhere. The West **was blamed** as the source of all ills, a half century after the end of colonialism. Antagonism toward Israel became the only acceptable outlet for political expression. Divisions of tribe, ethnicity and religious sect **were manipulated** as a means of holding on to power, or taking it away from somebody else.
>
> But the events of the past six months show us that strategies of repression and strategies of diversion will not work anymore. Satellite television and the Internet provide a window into the wider world—a world of astonishing progress in places like India, Indonesia and Brazil. Cell phones and social networks allow young people to connect and organize like never before. And so a new generation has emerged. And their voices tell us that change cannot be denied.

Obama's use of the passive voice (highlighted above) omits agency—or blame—for past grievances with the Middle East. The closest that Obama comes to attacking the Arab countries is identifying "antagonism toward Israel," largely to show his support for Israel rather than to denounce the Arab countries. The second half of Obama's excerpt features more direct agency (with active verbs), highlighting the more liberal agenda of outreach, shared progress and growth, and greater willingness to see America in a global context.

In either case, the speech has multiple audiences—both America and foreign countries. The words of these policy statements reveal both the present reality (the window) and the desired action (or mirror).

Consider the following prompt:

> Choose three documents from this chapter that characterize the United States' changing role in the world between 1975 and 2013. In what ways do these documents represent broader shifts in the country and the rest of the world?

STEP 1 *Understand the prompt, and identify the key words*

STEP 2 *Generate a working thesis*

STEP 3 *Identify and organize your evidence*

STEP 4 *Outline your response*

By recognizing the authors or speakers as both windows and mirrors to the larger society, the analysis of voice and audience enhances your argument. The focus on America's "changing role" invites a discussion of voice and audience.

One possible organization is to approach it like this chapter's Applying AP® Historical Thinking Skills exercise on periodization and comparison, where you monitor two distinct eras between a pivotal point, such as 9/11. A second choice is to use historical themes as a benchmark of these actual changes. For example, much of this chapter focuses on American identity and the United States' role abroad. So a second theme is America in the world. Given that American foreign policy has shifted dramatically over the last forty years, you may identify changes that have occurred to our national identity and subsequent changes in foreign policy. Such an outline appears here (the comparisons begin with the introduction of the second point of view):

   I. Introduction

  II. American identity 1975 to 2000

      A. Conservative point of view

      B. Liberal point of view

  III. American foreign policy 1975 to 2000. In examining foreign policy, draw attention to the relationship that the United States has with its intended audiences. Your analysis of different points of view should take into account their intended effect on audiences at home and abroad.

      A. Conservative point of view

      B. Liberal point of view

  IV. American identity 2001 to the present

      A. Conservative point of view

      B. Liberal point of view

   V. American foreign policy 2001 to the present

      A. Conservative point of view

      B. Liberal point of view

  IV. Conclusion

STEP 5 *Write your essay*

The New Right

Is there a point at which the coming together of wealth and leisure can change the nature of the definition of *conservative* in America? America's history defines conservatism as a belief in the status quo. Now, increasing access to the American Dream offers a new day in the social and political destinies of American citizens. Historians must consider whether the promise of this pursuit moves beyond the economic realm into uncharted waters that would likely confuse the Puritans. Did the fulfillment of a left-wing, populist approach toward access and equity create a New Right, a new norm, and a new sense of entitlement and what it means to have fulfilled the Dream? You have already read various sources that illustrate the differences between liberal and conservative points of view during this time period. Now read the two passages below and consider the extent to which the New Right represented a return to the states quo.

> The United States became a definitively suburban nation during the final decades of the twentieth century, with the regional convergence of metropolitan trends and the reconfiguration of national politics around programs to protect the consumer privileges of affluent white neighborhoods and policies to reproduce the postindustrial economy of the corporate Sunbelt. Since the rediscovery of Middle America during the Nixon era, the suburban orientation of the bipartisan battle for the political center has remained persistently unreceptive to civil rights initiatives designed to address the structural disadvantages facing central cities and impoverished communities. Despite the ritual declarations that the federal courts would not permit public opposition to influence the enforcement of constitutional principles, the historical fate of collective integration remedies for educational and residential segregation demonstrated the responsiveness of the judicial and policymaking branches to the grassroots protests of affluent suburban families. The color-blind and class-driven discourse popularized in the Sunbelt South helped create a suburban blueprint that ultimately resonated from the "conservative" subdivisions of southern California to the "liberal" townships of New England: a bipartisan political language of private property values, individual taxpayer rights, children's educational privileges, family residential security, and white racial innocence.
>
> —Matthew D. Lassiter, *The Silent Majority: Suburban Politics in the Sunbelt South* (Princeton, NJ: Princeton University Press, 2006).

> Although the political activity of the New Right and the threat of AIDS seemed to augur [predict] a retrenchment [reversal] in the behavior of many Americans, as the 1980s drew to a close it was not at all clear what the future would bring. Certainly the outcome of current controversies about sex would have to build upon the complicated set of sexual meanings that had evolved over generations. For instance, in seeking a restoration of sexuality to marriage, replete with

reproductive consequences, advocates of the new chastity had to contend with the permeation of the erotic throughout American culture, the expansive and varied roles available to American women, and a contraceptive technology that sustained the nonprocreative meanings of sexual behavior. A new sexual system that harkened back to a vanished world could not simply be wished into existence. . . .

—John D'Emilio and Estelle Freedman, *Intimate Matters: A History of Sexuality in America* (Chicago: University of Chicago Press, 1998).

Using the excerpts, complete the following three tasks:

1. Briefly explain one major difference between Lassiter's and D'Emilio/Freedman's historical interpretations of entitlement in America.
2. Briefly explain how one document from the time period not explicitly mentioned in the excerpts could be used to support either excerpt.
3. Briefly explain how one document from Chapter 22 could be used to support the excerpt you did not choose in question 2.

ACKNOWLEDGMENTS

Abigail Adams. Letter to John Quincy Adams. Reprinted by permission of the publisher from *The Adams Papers: Adams Family Correspondence*, vol. 3, *April 1778–September 1782*, ed. L. H. Butterfield and Marc Friedlaender (Cambridge, MA: Harvard University Press, 1973), 268–269. © 1973 by The Massachusetts Historical Society.

American Indian Movement Grand Governing Council. "Trail of Broken Treaties: 20-Point Position Paper." October 1972. Courtesy of the American Indian Movement Grand Governing Council.

H. Rap Brown. Speech at Free Huey Rally. February 1968. Pacifica Radio Archives, Pacificaradioarchives.org.

Rachel Carson. From *Silent Spring*. Copyright © 1962 by Rachel L. Carson. Copyright © renewed 1990 by Roger Christie. Reprinted by permission of Frances Collin, Trustee. All copying, including electronic, or redistribution of this text, is expressly forbidden.

George Cato. "Account of the Stono Rebellion." 1739. From *Stono: Documenting and Interpreting a Southern Slave Revolt* by Mark M. Smith. Copyright © 2005 by University of South Carolina. Used by permission.

Cesar Chavez. "We Shall Overcome." September 16, 1965. TM/© 2015 The Cesar Chavez Foundation, www.chavezfoundation.org. Used by permission of the Cesar Chavez Foundation.

Lawrence E. Davies. "Zoot Suits Become Issue on Coast." From the *New York Times*, June 13, 1943. © 1943 The New York Times. All rights reserved. Used by permission and protected by the Copyright Laws of the United States. The printing, copying, redistribution, or retransmission of this Content without express written permission is prohibited.

Betty Friedan. From *The Feminine Mystique*. Copyright © 1983, 1974, 1973, 1963 by Betty Friedan. Used by permission of W. W. Norton & Company, Inc.

Francis Fukuyama. From "The End of History?" *The National Interest* 16 (Summer 1989): 3–18. Used by permission of the author.

David J. Garrow. "Martin Luther King, Jr., and the Spirit of Leadership." *Journal of American History* 74, no. 2 (September 1987). Used by permission of Oxford University Press.

Martin Halpern. "'I'm Fighting for Freedom': Coleman Young, HUAC, and the Detroit African American Community." *Journal of American Ethnic History* 17, no. 1 (Fall 1997): 20–22. Used by permission of the Journal of American Ethnic History, Immigration and Ethnic History Society.

Elliott West. "Reconstructing Race." Copyright by the Western History Association. Reprinted by permission. The article first appeared as Elliott West, "Reconstructing Race," *Western Historical Quarterly* 34 (Spring 2003): 1–14.

John N. Wheeler. A Korean War Soldier's Letter Home. From *War Letters: Extraordinary Correspondence from American Wars*, ed. Andrew Carroll (New York: Simon & Schuster), 2001. Copyright © 2001 by Andrew Carroll. Used by permission.

Edmund White. Letter to Ann and Alfred Corn. © 1969 by Edmund White. Used by permission. All rights reserved.

Governor's Investigating Committee on Problems of Wisconsin's Spanish-Speaking Communities, Report to the Governor. 1971. Courtesy of Wisconsin Historical Society.

INDEX

in primary documents,
518–520
Voltaire, Declaration of the
Rights of Man and, 135
Voting and voting rights
15th Amendment and, 276
in Georgia, 124–125
for women, 345, 346–347
"Voyage to the St. Lawrence"
(Cartier, 1534), 18–19

Wages
of African Americans,
337–338
at Pullman Palace Car
Company, 363–364
Walker, David, "Walker's
Appeal . . . to the Coloured
Citizens of the World"
(1830), 179
Walker, Freeman, on Missouri
Compromise, 216
Wallace George, 460
Walsh, Mike, "Meeting:
Democratic Mechanics
and Working Men of New
York" (1842), 197
Wampanoag Confederacy, 37
Wampanoag Indians, conversion
to Christianity, 40–41
"War Message" (Polk, 1846),
237–238
"War on Terror," 507
Warren, Earl, 450
Wars and warfare. See also
Revolts and rebellions;
specific battles and wars
French-British, 86
in name of democracy,
412–420
Washington, Forrester B., "Study
of Negro Employees of
Apartment Houses in
New York City, A" (1916),
337–338
Washington, George
Battle of Fallen Timbers and,
155
expansion under, 86
Indians and, 103
National Bank and, 107 (i)
Treaty of Paris (1783) and, 104
Watergate scandal, 440–441
Weapons of terror, Bush, George
W., on, 507

Weatherman Underground,
"Communiqué No. 1"
(1970), 464
Weaver, James B., 322
Webster-Ashburton Treaty
(1842), 223, 229–230
Weld, Isaac, "Travels throughout
the States of North
America" (1797), 160
Welfare state, 362
"We Shall Overcome" (Chavez,
1965), 456–457
West. See also Expansionism;
Manifest Destiny
conquest of, 237–246
immigration in, 339
Native Americans in,
329–335
West, Elliott, 305–306
West Africa, slave trade in, 3,
17–18
Western Hemisphere. See also
specific locations
Columbus' discovery of, 2
enslaved Africans to, 46
as New World, 2
Western Reserve, 103
Westward movement
as national policy, 146
after Revolution, 86
"What Means This Strike?"
(DeLeon, 1898), 354–355
"What to Do with the Slaves
When Emancipated"
(New York Herald, 1862),
278–279
Wheatley, Phillis, "On Being
Brought from Africa to
America" (1770), 120
Whig Party, 238
White, Edmund, "Letter to Ann
and Alfred Corn" (1969),
462–463
Whitefield, George, "Marks of a
True Conversion" (1739),
73–74
Whitney, Eli, "Petition for
Renewal of Patent on
Cotton Gin" (1812),
193–194
Wilentz, Sean, 233
Wilmot Proviso, 225, 225 (i)
Wilson, Woodrow, 406
"On the League of Nations"
(1919), 413–414

"Remarks to the Senate"
(1917), 412–413
Winthrop, John, 71
"Model of Christian Charity,
A" (1630), 32–33
Winthrop, John IV, "Image of
John Winthrop IV"
(1773), 71, 71 (i)
Wisconsin
LaFollette in, 352
"Report to the Governor"
(Governor's Investigating
Committee on Problems
of Wisconsin's Spanish-
Speaking Communities,
1971), 481–482
Woman's Rights Convention
(Seneca Falls, 1848),
184
Woman suffrage
opposition to, 345
support for, 346–347
Women
civil rights movement and,
487–488
employment-hunting by, 366,
367 (i)
feminist movement and,
452–454
independence and, 117,
121–122
political culture of, 425
rights for, 184–185
Schlafly and, 482–483
in Second World War, 416,
417 (i)
Tarbell and, 372–373
Women of Lorain County,
"Petition against Woman
Suffrage" (1870), 345
Worcester v. Georgia (Marshall,
1832), 174–175
Workers
in 20th century, 425–426
factory girls in textile mills as,
198–199
industrial economy and,
371–372
Loom and Spindle: or, Life
among the Early Mill
Girls (Robinson, 1898),
198–199
political machines and, 197
Working thesis, 24, 80, 143–144,
379

World War I. See First World War

World War II. See Second World War

Wounded Knee, Native American occupation of (1973), 465

Writing skills. *See also* Historical thinking skills
  addressing exceptions in historical argument: the role of the qualifier, 272–274
  analyzing and evaluating persona in documents, 470–472
  avoiding either/or fallacy, 142–144
  beginning an argument with sources: the preliminary claim, 301–304
  comparison when assembling multiple body paragraphs, 51–55
  contextualizing historical argument, 324–326
  counterarguments in historical essays, 247–250
  evaluating context and multiple perspectives, 402–404
  evaluating evidence: discovering turning points, 379–380
  historical causation: the linear argument, 162–166
  implications in historical argument, 422–424
  incorporating secondary sources into historical argument, 485–486
  knowing what and when to quote, 206–211
  organizing and outlining a reason-based historical argument, 229–232
  organizing themes in historical arguments, 445–446
  patterns in historical argument, 188–190
  periodization in writing historical arguments, 356–357
  prewriting, 22–25
  rethinking audience and voice in primary documents, 518–520
  subordinated thesis statement, 79
  synthesizing themes in historical argument, 340–342

Yellowstone Park Timberland Reserve, creation of, 321

Yiddish words, boychick as, 364, 365 *(i)*

Yippies, 480

Yorktown, Siege of, 102, 104

Young, Coleman, 442

Youth International Party (Yippies), 480

"Zoot Suits Become Issue on Coast" (Davies, *The New York Times*, 1943), 399–400, 400 *(i)*

Zuckerberg, Mark, 514